Praise for *Padro Pio and You*

"Mary O'Regan's new book is quite aptly titled *Padre Pio and You* because she takes the reader on a personal journey that relives both the external events and the inner life of this great saint. For a thorough look at Padre Pio's entire lifetime, from his parents and childhood to his passing in 1968, this book is invaluable. While it is a complete biography of St. Padre Pio, it is much more than that. In chapter after chapter, O'Regan underscores the relationship between Padre Pio's life experiences and their practical application to the spiritual journey of the reader. As the author of several Padre Pio books myself, I can highly recommend Mary O'Regan's opus."

— **Frank Rega, Author, *Padre Pio and America***

"Mary O'Regan's book *Padre Pio and You* is a rare treat. It is a new portrait of St. Padre Pio, something like you've never seen before. The reader steps into his world and encounters him personally, in depth, from the beginning of his life to the end. To those who don't know him well, Padre Pio will become a true friend, and to those who do, a still better friend. In every chapter, you'll feel that he cares about you personally, and the advice he gives is priceless; this is a book to go back to again and again — each time a warm meeting with a best friend. Whether you know Padre Pio well or know nothing about him, this book is a gem."

— **Keith Berube, Ph.D. cand., Author, *Mary, the Beloved*; *Mary: The Rosary, the Relationship, and Dragons*; and *A Love Letter to Mary***

"This extraordinary work brings you into the presence of St. Padre Pio himself. Through high artistry and courage, O'Regan shares her deep and personal relationship with the saint in a way that leaves readers wishing that they, too, were one of his 'adopted children.'"

— **Tom Leopold, TV comedy writer and Catholic convert**

"Mary O'Regan is a beautiful writer and a beautiful person. Her warmth, mystical connection with God and her genuine love for Padre Pio come across wonderfully in this lovely book."

— **Jennifer Fulwiler, Bestselling author, *Your Blue Flame* and *Something Other Than God*; Host, *The Jen Fulwiler Show***

PADRE PIO AND YOU

MARY O'REGAN

PADRE PIO AND YOU

An Epic Story of Spiritual Fatherhood

SOPHIA INSTITUTE PRESS
Manchester, New Hampshire

Sophia Institute Press
Box 5284, Manchester, NH 03108
1-800-888-9344
www.SophiaInstitute.com

Sophia Institute Press is a registered trademark of Sophia Institute.

paperback ISBN 979-8-88911-508-3

ebook ISBN 979-8-88911-509-0

Library of Congress Control Number: 2025936148

Second printing

*For Mary, the Mother of God,
and the triumph of her Immaculate Heart.*

For Padre Pio's mother, Giuseppa, she who gave us Pio.

*For Padre Pio's sister, Felicita, the wife and mother
whose soul Pio said was better than his.*

Contents

FOREWORD

In the quiet corners of life, there are moments when the ordinary becomes extraordinary, when a simple encounter or a seemingly small event can change the course of a life forever. For fourteen-year-old Mary O'Regan, one such moment occurred during a summer vacation in Ireland, an event that would lead her down a path of profound faith and spiritual awakening. This book is a testament to her journey, which began with a fleeting encounter with Padre Pio — a moment that would forever alter the trajectory of her life.

It's often said that our paths are guided in mysterious ways, and Mary's story is no exception. On that fateful day, as she sat with a quiet Irish lady watching a film, little did she know that a comment about the mystical abilities of Padre Pio would ignite within her a spark that would grow into a blazing fire of devotion. As the image of a Franciscan friar began to form in her mind, and as he spoke those life-altering words, "I am waiting for you," Mary's soul was awakened to a journey that she never could have anticipated.

What follows is a beautiful, raw recounting of Mary's struggles, questions, and ultimate surrender to the divine. She faced doubts and skepticism, as many of us do when confronted with the supernatural or the miraculous. Yet, through a series of divine encounters, including a near-death experience that left her untouched by injury, Mary's belief in a higher power became irrefutable. Padre Pio's love and guidance became the cornerstone of her spiritual journey, his words and prayers offering Mary solace, wisdom, and unshakable peace.

Through these pages, Mary invites us into her world, in which prayer, faith, and devotion transcend the limitations of human understanding. Her story is not just about one young girl's encounter with a saint but about the universality of grace and the invitation to each of us to deepen our connection with God. Mary's relationship with Padre Pio becomes a symbol of spiritual fatherhood, of unconditional love that transcends time and space. As we read her words, we are reminded of our own need for guidance, for love, and for the ever-present hand of God in our lives.

This book is not only a personal account of Mary's experiences but a call to all who seek to deepen their faith and live lives of holiness. Through Padre Pio's example, Mary discovered the importance of Confession, contrition, and devotion to the Blessed Mother. Padre Pio's unwavering love for his spiritual children is evident in the way he continues to impact Mary's life, and it is my hope that through Mary's words, others will feel drawn into Padre Pio's spiritual family.

May this book serve as an invitation to those who are searching, to those who are questioning, and to those who are yearning for the divine. Mary's journey is a powerful reminder that no one is ever alone on this path of faith. As you read, may you feel the presence of Padre Pio, and may his love and guidance lead you closer to the heart of God.

Susan De Bartoli
April 3, 2025

INTRODUCTION

I am waiting for you.
— Padre Pio

The first time I heard the name "Padre Pio," I was fourteen, on vacation in a rural neighborhood in the West of Ireland. I was in the living room of a crumbly old farmhouse, decorated with baskets of freshly cut turf. An Irish lady sat before an old TV set that blared a trashy 1970s horror movie about a female psychic who could be in two places at the same time. I was beginning to feel uneasy, when suddenly the lady spoke up, solemnly declaring, "That psychic can bilocate, can be in two places at once. The only real person I've ever heard of who could actually bilocate was Padre Pio."

I did not have the foggiest idea who Padre Pio was. I'd never seen a picture of him, but the second the lady mentioned his name I had a mental image of a Franciscan friar in a robe as brown as turf. Brown-eyed, with a face framed with a white beard and white hair, this friar sat in a tiny white-walled cell, his eyes glowering with displeasure. Then, to my great surprise, he spoke. "I am waiting for you," he pronounced somberly. His thin carmine lips were tightly drawn; his solemn expression told me this man would play a crucial role in my life.

So inexplicable was the vision, I brushed it aside. I mean, was this Padre Pio even a priest? (I did not know that *padre* meant "father." By his garb I knew he was Franciscan — that was reassuring because I'd had positive experiences with gentle Franciscan friars in my hometown of Cork.

At the time I had no faith in Christ or His Church, and didn't have any particular respect for priests. And yet I could not square the fact that, although the horror film had disquieted me, the vision of the friar in brown had calmed me completely. Had he really spoken to my soul that way? I quietly dismissed the idea.

I thought no more about it until a little while later, when I was visiting a home and looking at its bookshelves. I saw an old book, the cover of which bore an image of the exact same Franciscan friar. "That's Padre Pio," I realized, looking at the title. Again, to my complete surprise a certain serenity soothed me.

I turned the book over and read the description. He had indeed been renowned for the rare ability to bilocate, so that as a priest he could serve two sets of people in two different locations at the same time. I also learned he had been from a conservative Franciscan order known as the "Capuchins." By this time, the Capuchin priest had been gone thirty years, and yet his intense stare unnerved me a bit.

The back of the biography contained a laundry list of Padre Pio's mystical gifts; I had never heard of most of them, including the stigmata. I read that he had been born in the rustic Italian countryside in 1887 and later had a priestly ministry in a town nestled in mountains. Apart from that, everything about him seemed beyond my IQ level, and the text may as well have been in Greek.

Although I could accept the idea that he could bilocate — I recalled the words of the large Irish lady who first mentioned him to me, and decided to believe Pio had bilocated because *she* believed he had — I found myself resisting some of his other supernatural abilities, such as the idea he could "read souls." How could anyone see a person's soul, or read it as one reads a page in a book? It sounded like something fresh out of a comic book, and as a teenager I didn't want to be caught up in childish constructs of a false reality. And so, in that moment I set aside the notion that this Franciscan friar was "waiting" for me; the very idea was ludicrous — especially since I had decided to give up all practice of the Catholic Faith.

A Brush with Death

About a year later, I was milling around my hometown of Cork one Irish summer's afternoon. Around three o'clock, I had just gotten off a red bus and walked behind the back of it, when I was struck full force by a truck. A second of harrowing pain gave way to unconsciousness as my skull was slammed and my body hit and thrown to the ground.

Then, in an instant, I was mystically lifted and absorbed in a great white space, a delicious peace came over me, and I was in a lovely ecstasy. I could see, all around me, every part of the white space at once, because I was not seeing with my eyes. I thought, "This must be death," to which an answer came: "No, this is not your death, your time has not come." I was shown a passage where I saw the years I had lived and a long stretch ahead, the years I was yet to live. Then I heard, "I am sending you back to the world 'til I call you to Me. You will return unharmed; you will not have one scratch." There was no desire on my part to return to the world, and neither was there any desire to stay in the white eternity of bliss. All I could do was obey.

"She must be dead," I heard an onlooker whisper.

"If she is alive, she'll be paralyzed for life," another murmured. "Or if she lives, she'll have very painful injuries."

To my surprise, the crushing pain had completely left me, and I felt not a twinge. Instead, a peace of such sweetness poured over me as I lay in the grime and grit of the ground, as the wheels of all the other cars passed by me. I was supremely happy.

The paramedics arrived and, finding I was still alive, quickly brought me to the hospital. The solemn faces of the doctors turned jubilant as they examined me and realized I had not sustained a single injury. I had not one scratch, not one bruise.

Up to that time I wanted nothing to do with God. During times of appalling suffering in childhood I cried out to God and prayed, but had never felt even a smidgen of consolation, not one answered prayer; only a black nothingness. Atheism appealed because it helped me evade the pain of feeling unloved by telling myself there was no One to give such love, so to seek such love was an impossible dream.

Thanks to the bracing encounter with the truck, I understood that I been saved from death because the Author of Life had a different plan for me. It just wasn't possible for me to deny God anymore. That gift of faith stayed with me and began to grow in my heart.

Another Encounter

Two years later, I was visiting someone who'd been seriously ill, and they had pinned at random places on their walls pictures of Padre Pio. Wanting to take a closer look at his face, I walked up to one picture. His face had an expression of great tenderness, and I was filled with love for him. Suddenly I felt myself standing before him. His face had a luminous glow, like he was made of light. Such awesome beauty was not owing to his physical bearing but to him being a saint with a perfect soul.

He smiled and looked at me so tenderly. "I love you," he said to me. It was more natural than breathing to love him in response: His perfection meant there was nothing not to love.

Although there was no denying the sharpness in his stare, there was, however, such tenderness in his eyes that he won me over. I was the object of the famous "Padre Pio stare" so often remarked on by ordinary men and women because of the way his gaze penetrated them. I was sure his gaze could see into my very soul. I was so mesmerized by him that my senses were arrested.

By this time Padre Pio had been dead for thirty-three years, but I felt the weight of his presence so strongly. I had intended to "see him" when I went to look at the picture, yet in that moment I had been allowed to see Padre Pio as he truly *is*, a glorified saint in Heaven.

Then, in my soul I heard the words, "Praised be Jesus," and Padre Pio instructed me to pray these words from my heart, which I did, having never said them before in my life. I did not realize the importance of this until sometime later, when I learned that as a young priest, Padre Pio was visited by demons who would appear in various forms and in clever disguises to trick him. Occasionally these fallen angels appeared to Padre Pio as the priest who was his closest friend, as the reigning pope, as Our Lady, and even as the Crucified Christ. It was hard for young Pio to tell the difference between real human beings and evil spirits, until he commanded them to praise Jesus. Evil spirits would vanish when asked to do this.[1]

Padre Pio asked me to say, "Praised be Jesus," and I did so. As a teenager I thought it was just something a saintly priest would ask you to say, but now it was my way of knowing he was of God, not a phantom created by the devil to deceive me. Had he not asked me to repeat, "Praised be Jesus," I would not be writing these words you are reading.

After a time looking at him, I felt I should turn away, out of politeness. It would have been greedy and rude to keep looking at him, asking for more smiles and more interaction. But the minute I turned away, the image of Padre

Pio stayed in my mind and a perfect portrait burned in my memory. I never lost the awe I felt in the face of his spectacular beauty.

Also, I never forgot the purity of his love. I knew Padre Pio knew everything about me, and this made me credit his love because it was based on knowledge. Later I would read more about Padre Pio's gift for reading not only souls but also hearts and minds. But from the minute I met him, I had known this. I had experienced it.

About This Book

During his lifetime, Padre Pio had been a spiritual father to multitudes of souls across the world, and he remained their spiritual father after he died. Many more millions of souls sought to be his spiritual son or daughter in the years after his death, and although they never met him in the flesh, they knew a true bond of their spirit with his spirit as he guided them from his place in Heaven.

Each time I encountered Padre Pio — whether unexpectedly or by reading about him — I longed to become his spiritual daughter and to benefit from his fatherly intercession. I wanted to know more about him, not just as a priest but as a spiritual father. Unfortunately, many of the biographies I picked up were very dry and focused on his priestly life. I wanted to know more about him as a person.

I thought being a spiritual daughter of Padre Pio would always be a very personal, private affair, not something that I would ever write extensively about. Then, when I was twenty-five, I moved to London, where I hoped to make my way as a writer and so founded a blog titled *The Path Less Taken*. I decided to post about Padre Pio, thinking this would scarcely get any attention and would just be treated as an obscure interest. I was proven wrong, as my posts on Pio were by far the most popular pieces I ever wrote.

There were times when, through selfish ambition, I would take breaks from writing about Padre Pio — whenever I knew someone who might offer me a career opportunity was put off by Padre Pio's fierce honesty with penitents in the confessional. But this people-pleasing game often ended badly, as the same people who resented Pio's truthfulness in decrying sin were not truthful with me and the opportunities they offered were often mirages. These letdowns were good for me because I learned it did no good to be occasionally disloyal to Padre Pio and abandon the call I'd received to write about him, when he had only ever been loyal to me. I was determined to write about Padre Pio in a way that explored the depths of his spirituality and offered analysis to readers that they could readily use to make personal goodness and holiness a reality in their lives.

To make up for the times when I'd failed to write about him, I wrote my most daring piece on him yet, using a testimony from a woman who went to Padre Pio's confessional in a hysterical state and confessed having had an abortion, but was refused absolution because Padre Pio told her she lacked true contrition. A year later she returned to Padre Pio's confessional and was granted absolution after Padre Pio saw in her soul that she was "truly sorry" for her sin.[2]

After I published this account in *The Mass of Ages*, the magazine of the Latin Mass Society of England and Wales, people started asking me more detailed questions about the difference between true and false contrition according to Padre Pio, and you may read in depth about this later in the chapter on mortal sin and Confession, which also contains full details of the healing of the post-abortion woman's mental health problems. I have curated everything Padre Pio said on true contrition being the spirit of peace, whereas false contrition is something that agitates and makes a person angry with themselves.

I felt myself being called to write a book on Padre Pio that took a reader through his life, a biography interlaced with exhaustive exploration of his spiritual wisdom with lots of insights from his conversations with the people whose souls he could read, in a bid for the reader to be able to learn more about how to receive healing from the God who wants to save souls.

In writing this book, I have found that Padre Pio's guidance and help are not the work of a moment; rather, it becomes part of who they are, thus establishing a true father-child relationship. Saint and spiritual child may not be biologically related, but the person who becomes Pio's son or daughter in spirit strives to develop more and more of Pio's sanctity in this life, so that they may spend eternity with him in the next.

As I began to write this book, I often thought of the first vision I had of Padre Pio, where he told me he was waiting for me — I understood for the very first time that he was waiting for me to reach others on his behalf. As Padre Pio's daughter in spirit, I felt called to introduce others to him, and I ask that you think of this not so much as a biography but as a daughter recounting her father's life; a daughter who has painstakingly collected his pearls of wisdom, our spiritual inheritance. Just as genetic inheritance (from our biological parents) informs our bodies, our spiritual inheritance from our spiritual mothers and fathers (in this case, Padre Pio) informs our salvation. Pio learned hard truths from his savage battles with the devil, whom he called "the enemy of our salvation"[3] and I believe these need to be known by every Christian. My priority is to show you how Pio won these battles the devil, so you too may learn how to triumph in such spiritual combat.

Padre Pio and the Blessed Mother

Padre Pio loved Our Lady and frequently employed her intercession. I have felt an urgency to present every precious detail of Pio's teachings on Our Lady's role in our greater good in this life and how she may help us achieve eternal bliss in the next. Pio expressed her singular role in relation to God: "She alone is capable of capturing the streams of love which pour from the Heart of God. She alone is worthy to discourse with Him."[4]

Pio took pains to explain that Our Blessed Mother speaks on our behalf to the Almighty, and she also takes care to make us as presentable as possible before we approach her Son. Pio spoke of Our Lady as the mother who launders our clothes and cleans us, and he claimed that God is merciful when Our Lady does so: "God is merciful when He sees Our Lady is about to wash our rags."[5]

Pio said we only profit well from confessing our sins by nurturing our love of Our Lady. "The sacrament of penance was instituted for man, not vice versa," he said, and "only through tender devotion to Our Lady will you find the way to make good use of it."[6] Loving Our Lady and making good Confessions are intimately bound together.

Most crucially, there are Pio's extraordinary notes on prayer, which need our urgent attention, and I've done my utmost to present these in a manner that you may be able to put into practice in your prayer life as soon as you read them. These eternal truths need to be embraced by everyone. Every spiritual son or daughter is different, and some may follow Pio more closely than others, or possess different kinds of spiritual gifts. For example, Pio had the gift of tears when he was in seminary: When he prayed, rivulets fell from his eyes, and when he contemplated that Our Lord died for his sins, Pio was seen to be in floods of tears.

Like many of Pio's gifts, the gift of tears is given only to a few, select souls. Pio had intense dark nights of the soul: His soul would be immersed in black every time he was on the verge of reaching a new height in the spiritual life. He wrote about the role of darkness and dryness in preparing the soul for greater union, and this forms the essence of the chapter "Pio's Dark Night of the Soul." Only the very holy are given these times of darkness, so they may graduate to a higher level of holiness afterward.

An Invitation

As you begin to read this loving testament to the life of Padre Pio, I ask you to close your eyes for a moment and ask Padre Pio to speak to you. Ask him to offer you his hand to hold, to guide you through this life and eventually lead you through the gates of Paradise. As you take the hand of my spiritual father, once punctured with the wounds of Christ's Crucifixion, never shirk sharing as much as possible in the spirituality of Padre Pio. Let us rather see ourselves in the man who went to Padre Pio for advice and then asked Pio if he thought of him as his spiritual son. The solemn reply from the saint was, "I have bought you with the price of my blood."[7]

Padre Pio's profound mystical gifts led me to marvel at the glories of his Creator, God the Father. I worried for a time that I loved Padre Pio more than God, and I found solace in the account from the boy who approached Pio, telling him he feared that he loved him more than God. Padre Pio told the child, "You must love God with an infinite love, through me. You love me because I direct you to good, and to God the Supreme Good." Mindful that love for him owed entirely to his being a vehicle to God, Padre Pio further said, "If I directed you not to God but to evil, you would not love me anymore." The ever-humble priest said to the boy, "I am just the means that carries you to God."[8]

You may already have become a spiritual son or daughter before reading this, and this book is not necessary for you to become Pio's spiritual child. I was not led to Pio by a book, but by his direct intervention in my life, and there are many ways to Pio, who leads you to the Way, the Truth, and the Light — but I hope and pray with all my heart that this may be one such worthy route to Pio.

All the while I ask you to keep as utterly important in your mind that Padre Pio said he saw "all" the souls entrusted to him when he offered the Holy Sacrifice of the Mass.[9] Thinking of Pio at the altar, beholding a vision of all the faces who would go to the Lord through him, I feel called to encourage you to ask this question of yourself: Did Pio see you? I believe this is highly probable. If you feel a call from Our Lord to follow Padre Pio, he may have seen your face when he was at the altar. When Pio said he saw "all" the souls he was to care for, he meant all those alive when he was alive and all those who were yet to live — which may include you.

Yes, we are talking about large numbers of people whom Pio saw when he offered Holy Mass, and credence is given to it being a large number, certainly millions and possibly billions. There is an extraordinary prophecy that predicts a Franciscan will bring a third of the world to Christ. When Pio was asked about this prophecy, he did not deny that it concerned him, but he showed himself dissatisfied: "What do I want with a third? More! More! I want to bring everyone to God."[10] On another occasion, a most beloved spiritual daughter asked him about the same prophecy, and he tacitly agreed, but again exclaimed that he wanted "More! More!"[11]

This is also a joyful explanation as to why Padre Pio was given such a marvelous array of charisms and gifts: Such supernatural abilities allowed him to fulfill his mission on earth. It can be argued that millions came to Christ through Padre Pio during his lifetime. But Padre Pio often used to tell people that he was going to have more influence in Heaven, where he could bring many more souls to God.

To take Padre Pio as your spiritual father means you become a spiritual sibling of his other children, and we may all pray for each other and help each other as best we can. You and I are part of a big family. We also have spiritual grandparents: Pio's parents. We owe an enormous debt of gratitude to Pio's mama and papa, Grazio and Giuseppa. We cannot honor Pio without honoring them. But first we must know them, and for this reason, I start the book with them, on their wedding day.

1

A Wedding Fit for a King and Queen

On his wedding day in June 1881, Grazio Forgione was so nervous and self-conscious that he was like a stranger to himself. Grazio was normally ebullient and supremely comfortable in his own skin, the definition of confidence. With a robust oval face and cheekbones round like apples, Grazio had a broad, natural smile that made his dimples pop. His teeth were whitened by the sun and his cheeks were burnished a dark rose from shepherding goats in the sunlight. His liquid brown eyes had a sheen of golden honey, and his mop of thick brown-auburn hair accented his lively eyes.

But today, standing in his parents' cramped stone house, Grazio was nervous. His unease was not due to any doubts about his bride. Giuseppa, with her crystal-blue eyes, was the love of his life, and he'd been totally consumed with gratitude that she'd agreed to be his wife. And yet he knew beyond a doubt that his life was about to change forever. He was going to walk out the door as a single man and come back as a husband. The awesome certainty overwhelmed him.

In his elaborate wedding costume, Grazio looked like a medieval king. His large doublet and black padded jacket filled out his slender build and made him look muscle-bound; the sparkling gold buttons glinted in the sun like so many medallions. His thin legs were covered in white stockings festooned with ribbons, a pair of gleaming white shoes on his feet. It was a foreign feeling for a farmer who was used to wearing rough trousers, cotton shirts, and boots covered in grime. No doubt all the guests would stare at him. But it could not be helped. Grazio was dressed as all Southern Italian men were expected to dress on their wedding day. His regal costume was the traditional dress of his people, the sun-bronzed natives who worked the land of the Mezzogiorno.

One day Grazio Forgione would be known throughout the world as the father of the friar, Padre Pio, the first priest in history to be given mystically the wounds of Christ, the stigmata. Grazio would grow accustomed to being in the spotlight as the man who had fathered a spiritual giant and a saint. But on that June day, he was struggling to leave for his own wedding. No one came to bolster him, because no one could have guessed he needed encouragement.

Grazio usually spent his summer days watering his olive trees, checking the progress of his wheat crops, and milking cattle. His spare time was devoted to thumbing his rosary beads and offering countless Ave Marias. But today all his usual duties had been delegated, friends and relatives taking turns tending his animals and picking up the ears of corn that fell to the ground, while he prepared to join his Giuseppa in Holy Matrimony.

As Grazio mustered the courage to walk out the door to meet his bride, his eyes caught sight of the many goblets filled with wine that were on the tables around him. His family home had been transformed into a banquet hall ready for the wedding feast. It was unthinkable that the guests would have to wait for their wine to be poured, when the plan was for everyone to rush in and be ready to toast the couple when Grazio carried Giuseppa over the threshold.

Impulsively, Grazio grabbed a goblet of the ruby-red liquid and gulped it down, breaking the fast he'd been keeping since midnight in anticipation of receiving Holy Communion, and felt his nerves soothe as a warm feeling replaced his jitters. Grazio never told a soul, not even his bride, about his weak moment when he'd gulped wine to steady his nerves. "No one will ever know," he told himself.

Three decades later, a priest confronted Grazio with what he had done and reminded him to confess it. Who was this priest who had jogged his memory? His own son, Padre Pio, read his father's soul and reminded him of an event that had happened six years before Pio was even born.[12]

A Bridal Procession

Grazio's mother and stepfather came to escort him to the home of his bride. Together they walked through the streets of Pietrelcina, a maze of stone houses set along winding lanes that had been built around the ruins of an old Norman castle. His bride, Giuseppa Di Nunzio, didn't seem nearly as nervous as her husband. She was dressed like a medieval queen, but the stares of onlookers and guests did not worry her.

Giuseppa was accustomed to people staring at her. She was tall, blade thin, had perfect posture, and carried herself with supreme dignity. She was known for her tiny, exquisitely pretty feet. All the villagers regarded her as having a distinctly regal bearing, and she was fondly called "the Little Princess."[13]

Normally Giuseppa dressed in gleaming white linen from head to toe, but on this, her wedding day, she was resplendent in a crimson-red satin dress. The bodice was embellished with gold brocade and a bright azure-blue apron fell from her waist and reflected the intense blue of her eyes. A white veil swept around her head and covered her nut-brown hair, and not a strand was showing. Around her neck was a precious scarf, embroidered with the faces of thirteen male saints. Local tradition had it that these thirteen intercessors guarded the bride's fertility, ensuring that she would bear many children.

Giuseppa was an only child, so her train of bridesmaids came from her group of friends. These young women were dressed in red silk dresses, maybe a little less stunning than the blazing, passionate red of Giuseppa's gown, but a bride in red satin flanked by her bridesmaids in red silk nonetheless made for a spectacular scene. The sun played on the red, gold, and blue of Giuseppa's dress, and her bodice was ablaze with dancing flickers of golden light.

As Grazio and his parents approached, Giuseppa knelt before Grazio's parents in her noble way, and she meekly kissed their hands. They walked to the town hall for the civil ceremony, a perfunctory affair by which the government said they were married in the eyes of the state and they signed the official records.

Grazio could hardly keep his eyes off Giuseppa. He was madly attracted to her, and as they strode hand in hand together on that sunny June day, Giuseppa and Grazio looked majestic. The lines of gold buttons on his bulky jacket matched the sparkling gold brocade of her bodice. The pure white of his stockings and shoes and her gleaming veil was symbolic of how remarkably chaste they had been in their courtship, which, though it was expected of them at that time, hadn't necessarily been easy.

They were in the prime of youth: Grazio was twenty and Giuseppa a bit older at twenty-two. That she was eighteen months his senior was slightly unusual for that time, but Grazio was so enthralled by Giuseppa that he'd given his all to courting her. In her mellow moments, her blue eyes could look like the wild-flowers; her gaze was steadied by her inner stability, like the stillest blue pond.

She was always totally sincere, and her face only ever wore her true emotions. Never had she compromised her natural gracefulness to put on airs of being a great lady; she was that and more by just being herself. Instead, she was a most pure and honest woman. It had been her purity of heart that led her to say yes to Grazio's marriage proposal.

It was common knowledge that she was Grazio's first true love. Before he fell madly in love with Giuseppa, Grazio had been something of a flirt. He wasn't a cold-hearted player, but he enjoyed the attentions of women. Grazio had a good singing voice, and he had often been asked by local bands to serenade the girls of the village. The band members would strum their guitars and mandolins while Grazio sang passionately the most rapturous love songs to the pretty ones. But after he gave his heart to Giuseppa, he could never adopt the persona of a singer in love again.

Grazio's family was not as wealthy or influential as Giuseppa's family, the Di Nunzios. Some of Giuseppa's relatives had disdained her choice of husband; they voiced snobbish opinions that Giuseppa was marrying down. Furthermore, there were grounds for worries about Grazio's mother, Felicita, who had a mean streak, even toward her own son, the joyful and sweet-tempered Grazio. Some of Giuseppa's family worried that in time Grazio would take after his mother, and that he would mistreat the lovely Giuseppa. Maybe they feared that having a woman like Grazio's mother in their familial fold would make life much harder.

In the end, Giuseppa's relatives set aside their hesitations and honored her choice of husband. Most everyone in the village took delight in Grazio's personality and his goodness, and Giuseppa's parents conformed their will to hers: If their sensitive Giuseppa loved this man, there had to be good reason for this love.

Early Memories

Grazio never spoke badly of his mama, and he never complained of her lack of motherly gentleness. Life had been hard for her as a young widow, until Celestino married Felicita out of the goodness of his heart. His new stepfather instilled in Grazio a sense of dignity and self-confidence that stayed with him all his life.

One example from Grazio's childhood shows how his stepfather helped to shape his stepson's character. When Grazio was a young shepherd, his mother Felicita had made a pair of trousers for him that were so coarse and tough that they stood on the ground by themselves like a piece of furniture. Like his mother, there was no softness or suppleness in the fabric, which was more like wood than anything, chafing poor Grazio's legs almost raw. Felicita forced her son to wear them to the fields anyway, and Grazio obeyed her. After reaching the fields, Grazio made sure his sheep were grazing happily before he took off the pants, found a stone, and battered them with it, in a bid to tenderize the material. But however hard he tried, he could not soften the fabric.

When Grazio returned home that evening, Celestino saw him and was appalled at the sight of his stepson's chafed legs. He upbraided Felicita and demanded she make another pair of trousers then and there. Celestino was like a guardian angel to Grazio, and Heaven knows how horribly his mother would have treated him, had Celestino not given young Grazio the benefit of his fatherly protection — the same protective instincts that would one day make Grazio such a fine husband and father.

Grazio survived his mother's tendency toward callousness. In fact, he was the opposite, an energetic empath. Grazio was often seen dancing over ants that scurried along the ground in the fields, instead of letting his boot crush them. When asked why he was jumping over an insect, he would reply, "Poor little creature, why should it die?"[14] He was quite a witty fellow, who could tell entertaining stories, and he loved to sing spontaneously in a booming voice. There was an eternal boyishness about Grazio, and his loquaciousness found a welcome home in Gisueppa's intense ability to listen.

Though Grazio had less money and less social standing than Giuseppa, she married him for love. Giuseppa had a tender, sensitive soul like Grazio's, but for very different reasons. She had been carefully reared, the only child of farmers who doted on her and provided her with every possible comfort. The attraction that she and Grazio felt for one another, the complementarity of their characters, and their vision of a life together where they would raise a brood of children as husband and wife was all part of the glue that held them together. But Grazio and Giuseppa's true bond was their shared Catholic Faith; they shared the same desire to sacrifice themselves totally within the vocation of marriage for the good of each other's soul.

From the first time they met, they knew that they mirrored each other in their prayer lives. They assisted at Mass together every morning and they prayed the Rosary together every evening. In this they may seem the stereotypical couple of the 1880s, prayerful and God-fearing. But Grazio more so than Giuseppa was something of a holy outlier, even for the times. In Southern Italy, piety was more common among women, because it was sometimes seen as feminine; for a man to be on his knees so much showed too much docility to the Divine. A common sight was men huddled in groups outside the local church while Holy Mass was being celebrated inside. They chain-smoked and gossiped with shoulders hunched while not daring to enter the church. They thought they were advertising masculine superiority.

More often, prayer was left to the women. Grazio, however, was remarkably reverent before the Blessed Sacrament, and in his home he had as many pictures of the Madonna and Child as he could get his hands on. In the field, he held his rosary beads with much affection, and he never hid that he prayed as many Rosaries as he possibly could.

Regrettably, the Italian peasants who were Grazio and Giuseppa's peers would sometimes curse God openly when they did not get the precise answer they had sought in prayer, because the Almighty had not bent to their will. However, Grazio never let misfortune or misadventure change the consistency of his courageous love of God. He'd lost his dad at a young age and had never let it make him bitter. For her part, Giuseppa made it a regular habit to make reparation for the blasphemy of the people around her. When she heard a blasphemy, she instantly dropped to her knees and prayed aloud, "Bless'd be God."[15]

Grazio and Giuseppa lived out their callings very differently, yet each respected and encouraged the other to embrace their callings with all their hearts. Grazio was more pious in that he said more Rosaries, and on an average day he offered a minimum of twelve of them. Giuseppa, however, was more practical. She fasted from meat three days a week in honor of Our Lady of Mount Carmel and Our Lady of the Rosary of Pompeii. She also had a heart for the sick, and took baskets of food to the people who were so ill that they could not cook for themselves. But she did so with Grazio's express blessing and encouragement.

Even before they married, the couple had a tacit agreement that some of the crops Grazio grew would be used for meals for the infirm. Grazio admired

Giuseppa, who had come from a family of means where there was always plenty of food yet had such empathy with those who were weak and hungry that she fed them the best meals she could make. She never bragged about her good deeds, her marathons around Pietrelcina to give nourishment to the needy. In fact, she did not speak of it at all, but simply accomplished these corporal works of mercy with quiet determination.

At the Wedding

It was with this same determination that Giuseppa accepted Grazio as her husband. She had found someone who loved Our Lord and Our Lady as much as she did. And so, on her wedding day, Giuseppa strode hand in hand with Grazio, with her head held high, toward the village church of St. Anne, where she was to become his wife in the house of God. They came to the church, left the sun-splattered streets behind, and entered the dark interior illuminated by yellow candles. They walked up the center aisle, their family and friends seated on either side, and took their place in two chairs before the priest. Giuseppa made sure to tuck the hem of her dress between Grazio's knees, to follow a local tradition that she had mistaken for pious devotion, which she believed kept evil tidings away. It may have appeared as a strange sight to the priest that Grazio's white-stockinged knees had the end of Giuseppa's dress tucked between them, but the priest was used to the intense fervor of wedding customs followed by the Southern Italians, and he knew all brides did this as a matter of habit. Giuseppa also had a tiny pair of scissors sequestered in her pocket, which was meant to deter anyone from wishing her ill or giving her the "evil eye," something Giuseppa took ever so seriously.

After they had exchanged vows, Grazio and Giuseppa left the church and were followed through the streets of the village by a band who belted out party numbers. When they reached the door of Grazio's family home, Grazio scooped Giuseppa up into his arms and the folds of red satin fell around him as he caried her into their home, located in the oldest neighborhood of the village. This was the exact site where Pietrelcina was founded.

The jubilant guests flooded in, dressed in their finest clothes, and each took a heavy goblet in hand. The happy couple stood at the center and a toast was raised to them. Cries of *"Salute!"* punctuated the air. In a poignant moment,

Grazio raised a glass to his late father, Michele, who had died when he was only a little child. A great feast was laid out, grace was offered, and the guests greedily ate all provided and drank more than their share of *vino*. It was usually frowned upon to take more than a little with dinner, but on the grand occasion of a wedding they drank up and were filled with merriment.

The Sacrament of Marriage had been performed, and so the handwringing and muttering about Grazio ceased. Everyone understood that the couple were now joined forever in the bond of matrimony, and no one dared to pick at a union consecrated by God. Grazio was bursting with joy, an exuberant extrovert who enjoyed regaling a crowd of fellow farmers with his witty banter. Like Giuseppa, he had never learned to read or write, but he had memorized many stories from Sacred Scripture and could hold a small audience captive by reciting them with theatrical flourish. Although he worked hard from dawn to dusk in the fields, he never gave into worry and his smooth face had not one worry line. He never fretted because he had a remarkable ability to talk out a problem among his family and with his stepfather, and together they hammered out a solution that they worked together to enact.

Giuseppa, however, was much more solemn and at times so serious that her tense thoughts caused her brow to furrow. Although she did not ruminate, her blue eyes displayed sympathy pangs for others who were suffering. Grazio could talk a mile a minute and was highly entertaining company, but Giuseppa was much more reserved. She was, however, intensely discrete. They both shared an aversion to gossip and talking about others behind their backs. In turn, their neighbors never had a bad word to say about chatty Grazio and his wife of noble silence. Here the careful Giuseppa who paused before she spoke was a good influence over garrulous Grazio, and in each other's company their good qualities became better and their bad qualities became less.

At the wedding feast, the guests sat around the tables covered in white linen and eagerly partook of the delicacies. The one guest who abstained from some of the delights was Giuseppa. As she sat next to Grazio and he eagerly munched the meat dishes, Giuseppa ate like a pescatarian and allowed no cured ham to pass her lips, because she always refrained from meat on Wednesday and, auspiciously for her and her husband, their wedding was celebrated on that day, the day of the week that is dedicated to St. Joseph. The turnips and red bell peppers contented her because she relished vegetables, and she delighted in the fish soaked in sweet sauces. This act of self-sacrifice gilded her piety but also marked her as a woman from a wealthier background than most, because going without meat was for her a choice, in a time and place when a sizable number of the population had no meat for their plates on a regular basis. Her love, Grazio, had grown up eating meat less often; instead he ate mostly vegetables, fruit, eggs, bread, and pasta.

But today, at their wedding breakfast, Grazio did not abstain from meat, and as a woman who was determined to obey him, Giuseppa did not dream of asking him to abstain as she did; and as he did not want to control her, Grazio did not insist she eat meat. Rather they both had a mutual respect for the other's way of practicing their faith, and their personalities were such that they allowed the other flexibility.

After the guests had dined and were well-wined, they swiftly left the happy couple so they could go to the home of the Di Nunzios to enjoy their first night as newlyweds. They were to spend the first year of their married life with Giuseppa's parents. When they were finally alone, Grazio and Giuseppa took out their beads and prayed their first Rosary together as a married couple. That first night of their married lives, Grazio and Giuseppa instantly started a tradition of prayer in their marriage that they never failed to honor. Their wedding night was the first time they were alone together in a bedroom, the first night of the forty-seven years of their marriage.

2

Giuseppa Gives Her Baby to St. Francis

In June 1882, one year after their sublime wedding, Giuseppa gave birth to their first child, a boy they named Michele in honor of Grazio's late father. He was a healthy little mite, born in his grandparents' home and adored as the first grandchild. Michele had a pointed head and longish face and he took very much after his mother's side of the family. From the beginning he was an assertive firstborn who had a serious temperament with a generous nature that balanced his natural solemnity. He had a keen survival instinct and a strong will. Contrary to his parents' plans to give him a sibling as soon as biologically possible, he was to be an only child until he was five years old.

The Family Grows

After Michele came, they needed more room, and so twenty-one-year-old Grazio and twenty-three-year-old Giuseppa moved to a street called *Vico Storto Valle*, or Crooked Valley Lane. The road was as curly as a noodle. Their nest was two stone houses side by side. Number 27 was one room that served as their bedroom, and it was where all the rest of their seven children would be born. It was four walls painted in lime. Many crucifixes blessed the walls, as well as pictures of the Virgin Mary and St. Francis. Though neither Grazio nor Giuseppa could read, they started collecting books which were like a library for their children to inherit.

Next door, number 28, had two rooms, one of which was the kitchen. The young couple also had a third building, a tall structure called "The Tower." It was a solitary chamber that was accessed by a set of steps so steep they were like a vertical ladder. From the top of this turret, there was a marvelous view of the Sannio Hills.

A year after moving into their own place, in the heat of a blistering hot summer, Giuseppa gave birth to her second baby boy, who was named Francesco after

St. Francis, the stigmatist founder of the Franciscans. Giuseppa had a profound devotion to St. Francis, and with Grazio's blessing, she was determined to name a son after him. But this first Francesco perished before the end of that sweltering summer, and he was buried soon after in the warm earth. When their third baby, Amalia, died as had her brother, Giuseppa was already carrying her fourth child.

At twenty-eight years of age, Giuseppa wasn't, by the standards of the time, young to be having a fourth pregnancy. Farming people often had hard and short lives. Giuseppa spent her pregnancy trying to discern how she might obtain the grace for this child to live past infancy. She didn't know if she had the strength to bury a third baby in four years. Yes, she knew many people who had confided their dead children to the cemetery; however, she feared that if she lost this child, it would be her last. Michele would be, like her, an only child.

Giuseppa was determined that Michele would have at least one brother or sister. She nurtured in her heart a desire to make a solemn pledge to St. Francis, that if this child that she currently carried in her womb were to live, she would give St. Francis something exceedingly precious to her as a profound offering of her heart. But what was most precious to her?

Then the day dawned that she proffered her sacrifice for acceptance. On Wednesday, May 25, 1887, a little boy was born. At five o'clock in the golden sunshine of late afternoon, the midwife handed a chubby-faced baby with curly blond hair to Giuseppa. A white caul — a membrane like a gauzy wedding veil — covered the baby's head, and the midwife was delirious with joy over such a good omen.

Her labor just finished, Giuseppa mustered the strength to ask the Lord that this child be allowed to live. She again named her third son after St. Francis, the merchant's son who had renounced all the things of the world, but she went one step further: She promised from her heart that if he interceded for the boy to live a long life, she would give him entirely to St. Francis and she would let St. Francis do what he willed with her second Francesco.[16]

On that sun-filled evening of May 1887, the fetid smell of the labor still in the air and her newborn's body still slick from her womb, Giuseppa in her humility had no inkling that not only would St. Francis take her at her word but that her second Francesco would be known throughout the world as the "Second St. Francis."

Little Francesco rested his head in the crook of Giuseppa's arm, a fine fuzz of blond hair splayed on her arm as his large cheeks cushioned her breast and he fed on her milk. She again invited St. Francis to intercede for this child. Yet it wasn't enough for her that Francesco live, it was better that he be as holy as the saint he was named after, and this was Giuseppa's prayer that accompanied her offering. It was a bold move, to call a child after so high a saint, but she knew the power of prayer; and if this child could approach St. Francis in goodness, then he would do her and his namesake proud. Scarcely could Giuseppa have even fantasized that she was suckling the babe who would grow to be the saint who would be put on par with St. Francis. Had anyone dared say this to the devoutly modest Giuseppa, she would have no doubt said they were indulging in delusions of grandeur and that all she hoped for was that her son would live, and even more be good and holy.

Il Bello Franci

The midwife wrapped little Francesco in swaddling clothes. His fine blond hair curled, later growing into ringlets that fell over a full face. Giuseppa was overcome with awe looking at his adorable face. He had large chocolate-brown eyes. Two long ears framed his face. Exhausted though she was and lost in admiring him, she asked if it was still possible to have him baptized that very evening, because local custom had it that if a baby was baptized on the day he was born, a soul would be released from Purgatory. Giuseppa, always longing to relieve suffering, wanted her little boy cleansed of the stain of Original Sin so a soul could leave the purgatorial fires and go to Heaven. But it was already too late for Francesco to be taken to the baptismal font.

As an infant, it was thought that Francesco was too "adult" a name and so he was called "Franci" (Frahn-chee) until he was nearly ready to become a seminarian. Ironically, he was hardly ever called *Francesco*, except in the most formal of settings. From his earliest years, he was known as *Il bello Franci*, or "the beautiful Franci." It was said that he looked "like an angel."[17]

Laying like a cherub in Giuseppa's arms, Franci drew many admirers. He seemed to have a charisma that kept people staring at him. Neighbors enjoyed a warm sense that he loved them. On a daily basis, Giuseppa felt her heart being sliced in two as she handed Franci to her mother or relatives who cared for him while she rode on a donkey to join Grazio in the fields. She needed help such as this; she couldn't bring a tiny baby into the fields while she dug up sordid soil to plant seed.

She hated being apart from her little chap, with whom she felt a supreme attachment. She had to stop herself from idolizing him and from giving him preferential treatment, even though the tenderness in her heart for him showed in her every gesture. It was a taste of Heaven to run her fingers through his silken curls and hold his soft body next to hers. But Giuseppa's workday was so filled with onerous activity that it never left her with enough time to cuddle Franci.

Farm Life

There was so much farming to be done on their five-acre plot of land outside the village! Giuseppa learned from Grazio, who was expert in raising a wide variety of animals. He raised sheep, goats, ducks, and rabbits and kept milk cows and hogs. These creatures needed feeding and nursing when they were sick, until they were ready to slaughter.

Giuseppa also had many tasks in running the house and keeping food on the table. She fetched pails of water from the well, carrying them back to the one-room house on her head. Known throughout the village for her bread-making, Giuseppa would knead the dough, then take it to the community oven where it was baked. Giuseppa also kept hens, feeding the pecking poultry with leftovers and cleaning out their nests with meticulous care. Selling eggs was Giuseppa's side-hustle, and she also used the eggs to barter for services; the shoemaker was paid with a basket of shiny eggs.

Franci's Tears

Although he was perfectly healthy, Franci often cried. Giuseppa sensed that, even as an infant, he had already known great suffering. She would look deep into his eyes and see unmistakable flickers of pain, though she didn't know the cause. Even when he wasn't crying, Franci had a strong and solemn stare; she could feel how much he loved her.

She had prayed so much for him, even while he was still in the womb, unaware of any turmoil he was enduring. Looking back, she feared that he'd already had demons — the invisible, bodyless spirits — pester and harass him when he was growing inside her. What a cruel irony, that these evil entities knew more about her son's capacity for heroic sanctity than she did.

Neither she nor Grazio understood why, as a little baby, Franci started to cry and shriek all night long. Night after night, Franci wailed. Giuseppa and Grazio grew more and more exhausted as they went from sleepless night to sleepless night. Every night, as soon as they quenched the lamp and Franci was laid in his wooden crib, he screamed uncontrollably, and no matter how they tried to soothe him, Franci was inconsolable. He winced in agony and his face was red with hot tears. It was deeply mysterious; he was not sick and for the most part he was a joyful baby who delighted others. Yet it was clear his suffering was both real and unrelenting.

A night came when Giuseppa and Grazio tried to settle in their bed, but Franci's sharp cries pierced the air without ceasing. Grazio, half out of his mind with lack of sleep, jumped from bed, seized Franci from the crib and started to shake him while he shouted, "The good Lord must have sent a little devil into my house instead of a baby!" Tragedy almost struck when Franci slipped from Grazio's hands and his fragile body crashed to the brick floor. Giuseppa leaped from bed to scoop up her precious infant. Amid Franci's ever more hysterical sobs, Giuseppa furiously shrieked at her husband, "What are you trying to do, kill my child?"[18]

Frantically she searched her son's body, but she found no trace of injury, and as always the reason for his ballistic bawling remained a secret. The weary and worn-out parents were not to know the scary truth: Their little baby was crying because the devil himself was picking on him mercilessly. Many years later, when their boy had become a priest, he revealed, "It was the devil tormenting me!"[19]

The fact that the prince of darkness was singling out little Franci for intense persecution at such a young age is revealing but also indicative of the holiness the devil and his minions foresaw in him. Had the devil had his way, and had Franci died from being dropped to the hard floor, the world would never have known Padre Pio. But for his mama and papa's part, Grazio and Giuseppa saw no evil spirits, they only saw their child cry in desperation at the hideously malevolent shapes that sneaked up on him in the night, trying to panic him just by being themselves.

This started a trend that was to continue for the rest of Pio's life: He was terrorized by demons who came in all their extreme ugliness. From the time he was being rocked in the cradle, Franci had the added isolation of one who could see the devil while those around him only saw the victim writhing in distress. Truly, his most harrowing agony was demonic persecution. He had to learn the hard truth that salty tears and merely human intervention were no means of counteracting the demonic. And after that night when his body collided with the floor, he was a little quieter, because he had seen the futility of screams against the satanic. Still, he passed quite a few nights in tearful agitation.

At their wits' end, Giuseppa and Grazio decided to take Franci to the local mystic, a man called Giuseppe Fajella, who had healing charisms and who was visited by many of the villagers when they sought a miraculous intervention for a mysterious condition. The mystic looked at Franci and uttered a very enigmatic, paradoxical prophecy that left Giuseppa and Grazio reeling: "This baby will be honored throughout the world. Through his hands will pass vast amounts of money, but he will own none of it. He will suffer much and one day everyone will want to touch him without being able to do so."[20]

Giuseppa wondered if this meant her Franci would be like St. Francis, who gave up a colossal inheritance so that he could beg. But she and Grazio had no such inheritance to give their son. Grazio had this thought: "Maybe when he is grown up, Francesco will go to America and make a fortune, but he will not be able to invest his money."[21]

As time went on, Franci's nighttime wailing stopped, almost as though he knew his tears were not the weapons of spiritual warfare. When Franci left babyhood and become a toddler, his curls darkening to a rich gold, Giuseppa had the sweet relief of being able to take him with her when she went to the fields and tended crops with her hands. In this plot of land, she also had her rose garden. For Giuseppa, flower gardening was a joyous hobby that gave her catharsis. There was such pressure on her to plant crops that could become food for the table, but no one would go hungry if roses did not bloom. Her fingers and thumbs were hardened from growing crops but also from pricks from thorns. Yet, to see roses blossom and burst with perfume gave Giuseppa great satisfaction. Little could Giuseppa have known that in a few decades her Franci was to bear wounds on his hand and feet that would smell of roses.

Franci's Sisters

In a short few years after his birth, Franci was joined by three younger sisters. Although it was not Giuseppa's intention to show favoritism, none of the girls attracted people in the same way that Franci did, and Giuseppa didn't appear to have the same longing to be with them as she did with Franci. When she had to be away from them, she did not seem to be splitting in two with separation angst.

When Franci was two years old, Felicita was born. There was an instant harmony between Franci and Felicita; Franci must have gurgled in delight as he played with his dark-haired baby sister with the serious brown eyes. Franci loved her and glowed with fondness for her. Next came Pellegrina, with crystal blue eyes and glistening auburn hair. Her lips formed a tight knot. She was a great beauty, but there was a feeling that she was so different as to be separate. Pellegrina became the middle girl when Graziella was born at Christmas 1894. Graziella had a little face with quite a large nose, and she was placid but also shy.

One final pledge of Grazio and Giuseppa's union came into the world: Mario, their eighth child. But he died shortly after his first birthday. Three children had died, five had lived, and for the rest of his life, Franci considered himself the fourth of eight siblings.

The Growing Years

As a little boy, Franci craved the company of his sister Felicita, his mother craved his company, and the youngest two girls, pouting Pellegrina and quiet Graziella, tolerated each other. Grazio busied himself teaching Michele how to be a farmer. Michele disliked being indoors intensely. He was happiest when he was roaming the fields or learning how to plant corn. Michele was meant to attend night classes, but he played truant continuously and instead he went on long walks. He stayed illiterate all his life. The fact he was missing out on education didn't bother him; he wanted to be just like his dad who could not read or write.

Michele and Franci shared a room — the Tower — down the street from their parents' bedroom. The house in the middle served as the kitchen and the girls' bedroom. The two boys and three girls not only had separate sleeping quarters but separate houses! Of the three girls, Pellegrina might have had reason to be hurt or resentful. She didn't have a close relationship with a parent or a sibling, and she must have felt like an outsider. She wasn't admired the way Franci was admired, and she wasn't cherished in the way Franci cherished Felicita. She didn't enjoy her father's attention in the same way that strong Michele who was the heir to the farm did, nor did timid Graziella have much affection for her. But her big sister Felicita was always kind, gentle, and compassionate with her. Pellegrina, however, returned Felicita's love with vindictiveness and developed a will to injure this sensitive girl. Pellegrina was the only one who had inherited her mother's regal good looks, but instead of concern for others, Pellegrina had a look of seething. She wasn't so much the black sheep as the bitter sheep. She attended daily Mass with her family and joined in the evening family Rosary, but none of it seemed to give Pellegrina a love of Christ and His Church. As soon as Pellegrina was old enough, she abandoned it all and never frequented the sacraments. She appeared to never have felt loved by her family or by God. The Forgiones were known as "the God is everything family,"[22] but even Giuseppa and Grazio's intense efforts meant the Faith did not get passed on to Pellegrina, who remained resistant.

From their earliest years the brothers and sisters were shepherds in training. Much of Franci's early life was spent as a shepherd. Franci, his sisters and older brother, and the children of the other farming families delighted in playing in the lush green fields. It was a sublime environment. Fresh spring water irrigated the land and cooled it. Franci had a nice group of childhood friends. Later, when he was grown up, Franci reminisced that they "roamed like little kings in a kingdom without confines, whose only law was that of the Good Creation."[23]

Down the lane from the five squares of land that the Forgiones farmed there was a row of tiny cottages. Each stone cottage was owned by a local family and had two rooms and earthen floors. The Forgiones' cottage was the summerhouse for the family and was the site of some of Franci's happiest childhood memories. The animals even slept in the cottage. During the long, hot summer nights, the families came together and sang with their children under the moonlight. Giuseppa's mother, Giovanna, was a wonderful storyteller.

Heavenly Visitations

When he was five, Giuseppa dedicated Franci to the Lord, to Our Lady, and to his patron, St. Francis, which was like a renewal of the vow she'd made. Giuseppa didn't know that at this exact time, amid this healthy, happy childhood in a farming community in Southern Italy, Franci was having heavenly visitors. Jesus and His mother, as well as the boy's guardian angel, were appearing regularly to him, and Franci was in total ecstasy when he beheld the Son of God, His awesomely beautiful mother, and his sweet-singing guardian angel. Yet, he never spoke about the most astounding intimacy he was enjoying with Jesus and His Blessed Mother, because he thought all his peers were having the same experiences! This sense that his mystical experiences were normal was enhanced by how Giuseppa and Grazio spoke of Jesus and Mary as real people who were worthy of the highest reverence. But Franci just thought these apparitions were totally normal. Our Lord did not make Franci aware that he was in receipt of exceptional graces. The boy knew and understood the importance of prayer and the sacraments and he worshipped Jesus as God, but he never thought himself special in any way because Jesus came to him so often.

Contrary to some reports, Franci did not regularly give lectures on the Faith and prayer to other children. He did not feel the need to preach at all because he assumed everyone else knew what he knew. His boyhood personality was characterized by a peaceful quietude and by a listening ear that heard the Holy Spirit speak to his heart. Even though he was so little, Franci had an insatiable desire to be in the local church as much as humanly possible. And when he was only five years old, the Lord invited Franci to make a complete offering of himself, a total gift of self, so that the Lord could do whatever He wanted with his life. Franci fully embraced this call to give himself wholly.

Not long afterward, one day when Franci was deep in prayer before the high altar in the local church of St. Anne's, Jesus appeared to Franci with His Sacred Heart exposed in all its glory, and he beckoned to Franci to come closer. Franci edged closer and knelt before Jesus's Heart. Jesus placed His hand on Franci's head and treated him like a beloved son, and this gesture sent a deep message to Franci's soul that Jesus had accepted his total offering of his life to do with it as He willed.[24]

When it came time for Franci to leave the church and eat dinner with his family, he saw no reason to tell them that he had seen Jesus's Heart, the vessel filled with His Precious Blood, and that Jesus had conferred His blessing on a very special offering Franci had made. Franci just assumed that the exact same thing had happened to his mama and papa. In his simplicity, he saw no reason to tell them.

Our Lord Jesus did not tell Franci that these visits from Him were a most spectacular grace, nor did He correct Franci in his misapprehension that He appeared to all Franci's peers. Perhaps he was protecting Franci from pride and narcissism, the feeling of being more special than others, even if it was in fact the case that Franci was receiving the most special mystical experiences. In any case, this apparition of Our Lord's Sacred Heart prefigured the grand occasion in Franci's future when, as a young priest, Jesus would take Franci's heart and join it to His.

From the age of five, Franci was deeply attuned to the things of God; though he went about life as usual, this sensitivity would reveal itself in unexpected ways. For example, because Franci was having close conversations with Jesus and Mary, he could not bear profanity — he felt a curse against God as painfully as if someone insulted his mama or papa. From his earliest years, Giuseppa had also instilled in Franci a horror of blasphemy. If anyone took Jesus' name in vain, Franci ran from them. Franci's mischievous friend, Mercurio, put this to the test one day when he and Franci were engaged in some boyish wrestling, trying to see who could pin the other to the ground. Mercurio swore, and as soon as he did, Franci let loose his grip on him and sprinted away.

When he was old enough to mind the sheep on his own, Franci would often hear the Holy Spirit instruct him solemnly on how to prepare for his mission ahead. One day when Franci was with his white woolly wards, he heard in his child's heart, "Sanctify in order to sanctify."[25] Franci knew this meant he had to make himself as holy as possible before he had a hope of calling others to holiness and before he could be a useful instrument in the salvation of others. He could not call others to a state he did not have, or ask others to do what he had not done.

This inspired in him a yearning to sanctify himself by whatever means he could find. From that moment on, he spent all the free time available to him while guarding the sheep in prayer. This was training for his future, when he would guard his spiritual children and pray for them. He adopted Grazio's practice of constantly saying the Rosary. Once, Giuseppa visited the Tower and had a rude shock when she saw Franci whipping himself mercilessly until his fragile back was ripped raw. When she begged for an explanation, Franci was unusually defiant. He said he had to scourge himself as Jesus had been scourged. He seemed always to have wanted to share in the pain of Jesus' Passion, and this started when he lashed himself as Jesus had been lashed.

The Christmas Crib

There was one exception to Pio's life of shepherding, prayer, and harsh penance. He had great joy making a Christmas crib — throughout his life from early childhood to old age, the celebration of Our Lord's birth was his happiest time of the year. As early as October, when the sheep were grazing, Franci dug mounds of clay from the ground and, with his busy fingers, he molded statues of Joseph, Mary, Baby Jesus, the shepherds, and the kings.

He was especially careful to get the figure of the Christ Child just right, starting over and over until he had rendered a likeness of the Lord that he thought good enough. Surely, he relied on the visions he had of Jesus and used his personal memories to guide his execution of the statues. He also made statues for his friends. There was no electricity to light the crib, so Franci went about the field finding empty snail shells that he cleaned thoroughly, filled with oil, and then placed a little wick in the middle of. These were the tiny lanterns that lit his manger scene.

A Life of Penance

During these years, more shocks awaited Giuseppa. She prepared a lovely bed for Franci in the Tower, and she was perturbed to find he had not slept in it at all. How could he have passed up the white linen sheets she had so painstakingly washed for him? Might they not have been good enough for him? No answer came from quiet Franci. But one day she left the house to find Franci asleep outside on the earthen mattress, his head on a rough rock as his pillow. He had taken the crudest rock with deep, jagged fissures and used it to rest his head.

Giuseppa found no easy answer forthcoming from Franci and she resorted to interrogating him. He made known to her in terse sentences that his appetite for penance was growing faster than his ability to sate it and that he was making reparation for sinners. These episodes when Giuseppa was shocked by his acts of self-injury and mortification must have inspired in young Franci a growing awareness that he was a little different — if his sweet mama found it so unnerving, then it must not have been that normal.

Yet, for each stage of his childhood there was a tailor-made attack from the demonic. In the years before Franci realized his vocation to be a Franciscan priest, he came home from the fields and outside his house he met an intimidatingly malevolent figure: a man dressed in black stationed outside his house. The stone-faced man did not let Franci enter his own home but stood as a menacing barrier. On every such occasion, there would appear a beautiful child who traced the Sign of the Cross and the man disappeared. This was perhaps the earliest apparition of the Christ Child to young Franci.

On other occasions, he was also beginning to see that Jesus was giving him select knowledge that was not simultaneously being given to others. One day, Grazio dug a deep pit and hoped to find water. When no water spurted forth, Franci showed him another spot and told him that water would be found there. Grazio followed Franci's lead and water poured from that place. When questioned, Franci said simply that Jesus had told him water would be found there.

A Healing Miracle

Franci assisted at his first miracle when he was only nine years old. One summer day Grazio took his little boy far into the mountains to the shrine of St. Pellegrino. They reached the church and found it jam-packed with people. The smell of sweaty bodies, garlic, and wine filled the air, while their ears were greeted with the din of a woman shrieking angrily before the statue of St. Pellegrino. She clutched in her arms her son, who had profound physical and mental disabilities. His body looked pitifully misshapen, and there constantly issued from his throat a crowing cry of "Graaak."[26]

The mother became hysterical, begging the saint to make her child well. When her child remained as he was, she actually cursed St. Pellegrino and uttered foul oaths against him. Hearing this, Grazio wanted to leave straightaway, but Franci bade him stay. Franci broke the rule his mother had given him, that he was to absent himself from the presence of one who cursed, and despite his father's attempts to take him out of the church, Franci remained rooted to the spot.

Finally the mother bellowed at the statue of St. Pellegrino, "Why don't you cure him? Well, keep him, he's yours!" And with that she hurled her boy at the statue. The little boy ricocheted off the marble and landed on the floor. Then he got to his feet and ran to his mother, calling out "Mama!" He had never walked or talked before that moment. But now he was completely well, his body healed, and he looked as though he had never been physically disabled. Resounding shouts of "miracle" went up from the teeming congregation of peasants.

At a spot further back in the church, young Franci remained praying for the boy and his mother. He knew the woman's melodramatic hysteria was not the way Giuseppa conducted herself, yet the healing showed Franci the great mercy of God, who deigned to heal a child miraculously, even though his mother had cursed a saint in Heaven.

3

FRANCI AND THE LURE OF WHISKERS

Giuseppa loved and cherished her darling Franci and longed to have him with her as much as possible. She even took him with her when she did works of mercy such as bringing plates of food to the sick and hungry in their primitive homes lit by gas lamp.

As was her way, the meat that Giuseppa abstained from on Wednesdays, Fridays, and Saturdays was given to those who could not afford food themselves. Each time she came into a house in her gleaming white dress to present a hungry person with a plate of delicious chicken and vegetables, she never mentioned that this food was spare because she had been fasting. Hers was a joyful offering, out of love for Christ.

When Franci was nine, he followed Giuseppa as she visited patients in the hospital at Benevento. They had gone by train to the town about five miles distant, where the nearest major hospital was located. Every time they went there, Giuseppa did the rounds of the wards, greeting and praying with patients for their health to return.

One such day, mother and son came across a soldier who had been maimed in battle. At the soldier's bed was a priest and nun who were trying to raise his spirits despite the soldier's protestations that he was about to die. The young soldier was already mourning separation from his mother and he poignantly cried out, "I'll never see her again. I feel like I'm dying and I'd like to see my family, especially my mother, who loves me so much, for the last time."[27] Then the officer hung his head and went to God.

Giuseppa did not pull her son away from this deathbed scene or cover his eyes. Instead, Giuseppa quietly held court, praying mentally for the soldier's soul and letting her son hear the dying words of the warrior who had pined for his own mother. Giuseppa allowed the sight of death to seep into Franci's soul. But so shaken was Franci by the sting of death that he didn't eat for the next two days. This encounter with death happened just before Franci was called to be a Franciscan.

Meeting Br. Camillo

While Franci knew he had been named for St. Francis, he did not want to become a friar until he met a young Capuchin named Br. Camillo in 1897, on a day that at first seemed like any other day.

Ten-year-old Franci had noticed that other children were buzzing with excitement: Br. Camillo, their favorite friar, was walking into the village. The children rushed at the Franciscan, squealing with glee. But Franci stood spellbound, his eyes wide as he took in Camillo's appearance. He was hugely impressed with this young friar — Camillo was twenty-six and had a flowing brown beard that utterly captivated Franci. True joy and holiness radiated from him. As was the custom, his crown was shaved, looking as though he had a wreath of brown hair around his head. Franci could not take his eyes off Br. Camillo's bearded face as Camillo was swamped by the local children.

A manly charisma came in waves off Camillo, whose face spread itself in a natural smile. With great tenderness, Camillo handed each child a holy card or medal as though he were giving them a precious gem. The late morning sun shone higher in the sky and caused Camillo's beard to glitter. When Franci approached the zealous Camillo and asked him what he would have to do to become a bearded friar, Camillo did a little promotion for the Franciscans and said to the boy that all Capuchins had to grow beards. At that very moment, Franci was determined to become a Capuchin friar.

Camillo could not have known that his combination of virility and holiness, tenderness and reverence, strength and Christlike presence had led the boy who was to become the Second Francis into his religious order. Camillo had been in Pietrelcina to beg. He traveled through the Southern Italian terrain, sack on his back, and begged for food and money, just as St. Francis had been a "holy beggar" to obtain the means to feed the men who were becoming his followers.

Franci announced to Giuseppa, "I want to be a friar with a beard." His manner was so serious that at first she found it funny. "With a beard!" she exclaimed. "Why, you're still a little child. You don't know anything about having a beard or not having a beard."[28] Then Giuseppa was most likely sharply reminded of the promise she had given St. Francis. She was being asked to give her beloved son, and although there were some years left before she would have to say goodbye to him, she already felt separation anxiety creep up on her. She'd known for a long time that Franci's strongest desire was to spend as much time as possible praying in their local church. But she had never suggested to Franci that he become a Franciscan priest; she'd known better than to supplant the voice of God in her son's soul. Giuseppa knew that the quicker she worked to pave Franci's way to the priesthood, the sooner she would keep her promise to St. Francis.

She was moved to her marrow by her little boy's resolve. When someone else suggested to Franci that he become a Benedictine, he refused outright: "No, I don't want to go there because they haven't got beards."[29] Franci, of course, had no idea of the pledge his mother had made, but years later when he was an ordained priest, the Holy Spirit revealed to him the offering she made of his life to St. Francis. When he would recount his vocation story, he admitted his obsession with Br. Camillo's beard: "Brother Camillo's beard was vividly before me all the time and nothing could make me change my mind."[30]

Giuseppa Keeps Her Promise

The mere thought of Franci moving away to seminary was already cutting at her heart, but Giuseppa felt she owed his life to St. Francis's intercession, and she had to hold up her side of her promise regardless of the sacrifices she had to make. And true to her efficient nature, Giuseppa wasted no time. The next time Br. Camillo came to the village to beg, she marched up to him and declared, "Brother Camillo, we've got to make this boy a monk."[31]

Br. Camillo already had an intuition that Franci was going to be a friar, and he spoke as though it was a foregone conclusion when he replied to Giuseppa, "May St. Francis bless him and help him to be a good Capuchin."[32] Br. Camillo invited Giuseppa to his friary to talk to his superiors about Franci joining the community when he was fifteen. She accepted their proposal, and shortly afterward, Giuseppa and Grazio traveled by train to the friary at Morcone, about seventeen miles by rail. The brown-robed superiors liked Franci, and they offered him a place.

When Grazio and Giuseppa came home that evening, they found Franci waiting for them, anxious to know if he'd been accepted. When they told him that there was a place in Camillo's friary, he was delirious with joy. "They want me! They want me!" he cried.[33]

Preparing for Seminary

Franci could not rush headlong into the seminary. He had to finish school first. Although Grazio and Giuseppa were overjoyed that Franci was going to be a priest, they had no spare money to pay for his tuition. He'd had three years of public school, but that was all that came free. The Forgiones worked to grow food for their table; they didn't get paid salaries.

Times were hard. Already three in ten men from Pietrelcina had left to find work in other parts of the world — and Grazio was quite a bit older than most of them. Grazio and Giuseppa were then in their late thirties, yet they both embraced the challenge with joy. Grazio, in his characteristically jovial way, even quipped that his choice was "emigrate or steal."[34] Both man and wife were called to make sacrifices, but they did so without a trace of resentment and with a buoyancy born of joy that they were sending their boy to the priesthood.

Grazio's Travels

The day came when Grazio had to bid *arrivederci* to his family. His five children and Giuseppa waved him off as he left for Naples, then set sail for Brazil. It was an arduous (and expensive) passage, yet Grazio went there with high hopes. He had a friend who had moved to South America and written home to report that there was a killing to be made — and that the houses had gold roofs. Grazio didn't see the brags for what they were, and he spent weeks on a ship. He was in for a rude awakening when his ship docked and he found no gold tiles and his friend working in a restaurant, washing dishes. The man was so embarrassed that Grazio didn't have the heart to upbraid him.

Poor Grazio had to borrow the money for the journey back to Italy. Later he was able to pay the money back, but the Brazil misadventure was a harsh penance for poor Grazio. Yet he refused to give up on finding work, and he soon resolved to emigrate once again, this time to the United States.

Grazio decided he would join some of his cousins who were working in Mahoningtown, Pennsylvania, tilling the soil of the Myers family farm. When he arrived, Grazio spoke no English, but he was such a hard worker, with fine expertise in raising crops and animals, that he was promoted to being a manager of other farmhands. Back home in Pietrelcina, the ever-energetic Giuseppa ran the farm by herself and had to take on some extra laborers. The sign that their marriage was very strong was that it was not strained by the thousands of miles put between them.

Every week without fail, Grazio sent nine dollars home. Letters went back and forth: Grazio had someone write his letter for him and Franci wrote letters in reply. When Giuseppa had enough money saved, she enrolled Franci in a school run by Maestro Domenico Tizzani. Tizzani was a tight-lipped man with a sour expression suggestive of his depressive nature. He had once been in the priesthood, but had left, been laicized, gotten married, and had children. Despite this change of vocation, Tizzani had a good reputation and was not known to be guilty of anything resembling malevolence or misconduct. He was thought well of as a teacher but was silent and joyless.

Franci, however, was deeply uncomfortable being taught by Tizzani and could not calm his mind to the point where he could learn. Soon he was getting bad grades. Tizzani deflected the blame, telling Giuseppa that Franci spent an inordinate amount of time praying in the village church and wasn't using his time to study. This upset Giuseppa, whose beloved husband was slaving to send money home to pay for Franci's education, whereas Franci was failing.

Swiftly, she confronted Franci: "What am I going to write to your father, who emigrated to America to pay for your studies to become a monk?" Franci then gave his mother the unvarnished truth, in an equally direct way: "Mama, it isn't my going to church that prevents me from learning. It's just that that man is a bad priest."[35]

Giuseppa was taken aback by her eleven-year-old boy's assertion — which he made in the present tense — that his teacher was an erring man of the cloth. Tizzani had not been in active priestly ministry for some years, but the Church holds that when a man is ordained, an indelible mark is placed on his soul which remains forever. When Franci saw Tizzani as a priest, this was one of the earliest occasions of Franci reading the soul of another. Young Franci did not complain that Tizzani had left the priesthood; rather that he *is* a "bad priest." Could it have been that Tizzani had abandoned prayer, and projected his own failure on the boy who spent so much time in church?

For the young boy, on the verge of his teens, Franci may have felt that Tizzani's leaving behind his vocation was something of a betrayal of Christ, whom, even during Franci's tender years, he loved most of all. Meanwhile Grazio thought it quite the contradiction for their son to be prepared for the priesthood by one who had left the celibate life, and he instructed Giuseppa to pull Franci out of Tizzani's school. Giuseppa was forced to find a new teacher — and she had to be wily. Angelo Caccavo was a good teacher who was also a strict disciplinarian with a hot temper. But he refused initially because he feared offending Tizzani. So, Giuseppa had to rally her family, the Di Nunzios, to ask Caccavo as a team, until he relented.

Caccavo was not particularly prayerful, but his lack of great holiness did not bother Franci. His two teachers evoked different reactions in young Franci, starting a trend that was to continue for all Franci's life. He was displeased to despondency when a priest or nun showed anything less than a total commitment to piety and perfection of soul, but with laypeople he was much more patient, even if he did speak to them in equally direct, pithy terms.

On his first day at this new school, Giuseppa informed Caccavo that she wanted her child to be clouted and not coddled: "Teacher, I have to work on the farm, so I am leaving him in your hands. Beat him if necessary."[36]

While Caccavo could be heavy handed — he would smack a child on the head with a book — he rarely punished Franci, with one notable exception. Once, Caccavo received an indecent letter, signed in Franci's name but actually written by a girl in the same class. Enraged, he bitterly rebuked Franci, pounding the boy with his fists until his wife rushed in and put herself between them. Later, when Caccavo found out he had been tricked, he was deeply ashamed of having punched the boy of whom he was so fond.

This beating episode shows that, while Franci was a mystic and miracle-worker, he was not all-knowing. Although he had seen his guardian angel from infancy, heard the words of Jesus that guided him to a bountiful spring of water, and assisted in healing the profoundly disabled boy when he was nine, Franci did not know the prank that was about to be played on him; otherwise he could have intervened and prevented the punishment. The incident was an outlier, however, and Franci completed the three-year course in two years, graduating first in his class.

Although Franci never gave Caccavo cause to scold or slap him, he was no shrinking violet and often gave as good as he got. Franci could be rambunctious in his play. Once, his best friend, Mercurio Scocca, found Franci sleeping and he piled corn husks on top of him. When Franci woke in pitch darkness, he screamed violently. Later, Franci retaliated when he discovered Mercurio napping on top of a farm wagon. He pushed the wagon up a hill and then let it roll. Its wooden wheels sped down the slope's lush green grass, with Mercurio wailing, until it hit a tree. Mercurio was unscathed, but he now appreciated better Franci's mettle.

Felicita was not only Franci's favorite sibling but his favorite person, and yet he would tease her as well, coming up behind her while she was in the bath and pushing her head into the water. She was too gentle and too consumed with the desire to forgive to retaliate, and she just said, "Hey Franci, you never stop playing, do you?"[37]

The topper of all his childhood naughtiness was when he was fourteen and went on a pilgrimage to see the shrine of Our Lady of Pompeii in Naples. He did not tell Giuseppa where he was going, and she was severely anxious when he had seemingly disappeared. She complained of this to Grazio in a letter that Franci wrote for her. Grazio reprimanded Franci by letter, and his contrite son then sent an apology letter to America. This parenting by long-distance mail is an indication of how Grazio and Giuseppa were more diligent in seeing to Franci's character formation than they were with the other children's. He was the one who needed the most sacrifices.

Grazio and Giuseppa were not the only ones who sacrificed. The two youngest girls, Pellegrina and Graziella, did not have the same closeness with their father as the older three. They just didn't have as much time with their daddy, and he was away for such long spells — even years at a time. When Grazio did cross the ocean by ship and come home for hurried vacations, his two little daughters were uncomfortable when he tried to cuddle them. Pellegrina appeared to be lonely and left out. Later, when she was a young woman, Pellegrina went to great lengths to get attention from men, even causing her older sister extreme pain — maybe because she was seeking the affections of men to compensate for the attention from Grazio that had she missed.

4

THE LIE THAT NEARLY COST A VOCATION

When Franci turned fourteen, a new priest arrived in town who had a remarkable influence on his vocation. His name was Salvatore Pannullo. He was fifty-two years old, very smart, and a little odd-looking, though he was quite outgoing. He had a sharp nose and jutting jaw with large eyes that protruded from his face like golf balls. His hairline had receded, but his remaining hair was white, and so straight and coarse that it stood on end.

Don Salvatore had been a college professor and had a photographic memory; he'd memorized the Gospels and could recite them at will during Holy Mass. He was a great intellectual, and although he was truly pious, nothing in his life had adequately prepared him to guide Franci. Yet the priest had a stout heart and a courageousness that was to serve Franci well in the battles that lay ahead.

For the next twenty-five years, Fr. Salvatore would prove himself to be a loyal and valuable friend. From the start Fr. Salvatore was impressed by Franci's holiness and did everything to accommodate it and nurture his vocation. He heard Franci's frequent confessions and made special provision for Franci to have as much time as possible in the chapel, praying before the Blessed Sacrament. He warmly encouraged the young boy's dream of becoming a Franciscan friar. Franci served Salvatore's Mass, gave the responses in Latin, and had an angelic disposition. He was the priest's favorite server. Franci even called him "Daddy." Don Salvatore could hardly have guessed that in forming Franci's soul, he was fashioning he who would be the first priest to bear the wounds of Christ. Nor could he have imagined that he would be the first priest to whom Franci would confide the details of receiving the stigmata. Neither could Franci have intuited that nine years later, Fr. Salvatore would help him obtain the grace to keep the stigmata secret.

Don Salvatore considered it his honor to give a glowing letter of recommendation to the Franciscans who Franci hoped with all his heart would accept him as a seminarian. And he was overjoyed when a letter came with the gladdest of news: Franci had been accepted by the Franciscans of Morcone, seventeen miles from his hometown. When he heard the news, Franci could not contain himself and jumped up and down. He had not been at all certain they would give him a place, showing his humility and lack of awareness that he was a perfect candidate.

One day Franci's vocation and relationship with Fr. Salvatore were suddenly thrown into jeopardy. Salvatore received an unsigned letter, which claimed that Franci had been sleeping with the daughter of the stationmaster. In fact, Franci did not even know the girl. Imagine poor Fr. Salvatore's shock when he had cause to doubt Franci! Would he have to retract the recommendation?

Salvatore temporarily dismissed Franci from his altar serving duties. Franci did not know the reason, he just obediently did whatever Don Salvatore asked, and Franci was not given any special mystical insight that he'd been accused of having a premarital sexual relationship. Thankfully, Fr. Salvatore launched a thorough investigation and uncovered the writers of the meddling missive: two boys who wanted to make Franci look a hypocrite. They were also altar servers and had been motivated by envy of the high esteem in which Salvatore held Franci. But if anything, the incident made the big-eyed, big-hearted priest think more highly of Franci; he'd not uttered a word of complaint when he was let go, and when his name was cleared, he returned to serving on the altar with the same ungrudging dedication to perfection.

When Accusations Strike

Perhaps you have been a victim of jealousy. Maybe someone threw dirt on your good name and caused you to be less in the eyes of those who liked and admired you. By this means they assuaged their jealousy, because having damaged your reputation they had less reason to be jealous. I submit that Franci's response to those who calumniated him is a good way forward.

As one would expect, he never became bitter or took revenge. Instead, he gave them over to the Lord: "At times I did mention to God, 'My Lord, if it is necessary to give them a whipping or two to convert them, please do it, as long as their souls are saved in the end.' "[38] Later, when he had been a priest for some time, he saw this incident as part of God's plan to make him see that love of

God trumps love of creatures. "With what was almost jealousy for His Son," he reflected, God "often allowed those who were attached to the earth to illtreat me, to shower ungrateful blows on me so that I might understand how false and mistaken was the love which in my innocence I bestowed on creatures."[39]

A Supernatural Vision

Just after celebrating Christmas with his family, Franci was set to leave for seminary in the early days of 1903. On New Year's Day, after he had received Holy Communion, he had one of the most dramatic supernatural visions of his life. The vision foretold the epic battle he would fight with the devil on behalf of Christ and His kingdom. As his reward, he was promised a crown of victory, and then promised an even more beautiful crown if he kept up a continual, all-out fight against the devil.

This mystical revelation began with Christ appearing at Franci's side as "a majestic man of rare beauty, resplendent as the sun."[40] Christ led him to a big field. Two enormous groups awaited him. On one side were "men of beautiful countenance clad in snow-white garments." On the other were "hideous, black-robed figures like so many dark shadows." Christ brought Franci right into the middle of the two divisions, and Franci wondered why he was in the space between them. He did not wonder for long.

Suddenly the devil came at him. He had "the face of a hideous black monster," and he was so tall his face touched the clouds. Christ informed Francesco that it was his mission to fight the devil and that He would help him. Francesco turned pale, trembled, and fainted in panic, but Our Lord prevented him from falling to the ground by supporting him on His arm. Regaining consciousness, Francesco begged Christ to spare him from the devil. Christ acknowledged that the devil was so strong that the united strength of all men could not defeat him.

This is very instructive for us. None of us can ever win out against the prince of darkness on our own strength. Relying on Christ's grace is our only hope of successfully fighting the evil one. Christ told Franci that His will was for him to fight the devil and that He would not allow him a free pass. "Your every resistance is vain. You must fight.... Take heart. Enter the battle with confidence. Go forth with courage. I shall be with you. In reward for your victory over him I will give you a shining crown to adorn your brow."

Francesco mustered courage and rose to the challenge. The devil assaulted him ferociously, but Christ never left his side. Eventually Francesco threw the devil to the ground and the fallen angel was forced to flee. The group of foul creatures took flight, howling ear-splitting cries and curses as they left. The group in white robes applauded Francesco's victory and sang praises to Christ. Christ took from within His robes a crown of rarest beauty and placed it on Francesco's head. But then Christ removed it and promised, "I will reserve for you a crown even more beautiful if you fight the good fight with the creature you have just fought. He will continually renew the assault to regain his lost honor." To this Christ added a powerful assurance: "Fight valiantly and do not doubt my aid." Christ stressed to Francesco that he was to be alert; the devil would try to take him by surprise, but he was not to allow himself to become fearful. Christ promised Francesco that He would always succeed in conquering the devil.

We may not receive a vision as stunning as the one that was given Francesco. We may, however, garner many gems of insight as to how to win our own war against the devil. We must first acknowledge that a real war is raging here and now for our souls. The devil is as he appeared in Francesco's vision: a foul brute whose frame fills the space between earth and sky, signifying that he is the prince of this world. If this truth scares us, we are in good company. Nearly twenty years after this vision, when Franci had become Padre Pio, he admitted he had been terrified and that even recalling it provoked fight-or-flight symptoms. "The mere recollection of that interior combat makes the blood freeze in my veins," he confessed, adding, "It was a sight to make the strongest tremble." Yet, he also revealed that Jesus had shown him this battle scene as a sign of "His infinite mercy."[41] You, too, might meditate on the vision given young Franci, and allow yourself to be thankful for Our Lord's mercy in sending one like Franci to fight the devil on behalf of his spiritual children.

Guard Against Our Adversary

In later years, when Franci became Padre Pio, he used to call the devil "the enemy of our salvation." Although that may sound extreme, to deny that the devil is our great adversary — and we his prey — is to engage in a deception that makes him more powerful, because we underestimate the danger he poses and do not adequately prepare for the threat.

Padre Pio said, "Here on earth we are on a battlefield."[42] We cannot rely on our own strength any more than Francesco was able to do; by acknowledging this, we do not denigrate ourselves but act in accord with truth and humility. As Christ told Franci, even the strength of all humans combined is no match. Rather, we must do as Francesco did, and on perceiving the devil's advance, we must lean on the arm of Our Savior. In the heat of battle, we must rely on Christ's strength and let this confidence replace all fear. Padre Pio used say, "Do not let the infernal beast frighten you. God will fight it with you and for you."[43]

In our battles with the demonic, we may be applauded by the holy angels and saints. And the population of Hell will react to our victory with howls and curses. The deafening noise made by demons is not a metaphorical sound effect. Padre Pio used to inform the people who flocked to him that such noise was actually a positive harbinger: "If the demon makes a lot of noise it's a sign he is still outside, and not inside. What should frighten us is when he is at peace and in harmony with our human soul."[44] In short, the roaring of the devil means he has not gained access. Another piece of wisdom Padre Pio shared is that there can be a period of artificial calm when first a soul falls for a ploy of the devil. "What comes from Satan begins with calmness," he warned, "and ends in storms, indifference and apathy."[45] This false "calmness" is not the lasting peace of God; it's good to know that Satan can confuse souls with fake peace that ends badly.

Christ also told Francesco that the devil would try to catch him off guard, but He pledged to Franci that He would always win out over the devil, so we have no reason to be fearful. The shadow of Satan ought not to scare us. The vision fortified Franci. Although such combat made his blood run cold, he was at the same time much braver, and after the vision he said he had "great courage" and felt "strong and generous in bidding farewell to the world."[46]

A Painful Goodbye

When Francesco prepared to leave home for the first time as a boy of fifteen, he had never been away even for a weeklong vacation. He felt his very bones being crushed because of the pain of parting. "I felt two forces within me, who were struggling against themselves and lacerating my heart," he wrote. "The world that wanted me for itself, and God who was calling me to a new life."[47]

On the day before he was to leave home, Our Lord gave Francesco a vision that took away the sorrow he felt at leaving his family and the world behind. Jesus appeared in all His glory, and beside Him was His Blessed Mother. They told Francesco how much they loved him. Once again Jesus placed His hand on Francesco's head, just as He had when he appeared to five-year-old Franci when he made a complete offering of himself to God. His pain vanished, and Francesco did not cry as he left the winding street where he had been born.

Giuseppa was only forty-three when she had to kiss her beloved Franci and bid him goodbye as tears fell from her eyes. The day had come when she had to honor her promise. She was letting her boy go and delivering him into the arms of St. Francis. A minute before he left, he knelt before Giuseppa for her blessing. "My son," she said plaintively to him in an echo of her vow, "my heart is bleeding, but St. Francis is calling you and you must go."[48]

He left behind the stone house of his birth and took the one-hour journey by train to Morcone, a town carved out of the side of the Matese Mountains, whose peaks were bright white with heavy snow. Morcone had an atmosphere of quiet and deep prayer; it had long been a nerve center for monastic life.

On arriving at the seminary, Francesco was greeted by Br. Camillo, who opened the front door and exclaimed, "Ah, Franci! Bravo! Bravo! You've been faithful to your promise and to the calling of St. Francis!"[49] How fitting that the same friar who had inspired his vocation would be the one to welcome him to religious life. Francesco was then shown to his cell. There was a wooden cross on the wall, a simple table and chair, a mattress filled with corn husks, and a nightstand with a jug for water. There was no welcoming party or session of handshakes and grinning introductions. Instead, Franci was greeted by silence.

5

A River of Tears

As a boy Francesco had never gone barefoot, as he did now as a novice. He took off his boots and never put them on again. His feet were to know the hard stone ground as he began a life which was divided between his cell and the chapel.

After arriving, he spent many days in intense meditation on his own. Whereas these days of solitary meditation may seem isolating to us, it was the best way for Francesco Forgione, the novice, to orient himself to God. He was to be like Elijah, who went to the mountaintop and found God in silence. The mountains of Morcone were to Francesco what Mount Sinai was to Elijah. In later years Padre Pio would say, "By meditation one finds Him."[50]

As a novice Francesco was under the stern direction of the novice master, Padre Tommaso. At the age of thirty-one, Tommaso had the look and demeanor of a vicious guard dog, with a glare that could melt the snow off the mountain peaks. Tommaso was the first to call Franci by his new name, "Pio." This name change took place just sixteen days after his arrival, during the solemn investiture ceremony.

Francesco and the other novices gathered in the chapel, and when his turn came, he knelt at the foot of the altar. Fr. Tommaso took off Francesco's jacket and prayed aloud, "May the Lord strip from you the old man and all his actions."[51] Francesco was then given his brown habit to put on while Tommaso intoned, "May the Lord re-clothe you in the new man who is created according to God, in justice, holiness, and truth." When Francesco had put the brown hood over his head, Tommaso prayed, "May the Lord put the hood of salvation upon your head to defeat the wiles of the devil." Francesco then tied the white cord around his waist and Tommaso prayed for the virtues he would need to remain chaste: "May the Lord gird you with the cord of purity and extinguish within your loins the fire of lust, so the virtues of continence and chastity might abide in you." Tommaso gave Francesco a lit candle to cup in his hands while instructing him, "Take the light of Christ as a sign of your immortality, so that dead to the world, you might live in God. Rise from the dead and Christ will give you light!"

Then and there Francesco's head was shaved at the top and at the front until he had a wreath of dark auburn hair around the sides. Fr. Tommaso informed him that his new name was "Br. Pio." This name had been decided by his superiors, and he had had no say in the matter. Why Pio, you may ask? "Pio" is the Italian for "Pius," and he was called Pio in honor of Pope St. Pius V, the pope who led the Rosary campaign that gave the Christians the grace of victory at the Battle of Lepanto in 1571. Henceforth Pio always celebrated May 5 as his name day, which is the feast day of Pius V.

Monastic Life Begins

The clanging of a bell was the alarm clock that woke Br. Pio every morning except Sundays, when the friars rested. Retiring at nine o'clock each evening, he got out of bed at thirty minutes after midnight and made his way to the chapel for his personal prayer time. Then he and the other fifty members of the community recited two hours of the Divine Office. They returned to their cells at 2:30 a.m. for two and a half more hours of sleep before waking at five. These tiny windows of sleep were all the rest given Pio, the aspiring ascetic.

At five o'clock they all gathered in the choir for an extensive period of prayer, including the Litany of the Saints, in preparation for two Holy Masses. After receiving Holy Communion, they had breakfast, a spare meal of bread and oil. Early on Br. Pio was in the habit of passing parts of his meals to the other novices, who gladly accepted the extra bread.

Breakfast eaten, they flocked to the chapel to pray the Divine Office of Our Lady. Br. Pio would then join the other novices who were being schooled by Padre Tommaso on memorizing the Rule of St. Francis. After taking instruction from Tommaso, they had time to study before going to the chapel to pray more of the Divine Office. After offering the Angelus at noon, they went to dinner, where most days the community ate like most Catholics eat on Good Friday: one meal and two smaller meals, with these two combined not exceeding the portions of a full meal. In addition, they fasted from November 2 until Christmas, and from February 2 to Easter Sunday.

After Br. Pio had eaten his dinner, he took a nap before joining the rest of the community to recite the Vespers of Our Lady. There were no maids in the employ of the friars, and the novices were given domestic tasks to do, such as scrubbing floors.

Br. Pio was never one to utter even a tiny word of complaint about the austerity of his cell, the tiny food rations, or the bitter cold. There was no central heating, and the friary was warmed by a single fire that eased the chill in a friary of fifty residents. Yet Pio could not stand the way other novices grumbled, and he left their company when they griped. Pio was a living embodiment of the Franciscan ideal that it is hard to satisfy the senses without slipping into sinful self-indulgence.

The novices' stomachs were swiftly shrinking with each meager meal. Every novice had to get the approval of Fr. Tommaso before eating by going on their knees before him and asking him to bless them. If Tommaso did not answer, the novice had to stay kneeling there and could be kneeling there until the rest of the community had finished eating. If, however, Tommaso gave them his blessing, the novice took his place and ate his meal. If a boy had displeased Tommaso, he could be told to take his food and eat off the floor like a dog. In fact, if a novice failed to keep an aspect of the Rule of St. Francis, he came to know how authoritarian Tommaso could be. In the event that a novice did not meet Tommaso's standards, he could expect a wooden collar to be put around his neck or to be blindfolded. All of this was done with the aim of supplanting the will of each novice with the will of their immediate superior, to make each newly minted Franciscan as obedient as possible.

There were other forms of physical penance as well. A novice could be told to flagellate himself while contemplating Our Lord's Passion. This act of whipping oneself was called "the discipline" and was part and parcel of Capuchin Franciscan life in those days. It was not out of the ordinary for novices and ordained priests to do it of their own free will. The violent punishment was intended to imitate Christ, who let His flesh rain with blood to cleanse us of our sins.

Br. Pio saw that these formative practices served an important purpose: He had to learn to die to self and become an ever more faithful replica of the wounded Christ. Therefore, Pio was willing to accept every punishment offered, but Tommaso could find no fault in Pio; he even gave Pio a high compliment when he commented, "This boy seems to know and observe the Rule better than we do."[52]

One day Tommaso forbade Br. Pio from taking the Eucharist at Mass. Tommaso gave no reasonable explanation, but when Pio did not receive Jesus in Holy Communion, he became suddenly so deathly ill that the friars thought he was dying. Tommaso never asked Pio to forgo receiving the Body and Blood of Christ again. Fifty years later, the memory of being forbidden from receiving Holy Communion brought Pio to tears.

Another novice pressured Pio to leave because he thought Padre Tommaso was so mean he could be of the devil. But Pio, even though he'd been reduced to lifelessness by Tommaso's insistence he go without the Eucharist, saw things differently. He replied to his peer, "I could never agree to this. You'll see, with Our Lady's and St. Francis' help, we too, little by little, will get used to this new life just as others before us did.... No one is born a friar."[53] Pio was willing to undergo any ill-treatment to become a friar. This shows us how badly he wanted to be a friar, to be like St. Francis, when he could have left and become a priest elsewhere. He'd been promised to St. Francis as a baby, and St. Francis was interceding for him from Heaven to receive graces of perseverance. His die-hard commitment to become a Franciscan eventually won him the respect of Tommaso, who lauded him as "an example to all."[54] From such an implacable judge, this was praise indeed.

We might be tempted to think of Padre Tommaso as a sadist who derived pleasure from ordering young boys to inflict pain upon themselves, and who caused Pio immeasurable grief by keeping him from Holy Communion. Certainly, people have said this was abuse. But it is more likely that Tommaso did not do it to derive pleasure from the pain of others, or even to derive pleasure from the pain inflicted upon himself, because we must bear in mind that Tommaso flagellated himself, too, and he earned respect because he asked others to do unto themselves as he did unto himself. He was in a sense a bodyguard for the Franciscans. He used these harsh methods to help him sort through the novices to find the ones whose vocations were so genuine they were willing to sacrifice their own autonomy and even sacrifice their dignity to become a Franciscan.

The time in history in which Tommaso was a novice master must also be kept in mind. Life with him was harrowing, and he regularly reduced the novices to such ignominy that they ate off the floor, yet it may not have been as hard as remaining in the world. As a novice there was a guarantee of at least some meager food and a room of one's own. In the Southern Italy of the early 1900s, crops failed, poverty was rife, and people often went hungry.

Under Padre Tommaso's iron fist, these teenage novices were being ground down and sorted like wheat from chaff. The fiery intensity of Tommaso's rigorous standards was purifying them like metal in a fire. If they were not the genuine gold of a true vocation, they would leave, which they often did. If, on the other hand, they withstood the humiliations, they were seen to be sincere and were not just becoming a friar so they could escape real-world suffering. Only a special grace such as that given Pio would have allowed a novice to subject himself to all this in the hope of being a Franciscan.

A Family Visit

The fact that Pio withstood Fr. Tommaso tells us a lot about his determination to give himself entirely to God, even as a young man. About a year into his formation, Giuseppa paid a visit to her son. She had given him so generously to St. Francis, who was now molding him into his successor as a stigmatist. She could have offered her son to any saint, but she offered him to St. Francis and gave him without reserve.

When she arrived at the friary, Giuseppa was faced for the first time with the pain of having given away her son. No one had primed the proud mama for what to expect, and she was in for a rude awakening. When she met Br. Pio in the monastery's guest room, her son, who had always been so affectionate, now seemed like a stranger. He looked drained of love and of his personality; in Giuseppa's presence he kept his head and eyes lowered. There was a chill in the air when he accepted the gifts Giuseppa had brought him and said perfunctorily, "Thank you, I will take them to my superior."[55]

"Son, what's the matter?" she asked him anxiously. "Why have you become mute?"[56] When she got no answer, she left in tears. She had offered up her son with total generosity and was being rewarded with his hostility. She did not complain to Pio's superiors or suggest to him — as his peer had done —that he leave. Rather, she grieved the loss of her son, who was breaking his bonds to his family by withdrawing all affection from her. St. Francis was taking her entirely at her word, but it was not easy, and Giuseppa suffered more at this time for her boy's vocation than at any other. She was being treated as though she had been an abusive mother, when she had been nothing of the sort.

Soon after, Grazio came home to Pietrelcina for a vacation and became irate when Giuseppa told him how Pio had treated her with such coldness. He rushed to Morcone and demanded to see Tommaso, ready to ask that his son leave the seminary. Tommaso assured him everything was well with Pio. So determined, however, was Pio to do as he had been instructed as a novice and break his undue attachments to family that he did not even offer his mama and papa the barest of explanations. Years later, he would reflect on this incident and admit, "As soon as I saw my mother, my impulse was to throw myself into her arms. But the discipline of the novitiate did not permit this."[57] Pio also refused an invitation to Michele's wedding back in Pietrelcina. Michele had met a lovely, big-hearted girl, and Grazio came from America for the nuptials. Although Pio could have gotten permission, he steadfastly declined to come, but he had to write Grazio a sensitive letter excusing himself lest he cause offense.

The River of Tears

That first painful visit between mother and son marked the beginning of a series of sensitive struggles that would continue for years to come. Pio began shedding tears, too, but they were a different caliber of crying altogether. He had the gift of tears and was seen as one who sobbed when he prayed on his knees or while walking through the friary or while praying in choir. Pio was totally consumed in meditating on Christ's Crucifixion; the Savior nailed to the Cross dominated his thoughts. When he was among the others in choir and they were praying, rivulets of tears fell from his eyes. Pio kept a white handkerchief at his side, which quickly became saturated with the salty water of his tears. And his tears fell in such steady streams that they stained the ground. The reason he cried is most revealing. Under obedience, Pio admitted, "I cry for my sins and those of mankind."[58]

Although it was the case that he spent most of his day praying and then prayed again during the night, it was his piety that singled him out among his peers. The others would see him in his room on his knees consumed in prayer. Now that you've learned of this regime of prayer and worship, as well as how much Pio prayed on his own, the question may occur to you whether it was too much. But it was never against Br. Pio's will to spend that much time in prayer, and it was the essential training and preparation for one who would spend fifty-eight years as a priest in the deepest of deep prayer for other people. During Pio's lifetime, people who were recipients of his prayers and who were cured of hideous afflictions and deadly diseases never complained that Pio prayed too much. Those who were snatched from Satan's grasp and escaped Hell never bemoaned Pio's prayers. It was through prayer that Pio brought so many, many souls to God — arguably your soul and mine, too.

Memento Mori

The picture I've painted of Br. Pio is a true one, but he may present as someone so strict and dour that others were repelled by him. By all accounts, however, the other novices and friars loved being in his company. The same fellow who had been a prankster in childhood wasn't always so straitlaced in seminary that he never played a practical joke.

Once, in the early hours of the morning, Br. Pio was returning from the bathroom when he spotted another novice who was quite nervy. Near them was a room which was completely dark — this room was the home of the *memento mori*, a large human skull which sat on a stage, serving to remind all who beheld it of the temporary nature of this life and the inevitability of death. Br. Pio went behind the skull, and when he saw the jumpy boy in the doorframe, he put out his hand, dangled his towel, and groaned. The boy screeched and ran for his life. Pio ran after him with the intention of telling him, but when the boy heard footsteps, he became more petrified. He stumbled and fell, only to have Pio fall on top of him like Basil fell on Manuel in *Fawlty Towers*. Far from being embarrassed by the memory of this, Pio loved regaling people by retelling it in dramatic fashion.

At the end of the novitiate, a meeting was held to decide which novices they would keep. Pio worried he would be asked to leave, and he spent the time during which his superiors were deciding his fate in prayer and nearly always shedding tears. Instead, he was invited to stay and make temporary vows to last three years. On January 22, 1904, Pio wholeheartedly vowed to be poor, chaste, and obedient.

6

PADRE PIO'S FIRST SPIRITUAL DAUGHTER

Padre Tommaso was unusually emotional. Not that he shed a tear, but he looked glum saying goodbye to Br. Pio. Tommaso had been humbled by this young man whose commitment to Franciscan perfection at age sixteen was so great that Pio had been like a teacher to him.

On a frigid day in January 1904, Pio left Morcone for the Friary of St. Francis of Assisi in the woodsy hamlet of Sant'Elia a Pianisi. Sant'Elia, with its medieval castle ruins and preserved thirteenth-century church, had been a stomping ground for royals down through the centuries, giving it the feel of having an ancient history.

Br. Pio and Br. Anastasio traveled barefoot and arrived frozen with cold. They were ushered in and sent before the fireplace to thaw. The next day, Pio was given his first pair of sandals and thus he began six years of study to become an ordained friar. Pio was to do the rounds of several friaries and take the courses that each seminary offered. His studies included philosophy, Sacred Scripture, theology, logic, canon law and the Rule of St. Francis, which he knew in forensic detail even before he was taught it at length. His years in seminary were not to be nearly as dramatic as his later years, as he was being given special graces of protection from temptation and distraction to make it to ordination. He was known as exemplary, but not as extraordinary; he didn't arouse intense curiosity and certainly did not invite celebrity, which meant he could be formed in the mold of St. Francis in peace and privacy. He did, however, graduate to a new level in the spiritual life, when he was granted the ability to bilocate.

A Gift of Bilocation

Pio was only seventeen when he bilocated — was present in two places at once — for the first time, and he was himself totally confounded at what was happening to him.

The first time it happened, on January 18, 1905, Pio was in the stone chapel, kneeling next to Br. Anastasio, both of them lost in prayer like angels before the throne of God. Then, in two shakes of a lamb's tail, Pio found himself transported hundreds of miles away to Udine, in the northernmost part of Italy, the very rim of Italy's boot. Pio was in the South of Italy and the North at the same time.

It was a gloomy winter night, and he found himself in the halls of a beautiful palace of a noble family. He had gone from the austerity of the friary to a place of royalty and opulence. Our Lady appeared beside Pio, which was no surprise because he saw her every day, and she said, "You see in that room a man is dying? He is the head of the family. He is saved through the prayers and tears of his wife, and by my intercession."[59] She instructed Pio, "Pray for him," and then Pio went near the dying man and, obeying Our Lady without question, he prayed with all his soul for the dying man.

Pio prayed behind the man's wife, who wept bitter tears. The wife, Leonilde, was heavily pregnant and dressed in a grand black Victorian dress that swept the floor and had a high neck. She did not know she was about to give birth to Pio's first spiritual daughter that same night and she sobbed her heart out, not so much because her husband was about to die, but because she feared he would lose his soul. Her husband, Giovanni, had been a diehard Freemason. And his fellow Masons were patrolling the palace gates. A priest was there, too, but so determined were the Masons that Giovanni was not to be shriven and receive the last rites, they prevented the man of God from entering.

Leonilde did not know that the Virgin Mary was there and had led Padre Pio in praying for Giovanni. But unexpectedly, Leonilde saw Pio leave the room. She called out to him, but he vanished from her sight. Suddenly she heard their dog howl mournfully as he sensed his master was dying. Not able to bear the constant yowling of the dog, Leonilde went outside to calm the pet, but no sooner had she done so than she went into labor! One of her menservants helped deliver the baby, and with her newborn baby girl in her puffy-sleeved arms, she returned to her dying husband. The same servant who helped Leonilde give birth saw an opening and courageously he walked up to the Masons and advocated, "Let the priest enter. You can stop him from assisting the dying man, but you have no right to prevent him from baptizing the little baby." The Masons relented and let the priest through the gates; he rushed to the dying man and administered Extreme Unction. Giovanni died with a prayer on his lips that beseeched God's pardon. The priest then hastily baptized the newborn baby girl, named Giovanna after her dad.

Our Lady informed Pio that Giovanna was his first spiritual daughter. "I entrust this creature to you," she told him. "She is a precious stone still in a rough state. Work on her, polish her, render her as brilliant as possible, because one day I wish to adorn myself with her."

Pio was perplexed. "How is this possible?" he asked. "How can I take care of this child when I am so far away?" Our Lady replied mysteriously, "It is she who will come to you, but first of all you will meet her in St Peter's." With that Padre Pio found himself back in the chapel in the click of a finger. He had never left the seminary, yet he had also been in the palace where Giovanna was born. In time he would become used to bilocating all over the world, including to places as far as Hawaii, but during all these mystical trips, he never once left his native Italy!

Mystical Influences

Pio would go on to call Giovanna Rizzani "the firstborn of my heart."[60] After she was born, her mother moved the family to Rome. She did not have the foggiest idea that Our Lady had entrusted her to a seminarian named Br. Pio. She didn't even know such a man existed. This is very telling because it goes to show that the Queen of Heaven put her under the care of Pio without her knowledge. Would we ever dare to think that we might be like Giovanna Rizzani? Perhaps Our Lady entrusted us to Pio as she did Giovanna, and maybe Pio was present for our births, as our parent-in-spirit. We may even be jagged stones that are being polished by Pio and destined to adorn Our Lady in Heaven.

Pio and Giovanna would have a long history, and she would be present at his death. Their lives paralleled each other's, and we will meet her again later in this book and discover the essential truths that Pio gave Giovanna, truths that we may inherit today. But after the seventeen-year-old Pio bilocated for the first time, he resumed seminary life as normal, as humble and unassuming as could be, and no one could have guessed he was enjoying such feats of mysticism.

Not all his mystical experiences were pleasant. Just as when he was a babe and the devil bullied him, the teenage Pio was dogged by the devil. During the summer of 1905, Pio was in his cell, his window and door open wide to circulate air. He was offering Rosary after Rosary. Suddenly, he heard a great deal of noise and footsteps coming from the cell next to his, which belonged to Anastasio. As it grew louder, Pio called out to Anastasio and asked why he was making such a racket.

Suddenly, Pio caught the stench of sulfur and saw a huge dog come at him with smoke wafting from his mouth. Pio said he was "terrified.... I fell on the bed and I heard a voice from the dog that said, 'It this one.' "[61] Instantly Pio realized it was the devil in the form of a monstrous mutt. The evil one had been watching for a second St. Francis, and when he pronounced, "It is him," he was recognizing Pio as being the successor of Francis.

In those distressing moments Pio held tightly to his rosary. The devil did not linger but sprang out of the window onto the roof and vanished. Pio had not struck him, or even verbally threatened him, but he was able to drive out the devil because he was offering the Rosary, which he always referred to as "the weapon" against the devil.

The Rosary: Weapon of Mary

One of Pio's pieces of urgent advice was, "Always hold the weapon of Mary tight in your hand. It will bring you victory over your enemies."[62] Our Lady can crush the devil's head and thus disempower his satanic agency. Satan and his minions cannot abide to be in her presence. It is called a weapon for a reason: It forces the foul fiends to flee. The devil may not appear to us as a savage dog, but he may still prowl and intimidate us, and our means of active defense is the Rosary.

If there are people who have tried to dissuade us from praying the Rosary, let us pluck their words from us as we would a shard of glass stuck in our hand. Their lack of faith in the Blessed Mother and the Rosary hurts us in the same way an injured hand prevents us from manually defending ourselves, and neglecting the Rosary means not having adequate defense against demons. Let's boldly replace the faces of those who may have maligned the Rosary with the face of Pio, who told us, "The Rosary is a powerful weapon to put the devil in flight, to overcome temptations, to win the heart of God, to obtain graces from Our Lady."[63]

Pio, the teenage seminarian, could not yet offer Mass or hear Confessions, but during these years he trained himself as a Rosary warrior. This was also a time when he was not leading souls but rather was being led. We are about to meet two Franciscan priests who had a seismic influence on Pio; in fact, Pio was shaped so much by them that if Pio is our spiritual father, these two extraordinary men of the cloth need to be honored as our spiritual grandfathers. Had they not molded Pio into the mystic and wonder-worker he became, he could not have molded others.

Padre Benedetto and Padre Agostino: Spiritual Grandfathers

When the friary in Sant'Elia a Pianisi was undergoing essential renovations, Pio and his Franciscan brothers were moved to the friary in San Marco la Catola, which was a quaint little town that sprang up around the crumbly walls of an old castle. It was here that Pio met Padre Benedetto. Benedetto had a huge mane of dark hair and a beard to match. His hefty build matched his colossally strong character. His lively, dancing eyes gave a clue to his prodigious intelligence.

Benedetto was a polymath. Not only was he professor of Italian literature and of science, he also taught painting and sculpting. He was revered as a splendid theologian. But his true genius lay in guiding mystics and in the spiritual direction of those with high callings. Benedetto's first impression of Pio came when he saw the teenager kneeling for long hours praying before a painting of the Blessed Virgin Mary. He was appointed Pio's spiritual director and, under obedience, Pio had to reveal to him the spectacular feats of mysticism to which he was graduating. Benedetto alone had the intellectual capability to guide Pio expertly.

The second amazing priest who informed Pio's formation was Padre Agostino. They met when Agostino taught Pio sacred theology at Serracapriola, a town only a few miles from the Adriatic Sea. He was only seven years older than Pio, whereas Benedetto was in his thirties. Thus, Fr. Agostino was more of a peer, and he and Pio became the closest of friends.

Agostino was as wide as he was tall. A little ball of a man, he had round spectacles and cheeks that had a bright raspberry hue. His beard was a sharp V-shape. He was not exceedingly smart, but he was a great empath and had the softest heart of all. His warm empathy was a healing balm to Pio during many harsh struggles. Over the years to come, Benedetto was the head and Agostino the heart of Pio's priestly formation. But circumstances were about to separate Pio from them.

The separation came about like this. When Pio was about to turn nineteen, he and some of the other seminarians went by foot to a shrine of the Virgin Mary, to venerate her under the title of "Madonna della Difesa," or Our Lady of Defense. On the way there, a downpour drenched their brown robes. The others recovered, but Pio fell so ill that he was confined to his bed for the next three weeks.[64] He had a horrible cold and hacking cough.

Pio later pinpointed this as the time when a serious illness rooted itself deep in his lungs, which at times became life-threatening. As we will see, this sickness caused much upheaval for the next ten years, and it forced Pio to spend a lot of time at home in Pietrelcina because, whenever he was in a monastery, he became deathly ill. But, as you will see, the illness also caused him to be ordained a year earlier because his superiors feared he was dying. Pio was destined to be the first priest to bear the wounds of Christ, and a month after he was ordained, he received the stigmata which he had until his death, fifty-eight years later. His priesthood and the stigmata were one and the same. But he was ordained at the age of twenty-three instead of the required age of twenty-four. Perhaps the illness was providential, in that it gave Pio an extra year to offer the pains of Christ's Crucifixion on behalf of sinners.

7

A Healing Homecoming

Pio's superiors were heartsick. They didn't want to send the sickly Pio home, yet they felt they had no choice. His illness was so bad that they hoped resting at home with the loving care of Mama Giuseppa might just restore him to health, or if the worst happened, he could die in her arms. But they held on to the hope that sending him back to Pietrelcina might save his life.

Since the day Pio had gotten soaked to the bone and returned to the seminary in a habit weighed down with rainwater, he'd been helplessly ill with debilitating flu, raging fever, and uncontrollable vomiting. It was all very well to make the decision for this most prayerful young man to leave, but when he did, his superiors spoke of how intensely they missed him, and this speaks to how much Pio was loved by his confreres. His superiors were a group of older Franciscans who had spent years detaching from their emotions and had broken all undue attachments to their own families, yet they were pained when Pio had to leave them. They were not to know that this pattern of Pio becoming ill, then going home to recover, and then returning to a monastery only for him to become so sick again that he had to return to Pietrelcina, was to continue for the best part of a decade.

Pio's superiors could not fathom his health condition. There was, however, an occasion when Pio got ill on wine — even though he hadn't drunk a drop! Pio had the task of bottling wine in the close confines of the cellar, and the vapors made him dizzy and unwell. "That was the only time in my life that wine made me lose my head,"[65] Pio later said of the incident of intoxication. But at all other times, Pio's symptoms baffled his betters.

Then, when Pio was twenty-one years old, the older friars got Pio a doctor who diagnosed tuberculosis, a contagious disease that was turning many parts of Italy into morgues. Given months to live, Pio was sent back to Pietrelcina into the embrace of Giuseppa, who was overjoyed to have her son back. She didn't quite buy the diagnosis of tuberculosis, and neither did Grazio, who was home on vacation. They decided to get a second opinion from Dr. Andrea Cordone, an amazing young medic. The handsome Cordone had a bright smile and broad forehead with thick black hair. He was to play a major role later as the first physician to examine Pio's stigmata, but for now, when he put his stethoscope to Pio's chest and gave him a thorough physical, he found no tuberculosis; rather, he pronounced chronic bronchitis, a deep infection in the sacs of Pio's lungs.

Cordone sent Pio to Naples to see a specialist for another intense probing of his body, and this doctor concurred with Cordone. Perhaps it was providential that Dr. Cordone got to know Pio so well at this stage, so that he came to know Pio's good, cheerful character under reasonably normal circumstances. After all, normal folks get infections in their chests, and in the years ahead Pio would be thought of and spoken of as abnormal and even mentally deranged because his hands were pierced with the wounds of Christ, which his detractors claimed were the result of fixation on the Passion of Jesus to the point he developed lesions as though nails had been driven through his palms. The diagnosis of tuberculosis, although alarming, along with the strange symptoms that caused so much suffering to Pio, did occasion his visits to Dr. Cordone, and this was apt preparation for a time when Dr. Cordone was going to have the role of doubting Thomas in the life of Pio.

There is also Giuseppa's blissful happiness in having her boy back, the son she had so selflessly given away so completely. He was going to be with her a lot in the next seven years, and this time was like the reward she never thought she'd have on earth, time with her beloved son. And he needed her: needed her compassionate blue eyes looking over him, needed her to bring him delicious home-cooked meals when he was too sick to get out of bed, needed her to fetch Dr. Cordone or our old friend, big-eyed Fr. Pannullo. When he was with Giuseppa, Pio always saw himself as her little boy. This would hurt Giuseppa in later years when he didn't allow her to bestow certain honors on him, but for now, the mother-child bond was restored and Giuseppa knew a lovely contentment that she may have thought she'd lost for good. She still called him "Franci," but to everyone else he was now "Pio." Grazio and Giuseppa decided it was time he had his own place. He took up residence a short distance from where he'd been born, in a house his father had paid for with money made in America.

Padre Pio's Letters

In the quiet seclusion of his room, he hid himself, studied, and wrote letters to his two spiritual fathers, Fr. Agostino and Fr. Benedetto. Pio shifted sheets of paper in his hands and used pen and ink to write them. Since the oxygen of his hometown was the only thing known to keep him alive, it meant they had to exchange letters, which chronicle Pio's graduations in the spiritual life, the attacks from the devil that he fended off, his dark night of the soul, and most importantly, his stigmata. We may think of it as fortunate that the hand of God placed Pio in Pietrelcina and kept the mailmen busy ferrying letters between him and his spiritual directors. Had Pio not been compelled to put in writing the levels of holiness and mysticism to which he was constantly graduating, we would not have an accurate record of them.

The letters come to 1,300 pages and their existence means that every generation of Pio's spiritual children may read them and see Pio's soul in all its glory. Under holy obedience, Pio had to reveal all to Fr. Benedetto, and for this we are grateful, as will be every spiritual child yet to come.

At one time, Pio was tortured with thinking his poor health was a chastisement from God for his sins. Benedetto informed him that those thoughts that he was being punished were a ploy of the evil one: "Your sufferings are not punishments, but rather ways of earning merit that the Lord is giving you, and the shadows that weigh on your soul are generated by the devil, who wants to harm you."[66]

We may allow Benedetto's clear-minded advice to help us when the devil muddies our thinking; often the devil may fool us into thinking that suffering is God striking us for our sins, when rather our suffering may be given to us by God for us to gain merit. Pio was adamant to Benedetto that he wanted to die a thousand deaths rather than commit one sin.[67] Here we see Pio's spirit more clearly than ever; he would have preferred his life be blotted out than that he blot his soul and offend God. To understand Pio's absolute aversion to sin is to understand him: He strove for sanctity by being more scared of sin than of his own demise. As his sons and daughters in spirit, if we want to follow him most closely, we need ask in prayer for the same allergy to sin that he had; only in this way will we be truly like our spiritual father.

His health began to fail drastically in Pietrelcina, too, and he often had stabbing chest pains. It was thought Pio was about to die, and rather than be fearful or unhappy at the thought of going to God in his early twenties, Pio was quietly ecstatic and confided in Benedetto that "the idea of death seems to attract me greatly"[68] and "I shall die very happy."[69]

Pio was a fledgling mystic who thought it possible he would die young, though it would later be revealed to him that he would die at eighty-one years of age — during his priesthood, Pio foretold his own death many times with eerie accuracy. At this time, prior to ordination, he had no awareness of the awesome mission the Lord had for him, but in his desire for death we see his holiness and freedom from sin; only the truly holy and those who are as sinless as possible can be that confident about going to God happily. He even wrote to Benedetto that the thought of ever being well again was so fanciful as to be foolish.[70]

Again, Pio had no inkling of the great plans Our Lord had for him, no idea he would be a world-famous wonder-worker or that he would go on to hear one million Confessions. His desire for death, however, would become greater and greater until it became a craving that consumed him. It would be a deceased spiritual daughter who would tell him it was not Jesus' desire for him to die young.

But Pio's body was also exhibiting phenomena that made him look immune to death. His body was often so hot, it was as though he was on fire! His body temperature was often 120 degrees Fahrenheit. Inside his heart was an actual fire that radiated intense heat to his every pore. Pio revealed that he kindled "a mysterious fire which I felt from my heart," and he often felt this flame was "consuming" him.[71] Pio had no ordinary, mortal heart, and within its fleshy walls there burned a fire which he felt was devouring him but which never seared him until he was a smoking corpse. Rather, this flame was from the fires of the Divine Love of God and furnished him the fervent love he needed to give himself totally as an offering for sinners.

Padre Pio Is Ordained

Considering all this, Padre Benedetto felt strongly that Pio was to die soon, so he hastily did all the necessary paperwork for Pio to be ordained at twenty-three. A dispensation was granted and Pio's ordination was set for August 10, 1910. This was the anniversary of the date that the Greek princess St. Philomena was martyred. Philomena was especially beloved by Pio, and he hailed her as "the Princess of Heaven."[72] At age thirteen, she caught the eye of the Roman emperor, but she refused his advances because she had promised herself to Christ. The emperor repaid her rejection by chopping off her head. Philomena was always cherished by Pio as one of his all-time favorite saints,[73] and it was a special treat for him to be ordained on the day she went to Heaven. The day was also a Wednesday, the day of St. Joseph. Pio's parents had been wed on a Wednesday, Pio had been born on that day, and he was about to become a priest on that day, too. Throughout his life, this day was the most tranquil of all the days of the week; the day when St. Joseph, terror of demons, interceded especially for Pio to be given respite from the devil. On that peaceful day, Pio and Giuseppa climbed aboard a horse and buggy. Grazio's presence was missed; he had not been able to make it home from America. The driver cracked the whip and they set off for Benevento, the nearest city. They traveled over a bumpy dirt road and felt the wooden wheels roll their way through the soft earth that was baked to a congealed paste by the sun on one of the most sweltering days of the year. Giuseppa was resplendent in her white dress and glistening white veil. This was the day when she was to honor the solemn promise she had made to St. Francis. They stopped outside the Benevento cathedral, and mother and son beheld the grey Romanesque facade of the duomo. Once inside, Pio went face down before the altar and was ordained "Padre Pio" by the octogenarian Archbishop Paolo Schinosi.

Afterward, they traveled back to Pietrelcina, and their carriage was met by the town band, which belted out celebratory tunes. The local people processed around mother and son, cheering and clapping. When they reached the room where Pio had been born, Giuseppa put on a lavish spread of the finest food. She had prepared a delicious banquet. Of course, she did not partake in any meat: It was Wednesday, and even her son becoming "Padre Pio" did not interfere with her abstinence in honor of Our Lady of Mount Carmel. The high point of the party came when Pio handed out prayer cards to everyone. The prayer Pio wrote on the card proved prophetic: "Jesus, my life and my breath, today I timorously raise Thee in a mystery of love. With Thee may I be for the world the way, the truth and the life, and through Thee, a holy priest, a perfect victim."[74] Pio was giving himself entirely to the Lord for Him to do with him whatever He willed. This plea of Pio's to be "a perfect victim" would be heard and answered in the form of the stigmata — though at this time he had little idea of the plans the Lord had for him.

Pio could now do what he had spent his life longing to do: offer the Holy Sacrifice of the Mass. He offered his first Mass — what we would now call the Traditional Latin Mass — on August 14, 1910, in the Church of Our Lady of the Angels. Pio's spiritual director, Fr. Agostino, came to give the sermon because Pio had not been given permission to preach. There were concerns among Pio's superiors that he lacked sufficient theological education to lead the faithful by way of sermons. He had missed many classes during his seminary years. Pio could not preach and could not hear Confessions, but he was given full permission to offer the Tridentine Latin Mass, and for the rest of his fifty-eight years of priesthood, this was the only form of the Mass that he ever offered. In the entirety of his priesthood, Pio offered over twenty-one thousand Latin Masses.

8

PIO BECOMES CHRIST'S SELF-PORTRAIT

Pio walked gingerly into Padre Salvatore Pannullo's office and put out his palms, which looked like they'd been stabbed in the center. Big-eyed Fr. Pannullo stared at the lesions; they did not shed blood, yet they appeared to reach right through Pio's hands and were the same on both sides; penny-sized, carmine piercings.

Pio had been a priest for less than a month. He told Pannullo that he had been praying in Piana Romano, the green pasture where he tended his sheep as a young boy. He'd been sheltering under the egg-shaped green leaves of an old elm tree. Usually, he hid from the scorching sun under the thatch of branches and said his breviary. Suddenly, Jesus and the Virgin Mary appeared to him and bestowed on his hands and feet the wounds of Jesus' Crucifixion.

The wounds caused him sharp pain, as though he were being crucified. But that was not the worst of it. Pio confided in Pannullo that he was unbearably humiliated by the glaring red marks of Jesus's Passion being on full display. He wanted them to be out of sight or invisible. So he beseeched Pannullo for his prayers, saying, "Let's pray together to ask Jesus to take this annoyance away." Pannullo agreed to join him in praying for Pio to be crucified inconspicuously. Pio, however, abided by one condition. Pio gave himself over totally to Our Lord's will by saying to Him, "Do with me as you please."[75]

Pannullo persuaded Pio to show the wounds to the brilliant Dr. Cardone, who examined them thoroughly, pressing his fingers into the holes and causing Pio excruciating pain. Pio asked Cardone, "Are you trying to be like St. Thomas?"[76] Cardone humbly conceded he had no medical explanation for the lesions. While he had the visible red marks, Padre Pio did not show them to his doting mother, and he used the sleeves of his brown habit to hide them from her. He did, however, tell his childhood friend Mercurio. Fortunately for Mercurio, he had survived being sent down a hill in a wagon as a child, and he lived to be one of the first witnesses to Pio's stigmata.

The Stigmata Is Made Invisible

One week after Pannullo and Pio offered a prayer asking the Lord to take away the physical signs of the wounds, the red piercings became invisible to the human eye. There is a beautiful instruction here for us. First, Pio needed Fr. Pannullo's prayers to be united with his, because only after he had invited these prayers was his request granted. When we are given a trial we had not expected, rather than asking for it to be taken away entirely, we may ask for the part that stings us the most, that which we find unbearable, to be taken away. And like Pio we may confide in a trusted soul to pray with us to double our prayers in real time. Pio may also have known that Fr. Pannullo was the person to ask; he may have known that the Lord intended to give him the grace of invisibility if Pannullo asked for it. Throughout his priesthood, Pio demonstrated a knowledge of who ought pray to obtain which grace, and he had a certainty in asking Pannullo that suggests strongly he knew it was he whom the Lord would answer.

During the next year the visible red wounds reappeared and then disappeared. But the stabbing pain remained constant. Giuseppa knew nothing about it, but once she came close to discovering the truth. One day, Giuseppa was bringing Pio a meal and she saw him come out waving his hands frantically because they were seized with such agonizing cramps. On seeing this, Giuseppa inquired wryly, "What's the matter, Padre Pio? You look as though you're playing the guitar." Pio humbly made light of his suffering: "It's nothing, mama. Little stabs of no importance."[77] He did not conceal them because he was secretive; rather, Pio did not want his mother to venerate him. He did not want her reverence, when she already lavished him with affection and showed him so much favoritism. Had she known that he had been given the wounds of Christ, she might have gone from loving to adoring him, and this is something Pio did not want for his mama.

One year after becoming a stigmatist, Pio told Fr. Benedetto for the first time. In a letter, Pio committed this description to paper: "In the center of the palms of my hands a red patch appeared about the size of a cent and accompanied by acute pain in the middle of the red marks." The pain was not equal in both hands, and he described how "the pain was much more acute in the left hand and it still persists."[78]

When we hear that Pio waited a year before telling Benedetto, we might assume Pio did not trust him adequately. The reason Pio could not bring himself to tell Benedetto is the same reason he asked Our Lord to make the wounds invisible: He felt unbearable humiliation at being seen as alike to Christ, something he felt so unworthy of being. As Pio explained so apologetically to Benedetto, "Do not be disturbed by the fact that this is the first time I have mentioned it, for I was invariably overcome by abominable shame."[79]

The use of the word *shame* ought command our attention. It may mean demonic interference played a role in making him feel so self-conscious, so as to make him feel ashamed of the gift of the sacred wounds of Christ, and in not telling Benedetto for one whole year he was stretching his bond of obedience to tell Benedetto everything.

Pio, however, never denied that these wounds were gifts. We'll recall that Pio had asked to be a "perfect victim," and on the day of his ordination all his family and friends prayed for his intention, as printed on the holy card, that the Our Lord would deign to make Pio an impeccable victim. His petition to be made a flawless victim tells us he did not assume he was already good enough to be a victim, but he was of the mind and the will that he had to offer prayer to be made into one. This points to him feeling unfit to be accepted as a victim when, in the earliest days of his priesthood, he experienced the unbearable humiliation of bearing the wounds visibly and of telling Benedetto. Yet most importantly, it instructs us as to the nature of being a victim soul. A person who, like Pio, feels a tremendous desire to make a total offering of themselves and asks the Lord to give them whatever suffering He wills may find that the suffering that comes carries trials that they could never have imagined. Certainly, Pio never thought he would bear the wounds of Christ. He thought he was to die shortly after ordination, yet he gave himself to the Lord to do with him whatever He willed, and Jesus willed for him to be a living replica of Him, even if for Pio this meant dire psychological pain, such as he felt when the wounds were visible. At this time, however, Pio was given respite and was allowed to suffer the Crucifixion in private.

An Exquisite Suffering for Souls

During the fifty-eight years he was a priest, Pio was simultaneously a stigmatist.[80] He received the stigmata in September 1910, and he died in September 1968. He was a crucified priest, living a living crucifixion. For the first eight years of priesthood, Pio had *invisible* stigmata. Then, for the remaining fifty years of his life, he bore the wounds visibly and they could be seen in all their bloodiness by human eyes. Pio's priesthood and the stigmata were inseparable. In those years when Pio was in his twenties, however, the invisible wounds did not attract notoriety. A few months after he first received the wounds, Pio knew for *whom* he felt called to offer his pain. He sought Padre Benedetto's permission to offer it for two sets of souls: "My dear Father, I want to ask your permission for something. For some time I have felt the need to offer myself to the Lord as a victim for poor sinners and for the souls in Purgatory."[81]

Benedetto replied energetically, "Make the offering." He further encouraged Pio, "Extend your own arms also on your cross and by offering to the Father the sacrifice of yourself in union with our most loving Savior, suffer, groan and pray for the wicked ones of the earth and for the poor souls in the next life who are so deserving of our compassion."[82] This letter, written over a hundred years ago, did not just apply to the people living at that time, but to all the people who would ever live who would benefit from Pio's sacrifice. We could be among the people for whom Padre Pio offered up his agony. It may take the gift of humility to accept this, but we are part of the group of "poor sinners" whose debt would be diminished by Pio.

Throughout all this, Pietrelcina remained the only place where Pio was well enough to function. He even had the strength to fend off a suggestion that triggered him. His old buddy Mercurio was rather red-blooded, and even though he knew Pio bore the holy wounds of Christ, he had the audacity to say to Pio that his illness was caused by sexual frustration and that he ought to get married. Pio grabbed a pitchfork and swung it at Mercurio as he chased him away.

We may well ask what was so special about Pietrelcina; why was Pio only well there? Pio was given the grace to be there because he was so dearly loved by his native people that they prayed their hearts out that he could stay in their company — and the Lord answered them. In fact, Pio said, "The Lord intends to hear the prayers of all these devout people here who want, it would appear, to keep me against my will in their midst, by sending up prayers and almost doing violence to the Heart of God to obtain their great desire."[83]

The powerful prayers of the people of Pietrelcina kept him with them, and to think, they didn't even know they had the Second St. Francis as their neighbor!

But Pio showed great charity to all. He rose to the challenge of being a school-teacher and taught math. His pupils knew him to be exceptionally patient, especially with those who struggled. One former pupil shared the memory that Pio worked tirelessly with him until he could solve math problems. If, however, Pio heard a boy cursing or blaspheming, he would take off his sandal and swat him with it. Among the adult population the level of illiteracy was high, so Pio arranged for adult education alfresco. He held lessons in reading and writing in the open fields for farmers and laborers. Pio would have done none of these works of charity among his own kin had he been well enough to live in a monastery. But the symptoms that could not be treated by the best doctors were not owing to weakness in Pio's physical makeup; rather, Pio revealed that the cause of his illness was "entirely spiritual pain."[84] Certainly, Pio was suffering intense demonic persecution, and Satan was trying to oppress Pio in mind, body, and soul.

Resisting Evils of the Mind

In a bid to control his thoughts, Satan tried to get Pio to hate himself. Pio told his spiritual fathers that Satan was in the practice of representing "a most dismal picture" of his life. Our Lord permitted the devil to disturb Pio's peace of soul by tempting him to impurity and despondency. In 1911, when Pio was about to celebrate his first Holy Week as a priest, he wrote to his director, "Even during these holy days the enemy is making every effort to induce me to consent to his impious designs. In particular this evil spirit tries by all sorts of images to introduce into my mind impure thoughts and ideas of despair." And these attacks were inexorable: "Temptations pursue me more relentlessly than ever and they are a source of great suffering." The devil was actively tormenting Pio during the night: "Even during the hours of rest the devil does not cease to torment my soul in various ways." After he read this, Benedetto enlightened Pio as to why Our Lord allows the devil to tempt us: "Temptations are the sure sign of divine favor and the fact that you fear them is the clearest proof that you do not yield to them." As for the ferocity of the attacks, "the more violently the enemy attacks you the more you must abandon yourself to the Lord, confident that He will never allow you to be overcome."[85] We need to do as Benedetto instructed Pio and practice abandonment to the Lord. Instead of seeing temptations as a sign of God holding us in contempt, we should see them as a special privilege — though to attain the spiritual maturity to see them as such may take much prayer.

Benedetto led Pio in these times of tremendous temptation, but he deferred to Pio to give him insight into the soul of a woman who had been on her way to Heaven but through her presumption seemed to have turned onto the path to Hell. Pio never met this lady, but he could see her soul and he disclosed:

> This is how that soul was snared in the devil's net. She saw that she was so favored by God.... But the enemy who is always alert, seeing such affection, convinced her that such great confidence and certainty could never decline.... He put into her heart a clear vision of the heavenly prize.... The devil used this immoderate confidence to make her lose that holy distrust in herself, a diffidence that must never leave the soul, no matter how privileged it is by God. Meanwhile, having lost, little by little, this distrust, she was cast sorely into temptation, still persuaded that she had nothing to fear.[86]

She trusted herself too much, presumed her place in Heaven, and gave into temptation, which Pio concluded "was the origin of her final ruin."[87] The only solution Pio posited for her was prayer. This woman stands in stark contrast to Pio, who although he was given extraordinary gifts, didn't lose his distrust of self and placed all his trust in God. For us this means not placing our confidence in our flawed human nature but instead placing all confidence in God. We humbly acknowledge our weakness and know there is no basis for trusting ourselves. For all his holiness, Pio never became spiritually self-entitled as did the presumptuous woman. She became convinced of the devil's lie that no matter how much she sinned she would not lose out on the heavenly prize.

Unrelenting Temptation

Benedetto made demands on Pio to return to monastery life, and late in 1911 he went to a friary in Venafro, about sixty miles from Pietrelcina. Here he lived for a short time with Fr. Agostino. While in Venafro Padre Pio was often in states of divine ecstasy, but in between ecstasies he was visited by Satan. Fr. Agostino witnessed the devil come in a dizzying array of disguises and recorded in his diary that the devil first appeared to Pio as a monstrously ugly black cat.[88] Then the prince of darkness came as naked young women who danced lusty dances to incite Pio so he would sin against purity. The third time, the devil was invisible but spat in Padre Pio's face.

Next the devil manifested his presence by making an ear-piercing noise. After that the devil came in the form of an executioner who flogged Padre Pio's flesh. He thrashed Pio's flesh as punishment for not giving into temptation. Pio was subject to severe psychological and bodily assaults in much the same way as governments capture and torture prisoners of war in a bid to make them defect. The sixth time, the devil came as a crucified man, maybe in a bid to compete with the Crucified Christ for Pio's affections. The seventh time, the devil tried to pass himself off as a young man who was a friend of Pio's and who had just paid him a visit.

The devil was trying to fool Pio and was posing as friends and intimates to gain Pio's trust and to get him to listen to him and talk to him, so he could fill him with his lies and manipulate him in the vain attempt to get Pio to sin. The eighth time, he even appeared as Padre Agostino, Pio's beloved director, and the ninth time he appeared as the provincial, the highest-ranking Franciscan, the one who had authority over all the friars of that region. When the devil posed as authority figures to whom Padre Pio was obedient, it was an attempt to dupe Pio into obeying him. The tenth time, he appeared as the pope, who at the time was Pius X. Although it may seem outlandish, the devil pretending to be the Vicar of Christ, he was trying to elicit the awe and respect Pio had for the pope and cover himself in glory, however fraudulently. There were other times when the father of lies came to Padre Pio taking the form of his guardian angel and even Our Lady. But he also came as St. Francis, which is especially interesting, since it was St. Francis who won Lucifer's throne in Heaven. When St. Francis walked the earth, it was shown in a vision to one of his followers, Br. Pacifico that the throne Lucifer forfeited was to be awarded to Francis. What Lucifer lost through pride, Francis gained through humility.[89]

The devil wanted Pio's defection from the divine law of God. But the devil would not succeed and his efforts would backfire: The way he tempted and persecuted Pio only made Pio holier. Though the devil failed repeatedly, we should not underestimate how much the devil wanted to possess Pio. During his life Pio frequently said something that he first said to Benedetto: "The devil wants me for himself at all costs."[90] But eventually the devil failed spectacularly. The attacks he made on Pio were futile — Pio did not despair or become impure — and here we see the devil humiliated. Pio was making a complete offering of himself so as to save his own soul and as many other souls as possible. This total self-sacrifice for the salvation of souls provoked the rage of the devil, because God would use Pio to save souls from going to Hell; hence the devil's losses would be immense.

The battle between Pio and the devil may seem removed from our lives. But we may take it personally that the devil wanted Pio for himself — to steal a saint who could be of help in saving our souls. In struggling for Pio's soul, the devil was also struggling for my soul and yours. As already noted, in his letters Pio used a moniker for the devil, "the enemy of our salvation," which, if we adopt it today, impresses in our minds how much the devil seeks to snatch souls and rob them of their eternal happiness with God in Heaven. But God never allows a soul to be attacked without giving that soul the graces to withstand the enemy's fire.

In tandem with demonic attacks there were also awesome visions of the Lord which give simply spectacular instruction. Padre Agostino overheard and wrote down the dialogue. On the first Friday in December, Jesus appeared crucified, but Pio protested, "Don't appear to me like this anymore . . . you tear my heart to pieces." Then Pio revealed, "It's true, then, that you bore the cross all the time of your life. . . . Your suffering was continuous." Then, two days later on the Sabbath, Jesus appeared to Pio and he was bleeding profusely, so much so that Pio lamented, "My Jesus, why are you so bloody this morning? . . . They did wicked things to you today? . . . Alas, even on Sunday you must suffer the offenses of ungrateful men! How many abominations took place within your sanctuary!"[91]

Pio begged pardon on behalf of bad priests and then spoke of a sword that Jesus seemed to be holding. Although Agostino could not hear the words of the Savior, he heard Pio almost commanding, "Lower that sword!" and "If it must fall, may it find its place on my head alone. . . . Yes, I want to be the victim!"[92] With all-consuming fervor, Pio offered himself for unfaithful men of the cloth, and we will see that it was priests like these who caused all his persecutions. As for this sword, there is a case to be made that it constituted part of an ongoing invisible stigmata that Pio said scored him from the inside. Pio referred to it in his letters when he wrote, "My heart, hands and feet seem to be pierced through by a sword, so great is the pain I feel."[93] This blade may have been the cause of a lifelong internal wound because, as we'll see, fifty-seven years later and near death, Pio referred to it again.

At Venafro, Pio became so ill that he had to be sent home to Pietrelcina for fear he would die if he stayed. He was brought home on December 7. The next day was December 8, the feast of the Immaculate Conception, and totally inexplicably Pio was well and able to sing Mass as if he had never been on the point of death just a day before. The prayers of the local people had again been answered!

He had been home in Pietrelcina for one month when he wrote to Agostino, "The ogre won't admit defeat. He has appeared in almost every form. He paid me a visit during the past few days along with some of his satellites, armed with clubs and iron weapons and what is worse, in their own form as devils. I cannot tell you how many times he has thrown me out of bed and dragged me around the room."[94] The fact that Pio said the devils appearing as themselves without disguise was "worse" than being clubbed is startling, but very revealing. Pio felt more abused by the sight of them than he did when they beat him mercilessly. He was a victim of demonic brutality, but he also revealed the source of his consolation: "The Lord and the other noble and heavenly persons make good all my losses by their frequent visits."[95] Then, in spring of 1912, the violence escalated, as Pio wrote, "I was still in bed when those wretches visited me and beat me so savagely that I consider it a very great grace to have come through it alive."[96]

This was the single worst time in Pio's life for demonic attack; he was subject to physical violence and to merciless and unrelenting temptation. All Satan's power to tempt him would end when Pio received and accepted the visible stigmata, but in these years temptations accompanied the invisible stigmata and were allowed by Christ for Pio's growth in humility. So humbled was Pio by the devil's demonstrations that he didn't easily feel pride at being so exceedingly privileged.

Pio had his single greatest mystical experience a month before his twenty-fifth birthday, and yet this was sandwiched between periods of dire demonic attack.

It was a seemingly ordinary April morning in Eastertide, just weeks after the satanic onslaught of spring 1912. He was alone in his room. Jesus appeared to him, and taking Pio's heart out of his chest, He took Pio's pulsating organ into His Sacred Heart and made Pio's heart one with His divine Heart. Pio wrote a letter to Benedetto about this ecstatic union: "The heart of Jesus and my own — allow me to use the expression — were fused." Jesus allowed for His Sacred Heart and Pio's human heart to become one heart, as Pio divulged: "No longer were two hearts beating, but only one."[97] Pio's heart beat in time to His Heart, the combined rhythm of the two hearts becoming one and functioning as one. Jesus allowed Pio's heart to become His Heart and to pump His divine Blood.

When Pio's heart was synchronized with Jesus', he felt an intense joy which made him weep profusely: "The very joy that filled my heart was what made me weep for so long."[98] Padre Pio's heart was not divine, but Our Lord treated Pio's heart as being good enough to be "fused" with His. In our times, Padre Pio's heart travels around the world, being reverenced by the faithful, and when we venerate Pio's heart this gives us intimacy to Our Lord in a direct way, because Pio's heart became Jesus's Heart, too. Pio's heart is a relic of Christ.

Yet, months after the Savior took Pio's heart and absorbed it into His, Pio told his spiritual fathers of an assault that lasted seven hours: "From about ten o'clock until five in the morning that wretch did nothing but beat me continually." Pio thought he was being battered to death: "I really thought that was the last night of my life." But the beating preceded a hellish chill: "When the wretch left me, my whole body became so cold that I trembled from head to foot, like a reed exposed to a violent wind."[99] The devil, during the same attack, tried to injure Pio psychologically with "many diabolical suggestions, thoughts of despair, distrust of God."[100] Then Pio feared he was losing his capacity to reason, that his mental health was suffering under satanic strain. Later, when Pio had a sea of souls coming to him, he never said he had been spared the onslaught of satanic savagery. Pio had been a victim of the vile assaults of the demons, and he instructed his children how to fight as he had fought.

Another guerilla warfare tactic of the demons was to isolate Padre Pio by interfering with his letters. In the winter cold of 1912 Fr. Agostino sent a letter to Pio that when opened was just one big blot of ink. Fr. Pannullo was asked for help and later gave testimony that "when the letter had been placed on the crucifix and sprinkled with holy water it was possible to read it."[101] More treacherously, Satan appeared to Pio as a Franciscan friar and said he had an order from the provincial. The order forbade Padre Pio from corresponding with Fr. Agostino ever again because such an exchange of letters was a breach of his vow of poverty. When he thought he would be forbidden from corresponding with Agostino, Pio burst into bitter tears. Mercifully, his guardian angel appeared and revealed to him that the "Franciscan friar" had been the devil trying to get between him and Agostino.[102] But let us consider how the devil had momentarily fooled Pio. The devil had claimed that sending and receiving letters from Agostino prevented the perfection of Pio's soul. This example offers a most valuable lesson: The devil is a liar and will use sanctimonious lies to snare a soul.

The young priest communicating by letter to his spiritual directors made the denizens of Hell furious. They made dire threats to Pio, such that if he was to continue his correspondence with Benedetto and Agostino, they would beat him severely.

In 1913, the devil tried to prickle Pio's mind with suggestions that he burn Agostino's letters without reading them. When Pio defied him and read the letters, demons hurled themselves at him, beating him and cursing him. They promised vengeance for his disobedience to them in opening Agostino's letters. These were not empty threats, as Pio wrote, "They kept their word, for from that day onward they have beaten me every day."[103] In the following weeks Pio revealed, "My body is bruised all over from the blows I receive at their hands." This serves as a sobering reflection on demonic viciousness. The fiends from Hell were hell-bent on Padre Pio's physical destruction. The vast majority of us will not be violently victimized by devils, but just how hungry they were for Pio's blood instructs us as to their uninhibited savagery. Still, many of us make a grave mistake when we read accounts of Pio being attacked. We may think that we are so entirely different from one such as Pio that the devil and his minions would not treat us the same way. Thinking we will climb to greater holiness without demonic attack is wishful thinking. Reviewing the attacks made on Pio as a young priest, we can see the demons are filthy brutes, but often they wish to pass themselves off as harmless so that we let down our guard and grant them entry.

9

PIO'S DARK NIGHT OF THE SOUL

From the time he was in his twenties, Pio was engaged in violent warfare with the devil, but Our Lord lavished love on Pio in between demonic attacks. Around the time Pio turned twenty-seven, the demons were not granted as much access to him as they had enjoyed, but Our Lord put him through a new purification of spiritual darkness that became worse and worse. Pio wrote to Benedetto that "darkness grows still deeper"[104] and that "this is much harder than all kinds of death together!"[105] He divulged that the pain of darkness rivaled that of damned souls in Hell. As horrific as this sounds, it was in fact the process for Pio's perfection. We need to note well that this new purification was a tribute to Pio's great holiness.

There are usually two misconceptions about dark nights of the soul. Many people mistake depression and grief for the dark night of the soul; others see the dark night as a useless burden, when it is instead the method the Lord uses to bring a most blessed and special soul closer to Him. Our Lord thrust Pio's soul into a night so black that Pio did not have enough light to see his own soul, but all the while, he had the ability to see and read the souls of others and give expert insight. Here we encounter one of the biggest ironies of Pio's earthly existence: He was able, even as a young priest, to see the souls of others and make accurate assessments of them, but he was not objective about his own soul. Yet, a period of great darkness always preceded a graduation in Pio's life to new heights of holiness and mystical gifts, and Pio was a living embodiment of the truth that dryness and darkness were the essential passage to greater union with God and to mystical milestones.

While Padre Pio was deep in the throes of the dark night, his spiritual fathers appointed him as a spiritual father to some spiritual daughters. He did not meet these ladies in person, but they exchanged letters. One such spiritual daughter was a noblewoman, Raffaelina Cerase, who became one of his most generous children.

Raffaelina and Our Lady of Pompeii

Raffaelina had round soulful eyes and brown hair, parted severely in the middle and gathered in a formal hairdo. She dressed in Victorian fashions; having been born in 1868, she was part of the last generation to be raised during the reign of Queen Victoria. Raffaelina lived with her sister, Giovina, in a rented apartment in Foggia. Both sisters were unmarried and had been born into a wealthy, aristocratic family. Yet they led hard lives because they fought bitterly with their older brother over their inheritance. He and his wife lived in the house that Giovina and Raffaelina had lawfully inherited, and the injustice especially galled Raffaelina, who yearned to live in her family home.

Raffaelina had a melancholic temperament; she could be overly emotional and was an incorrigible worrier. She'd known grief: Three of her sisters and a brother had died young. She told Pio she led "a sluggish, stupid life,"[106] that she'd committed "sins of every description,"[107] and that she was "very, very bad!"[108] We may think of her as crossing the line from being self-effacing to self-hating. But during the time she corresponded with Pio she, like him, was in darkness of soul. In her very first letter to Pio, she poured out her pain on the page: "It is deep night within me."[109]

Pio had the role of rescuing Raffaelina from herself, and he helped her see that the darkness and dryness in her soul was not a sign she was despised by God but that she was a most fortunate soul to be singled out for purification by way of darkness. Pio was twenty-seven, Raffaelina forty-six, but he treated her like she was his little girl and often told her to be more obedient. He lovingly encouraged her to write to him as much as she needed, that she was pleasing Jesus and doing him a favor. Pio also knew that her soul was so much like his that the advice Benedetto gave him could be copied wholesale and given to Raffaelina.

Early on Pio taught her to separate in her mind that which was spiritual darkness visited on her by the Lord and that which was depression caused by the devil attacking her imagination. "Don't listen to what your imagination tells you," he instructed her, "for it is upset and powerfully attacked by our enemy, who wants you to consider your life unproductive of good."[110]

Besides giving her detailed lessons on her soul in darkness, Pio also pressed her to do him a great charity, which would at the same time enhance her virtue of piety. Raffaelina had a special devotion to Our Lady of Pompeii, and credited the Virgin of Pompeii's intercession with helping her unite with Jesus. "At 21 years of age I made for the first time the fifteen Saturdays to our beautiful and dear Mother of Pompeii," she wrote. "This was the first link in the holy chain which unites me with Jesus, and it was all due to my good Mother."[111] Pio asked her to offer the fifty-four-day Rosary novena to Our Lady of Pompeii three times in a row. This meant she was to offer fifteen decades of the Rosary for his intentions for twenty-seven consecutive days while also offering her Holy Communions for him, then she was to offer the Rosary in thanksgiving for another twenty-seven days after that. And she was to do this thrice, essentially offering the whole Rosary for Pio for 162 days straight. Pio strove to make her see that she was not redundant, as she relentlessly said of herself. When she was entrusted with praying so much and for so long, this was a direct antidote to Raffaelina's feelings of uselessness. She was shown she had a role, as someone who was to pray for him and win him graces.

Raffaelina was stunned that Pio sought her prayers: "I am surprised, amazed, astounded that you ask me, *you*, to make the three novenas to Most Holy Mary of Pompeii and to offer my poor Communions. In order to obey you, I am doing what you ask. Are you satisfied?"[112] Padre Pio answered as to why he needed such intense prayer, "Keep up the novenas to the beautiful Virgin of the Rosary of Pompeii and offer your Holy Communions for me still, for God's hand is coming down on me more and more heavily. My poor soul is on the point of drowning in the waters of affliction and tribulations, and I see no way of escape except through the prayers of others."[113]

Pio fervently told her she was making reparations for him. "Pray and beseech more insistently the divine compassion of our God that He may have mercy on me and not be mindful of the sins of my youth," he wrote.[114] Pio encouraged Raffaelina toward a proper respect for receiving Holy Communion regularly: "To remain immune from sin and make progress on the path to perfection is not possible for those who remain for months on end without partaking abundantly of the immaculate Flesh of the divine Lamb."[115]

During the half year it took for her to offer three fifty-four-day Rosary novenas, Raffaelina blossomed in the spiritual life. She began to understand her value to Pio by her prayers for him, and she also saw that she was valuable to God, who was putting her soul through certain processes to make it perfect, so she would glitter in Heaven. At first, she had to be coaxed by Pio into prayer and self-sacrifice, but she graduated to being independent in prayer, ultimately deciding to become a victim soul and offer her life to God for Pio's return to monastic life and for him to become a confessor.

In the early days of their correspondence Raffaelina pleaded with Pio to let her know whether Jesus was happy with their exchange of letters. Pio was emphatic: "From my manner of dealing with you up to the present, you ought to have realized that Jesus is highly pleased with these holy colloquies and conversations of ours."[116] But even after she learned this, Raffaelina was a stubbornly hard judge of herself. "I remain perplexed, embarrassed, plunged in the depths," she wrote, "when I reflect on the mass of graces which our good Jesus has unexpectedly poured down on my undeserving, ungrateful, sterile soul."[117] Raffaelina was not content to know she was pleasing Jesus; rather, she was self-absorbed with her self-dissatisfaction and feelings of inadequacy. Pio took her in hand and told her frankly, "The discouragement you feel when you deplore your failure to correspond with grace comes from the enemy."[118]

To counteract the demonic message that she was not good enough for the many graces given her by Our Lord, Pio instructed her thus: "I should like you to imitate in this the brides of this poor world, who admire and take pleasure in nothing else but the fine gifts and qualities of their husbands, without bothering in the least whether or in what manner they correspond to their husbands' demonstrations of affection."[119] He called her affectionately a "little bride of Jesus."[120]

Light in Dark Times

Pio was educating Raffaelina as to the traps of the devil, and so instead of telling her to dwell on discouragement, he told her to do the opposite and to rejoice in her afflicted state. "The more you are afflicted, the more you ought to rejoice," he assured her, "because in the fire of tribulations the souls will become pure gold, worthy to be placed and to shine in the heavenly palace."[121] Raffaelina was filled with extreme fear, for which Pio suggested a remedy which is of great benefit to us, too: "Beseech our divine Lover to free you from these excessive fears, which instead of opening the heart to Jesus' love tend to close it."[122]

We need be on our guard against excessive fear. It closes our hearts to Christ's love. Raffaelina was blind as to the state of her own soul, and Pio's role was to see her soul for her, while he was fulfilling a duty in guiding her that would help him save his own soul. As for why Our Lord gives dryness to a soul, Pio explained, "He sends you this spiritual aridity, to unite you more closely to Him, to rid you of certain attachments."[123] He warned her that the devil would try to trap her by inspiring her with thoughts that her dryness was a sign she had been abandoned. On the contrary, Pio told her dryness was a sign that she was high in the Lord's favor.

Before he instructed her as to the role of darkness imposed by God, Padre Pio told her of the three signs by which she was to identify that light that comes from God:

> The first is that these lights produce an ever more admirable knowledge of God, who, while revealing Himself to us, gives us a deeper and deeper knowledge of His incomprehensible greatness. In a word, this light leads us to love God our Father more and more and to increase the sacrifices we make for His honor and glory. The second sign is an ever-greater knowledge of ourselves, a deeper and deeper sense of humility at the thought that such a wretched creature should have had the effrontery to offend Him and still dares to look at Him and tend towards Him. The third sign is that these heavenly rays produce in the soul an increasing contempt for all that belongs to this earth, with the exception of those things which may prove useful for the service of God.[124]

Although he was very tender with her, Pio did not flinch from giving her a stern reprimand on one occasion when Raffaelina made a jealous assessment of her sister, Giovina. Padre Pio and Raffaelina were both in the habit of calling Giovina a martyr, for she had such debilitating stomach problems that her ability to take part in the normal activities of life was curtailed almost totally, but Giovina had offered up her losses to Christ. Raffaelina complained to Pio that Giovina was so ill that her beauty, education, and social standing had been of no use. Although this comment was like something Raffaelina would say of herself, she had no right to say her sister's good looks and noble birth had been awarded her in vain, because Giovina had offered up her worldly opportunities as a sacrifice to Our Lord. Pio rebuked Raffaelina sharply: "May God forgive you, for this time you have made a really big blunder." He reminded her that Giovina had offered everything up to the Lord and that instead of being redundant and of "no use,"[125] Giovina would be rewarded by the generosity of Our Lord for the offering she made of herself.

As we go through the guidance Pio gave Raffaelina, we have a palpable sense of how much he loved her soul, and these words of Pio's reinforce our belief in his love for us: "I love my spiritual children as much as my own soul and even more."[126] Pio revealed to Raffaelina that through his intercession she was a bride of Christ: "I have espoused you to Jesus and I am jealous lest others ensnare you." He said he was in danger if he failed to help her to save her soul: "Woe betide me if I fail in this task."[127]

The devil tried to stop a letter from Raffaelina getting to Pio, and Pio said Satan had trapped it with his hoof, but he also saw the Virgin Mary sending Satan on his way and arranging for the letter to reach Pio. Pio received the letter, albeit much later than normal. As when the devil tried to obstruct the letters between Agostino and Pio, we see that the devil prioritized impeding communication between spiritual father and spiritual child. But the devil also wanted to stop you and me from benefiting from these letters, which are the cream of Pio's teachings on the soul's graduations and are part of our spiritual inheritance.

Pio gave meaning to Raffaelina's sufferings and told her that her pain was not in vain but that Our Lord imposed this darkness to purify her soul for a greater union with Him. The gems of insight Pio gave Raffaelina may guide you in your dark night. Pio told Raffaelina we must cultivate a reflex of automatic thankfulness not only when Our Lord manifests Himself to us but also when He hides Himself — we must always thank Jesus. "If Jesus manifests Himself, thank Him," Pio exhorted, "and if He remains hidden, thank Him just the same: all is a trick of love."[128] This was the most basic of Pio's counsel on "the game of love," a phrase coined by St. Catherine of Siena to describe Jesus' intermittent hiding from us.

Raffaelina wrote plaintively, "I yearn and long for light,"[129] and she made repeated pleas to Pio that he pray for her to be given more light. Pio agreed that Raffaelina was in "darkness," but he guaranteed her she would always receive "as much light as suffices to prevent you from yielding to despair." She was told by Pio she had "a horrible conflict" in her soul, owing to the higher part of her soul feeling drawn to God whereas "the lower part, that is to say the sensitive appetite, is torn and tormented by ennui, tediousness and many other vague feelings of a painful nature."[130]

Accidental and Substantial Love

Raffaelina wrote to Padre Pio about painful doubts. She felt God had withdrawn His love from her and that simultaneously her love for God was decreasing. She was not deliberately holding back from loving God as a way of retribution for feeling herself deprived of God's love; she wanted to love God as much as she could. She had, however, lost "sweetness" in her love of God. Padre Pio pulled the jagged thorn of doubt out of Raffaelina and assured her, "Your love for God is growing and being consolidated continually," despite her not consciously feeling it.[131]

This same lesson is one we all must take to heart. We must not measure our love of God by how much we feel it. Like Raffaelina, our love of God may be getting stronger especially when we do not feel it. Padre Pio defined the state of the soul that is growing in love of God but nonetheless in stubborn dryness: "In every devotional act it finds that the will usually remains dry and the heart quite hard, devoid of all feeling for supernatural things."[132]

Pio informed Raffaelina that God "wants to win us over to Himself by having us experience abundant sweetness and consolations in every one of our devotions, both in the will and in the heart."[133] Once He has won us over, He may start a process in the soul whereby accidental love signified by its sweetness is taken away and the soul has symptoms of withdrawal. Pio carefully instructed Raffaelina regarding the difference between "substantial love" of God and "accidental love" of God.[134]

Accidental love of God comes in two forms, the first of which is perceptible whereas the second is "purely spiritual."[135] Pio was at pains to tell Raffaelina that accidental love is surrounded by great dangers, because it is easy to become very attached to it and to place it above substantial love of God. A soul can want it like a child who wants only ice cream and never dinner. One may engage in devotion to God not out of the desire to put Him before everything else but instead to get the sweetness it brings.

Substantial love, on the other hand, is the better love and was defined by Pio as "that simple and straightforward choice by which the will places God before everything else because of His Infinite Goodness." Pio told Raffaelina that the person who loves God by always placing Him first "loves Him by an act of substantial love."[136] It is like preferring meat and potatoes over candy.

Most crucially, the Lord takes away accidental love, by way of removing the sweetness, because a soul can only become contemplative when it was been purified of accidental love. This is not a passive process because the individual soul must actively give up its attachment to sweetness, quit seeking it, and submit humbly to the purification of the senses. A distinction exists between a soul that is without the sweetness and still desires its return, which might strengthen its attachment, and a soul that is without the sweetness and actively gives up its desire for it, thus severing the attachment. The former soul will remain as it is, but the latter will progress to substantial love of God and contemplation. For this reason, Pio cautioned Raffaelina against being "attached" to accidental love, and encouraged her to defer to substantial love, a process that makes us "dear and pleasing to God."[137] Not all of us are called to be purely contemplative, as in the case of a cloistered nun, such as Mother Angelica who founded the EWTN television network, but never does Pio confine graduation to the contemplative state to religious life. Like Anna-Maria Taigi or St. Elizabeth Ann Seton, who were both married and who both graduated to the realm of mystical contemplation, the Lord can invite any soul of His choosing to go through dryness and darkness so they become contemplative.

When Our Lord sees that the soul "has acquired sufficient virtue to remain in His service without all these attractions and sweetness," He places the soul at a distance from "earthly things and from the occasion of sin." The purpose of this transition from a lower to a higher love is, as Pio put it, so that a person may have "greater holiness of life." When sweetness is no longer given to a soul by God, a person may think, as Raffaelina did, that God has abandoned them and that they are being punished for serious sins. But as Pio revealed, this is an erroneous misconception: "What the unfortunate soul calls abandonment by God is nothing else than a most singular and special attention on the part of the Heavenly Father." While Our Lord no longer gives sweetness, instead He gives a soul "great strength."[138]

Furthermore, Padre Pio encouraged Raffaelina to persevere, because for the soul who enjoys contemplation, everything becomes "delightful."[139] The purification, however, must come before the prize. A soul, even one as highly favored as Pio's, cannot become capable of contemplative prayer without first being purified of accidental love. The pain accompanying this growth owes to the breaking of the attachment the soul has to accidental love.

The next step is even harder and "most painful," to quote Padre Pio, because "the soul in this state can no longer pray and meditate easily but is left in the dark." Pio explained that the darkness persists because the old light has been removed. The soul's faculty of meditation is disabled deliberately — the light upon which it has relied to play scenes in its interior is taken away. God removes the old light from the imagination so as to make room for the new light, which is "a more perfect light."[140]

This better light is cleaner and not compromised by impurities that clog the soul's contemplation of God. When the soul's appetite is not filled with sweet, accidental sense love, the soul may enjoy "a much purer light by which he can fix his eyes on God and on divine things and without any words just contemplate Him with a simple gaze."[141] This light acts without the soul recognizing its actions, because it is not a visual phenomenon; it is not like being in a dark room and suddenly having the light switched on but is instead a gradual graduation from poorer abilities of the soul to heightened abilities for contemplating God that are enabled by this vastly superior light.

Pio prepared Raffaelina by telling her that though her soul could not "discern"[142] this light, her soul would be given greater powers. The soul does not feel the new light, which is part of its gift. Were the soul to feel it, then the conscious sensing of this light would distract and dilute from the object of the light: God. The soul's new ability to concentrate on God and see heavenly things in a way that was previously beyond its capability is none other than a fine preparation for the Beatific Vision.

We may wish to note well that the process whereby a soul is thrust into darkness, gutted of accidental love, and brought to a point where it can love God substantially is not the way of every soul, but as Pio revealed, "a very exceptional grace."[143] If you are such a soul undergoing this transformation, you may give prayers of thanksgiving. Pio informed Raffaelina that after she had completed purgation of the senses, she would enter the purgation of the spirit. He warned her that this purgation is "very severe"[144] and that it would consist of "absolute privation of all comfort of a purely spiritual nature."[145] When she was cleansed of accidental sense love, she would then be cleaned of "accidental spiritual love,"[146] the purgation of the spirit. Pio explained that the refreshment she had enjoyed thus far would now be taken away and that dire dryness would follow. "The aridity experienced during the purgation of the senses does not in itself prevent one from enjoying a certain spiritual refreshment," he wrote, but "the further purgation consists in being deprived of this refreshment."[147]

Pio put her on notice that "when the Lord shall be pleased to place you in this state you will suffer a pain so severe as to exceed any idea it has been possible to form about it before. When that happens, however, remember that the love of God is growing all the time in your soul."[148] Her spiritual guide then gave her a sign by which she was to know she was growing in love of God: "You will feel more and more willing to face everything that offers service and honor to God."[149] But she would have "no feeling at the spiritual level."[150] Instead, she would be "in deep darkness"[151] and would find that "all activity at the spiritual level will be difficult and repugnant."[152] Pio revealed to Raffaelina that "God has withdrawn from you His reflected light"[153] but also that "aridity and privation of the reflected light are not sufficient for spiritual purification."[154] In addition, "another painful interior process is also required,"[155] because she was being invited to a "perfect mystical union in love."[156]

This purgation would consist of a light that would have the purpose of causing darkness. "This is nothing but a very bright light," he explained, "which gives the soul a clearer view of its faults than we can possibly conceive and consequently plunges it into an abyss of darkness and most painful anxiety."[157] This light causes hideous pain — "They are not deceived in their judgment when they reckon that death itself does not bring with it as much suffering as they endure in their present state"[158] — and bears comparison to the pains of the damned in Hell. This is not pointless suffering, however, because the very same light that at first "invades the soul with such desolation and pain is later to raise it up to mystical and transforming union."[159] Pio finally gave Raffaelina much relief when he told her that this light "will join the soul to the divine Bridegroom in perfect loving union."[160] He instructed Raffaelina that this knowledge of God's plan for her should arouse gratitude in her and "serve as an incentive to lay aside all fear."[161] May we too have gratitude and not fear, if we are offered this special route to perfection.

10

A WILL SURRENDERED TO GOD

As a young priest, Pio had one last, poignant encounter with his old teacher, whom he had once called a "bad priest."[162] There was no bad blood between Pio or Tizzani; Pio always sent his best regards to Tizzani through his wife, and when he offered to visit his old teacher, lo and behold, Tizzani agreed. Pio went to hear the man's Confession; Tizzani sobbed for his sins, and died the next day.

His teacher's death swelled a deep longing in the heart of Padre Pio, who wanted his earthly sufferings to end so that he might join Tizzani in eternal life. Shockingly, Pio even implored Raffaelina to pray to God that he would die as soon as possible. When Raffaelina refused, he demanded, "Why am I denied this charity?" Then he begged, "By the bowels of mercy of the incarnate God, I still dare to entreat you," and warned her that if she refused, she would make of herself "a murderess."[163] Pio was adamant that he wanted her to "beseech the Bridegroom of souls to sever without delay the bonds that keep me united to this fragile body."[164]

Why did he want so much to die?

The timing of Pio's correspondence with Raffaelina coincides with the first half of World War I. The bloodshed appalled Pio so much that wished to be among the dead. He declared to Agostino, "I would rather die than witness such slaughter!"[165] Italy lost a total of 531,000 lives in the Great War. Pio himself had spent time in and out of army barracks. A pattern emerged: He would be drafted, found too ill to do anything, and then put on leave.

In November 1915, he was summoned for a physical, and even though he was diagnosed with tuberculosis, he was still assigned to the Tenth Company of the Army Medical Corps at Naples. He tried to do the work of a janitor, but he could not stop vomiting. His spirits were very low and he was most unhappy in uniform. Thankfully, before Christmas, Pio was found to be too ill to be of any use and given a year's leave.

To Raffaelina, Pio confided certain mystical insights about the war. He said their country had become "detestable in God's sight"[166] and that God was "justly angry."[167] But he conceded that, as angry as God was with their homeland, He still loved her because He was still on speaking terms with the Italian nation: "While heaven speaks, we are still loved." Yet Pio also said, "Wretched are those countries to whom the Lord doesn't speak anymore … this is a sign He has cast them off." He declared, "Tremble, all nations who no longer hear even the angry voice of our God." The spiritual solution was, according to Pio, repentance and contrition. He said to Raffaelina that God was waiting for "the voice of our repentance to silence his thundering" and waiting for "tears to extinguish his lightning."[168]

It is ironic, given how effective Pio's prayers were during his lifetime and the myriad people cured of both physical and spiritual illness, that God did not answer Pio's prayers for death as he wished. In this instance, when Pio prayed much for his own death, the will of God triumphed. This helps those of us who hold Pio in the highest esteem not to confuse him with the Lord; it reminds us that Pio was His servant — a powerful one, yes, but always in the service of the Almighty.

A Victim Soul

Although Raffaelina was not a mystic and did not have the supernatural gifts Pio had, her prayers were mightily meritorious all the same when offered in accordance with God's will. After Pio had been away from monastery life for nearly seven years, relations became strained between him and Benedetto, who wanted him to return to the monastery at all costs. Around this time Raffaelina's sister Giovina was so ill and emaciated she was thought to be approaching death. Doctors were giving Giovina morphine to ease her pain.

With an act of unselfish love, Raffaelina offered herself as a victim soul, to let the Lord take her life if He wished, for two intentions: for Giovina's return to health and for Pio's return to full-time community life in a Franciscan monastery, that he might become a renowned confessor. Raffaelina did not want Pio just for herself, isolated in his home village and thus able to write her detailed letters.

Evidently God accepted Raffaelina as a victim; a cancerous tumor sprouted in her breast. She had a mastectomy, but a handful of months later it was discovered the cancer had spread beyond hope. Raffaelina was dying. The lady Pio had asked for prayers for his own demise greeted Sister Death fifty-two years before he did. But not before she collaborated in the practical arrangements to make Pio a full-time member of a monastery again.

Agostino visited Raffaelina and spoke to her of the barriers preventing Pio from returning to a friary — namely, his history of collapsing when he was taken out of Pietrelcina and the violent protest he foresaw coming from the villagers of Pietrelcina, who hailed Pio as their own saint and did not want him removed from their midst. Raffaelina and Agostino devised a plan. Agostino invited Pio to come to Raffaelina's home, on the pretext that he could meet her at long last in person and hear her Confession, and as far as Pio and his own people were aware he was only going to Foggia for a short visit. After they had crafted their plan, Raffaelina said something prophetic to Fr. Agostino: "Make the Superiors give Padre Pio the faculties to hear confessions. He will save many souls."[169]

Pio Returns to the Friary

So, in February of 1916, Pio made plans for a short trip, telling his mother and friends he was going to Foggia to assist a dying lady. After he journeyed by train to Foggia, he was taken to St. Anne's Friary, where he thought he would be staying for merely a few days. To his surprise Padre Benedetto was waiting for him, and he gave him a pen and paper. "Write to your mama," he ordered Pio, "and tell her to send your belongings because, dead or alive, you're staying here at Foggia."[170] Pio obeyed.

When Pio settled in the Foggia friary, Raffaelina's first request was granted: Pio's health did not fail, as it had in the past when he was taken away from his home village. It wasn't long before Raffaelina's other request was honored as well: Her sister Giovina recovered completely. God had accepted Raffaelina's offering as a victim soul.

Raffaelina's Final Days

Fr. Agostino had the pleasure of introducing Pio to Raffaelina for the first time, and they delighted at being in the same room together. Agostino felt a debt of gratitude to Raffaelina, and to reward her he gave Pio permission to spend much time in the company of Raffaelina during her last days. Raffaelina faded fast, and on the feast of St. Patrick, in March 1916, Padre Pio described the journey of Raffaelina's soul with startling vividness: "She is already of the King. Before long she will be led into the nuptial banquet."[171]

It might seem strange to think of Raffaelina as a bride of Christ, since she was not a religious sister or a nun. But she had taken vows when she became a Third Order Franciscan, and Pio had espoused her to Christ and taken great pains with her soul so he could present her "to the divine Bridegroom as a chaste virgin."[172]

Raffaelina spent her last hours on earth with Pio by her side. Giovina overheard Pio ask Raffaelina if they could pray and ask Jesus to take him in her place. Raffaelina denied Pio's wish by saying, "I want to go first to Jesus." Nonetheless, she reassured him, "I will tell Him to send me to take you."[173]

In the early hours of the feast of the Annunciation, March 25, Pio saw Raffaelina go straight to Heaven, where she celebrated the wedding banquet with her Divine Spouse. Pio proudly told the others that they had a new intercessor before the Heavenly Throne. Raffaelina kept her word, insofar as she came to Pio as a glorified soul. But she told him that when she asked the Lord to take him, Jesus told her this was contrary to His will. Raffaelina was, according to Pio, a saint in Heaven, but her intercession on this occasion was futile because it ran contrary to Our Lord's will.

The Road to San Giovanni Rotondo

After Raffaelina died, Pio went on to spend six months at St. Anne's Friary, where he was often very ill. This was a heady time: The Great War raged and, as more and more men were lost, the Italian military authorities were increasingly desperately looking for any man who could fight in battle. The war lasted another two years, and during that time the army continued to summon Pio for physicals, to determine whether he could be in active combat. To his great relief, Pio failed each one, and so was able to escape life in a barracks — until the fall of 1917, when he had to spend a few months in the barracks at Naples.

While living at St. Anne's, Pio met Padre Paolino di Tommaso, who took a great liking to him. Paolino was highly intuitive and an excellent reader of people; he saw Pio's goodness and holiness and yearned for him to be a member of the friary where he was superior: Our Lady of Grace in San Giovanni Rotondo, twenty-five miles from St. Anne's. Pio and Paolino began a warm friendship. Paolino was only a year older than Pio. He was short, stocky, and short-sighted. His round glasses framed eyes that flashed with intelligence.

A native of the town of San Giovanni Rotondo, Rachelina Russo, was an enterprising entrepreneur who had become a spiritual daughter of Pio. Rachelina would travel to St. Anne's Friary, where she and Pio met so he could guide her soul in person. Rachelina had lively eyes, a long nose, and a gaunt face. She had a bright smile that lit up a room. She ran a clothing store, by which she was well able to make a living, and she generously shared the proceeds with the friars.

Rachelina longed for Pio to come to her town, and during one intensely hot July, Paolino invited Pio to spend a little time in San Giovanni Rotondo and inhale the fresh mountain air. Pio had not been sleeping well at St. Anne's, and Paolino argued that it was cooler at San Giovanni Rotondo and Pio could get some sleep there. Although Paolino evaded getting Fr. Benedetto's permission for Pio's vacation, the vacation came to pass, and Rachelina even paid for Pio's travel expenses.

When he returned from vacation, Pio sought Benedetto's blessing to spend more time in San Giovanni Rotondo, a town shaped in a circle with mountains ringing it, providing protection from the searing sun. Benedetto gave his consent for Pio to live there permanently, thinking that the oxygen-rich air filtered by the surrounding mountains might keep Pio healthy enough to function. So Pio moved there in September, and was overjoyed to be with Paolino full-time. Paolino wrote to Agostino that Pio was "truly happy," and that the feeling was mutual for all the community: "You can imagine the benefit we experience in the presence of Padre Pio!"[174] Pio had finally come to the town where he was to have a magnificent ministry for the next five decades.

Pio's Ministry to Souls in Purgatory

Because of his extraordinary spiritual gifts, Pio had a ministry to both the living and the dead. At the height of the Great War, during a frosty winter's evening, Pio was in the guest room, warming himself by a roaring fire, when an old man dressed in an old-fashioned cape crept in. Pio was a bit unnerved when the old peasant sat down beside him, and he was flummoxed as to how the man had gotten into the friary at such an hour. "Who are you? What do you want?" Pio asked pointedly.[175]

"I am Pietro Di Mauro," the old man replied. "I am still in purgatory. I need a Mass to free my soul from it. God has given me permission to come to you and ask you for your prayers." At the mention of Purgatory, Pio knew, as the dancing flames of the fire cast shadows on his face, that Pietro was dead. Pio was ready to honor his request: "Rest assured that tomorrow I will celebrate Mass for your liberation."[176] Then Pio accompanied Pietro to the front door and found the door locked; it had never been opened to allow Pietro in. Pio unlocked the door and Pietro walked out into the square that was thick with snow glistening in the moonlight. Then Pietro promptly disappeared. Pio felt faint and fearful. In time, Pio became so accustomed to souls from Purgatory coming to him for prayer that they didn't frighten him at all.

Lucia Fiorentino and the Tree

It was God's will that Pio come to San Giovanni Rotondo; some may even say it was predestined. Ten years before Pio's arrival, Jesus gave a woman who was to be his spiritual daughter, Lucia Fiorentino, a prophetic vision of an enormous tree that grew in the atrium of the friary.

Our Lord told Lucia, "This is the symbol of a soul who is now far away but will come here." He explained, "He will be strong and well rooted like this tree." Then the the Lord revealed, "All the souls who come . . . if they take refuge in the umbrage of this tree, they will be freed from evil." Jesus, however, emphasized the need for humility and made the glad promise to Lucia that "if they humble themselves before this worthy priest, they will receive counsel and the fruits of eternal life. . . . His mission will extend throughout the whole world."[177]

The Savior warned, however, that those who hated this tree would find themselves subject to His punishment. Jesus revealed to Lucia that the tree was Pio, who, when he met her in San Giovanni, instantly knew Lucia as his child. Lucia, like Raffaelina, wore proper Victorian dresses; she had a small, oval face but always had a serious expression. Her skin was smooth and uncreased because she rarely smiled; she was as stoic as she was sincere. She readily embraced suffering and didn't resent her faults. Rather, she quickly offered up the pain her sins caused her.

Padre Pio's two spiritual daughters had come from different social standings; Raffaelina had never had to work, while Lucia had been a seamstress from childhood. Lucia was a mystic who had been shown Pio's role in San Giovanni a decade before Pio even knew he was going there. In the 1930s, as we'll see, Lucia offered herself as a victim soul for Pio's ministry, for the intention that his "imprisonment" would end. And like Raffaelina, her request was granted. Despite their differences, both of Pio's spiritual daughters were moved by love of Pio, love of God, and love of other spiritual children — and believed that they could benefit from the guidance of their spiritual father.

The Early, Invisible Years

Were the ordinary people of the town initially aware of Pio being a stigmatist? No. The wounds were invisible for the first two years Pio lived in San Giovanni Rotondo. These years were to be the last quiet years of Padre Pio's life. He was far from idle though; he was a teacher in the school run by his fellow Franciscans, and he immersed himself in the lives of his spiritual sons and daughters. He spent long hours drafting letters to his spiritual daughters, and on occasion meeting with them in the confines of Our Lady of Grace Friary, where he prayed with them and offered them counsel for their growth in holiness.

In 1917, when Pio was thirty years old, Archbishop Pasquale Gagliardi granted him the faculty to hear Confessions. A few years later, in a bitterly ironic twist, this same archbishop led an unjust persecution of Pio. Many of the freedoms and activities that characterized Pio's early years of ministry — his close relationships with his spiritual sons and daughters, the long hours spent in the confessional, and his meeting ordinary people who visited him in San Giovanni — were curtailed during this first persecution.

Becoming Pio's Spiritual Child

At this time (from 1916 to 1917) Pio's superiors sometimes assigned Pio to give spiritual direction or serve as confessor to certain individuals, but he was reluctant to take care of a soul if he could not read their souls, if he did not know them "before the Lord." It was not actually a random, accidental process by which a man or woman came to be a spiritual son or daughter of Pio's. Pio said he was better able to serve a soul if the Lord had given him special insight. Then and now, Pio adopts souls who may not know he has special "illumination"[178] from the Lord into their soul until Pio introduces himself. Pio was completely willing to guide a soul for whom the Lord gave him "illumination," but when this light was lacking, it was difficult for Pio to divine the way forward for the soul.

In order to become a spiritual child of Padre Pio, you must first ask the Lord if this is His will, if He will grant the graces necessary. If the Lord wills it, He will give Pio the light necessary to guide you. Below is the Prayer to the Sacred Heart of Jesus, which Pio said every day for all his spiritual children and for all those who asked his prayers. If Pio knows your soul "before the Lord," as he used to say in his lifetime, he will make this known to you. To be a spiritual son or spiritual daughter of Pio's is to be a recipient of the glorious promise that Pio made as part of a "pact with the Lord": "I will take my place at the gate of Paradise, but I shall not enter until I have seen the last of my spiritual children enter."[179] If you want to be a spiritual son or daughter of Pio's, you may pray to the Sacred Heart of Jesus and ask Our Lord to entrust you to Pio. Ask Our Lord to bless your request.

Prayer to the Sacred Heart of Jesus

O my Jesus, you have said: "Truly I say to you, ask and you will receive, seek and you will find, knock and it will be opened to you."
Behold I knock, I seek and ask for the grace of … (*Mention your intention here. Then offer an Our Father, a Hail Mary, and a Glory Be.*)
Sacred Heart of Jesus, I place all my trust in you.

O my Jesus, you have said: "Truly I say to you, if you ask anything of the Father in my name, he will give it to you." Behold, in your name, I ask the Father for the grace of … (*Mention your intention here. Then offer an Our Father, a Hail Mary, and a Glory Be.*)
Sacred Heart of Jesus, I place all my trust in you.

O my Jesus, you have said: "Truly I say to you, heaven and earth will pass away but my words will not pass away." Encouraged by your infallible words I now ask for the grace of … (*Mention your intention here. Then offer an Our Father, a Hail Mary, and a Glory Be.*)
Sacred Heart of Jesus, I place all my trust in you.

O Sacred Heart of Jesus, for whom it is impossible not to have compassion on the afflicted, have pity on us miserable sinners and grant us the grace which we ask of you, through the Sorrowful and Immaculate Heart of Mary, your tender Mother and ours.

Hail, holy Queen, Mother of mercy, our life, our sweetness and our hope.
To thee do we cry, poor banished children of Eve: to thee do we send
    up our sighs, mourning and weeping in this vale of tears.
Turn then, most gracious advocate, thine eyes of mercy toward us, and
    after this our exile, show unto us the blessed fruit of thy womb, Jesus,
        O clement, O loving, O sweet Virgin Mary!
Pray for us O holy Mother of God,
that we may be made worthy of the promises of Christ.
St. Joseph, foster father of Jesus, pray for us.
Amen.

This prayer to the Sacred Heart is powerful. Padre Pio offered it every day of his life because of its amazing efficacy. The line "O Sacred Heart of Jesus, for whom it is impossible not to have compassion on the afflicted" tells us of Our Lord's great empathy and benevolence toward us.

In addition to the stigmata, another manifestation of Padre Pio's intimate union with Christ was the ecstatic union of Jesus's Sacred Heart with Pio's heart, when Jesus took Pio's human heart into His Sacred Heart and the two became one. When Pio prayed to the Sacred Heart every day for each and every person who asked his prayers, he was praying to the Heart that had taken Pio's heart into His. Jesus gave Pio's human heart a home in His divine Heart. And so, by praying to the Sacred Heart of Jesus, you are asking the Sacred Heart to give you grace through the intercession of Pio, whose heart beat in time with His. The shared function, the shared operation of their hearts speaks to a unity of purpose, a shared mission to save sinners from their sin.

11

Christ and the Blazing Blade

In 1918, Padre Pio's body became a living exhibition of Christ's Crucifixion for all to see: His invisible stigmata became visible. He went from looking like an ordinary Franciscan to looking as though he had been crucified. Before this event transpired, Pio would often say, "I am a mystery to myself."[180] All that he had endured up to that time was simply preparation for this momentous occasion, when he became a visible stigmatist.

During the months before Christ appeared to Pio, he had been in intense spiritual darkness, undergoing the most extreme and excruciating purgation of his spirit. His soul was in a place so black that Pio had no inkling of the plans Our Lord had for him to bear the visible wounds of His Passion. Pio was literally being kept in the dark as to Our Lord's designs for him. Had Pio known what lay in store for him, his struggle to conform his will to the Lord's would have been even greater. As it was, Pio logged his journey through desolation in the letters he wrote to Benedetto and Agostino. He told these spiritual fathers of having the light of God all but completely removed and that he fully believed he had "lost"[181] Our Lord forever.

Prior to this dark time, Pio had expertly guided Raffaelina in her soul's purification through darkness. It is one thing to be a guide to someone else, however, to hold the lantern of counsel and lead a person along the black road; it is another thing to be as Pio was, in "this most harsh and obscure prison."[182] All Padre Pio's previous experiences had not adequately trained him for this, and although he knew that the reason Our Lord purges a soul through darkness is to make the soul capable of a higher union with Him, Pio felt so removed from God and so far from His light that he could not bring himself even to acknowledge that he could be on the cusp of closer union.

Pio said, "I see hell opening beneath my feet.... I have already been down into hell,"[183] and he truly began to believe that God had rejected him totally and forever. These letters may seem melodramatic, speaking as they do of a pit of Hell, but Pio's darkness was so deep that he felt separated from God and his grief was like that of a damned soul. As we know, Pio had told Raffaelina that the sufferings of a soul in darkness can compete with the sufferings of the lost in Hell, and here he was living the reality of his own description. Pio was filled with self-loathing, which matched his belief that he was "contemptible" in God's eyes. This meant he did not resent his state; rather, he felt he deserved to be "cast off … rejected and abandoned" by God. He was experiencing the process he had described to Raffaelina, where he was in mortal agony because he was transfixed on his own failings and unworthiness of union with God, which is ironically the prelude to union with God. All the while, he feared greatly that he was going to sin against the Lord in some way. Pio felt he was locked away in some kind of prison, taken away from the light of God forever: "Cruel shackles seemed to close on me and bind me tightly and I felt I was about to die."[184] He was in agonizing grief because he truly believed he had lost Our Lord.

All the while Pio was in this deep darkness, he went about his priestly duties, teaching in the school, hearing Confessions and living as a Capuchin who celebrated Mass every day and observed the demanding timetable of continuous prayer. He wrote that his hectic ministry gave him relief. Pio was able to see the souls of his spiritual sons and daughters who came to visit him frequently and see the souls of the penitents who confessed their sins to him. He did all this while in "everlasting night."[185] He was less and less able to see himself, relying mostly on Benedetto's strength and Agostino's gentle support, which came in their letters. Pio's desire for God's love increased until he was wild with longing. He was convinced of total and permanent loss: "I have lost every trace, every vestige of the Supreme Good."[186] He was following the advice he had given Raffaelina, that the soul needs to submit to the purification in order to progress.

Grieving Spiritual Loss

A way that may help us understand Pio's grief is to think of a time when perhaps a loved one died or rejected us, becoming permanently estranged. Padre Pio's pain was yet more intense, for human love is limited and feeble compared to divine love, and when human love is taken away it can to some extent be replaced by the love of another human. As with human love lost irrevocably, we are powerlessness to restore divine love; it is entirely a grace of God, to confer when and if He wills.

Fr. Benedetto gave Pio an exquisite metaphor that we may wholly adopt if we find ourselves in the black waters of purgation. His one and only spiritual director told Pio to think of himself as a passenger on a ship, shut away in his cabin and unable to see the ship or feel the motion of sailing, yet traveling nonetheless.

Pio felt totally out of favor with Our Lord, when the opposite was true — he was highly favored. Pio felt like a useless piece of trash; little did he know the great mission Christ had in store for him and the use Christ would make of him. Drawing on Pio's experience, if you ever find yourself in darkness of the soul — a condition, remember, that Pio stressed as being an exceptional grace — it is good to note that a soul in darkness may lose perspective of its true state. If you feel that God is holding you in contempt, it may in fact be that the opposite is true. This may especially be the case after you have made much progress in holiness. Perhaps there was a time of deep darkness in your life when you felt God's absence, but later you saw this time was a precursor to being given a role uniquely suited to you and your talents, a way of serving God that was specific to how God made you.

At this time Pio believed he was experiencing "God's rejection."[187] Furthermore, he felt he deserved it: "God is rightfully spewing me out of his mouth continually."[188] The suffering friar even repeatedly committed to paper his most frantic plea: "My God, my God, why have You forsaken me?"[189] — an exact echoing of Our Lord's words on the Cross when he called out to His Father in Heaven. Pio was undergoing his spiritual crucifixion. He shared the same suffering spirit as Jesus had on the Cross when he felt forsaken even by His Father in Heaven.

Padre Agostino felt that this time of darkness was sent to humble Pio, to keep the saint from knowing how well he was fulfilling His holy will. Benedetto assured Pio that his black torments were part of being intimately involved in Christ's plan for the salvation of souls. Christ, with the aid of a blazing blade, was about to make Pio a bearer of His wounds, the wounds of the most perfect Son of God. Yet while he was lost in darkness, Pio did not know what was about to happen to him, and he was not filled with thoughts of how special he was or how close he was to God, but rather how inadequate he was and how much of an unbridgeable gulf there was between God and him. Pio was being thoroughly trained to serve Almighty God, who had shown His power by leaving Pio to languish in a hellish state, by means of withholding His love and light — a temporary measure that nonetheless felt eternal. Pio was being instructed in his own weakness, as well as in his total dependence on God.

Padre Pio's Transverberation

June and July of 1918 were bright outside, the dazzling rays of sun shining on the town where Pio lived the life of a busy priest, but inside Pio, his soul was in the darkest recess it had ever been in. He was about to have one of his two epic meetings with the Messiah, yet he felt at his worst.

Outside in the wider world, World War I was claiming millions of lives, and certainly Pio was not being sheltered from news of the barbaric bloodshed. Pio felt called to make an offering of himself for the end of the war. The very minute he offered himself, he found himself suffering like a damned soul, as he conceded in his letters: "I have felt myself in hell without even an instant's respite."[190]

On August 5, 1918, Padre Pio had a profound and life-changing encounter with Christ. Schoolboys from the school run by the Franciscans were lined up for Confessions, one by one kneeling before Pio. One boy was confessing his sins to Pio when suddenly the wounded Christ presented Himself to Pio. Jesus held a very long blade with a sharp point that seemed to spout fire. Christ hurled the weapon into Pio's soul with all His strength. The stab of pain was so sharp, Pio thought he was on the point of dying, so he told the boy to leave because he was ill and did not feel he would be able to continue to hear his Confession.

The blazing blade shot through Pio's internal organs, tearing and rupturing his body. This was Pio's experience of *transverberation*, the mystical piercing of the heart. No part of his interior was saved from the eviscerating blade, and the outside of his body also sustained a wound, initially shaped like a cross, which manifested itself on Pio's left side and was there for the next fifty years.

From the instant the weapon was thrust into him by Christ, Pio was in agony which lasted the rest of that day without any break, then the entire following day of the sixth, and did not cease until the morning of the seventh. He wrote a letter to Benedetto with an account of the assault and informed him that since

Christ thrust the weapon into his soul, "I feel in the depths of my soul a wound that is always open and causes me continual agony."[191]

Though at the time he recognized Our Lord as the one who held the blazing blade, Pio called the figure "a celestial person"[192] in the letters to Benedetto. Why did Pio make it a mystery? At this point, Christ had hidden Himself from Pio for so long as to become deeply mysterious to Pio, and Christ's meeting with him was so strange to one who had been in such darkness that Christ seemed a stranger to him.

Pio was confounded, asking his spiritual father if this was a "punishment."[193] Pio's will was arrested — he had never wanted to be seen as a stigmatist — yet Our Lord had given him unmistakable marks. Benedetto could not agree that it was a punishment visited on Pio but, instead, thought it a shared expiation with Christ for the sins of the world. As he knew Pio had been bearing the crucifixion wounds invisibly for a total of eight years at this time, Benedetto perceived the appearance of the side-wound as an event of epic importance. "The wound completes your passion," he wrote, "just as it completed the Passion of your Beloved on the Cross."[194] Benedetto described Pio's experience as proof of God's great love for him. Indeed, God the Father had elevated Pio so that he was more comparable to His Son.

The following month, on September 20, 1918, the stigmata became visible on Pio's hands and feet. That day Padre Pio had offered Holy Mass, and he retired to the choir loft to make his thanksgiving. He was lulled into a repose, like being soundly asleep; all his senses and his soul were consumed in a complete quiet, as he wrote later: "Absolute silence surrounded and invaded me," and he was filled with "great peace."[195]

Suddenly a great light shone in his eyes, and in the midst of this light, the crucifix on the wall came to life and there appeared the wounded Christ, with His hands, feet, and side dripping blood. Pio was terrified and felt that his heart would jump out of his chest. But the Lord strengthened him. Shafts of light and flame beamed forth from the wounded Christ and pierced Pio's hands and feet. When the vision of Our Lord ended, he found himself on the floor, his hands and feet shedding blood. Unlike just a month before, this time Pio had a better understanding that his wounds were a call to be a sacrifice offered for the salvation of souls, and when he went back to his cell, he sang hymns of thanksgiving to Our Lord. The physical pain was agonizing, he later confided to Benedetto. "Imagine the agony I experienced and continue to experience almost every day," he wrote. "I want to be inebriated with pain." That which he found to be "unbearable" was the shame and humiliation he felt because the wounds could be observed by himself and others — "these outward signs which cause me such embarrassment and unbearable humiliation." This humiliation was something so strange that he could not find the words to describe it. An important distinction is that Padre Pio wanted the physical pain, but not the visible marks: "I will raise my voice and will not stop imploring him until, in His mercy, He takes away, not the wounds or the pain ... but these outward signs."[196]

Yet this time his prayer was not going to be answered. This was to be a psychological passion as well as a physical one. All this time he kept these magnificent meetings with Christ a secret from the other friars, who sat with him at meals, prayed alongside him, and socialized with him in recreation. He did not breathe a word of it to Fr. Paolino, his superior and best friend in San Giovanni Rotondo. Benedetto chose not to disclose anything to Paolino either, whom he still distrusted. Paolino was an able administrator, energetic and efficient, but he had shown disregard for Benedetto when he arranged the vacation that led to Pio coming to his friary. Paolino was prone to overreacting to slights, and although it caused Pio unbearable anguish to reveal the details of his meeting with Our Lord to Benedetto, he may not have wanted to involve the young Paolino in the conversation for fear it would bother Benedetto, whom he needed so much as a Sherpa for his soul.

When his prayers that the wounds become invisible went unanswered, Pio gave himself up to bearing the wounds visibly and he offered the agonizing psychological humiliation along with the excruciating physical pain for the same reason Jesus gave Himself to be hung on a cross: for the expiation of our sins.

Praying "through the Wounds"

Praying to Christ Crucified by offering a prayer "through" the wounds of Pio is a potent method. There is no telling the miracles that wait upon making a request of Our Lord by sending the prayer to Heaven via the wounds of Pio. The prayer passes through the wounds and arrives before Our Lord in a cleansed, purified state, washed by the blood of this saint, making it all the more worthy to be considered by Our Lord. We may pray for the soul of a person we are hoping will convert by placing that soul inside the wounds of Pio and asking Our Lord to bless the soul after it has passed through the pierced hands and feet of Pio. Our Lord gave Pio the lived experience of His Passion for our sake, that Pio's agony, like Our Lord's own agony, would be the suffering offered in atonement for our sins. In sending our prayers through the wounds of Pio, we are doing as Pio did when he offered his prayers in union with the pain he suffered in bearing the sacred wounds of Christ.

An aid to the salvation of you and your loved ones may be for you to meditate on Pio's wounds and hold an image of them in your mind, or rely on a photograph of Pio with his wounds uncovered, and while visually meditating you place your soul or the soul of a loved one into the wounds and ask Our Lord to receive you or your loved one as they pass through the blood shed by Pio. We may honor the Passion of Christ by making the sacred wounds of Christ borne by Pio the route by which we offer prayer to Christ Crucified. Pio's pierced flesh is a passage for our prayer.

Our Lord chose Pio as His servant to bear His wounds, and in making the wounds of Pio the vessel for our prayer we are honoring Our Lord's plan for these sacred wounds. When we send prayer requests and ask for the conversion of a soul through the sacred wounds on the person of Pio, our prayers pass from us, through the wounds of Pio, up to Heaven. If asking for a prayer or grace "through" the body of a saint seems alien, I ask you to bear in mind that when we offer the prayer to the Sacred Heart of Jesus, we ask Jesus to give us the specific grace we ask "through" the Immaculate Heart of Mary, essentially requesting that the grace travel from Our Lady's heart to us. In the same manner, I am suggesting that Our Lord will give us a grace that travels through Pio's pierced flesh.

The magnificent merit of Pio's bearing of the wounds of Christ is that people who saw him during his lifetime and all of us who have seen photographs of Pio have a more intimate knowledge of Christ's Passion. We who were not there on Good Friday, under the Cross, watching the Sacred Blood rain from Jesus's wounds, may nevertheless see Christ's wounds on Pio and know Christ better when we behold photos of Padre Pio's punctured hands. Keeping mental images of them before our minds affords us a visceral appreciation of Our Lord's words on the eve of His Passion, that He had come into the world to offer himself in atonement for sin.

Thus, the one million people who came to Pio for Confession, when they knelt in front of him, could be in the presence of Christ's wounds from His Passion, which made the forgiveness of their sins possible. Obviously, there were no photographs taken of Our Lord's Passion. There were, however, photographs taken of Pio's stigmata, and meditating on them impresses upon an ordinary man or woman the reality of Our Lord shedding His Blood. The devil was defeated when Our Lord sacrificed Himself on the Cross and offered Himself as ransom for souls, which meant the devil's plan for total domination over souls was thwarted.

In like manner, the devil was diminished in his power to tempt Pio when he received the stigmata. We need to underscore Fr. Agostino's statement of a fact that during the year Pio received the wounds, the devil lost all power to tempt Pio on a personal basis: "From 1918 Satan was completely vanquished and the servant of God, Padre Pio no longer experienced the slightest temptation."[197] For the rest of Pio's life, however, the devil launched ferocious attacks on Pio's ministry, and he brutalized Pio again later in his life. There was a coinciding of Pio receiving the wounds of salvation and the devil being put at a distance — almost in the same way the devil fled from Our Lord's Crucifixion, he also fled from Pio when his hands and feet wept blood on account of his being wounded with the wounds of salvation. There was an exchange of suffering, because although Pio felt eviscerating embarrassment from being seen as a stigmatist, he was free from Satan goading him to sin.

12

A Death in the Family

A local schoolteacher, Nina Campanile, was on a mission to tell Padre Paolino that Pio had the stigmata. Nina was a cherished spiritual daughter of the stigmatist. She was only twenty-five but had a grandmotherly face, very full with creamy skin and large round brown eyes. She was tiny and her black mantilla covered her like a lace curtain.

Paolino was so incredulous when Nina told him that Pio had been marked with Christ's wounds that he giggled. He thought she loved Pio so much that she was extolling him as the Second St. Francis. The practically minded Paolino informed Nina that the red marks were acid burns. He reminded her that they were in the middle of a pandemic and that many of the boys at their school were direly ill with Spanish influenza. Paolino explained that he and Pio had been giving injections to the sick boys and that they'd sterilized the skin of the boys with carbolic acid. Not being medically trained, Pio and Paolino used pure, undiluted acid that burned the bottoms of the boys and burned their fingers as they applied it!

Nina needed no reminding of the pandemic; her sister Lucietta was pregnant and laid low with the flu. This was why, days before her visit to Paolino, Nina had visited Pio to beg his prayers for Lucietta, whom she feared was dying. Pio assured her that she was going to get better. Then, as usual, Nina tried to kiss his hand, and bending her lips to his palms, she discovered his wounds! This perturbed Pio, who griped, "If you only knew the embarrassment you cause me!"[198] And as he had once implored Fr. Pannullo, he now implored her to pray that the wounds would vanish.

Still Pio did not tell Paolino. Just as he had before, Pio tried to cover the coin-sized piercings in his palms with the ends of his brown cape. But the red edges kept peeping out. Paolino decided to find out for himself. One day Paolino entered Pio's room unannounced and saw the marks of Christ's Passion on his hands. When Paolino asked Benedetto about the matter, he was given the strict instruction to keep everything confidential. Meanwhile, Nina blurted her discovery to her mother and sister. Previously, Pio had assured Nina that Jesus loved her very much, and even though she had been loose-lipped, Pio remained very fond of her — yet he was mortified with embarrassment as the news of his stigmata spread among his spiritual daughters.

Pio did his best to distract people from becoming preoccupied with his wounds. But they were hard to hide. They were red and covered with a crusty scab that continuously oozed fresh blood. Pio started to wear brown mittens that soaked up the blood, and he wore white mittens at night that were drenched in blood by morning. But Pio did not become an overnight sensation — too many people were just too sick. San Giovanni had become like one big hospital, homes filled with bedbound people. Nina was petrified she would perish in the pandemic, and Pio gave her this advice: "Put yourself under the protection of the Virgin, do not sin and the sickness will not overcome you."[199] This is good advice for us all. If we are ever at risk of having our health compromised, let us take shelter under Our Lady's mantle and avoid sin at all costs. We can take heart that none of Pio's spiritual daughters died from the flu. However, Pio lost family members to it, and the grief almost devastated him.

Before the Forgiones were struck by illness, they'd had an extremely rocky few years. Felicita, Pio's favorite younger sister, had gotten married to Vincenzo and had three children. But her husband had cheated on her — with Pellegrina, Felicita's copper-haired younger sister. Pellegrina had given birth to a baby boy, Vincenzo's son. Pellegrina, it seems, had been jealous of Felicita and stole her husband's affection from her as a way of score settling. It was also rumored that Pellegrina had a drinking problem. Felicita forgave Pellegrina completely, but Michele, the strong-minded eldest, declared he would never speak to her again. Pio intervened and urged Michele to forgive her, and when he refused, Pio made him forgive her by saying, "If you don't forgive your sister, you'll never see my face again."[200] Michele didn't want to be on the outs permanently with Pio, so he forgave Pellegrina.

How is it possible that this could happen in the Forgione family, who had brought up such a wonder-working saint? All we can say with certainty is that Giuseppa and Grazio did their best, even when facing difficult times. Giuseppa had to take on the full-time running of the farm while Grazio toiled tirelessly in America to pay for Pio's education. The two youngest girls, Pellegrina in particular, missed out on their father being around. When he came home, they shied away from cuddling him. When Pellegrina became promiscuous, she may have been seeking out physical intimacy to compensate for the love she felt was not given her; she always had a spiteful, hard look on her face as though she felt unloved. Pellegrina fell away from the Faith, and it is uncertain whether she returned to the sacraments before death. Even the mother and father of a saint may have a child who hurts other family members horribly and leaves the Church. This example may speak to parents who have done their utmost to raise virtuous, pious children and yet have found that one or more of them have grown up to be the opposite.

Although Pellegrina's betrayal wounded Felicita terribly, Felicita forgave her husband. All Felicita's family fell ill with the Spanish flu. Felicita was nearly thirty and pregnant; she became so sick that she lost her baby. Then her four-year-old son died, and when Felicita realized that she, too, was about to die, she encouraged Vincenzo to make an honest woman of Pellegrina by marrying her when she was gone. The darkness of Pellegrina's deeds were the backdrop to the brightness of Felicita's heroic virtue. (Sadly, Vincenzo could not marry Pellegrina because she had an estranged husband who had gone to America.)

News of Felicita's death reached Pio by telegram, and when he learned she was gone, Pio was overcome with grief: The soul whom he hailed as better than him had gone to God, leaving him on the earth to mourn her and sing her praises: "She was a saint.... Even with all the woes that befell her, she was always smiling.... Everyone else in the family she surpassed in goodness and loveliness."[201] Those of us called to marriage may be edified that he said his married sister had the highest level of sanctity in his family.

Felicita's death in 1919 caused Pio much sorrow, but it was also during this year that Pio was physically and psychologically examined by doctors, who forensically scrutinized him and his stigmata. They wrote up anatomical descriptions of the stigmata. The first doctor to make a detailed report was Dr. Luigi Romanelli, who was a trusted friend of Benedetto, a highly respected surgeon, and genuinely devout. Romanelli examined Pio five times between

May 1919 and July 1920. He confessed to him, and he experienced joy when he was in Pio's company; he said he was greeted by a celestial perfume that emanated from the wounds.

Pio's Stigmata Examined

Romanelli had reason to be disinclined to believe in the stigmatist. Previously, he had passed messages through Benedetto to ask Pio to pray for a private intention, and these prayers were not answered. Yet it did not sour the doctor against Pio. Romanelli eagerly examined the stigmata, a phenomenon he hailed as a "living miracle."[202] His reverence for the holy person of Pio did not, however, prevent him from pinching and probing the wounds repeatedly.

He wrote in his report how he placed his thumb on one side of the wound in the hand and his index finger on the other side and pressed his thumb and finger at the same time, which caused Pio harrowing pain yet led Romanelli to conclude that "one has the feeling of emptiness," because he found his fingers "divided only by a soft membrane of skin which feels like sand, and there is no resistance of bone or flesh."[203] He measured the lesion in the center of the palm, front and back, to be approximately three-quarters of an inch in diameter. Romanelli refused to diagnose these as normal, human wounds because they did not begin the healing process at all and yet did not become infected, something for which biological science did not have an explanation.

In the heat of July, Romanelli finished his fifth examination of Pio. Only days later Pio was scrutinized by Professor Amico Bignami, an illustrious professor of pathology in Rome who was an avowed atheist. Bignami's assessment differed radically from Romanelli's. He said the wounds were not nearly as deep, that they were so shallow as to concern only the top two layers of skin. Bignami also caused Pio torturous pain when he stuck pins into the wounds.

His interest centered on Pio's use of iodine. Pio admitted he used this brown liquid to limit the bleeding. This prompted Bignami to perform a test. First, he ordered the removal of all medicines from Pio's room. Then he asked the friars to bandage and seal the wounds in the presence of witnesses. Every friar involved took an oath to tell the truth. These same witnesses were to check every morning and see if anyone had interfered with the sealed wounds. At the end of eight days the witnesses removed the bandages and checked if the wounds showed signs of healing. Bignami, however, submitted his report without waiting for the results to come back from the test.

Bignami's report proffered that either Pio had deliberately wounded himself or the wounds were symptoms of a disease. But Bignami's own test, the results of which he did not wait for, refuted his belief that there were scientific explanations for the wounds. After eight days had passed, the witnesses gave sworn testimony that the wounds remained the same except that "they turned bright red" on the eighth day, whereas on every day all the wounds bled and the blood seeped out through the sealings, as the friars could show from the bunch of bloody bandages. They included the telling detail that, "While Padre Pio was saying Mass, we were obliged to send a fresh bandage to the altar to stem the blood which was streaming down the back of his hands."[204] The continuous bleeding after the wounds were sealed in bandages could not be explained scientifically.

Bignami also conceded that the edges of the wounds were unlike longstanding injuries, which was a veiled corroboration of Romanelli's findings that the wounds could be claimed to be miraculous because they did not begin the healing process. Romanelli, however, had not dared suggest that the wounds were self-inflicted.

One celebrated doctor who examined the stigmatist opined that Pio's wounds were caused by his morbid obsession with Jesus' Crucifixion. When someone told Pio this, Pio gave this riposte: "Tell him to think intensely about being an ox. Let's see if he grows horns."[205]

Certain issues remained in dispute, despite numerous examinations: the cause of the stigmata and how deep the wounds were. Some doctors disagreed with Bignami's claim that the wounds were very shallow, but four years later Pio made a statement under oath that explained this discrepancy. Pio was visited by Bishop Raffaele Rossi, investigating at the behest of the Vatican, who asked him to swear on the Gospels and describe the stigmata. Pio revealed that the wounds had a changeable appearance. "Sometimes they look like they are about to disappear but they don't, and then come back, flourishing again."[206] While Bignami had examined Pio only days after Romanelli, it is possible that he saw them when they looked as though they were, to use Pio's words, "about to disappear."

In the years to come, other medical examinations of Pio's stigmata would vindicate Romanelli's findings, and the measurements he took of the length and depth of the wounds were shown to be correct, with slight variations. In the same year as Romanelli's examination, Dr. Andrea Cardone, the brilliant doctor who had known Pio from the time he was a sickly seminarian, said the wounds were even deeper than Romanelli had said they were, and that they "pierced the palms of the hands completely through so much so that one could see light through them."[207]

To this day, some people who hear of Pio have a reaction like Romanelli's — they believe there is no medical explanation and it is miraculous —and this tends to correspond to their belief in God. Others have a reaction like Bignami — they believe the wounds were self-inflicted by Pio because of a psychiatric disorder — often corresponding with their atheistic or agnostic beliefs.

The News Gets Out

When Romanelli's report landed on the table of the friary, Benedetto demanded that absolute confidentiality of its contents be maintained. But the report got leaked to a big newspaper in Naples, *Il Mattino*, which ran a story based on Romanelli's report. Thus the general public's first impression of Pio was influenced by findings of a faithful Catholic surgeon who believed Pio's wounds to be miraculous. The story caused a sensation and was the catalyst for Pio's celebrity.

Benedetto was incandescent with rage and ordered every member of the community to keep a strict silence about every aspect of Padre Pio's life, "under pain of mortal sin." Then four new friars arrived at the friary, including Fr. Anastasio —Pio's buddy from seminary— who had been praying alongside him when he had first bilocated to Udine on the night of Giovanna's birth. Letters flooded the friary. Close peers of Pio's, the young friars Placido, Basilio, Damaso, and Anastasio became like mailmen, opening and sorting the sacks of letters. They also heard the Confessions of the masses of people, mainly women, who descended on Our Lady of Grace Friary.

In 1919, the year after his wounds first became visible, Padre Pio became a celebrity in his native Italy. This notoriety appears to have been part of God's will for him. Our Lord could have chosen to leave Padre Pio's wounds invisible, as He did in the case of St. Catherine of Siena, who asked Our Lord to hide her stigmata (and her wounds remained invisible for the rest of her life). But Pio's wounds remained visible for fifty years, until his death.

As the summer sun grew hotter, the friary turned into bedlam. Pio was spending fifteen to nineteen hours each day meeting the spiritual needs of those who came to see him. He heard the Confessions of the women in his wooden confessional and the Confessions of the men in the sacristy. People of every description — from farm laborers to highly qualified professionals to people struggling with sickness and disease — came to ask Pio to intercede for them. Others felt they were under the control of an evil spirit and wanted to be exorcised. During this time when Pio was spending most his waking hours hearing Confessions, he was also subject to the intense medical examinations described above.

Pio's schedule was grueling, but his zeal was white-hot. He wrote to Benedetto, "All my time is spent in setting my brothers free from the snares of Satan," and, "The greatest charity is in snatching souls bound to Satan and winning them for Christ."[208] He was severe with any man or woman who approached the confessional with a bad intention or without a true aim of amending their lives. He had a particular aversion to anyone who came to see him as though he were an item on a bucket list.

Insincere souls angered Pio. He admitted to Benedetto that his choleric temperament troubled him. "My only regret is that, involuntarily and unwittingly, I sometimes raise my voice when correcting people," he confessed. "I realize that this is a shameful weakness, but how can I prevent it if it happens without my being aware of it?" Pio prayed for his temper to be cooled: "Although I pray and groan and complain to Our Lord about it, He has not yet heard me fully."[209]

Benedetto was gentle with his ward. "Don't be upset concerning those outbursts, although you should never be satisfied with them," he advised. "If the Lord doesn't give you the grace of inexhaustible and continual gentleness, it is in order to leave you means to practice holy humility."[210]

A Season of Miracles

All the while, Pio's fame was growing, and many people were desperate to have any tiny shred of something that had touched him. There was such a big market for fabric which had been on his body that eventually policemen guarded Pio, trying to prevent people from using scissors or their bare hands to claw cloth from his brown habit. Other priests bitterly begrudged Padre Pio's thriving ministry, which attracted so many people. Ill-feeling was spreading among the clergy in the town of San Giovanni, who took issue with Pio's practice of going to the window over the courtyard, where he would bless the huge crowd and wave a white handkerchief by way of greeting them.

In 1919 a local priest, Don Giovanni Miscio, began spreading rumors that the friars of San Giovanni were turning Padre Pio into a show so they could make money. At thirty-three, Miscio was approximately the same age as Pio, and he used many platforms to spread his suspicions; he even sent poison-pen letters to the archbishop of the diocese, Pasquale Gagliardi, who became one of Pio's greatest enemies.

As for the teeming hordes of people who were coming, how did all this sit with Pio's superior, Paolino, who was easily perturbed? Paolino complained to Pio that he and the others had no time to relax, but Pio would not entertain this grousing, and said they ought to be thankful so many souls were coming. Many were coming hoping for a miracle.

And miracles did indeed occur. One astonishing miracle concerned a disabled man named Francesco, who had clubfoot, his toes bent toward his heels. Mentally challenged, Francesco could not make a living for himself, and he came to Pio's friary often to be fed. He hauled himself around on his knees, his weight supported by tiny crutches.

One day Francesco was stationed by the doorway of the church when Pio came toward him. Francesco hollered over the din of the crowd, "Padre Pio, give me a blessing!" Pio kept walking but ordered Francesco, "Throw away your crutches!" The riveted crowd watched as Francesco set aside his crutches, raised himself on his feet, and walked normally for the first time in his life. Although there was no visible improvement to Francesco's feet, the fact that he no longer had to hobble about on his knees was an amazing grace for him.

Padre Pio's detractor, Fr. Miscio, complained that this was not a genuine miracle. He was not alone in this opinion, and Bishop Rossi (the Vatican official who later came to do a thorough inspection of Pio and his ministry) said that because Francesco's poor physical condition had not improved, it could not rightly be considered miraculous. But one thing is certain: Francesco had not been able to walk without crutches before, and after Pio interceded for him, he could.

Around the same time, miracles were happening to ordinary people who were better able to articulate that they had been cured. Maria Scotto Di Festa was a middle-aged woman whose right leg had been paralyzed for eighteen years. She came to see Pio and asked for his prayers before leaving San Giovanni. She had not asked specifically for a miracle, yet on her way home she felt sensation returning to her leg, and on arriving she walked perfectly.

Another miracle happened to the chancellor of San Giovanni Rotondo, Pasquale Di Chiara. Pasquale was a man in his mid-thirties, with a wife and family. He enjoyed the company of powerful politicians and was seen at illustrious gatherings. At one such gathering — a big party to celebrate the end of the Great War — Pasquale was walking down some stairs at a posh hotel when he fell head over heels and was horribly injured. He was bedridden for some months, and when he was able to get out of bed, he had a painful limp and had to lean heavily on a cane and drag himself about.

When he heard about Padre Pio, Pasquale thought about seeking him out — not for himself but for his little girl, Italia, who had infant paralysis. When he took her to see Pio, Pio told Pasquale and his wife to throw away the orthopedic device on Italia's leg. They didn't do so, and the next day the device suddenly broke, yet still Italia did not get better. When they returned to Pio, he told them that it was their fault Italia had not been cured, that they needed to trust in God fully. Soon, Italia was able to walk normally.

Later, Pasquale visited Pio in the company of his bosses at the chancellery. He was putting his weight on his cane, which provoked Pio to demand, "Throw away the cane!"[211] Pasquale let go of the stick but leaned on a nearby wall, at which Pio upbraided him impatiently in front of his bosses: "Man of little faith, go ahead and walk."[212] When Pasquale put one foot in front of the other, he felt a great sensation of warmth flood his foot and then his entire body. He was completely cured. For the rest of his life, he told people that Pio's words, "man of little faith," continued to ring in his ears.

13

YOUR EYE, YOUR ENEMY

Raffaello "Lello" Pegna was a Jewish man from Florence.[213] The only son of observant Jewish parents, Lello became blind as an adult and was told by doctors that there was no cure. His eyes were covered in black bandages.

Lello became friends with a priest, Fr. Carlo Naldi, who took him to see Pio. The stigmatist gave Lello a warm welcome, advising him, "Become a Christian first, and the rest will follow."[214] He told Lello that if he were to be baptized, then the Lord would give him his sight back. Pio had the mystical gift of seeing grace and he saw the grace that awaited Lello.

Putting his trust in Pio's promise, Lello was baptized. This was 1919 — the same year Pio's stigmata became known to the public — and his reputation as a miracle-worker was not yet well established, so Lello was taking a chance. Lello was disheartened when his cure was not instantaneous. But lo and behold, several months later Lello's sight mysteriously returned, and the doctors were baffled.

Healing Blindness

During Pio's lifetime, he was a conduit of grace for many people who wanted to be healed of their blindness — and an intercessor for a few other special souls, who chose not to accept the grace that would have restored their sight, believing that blindness was also a source of redemptive grace.

"The eye is the organ that brings us into the most sin,"[215] Pio pronounced solemnly to Pietro Cugino, a blind man whose friendship he cherished. When Pietro's parents died, Pio arranged for Pietro to move into the friary, where he was treated like family. Pietro was highly trustworthy, discrete, and diligent. He was good to all the friars, ran errands for them, and collected their mail every morning. Pietro had been born into a poor family and raised without any extravagance; thus he enjoyed the simple things.

Pietro was naturally kind and sweet-tempered, and he did not resent that he had inherited a condition from his dad that took his sight by age twelve. He resigned himself to his humble station in life. Although Pio knew the eye to be the bodily organ that "brings us into the most sin," he once asked Pietro if he wanted his sight back. With a pure spirit, Pietro replied, "If to see is useful for the good of my soul, then may the Lord restore my sight. But it if is harmful to my spiritual salvation, then I prefer to remain blind."[216] Pio told him that the grace for his sight to return to him was always available. But Pio often said it was marvelous that Pietro had elected to stay blind out of concern for his own salvation.

Pietro lived inches from Pio's cell, and had many occasions over the years to change his mind about having his eyesight. He was open to the healing, but only if it was "good" for his soul. From the fact that Pio did not assure him it would be good for his soul, we may deduce that it would not have been. So why did Padre Pio offer Pietro the chance of a miraculous cure? It's unlikely Pio would have offered Pietro the healing grace had he known it would lead Pietro to fall into grave sin, forfeiting Heaven.

For the multitudes of pilgrims coming to San Giovanni, Pietro was a living example of someone shunning healing for the sake of his own soul; one who endured the hardship of handicap, all for his greater good. And for us today, Pietro reminds us always to be mindful of our eye, our enemy.

A Cautionary Insight

Although it might seem strange to think of the gift of eyesight as a source of spiritual danger, the mere fact of Pietro's refusal to avail himself of the miraculous healing speaks to us of the danger our eyes can pose to our souls. Pio's true insight as to the eye chimes with Our Lord's words: "If your eye causes you to sin, pluck it out" (Matt. 18:9).

This may sound so severe as to make you shiver, imagining what it would mean to take this literally; and yet the danger is also real, and the warning needs to be equal in seriousness. Our Lord was not being arbitrary when He spoke of the eye; He didn't mention lopping off the nose. It has sometimes been asked if Our Lord was employing hyperbole here, but taken to heart it prompts us to ask ourselves if it is better not to see in this life for the sake of seeing Heaven.

In Flannery O'Connor's classic work *Wise Blood,* an unstable young man named Hazel blinds himself to atone for committing a brutal murder. Hazel is mentally ill, and his self-mutilation is an attempt to make his peace with God. The novel is a profound work of apologetics on the part of O'Connor because in it we see self-destructiveness done with the aim of making reparation and cleansing the soul, when sacramental Confession is really what is needed. O'Connor's work provokes the reader to ask if Hazel could have done something else to restore his soul to grace; sacramental Confession is the very thing, but Hazel is ignorant of it — unlike Padre Pio, who spent years in the confessional, trying to draw his spiritual daughters and sons closer to Heaven.

Of course, as much as he admired his young blind friend, Pio as Our Lord's servant never counseled anyone to blind themselves. Instead, he would explain to sinners that "sin against charity is like piercing God in the pupil of the eye — what is more delicate than the pupil of the eye?"[217] Rather than advocating blindness, Pio invited penitents — and invites us as well — to have a healthy fear of misusing the gift of sight, and to confess the sins which we commit as a result of the eye.

Of course, even when we are trying our level best, we do not always have control over what we see. How, then, is it possible to stop seeing something that causes temptation? Let us meditate on this: God has given us our eyesight so we may fulfill His plan for us. This was certainly the case with Pio — his earthy brown eyes had a piercing stare which could search the deepest recesses of hearts. Pio, however, did not take delight in his own ability to see. He even told Pietro that his blindness made him fortunate because, "You do not see the filth and rottenness of this world. You have less occasion to offend the Lord."[218]

More Miracles of Sight

Pio had another blind spiritual son, Salvatore Sciogliuzzi, who had a wife and a big brood of kids. Losing his sight in middle age, Savlatore could no longer hold down a job, and his family was plunged into poverty. He applied for a government pension (he had been a government employee), but it was delayed and Salvatore had serious money problems. In a state of depression, he made a trip to see Pio, but Salvatore did not ask for a miraculous cure. Instead, Pio said to him, "Trust in God and in a little while everything will work out."[219]

Cheered up considerably, Salvatore went home and the government check came shortly afterward, which delivered him and his family from poverty. Salvatore made an annual trip to see Pio, and on one of these trips his youngest son asked his dad, "Why don't you ask Padre Pio to give your sight back?" Salvatore replied, "Why don't you ask Padre Pio?" So, the little boy went ahead and asked the saint, only to be told to go back to his father and ask him why he had never asked for his sight. The little boy was getting dizzy going back and forth between his father and the Father, but he returned to his the side of his father, who revealed to him, "Padre Pio told me when I first came to him that any time I want to ask for the grace, the grace is there. But when I thought of how much Jesus suffered for us, I said to Jesus, 'I give my sight for Your glory.' "[220]

Salvatore's decision not to ask throws light on a glistening gold nugget of insight: We have a role in receiving a grace by asking for it. Too often we feel disenfranchised from divine grace, assuming the grace will be given without our having to ask, or we feel despair to the point of thinking there is no point in asking. Put simply, we may have to ask before the grace is given. By asking we evidence our faith in God, because our request shows confidence that such graces are a reality. The details of our request are important, too, as the following case illustrates.

Once a blind man asked Pio to pray that he would be able to see in one eye, which is exactly what happened. He was overjoyed to be able to see out of one eye — until he saw another blind person get the grace of sight in both eyes. The man with one good eye returned to Padre Pio and demanded to know why that man got sight in both eye. "You only asked for sight in one eye," Pio reminded him. "Never put limitations on God."[221]

Another friend and spiritual son of Pio was Giovanni Savino, an extremely holy young man who was so prayerful that Pio used tease him that he could have had a vocation. He provided for his wife Rosa and their kids by being a manual laborer.

One day, Giovanni was working with a crew in the garden of Pio's monastery, blasting rocks with dynamite. Before beginning work, Giovanni was told by Pio, "I'm praying to the Lord that you might not be killed." Giovanni was only thirty-five and in good health, so he brushed aside Pio's words and went to work. Moments later, a charge of dynamite blew up in his face.

Giovanni's face was ravaged by the blast and he was rushed to hospital, where it was discovered the explosion had destroyed one of Giovanni's eyes completely and left the other embedded with shards of rock, but because some of that eye was left there was a chance of saving it. Meanwhile Pio was asking all around him for prayers for Giovanni. Then he led eucharistic adoration, where he made a special offering: "Lord, I offer You one of my eyes for Giovanni because he's the father of a family."[222]

As Giovanni lay in his hospital bed, he decided to seek a miraculous cure, because he could not bear to stay blind. Late one night Giovanni was praying the Rosary, when suddenly the scent of fine tobacco surrounded him and he became aware Pio was standing by his bed in bilocation. Giovanni plaintively said to Pio that he could not bear to stay blind and he wanted the grace of sight back, at which Pio gently slapped him three times on his head.

The next morning, Giovanni's doctor, an experienced eye specialist, examined Giovanni. He was stunned when Giovanni said he could see him with the "eye" that had been destroyed! It was not so much an "eye" as a mesh of bloody tissue left after the eye had been shattered. The doctor thought that perhaps Giovanni was confused and could see out of the eye that had been pierced by rock rubble. But no, Giovanni was seeing with the shattered eye.

The doctor examining him, who had been an atheist, was converted on the spot. He immediately credited God with the return of Giovanni's sight; it was a miracle that defied the laws of biology completely. For the remaining twenty-five years of his life, Giovanni was able to see out of his "eye."[223]

This next story is hailed by many as one of Pio's greatest miracles. A grandmother brought her seven-year-old granddaughter to San Giovanni. Gemma had no pupils and had been blind since birth. Pio knew of Gemma because her aunt, who was a nun, had sent him a letter asking him to intercede.

The first signs of a miracle happened on the way to San Giovanni, when little Gemma for the first time in her life looked out a window of the train and saw a ship sailing on the sea. When they arrived and introduced themselves to Pio, he heard her first Confession and gave her First Holy Communion. He made the Sign of the Cross over her eyes, and Gemma could see, even though the biological makeup of her eyes remained the same.

This case of the girl who could see without pupils caused a sensation. Pio could be at his most curmudgeonly when invited to discuss Gemma's miraculous cure, saying, "Don't bring me into this," and when people would cite it as proof he was a wonder-worker he deflected the praise, saying, "It was not I, it was the Madonna." Someone once retorted that Our Lady had given the grace because he had asked her. "But all the same it must have been you who asked her for this boon," they insisted.[224] Pio was always a gentleman about giving credit to Our Lady.

Let us return to genial Pietro. After Pio told him the eye is the organ that brings us into the most sin, Pietro told him he was making an offering of his blindness: "Well, Padre, let God take my eyes, I offer them to Him for sinners."[225] Pietro was not just accepting his blindness for his own good, but as a gift for many others.

Which of these stories speaks to you? Do you see yourself in Pietro, who willingly offered his sight for the good of his soul and that of others? Or would you be more like Giovanni, whose piety was revered by Pio but who said he could not live if he were to stay blind and asked for the grace to remove his disability? Or do you see yourself in Lello, whose blindness caused him to seek out Padre Pio and led to his baptism? Or are you like Gemma's grandmother, bringing her loved one to Pio in the hope of a miracle?

If we are seeking a big grace, let's bear in mind St. Teresa of Ávila's aphorism, "You pay God a great compliment by asking great things of Him." Perhaps the story of the atheist doctor who treated Giovanni and was converted to the Faith reminded you of a friend or family member whose conversion you have been praying for. If you are granted a miracle and bystanders observe it, perhaps it may be the catalyst for their conversion.

However we see ourselves, Pio's warning about the eye deserves careful reflection. If we are longing for the bright lights of Heaven, let us see our eyes for the true danger they pose to our souls.

14

AMAZING MERCY

Pio had had the stigmata for a little over a year when he was examined in 1919 by a most extraordinary surgeon, Dr. Giorgio Festa. He was a dynamic fellow who had his own thriving practice in Rome, and he was the one appointed by the Franciscans to be Pio's personal physician.

Dr. Festa had a bold, striking appearance; he wore the most formal, precisely tailored suits, and a large pince-nez on his oval face substituted for a smile. His jet-black hair was thin at the temples, and he had dark eyes almost as penetrating as Pio's own. His beard was cut to a perfect square that jutted from his chin. His strict facial landscaping spoke to his extreme meticulousness.

He was the most exceptionally exacting doctor ever to examine Pio up to this point — and he turned out to be a loyal friend to Pio. When he applied his hands to Pio, Festa scrutinized the wounds in minute detail, then compiled a report which trumped the others in detail and length. He totally disagreed with Bignami that the wounds were shallow, and he explained that they looked skin deep because they were covered with a thick scab. Yet when the wounds were completely clean of dry and sticky blood, their depth could be measured accurately. Both Bignami and Romanelli had said that the stigmata on the palms were symmetrical to the ones on the back of the hand, but Festa contradicted them both and determined that the wounds on the hands did not line up exactly. Festa asserted something in his report that he later repeated in his groundbreaking book: that the center of the wound on the palm corresponded with the upper edge of the wound on the back of the hand.[226] But Festa took a humble stance and said that the wounds evaded any medical explanation that he could offer.

Festa analyzed Pio's personality by interviewing him for long periods, asking him many questions. His psychoanalysis of Pio was the first item on his report, and painted Pio as being warm and loving. It included that Pio loved witty banter, that he mixed well with the others, and that he had a cheerful smile. It noted that Pio's attention, however, became utterly absorbed when the conversation turned to the subject of holiness. Festa noted that Pio was exceptionally self-giving in the long hours spent hearing Confessions and in listening intently to the pilgrims to whom he gave his full attention. Festa also confirmed that Pio had extremely healthy mental balance.

Festa was unable to account for the aroma of Paradise that came from Pio's blood. After Dr. Festa first examined Pio, he mopped the blood from the side wound with a small cloth and brought the bloodied cloth with him to Rome for an examination. It so happened that Dr. Festa had no sense of smell. However, when he ferried the cloth in his railcar from San Giovanni to Rome, the other passengers in the car enjoyed an exquisite perfume of roses which came from the cloth. When Festa reached Rome, he stored the cloth in a cabinet in his practice, but the scent seeped out and many patients quizzed the doctor as to where the perfume came from. There was, however, no scientific explanation for this sensational scent.

Dr. Festa had not been a believing Catholic. One might say he'd been anti-Catholic, a Mason, but he threw away his white apron and repented, and so, too, did a lawyer from his illustrious family: Dr. Festa's cousin Cesare Festa. The story of his conversion from masonry is of vital importance to us today, perhaps one of the most important of all.

Pio and the Freemason

A highly successful lawyer, when he first learned of Pio, Cesare argued that the reports of Pio's supernatural charisms were exaggerations. Cesare held all priests in contempt, and he had been given a specific role by the Masons to fight the Catholic Church's influence in Italian politics.

One day, a strange desire grew in Cesare to seek out Pio, and he was compelled to go to San Giovanni. When he approached the stigmatic friar, Pio challenged him, "What, you here amongst us? But aren't you a Mason?"[227] Cesare was stupefied to discover Pio knew he was a member of secret society. "And what task have you in Masonry?" pressed Pio. "To combat the Church on political matters," answered Cesare. Pio gave him a smile laden with pity and told him the parable of the prodigal son, who left the fold only to find the world was a cold, hard place and then return to his father's house.

This parable of returning to one's family spoke to Cesare; his family was his pride and joy, and he was very close to his cousin, Dr. Festa, who had examined the wounds of Pio — the same stigmatist who stood before him and knew the contents of his heart.

One hour later, Cesare begged Pio to hear his Confession. After making a thorough Confession, he had a newfound happiness and wanted to tell everyone of his conversion and that he was going to free himself from the fetters of Freemasonry. Pio had been deliberately charmless in asking Cesare direct questions and elicited straight answers so that there was no fuzzy misunderstanding. Pio established the truth of the lawyer's life and used this as the basis for the conversation which led to the lawyer's conversion. Although we may have heard people describe Pio as blunt and rude, it is more the case that Pio was determined to get the truth from someone, because their soul was at stake. We may think of taking the same approach with someone like Cesare, so that they will be inspired to trade in their white apron for salvation.

When Cesare answered Pio honestly, he was already breaking with his promises to Freemasonry that he would never discuss his assignment with a non-Mason, and especially not a priest. But after talking to Pio, Cesare was determined to throw his white apron in the trash and go out and convert other Masons! When Cesare asked Pio how he might lead them to convert, Pio replied, "Do nothing now and wait. When the opportunity presents itself, the Lord will notify you." When he heard this, Cesare felt a tremendous happiness. He thanked Pio profusely, and afterward Cesare wrote a heartfelt letter to his dear cousin, Dr. Festa, and told him of the wonders Pio was working in his life.

Cesare felt called to make a pilgrimage to Lourdes, but once there he felt repulsed by the many sick people who surrounded him at the grotto. He kept in mind that St. Francis had been revolted by the lepers but had so overcome his revulsion that he became their servant. Cesare did everything he could to serve the sick and spent long hours by the side of the most vulnerable, attending to their every need. After his time in Lourdes, he was welcomed home by a mocking article in a left-wing newspaper, which ran under the headline "A Mason at Lourdes." He was in for even worse treatment when he went back to the lodge so he could tell the Masons gathered for their meeting that he was no longer one of them and that he wanted them to burn their white aprons. They threw the filthiest insults at him and made dire threats. He never lost his cool, however, and even when they warned what they would do to him if he did not become a Mason again, he refused to be cowed.

A little while later, Cesare found out the lodge was going to have a hush-hush meeting about him, but on the same day he received a letter from Pio which contained the most vital message, one which is even more relevant to us today: "Do not blush about Christ and His doctrine, the time has come to bring the fight into the open." How meritorious it is for us to learn from Pio that now is the time for "the fight" to be had in "the open."

Pio also gave Cesare this assurance: "The Doctor of every good will give you the strength." He took Pio at his word and the lawyer Festa went to the meeting — even though he was not invited and it had been arranged behind his back so they could plot against him. Although he was verbally attacked, he spoke about Christ and the urgent need for the Masons to convert. Cesare was given the divine protection he needed and their plots against him failed. His star began to rise in the Catholic world, and he became known as a hero who had left the privileges of being a Mason behind. Cesare was even noticed by the ruling pope, Benedict XV. When Benedict gave Cesare an audience, the pope had this to say about the stigmatist who had converted him: "Padre Pio is truly a man of God. You must assume the task of making him known. He is not appreciated by all as he merits." Cesare did exactly that. He made known his conversion story far and wide, and he caused other men to leave Masonry for salvation. In addition, Cesare became a Franciscan tertiary and an author on Franciscan spirituality. And he grew a long, wayward beard in homage to Sts. Francis and Pio.

The Conversion of Emanuele Brunatto

In the early years of Pio's fame, his stigmata and the miracles he worked on the sick were the catalysts for his celebrity. But at the same time, marvelous conversions of sinners were happening and these, for many of us, were the grandest of all Pio's miracles.

Emanuele Brunatto was a man who may well have been a sociopath. He still divides opinion; he is either loved or hated by those who read of his role in Pio's life. He went from being a sleazy con man to being one of Pio's greatest friends and defenders, a brave warrior who fought any battle necessary to defend his father-in-spirit. First, however, Emanuele had to acquire a conscience through Padre Pio's intercession.

When he first met Pio, Emanuele was twenty-six and a native of Turin, yet he looked like the perfect English gentleman, with a teddy-bear face and a proud bearing. But his hot Italian temper would explode with energy. Spectacularly smart, Emanuele had been raised in a wealthy Catholic family, and he had been brought up to be a spiritual son of St. John Bosco. His father had been one of the first and most generous benefactors of Bosco. Emanuele, however, had fallen away from his Faith and his family. He had become a con man.

During the war, Emanuele trafficked in the sale of goods on the black market. He was found out and was sent to the front line. After the war, he got into the fertilizer business but ripped off clients, and they reported him to the police. For Emanuele, it had become habitual to swindle people of out of money and shamelessly use women for sex. Possessed of a glib charm, extraordinary skill for poetic speech, and the polished etiquette from his privileged youth, he easily fooled people into parting with their money.

When Pio came to his attention, he was cohabiting with a woman and living among prostitutes in the Naples red light district, seemingly a hopeless case. An intervention came when he read sensationalized coverage of Pio in the press. He knew he was a younger contemporary of this priest who was being held up as a saint, which was a rebuke to Emanuele for the way he was living.

After he read about Pio, Emanuele could not stop thinking about him and was overcome with the desire to travel to San Giovanni. But because he'd lost his money in a recent scam, he only had enough for part of the trip and then had to walk ten hours. After walking all night, Emanuele walked into the friary as day was breaking and saw Pio hearing the Confession of a farmer. Emanuele instantly held Pio in contempt, thinking the priest had "a bandit's face."[228] Yet when Pio fixed him with a piercing stare, Emanuele was so shaken that he ran out of the friary and on reaching the garden sank to his knees, his eyes brimming with tears.

When he returned to the friary, he found Pio by himself, waiting for him. In the tiny time lapse between his first seeing Pio and this second time, Emanuele's impression of Pio utterly changed, and he now saw Pio's face to be of "surpassing beauty, radiating indescribable joy … in his eyes was love." Kneeling for Confession, Emanuele poured out the details of his life from his earliest years, but Pio stopped him and reminded him of a Confession he had made years earlier. "You confessed during the war and the Lord has pardoned your sins and put a great boulder over them, and you must not try to raise it. Tell me only that which you have to regret since that time." This part of their exchange is noteworthy for us because the idea of the Lord putting a gigantic rock on top of sins so they do not follow a person speaks to His amazing mercy.

When Emanuele continued his Confession, Pio aided his memory and gave him counsel which was "clear and compassionate." Later, when Emanuele wrote of this Confession, he remembered that when Pio attempted to absolve him, he had to start the process of absolution again and again, "as if he were struggling against an invisible adversary who was clinging to my shoulders." This unseen enemy was perhaps a demon trying to hold onto its prey. When Pio finally spoke the sacramental words of absolution, Emanuele said, "There came an intense perfume of roses and violets which bathed my face." With his soul shriven, he felt he had been "freed from a great weight."

Then, back home in Naples, Emanuele was given a vision of his former life, which he experienced for the first time as one with a working conscience. "All of a sudden my past life began to pass before me like the projection of an old film: the dangers run, the sins committed," he recounted. "The gifts and the graces, the flights and the returns all were reconstructed chronologically in a wonderful experience of my life under the incessant protection of the Mother of God. For long hours I lingered a simple spectator, moved to tears at the film of my past."

Did Emanuele trace this back to Pio's intercession? Yes: "One fact … was clear to me: the operator of this film was Padre Pio." As soon as he could, Emanuele returned to San Giovanni to live a humble life, making his home in a hut, dividing his time between raising chickens and devoting himself to prayer and meditation. In time this clever chap was given a teaching job at the school run by the Franciscans and a room in Pio's friary. Daily he made his way to the choir, where he recited the Office while sitting next to Pio.

One day another friar suggested to Pio that Emanuele might become a priest, but Pio shouted, "Never! Never! Never!"[229] As we will see, Emanuele remained a layman, but this worked out for the best, because as one who had not taken the vow of obedience he acted of his own accord when Pio was in trouble. In the years ahead Emanuele's antics, although they would bring Pio's enemies to heel, caused Pio to say, "Sometimes he seemed an angel to me, and at other times a demon."[230]

The Twelve Daughters

All the while, Pio was not just concerned with the conversions of high-profile people such as Cesare or colorful characters such Emanuele. He never failed to do his best by his local spiritual daughters, a growing group of women who would be his key supporters in the decades ahead. We've already met Rachelina Russo, a resourceful entrepreneur who paid his bus fare to San Giovanni; Lucia Fiorentino, who was given a prophetic vision of Pio; and Nina Campanile, who discovered his stigmata. These beloved daughters were part of a band of twelve women who were his closest spiritual daughters. No matter how famous Pio became and no matter how many thousands of people flocked to see him, he endeavored always to meet them twice a week in the guest room of the friary. He gave them a blueprint for their sanctification and instructed them on how to save their soul. Let us imagine we are there with them, in the little parlor, hearing Pio hold forth on the five tenets he gave them for their salvation, which were reception of Holy Communion daily, weekly Confession, meditation, examination of conscience, and spiritual reading.

The daughters assisted at Pio's Mass every day and took Holy Communion, encouraged by something Pio said often: "Unless you are positive you are in mortal sin, you ought to take Communion every day."[231] Soon, more and more people around San Giovanni Rotondo were following the spiritual daughters and receiving Holy Communion daily. Regarding weekly Confession, Pio made himself as available as humanly possible to them. Later, Pio would be criticized because he recommended to them that they confess so often, but we need to respect that Pio could see their souls and wanted them to be as filled with grace as possible. He compared the soul to a room that needs to be dusted once a week.

Pio also encouraged them to meditate frequently. "Meditation is the key to progress in the knowledge of self as well as the knowledge of God," he taught, "and through it we achieve the goal of the spiritual life, which is transformation in Christ."[232]

Keys of Meditation

Wow! Meditation is "the key" to both self-knowledge and knowledge of the Almighty, as well as being the way to allow Christ to transform us. Perhaps we need to request the grace to take Pio's words on meditation to heart — our souls may depend on it — and to put into practice the method he gave his daughters.

First, choose a theme for meditation. The themes Pio prioritized were the life, death, Resurrection, and Ascension of Jesus. Then we must put ourselves in the presence of God, and know that "with all the celestial court, he is there within your soul."[233]

Next, invite divine aid and "ask God for the grace to make good the mental prayer … so that you can derive the fruit that God most desires."[234] Ask the help of Our Lady, the angels, and the saints, so they may intercede to keep away temptation and distraction.

Thirdly, allow the scene in your mind's eye to consume your attention. Start with the mysteries of the Rosary and develop your meditation from there.

Fourthly, resolve to confront "that defect" of character that causes other sins and trouble. Then pray, asking for "all those graces and for all those helps"[235] that are needed to overcome these defects.

Next, turn your attention to prayer. Pio taught the twelve to pray for themselves first, then to turn their attention to others, leaving no one out: the living, the dead, unbelievers, heretics, and sinners. Finally, Pio said, "After you have done this, offer your meditation and your prayer, along with yourself and those closest to your heart. Offer them all to God, along with the merits of Jesus."[236] Pio wanted all his spiritual children to follow this exalted advice, using it like a ladder to Heaven.

The Good of Spiritual Reading

When he was back in Pietrelcina, Pio had already impressed on his beloved Raffaelina the great importance of spiritual reading, and he stressed to her that reading books such as lives of the saints is not less effective than prayer and meditation. Many of us think that the time we devote time to reading holy books ought to be spent in prayer and think of it as a second-best pursuit, but Pio wrote boldly to Raffaelina about "the need for such reading in the case of those who are seeking Christian perfection."[237] He maintained that "spiritual reading is as necessary to you as the air we breathe,"[238] and declared to Raffaelina, "I am horrified, my dear sister, at the damage done to souls by their failure to read holy books."[239]

Indeed, Pio said that reading holy literature can be a great help when the soul is in darkness and dryness, and can occasion "spiritual renewal." He was now telling a coterie of women what he had told Raffaelina: that reading holy works "conduces to great progress along the path to perfection."[240]

Pio said our primary motive ought not be to study or sate curiosity. Instead, our purpose should be to serve the Lord: We read about holiness, "solely to give Him pleasure and enjoyment."[241] There was a roomful of such books in the friary, and Pio made this the family library of his local spiritual daughters. He lent the Bible to them, making accessible a book that in the early twentieth century was in the possession of very few. To own a Bible, you had to be rich or a religious.

When they met in the parlor, Pio gave them conferences on Sacred Scripture. Pio's family of spiritual children was growing bigger; among this group of twelve local women was a young girl called Cleonice Morcaldi, who was only fifteen at the time these meetings began. Cleonice had been born into poverty but had worked her way up to becoming a schoolteacher. She'd lost her dad at a young age, and her grief had only begun to heal when she met Pio at age sixteen. Pio made it his solemn goal to become her adopted father and help her recover from her loss.

Barely five feet tall, Cleonice had classical Italian looks, with full cheeks, dark chocolate eyes, and thick brown hair. She became very special to Pio, more so than others, not because he showed favoritism but because he trusted her implicitly. In the decades to come, Cleonice showed herself to be so generous, so loyal, and so pure-hearted that Pio entrusted to her very sensitive tasks as well as giving her profound mystical insights that she recorded in her diary and which form the gold of our spiritual inheritance.

15

PIO'S PERSECUTORS

Not long after the publicity blitz that made Pio a public spectacle, the local archbishop, Pasquale Gagliardi, decided to ask the stigmatist for a special favor. He was determined to request Pio's prayers for his brother's daughter, a little girl who was a deaf-mute. Archbishop Gagliardi was in his sixties, short and sturdy with a constant look of fury on his tiny, round face. He had extremely dark, deep-set eyes and low-slung, round ears. His formal, purple robes looked too big for him, and his pectoral cross hung like an enormous weight on his chest.

A Southern Italian by birth, he was gifted with amazing academic intelligence, holding doctorates in philosophy and theology. Gagliardi met Pio for the first time in 1917, when he gave him faculties to hear Confessions, and at the time he thought of Pio as an ordinary friar. Now it was 1920, and Archbishop Gagliardi paid a visit, wanting a miracle for his niece.

When he arrived, Pio was in the confessional. Gagliardi was treated with all due deference by the friars, and the minute he came into the friary he was taken directly to Pio's cell. He waited with Agostino until Pio shuffled in. Pio instantly went on his knees and kissed the archbishop's ring, then Gagliardi asked for Pio's hand and he kissed his brown-gloved fingers. Pio sought Gagliardi's permission to offer Holy Mass. After Gagliardi gave it, Pio swiftly took his leave and went to the altar. Agostino and Gagliardi went to the choir loft, where the archbishop scrutinized the stigmatist as he offered the Sacrifice. After Mass, Gagliardi and Agostino went to the refectory, where Pio joined them for lunch. Pio pecked like a bird at his food as they spoke of the recent canonization of Joan of Arc; Gagliardi let slip that he had voted against her being declared a saint.

After eating, Pio, his fellow friars, and Gagliardi went to the garden for recreation. Once again, the archbishop sought out Pio. Agostino stood a bit apart from them but clearly observed the archbishop ask solemnly of Pio, "Father, pray hard for a little sick niece of mine."[242] Pio assured Gagliardi he would pray for the little girl and then knelt one last time to kiss Gagliardi's ring before the archbishop departed. When Gagliardi made this request — he treated Pio with reverence and believed in his prayers — there was harmony between archbishop and stigmatist.

An Archbishop's Ire

Pio prayed for the little niece, but she did not get better and remained a deaf-mute. Archbishop Gagliardi turned viciously on Pio. Perhaps Gagliardi thought that Pio was not genuinely holy or a man in high standing with God. He may have become bitter because other people were boasting that they and their loved ones were being cured of maladies and disabilities, whereas his darling niece could not hear or speak. Others were enjoying miracles — which were being sensationally celebrated in the media — attributed to Pio's prayers. Why had Pio's intercession not moved God to heal his niece?

There was the miraculous cure given to Maria Cozzi, a lady in Florence who had tongue cancer. She asked Pio's prayers, but she also prepared to go under the knife to remove the carcinoma embedded in her taste buds. On the day the surgeon went to slice her tongue, he found that the cancer had vanished without trace and Maria was perfectly healed and well.

Then there was a young man in Canada who was ravaged by tuberculosis so badly that his lungs were disintegrating. Pio visited him twice in bilocation, and afterward he was completely healed, with no trace of the white plague.

So why was his niece still not healed? Perhaps Gagliardi felt he might be partly responsible for his niece's condition. Apparently, when his brother's wife was pregnant with the little girl, Gagliardi had taken them to a convent in his arch-diocese of Manfredonia. When inside the convent walls, Gagliardi pushed past the mother superior, who did her utmost to stop them from entering the private rooms of their cloister. However, Gagliardi was determined to give a tour to his family and was impervious to the pleas of the mother superior that this was a sanctified space for nuns and that laypeople were trespassers on holy ground reserved for brides of Christ.

According to reports, the mother superior had a premonition, and she warned Gagliardi and his family that because they had trespassed, the pregnant woman would give birth to a deaf child. Her words came true, and this may have galled Gagliardi, who had behaved so arrogantly. He may also have been shamed in front of his family; he was the one who insisted they walk through the cloister.

The archbishop already had a dubious reputation. One of the more disturbing events was when Gagliardi gave an appointment to a priest who had been in trouble many times with the police for "continual and habitual pederasty."[243] He was also hated among the ordinary people for reportedly selling off sacred works of art — ostensibly to raise money for the poor, but it was thought he did it to line his own pockets. He had also been neglecting his pastoral responsibilities, and many young people in the area had not been confirmed. Was it any wonder, then, that the faithful were forsaking their churches and going to the friary at San Giovanni Rotondo to see Padre Pio?

The spiritual effects of the archbishop's bad example spread. The priests in the town of San Giovanni Rotondo had grown madly resentful of Padre Pio; the faithful were forsaking their churches, and many were only going to Pio's Mass, and even more were only giving their cash to the friars. Less and less lire were going into the collection plates at the Masses of the local clergy, and they were extremely upset about it.

Earlier we met a young priest by the name of Giovanni Miscio, who was the founding member of the anti-Pio faction. Miscio was thirty-something, volatile, and energetic. His love of money seemed greater than his love of souls, and his aim was to have Pio's ministry stopped, so the faithful would once again give him their offerings instead. He swamped Gagliardi with hate-filled letters against Pio. When the archbishop turned on Pio, he was delighted to have Fr. Miscio on his side, and he encouraged the local priest to write similar letters denouncing Pio to the Vatican.

Don Giuseppe Prencipe, Pio's Prodigal Son

Sadly, another priest-detractor was also Pio's spiritual child. His name was Giuseppe Prencipe. He had confessed to Pio, and he even said that Pio had "an extraordinary gift." But Fr. Miscio was leaning on Fr. Prencipe to castigate the Capuchin in public. Prencipe even went to Pio and complained, "I'm under great pressure … to denounce you, and you're not praying for me." Pio answered tellingly, "If I didn't pray, things would be worse."[244]

Regrettably, Don Prencipe succumbed to pressure and spoke out of both sides of his mouth. He tried to sow doubt among the faithful about the miracles that Pio was working, saying he personally doubted that they were true. At the same time, he was pressurizing Pio to perform miracles according to his demands. Don Prencipe wanted Pio to bilocate as a stunt to bring about conversions of unbelievers. He also wanted Pio to work a miracle in front of his friend, Dr. Francesco Ricciardi, a medical doctor, a hard-nosed atheist, and a harsh critic of Pio. We will have occasion to meet Ricciardi later, when Pio will intercede for his life —and his soul —to be saved. But at this time, Fr. Prencipe wrecked his own reputation. He became known as a hypocrite among the locals, who saw him confess to Pio but also heard him discredit the friar. They saw that he was benefiting from being Pio's spiritual child while also keeping his buddies happy by denigrating Pio's miracles.

Prencipe held in contempt many of the local people who had benefited from Pio's miracles. One such mother, Bambinella D'Enrico, had been so ill that her temperature shot over 102 Fahrenheit, and she believed she was about to die. Bambinella's husband was skeptical of Pio, and doubted when his wife told him that Pio had bilocated to their bedroom to pray for her healing. The husband said that he would believe in Pio if Bambinella were cured instantly, and no sooner had he made this statement than his wife leapt from bed, perfectly well. Straightaway she was able to breastfeed their little baby, even though her supply had disappeared during her illness. After speaking with the family about Bambinella's recovery, Prencipe labeled them "mentally disturbed."[245]

Another Pio Critic: Don Domenico Palladino

Frs. Miscio and Prencipe were joined by Fr. Domenico Palladino, who was about to turn thirty. Don Palladino lived with his mistress and projected his own scandalous misdeeds onto Pio and his relationship with his spiritual daughters. Palladino liked to give a sexual twist to the daughters' visits with Pio, he emphasized how much they wanted to touch Pio, and he criticized them when they wore pictures of Pio around their necks. They did this in much the same way ordinary women may keep a picture of their fathers in a locket around their necks, but Palladino made them sound obsessive and crazy, which was a slight on the characters of these women who Pio loved as his children and who were holy and charitable to their cores.

Palladino was also bursar of the archdiocese, and he was privy to all the financial records. He too was led by Gagliardi to send nasty letters about Pio to the Vatican. His motives were largely financial: Palladino knew how much money was coming into the archdiocesan coffers and of its diminished financial situation. Many locals were giving their offerings to Padre Pio for charitable causes.

Palladino seems to have been the priest whom the people of San Giovanni held most accountable for the campaign against Pio, and in a few short years, they would nearly make him pay with his life. At the time, however, the people were sometimes too quick to pounce on something that they could use against Pio's persecutors, even if it wasn't true. When the bell in the main church in town cracked, the locals immediately jumped to the conclusion that Pio had prayed for it to crack to get back at the priests who maligned him! Pio had never prayed for any such thing, but his followers were utterly convinced that this was God showing His displeasure at the anti-Pio faction. They made such a racket about the ruined bell that it was hot news all over Italy that Pio's prayers had sundered the bell. Perhaps they felt they could scare the priests into behaving well toward Pio, but it did nothing to deter the priests from their detraction.

In time, Don Miscio had a change of heart; he went from being a diehard enemy of Pio's to being contrite and profoundly grateful to Pio

A Fiery Conversion

In the meantime, Pio continued to be God's instrument in amazing conversions. Michele was a devout Communist sympathizer, an ordinary worker who lived some twenty-five miles from Pio's friary, right along the way the pilgrims passed to get to San Giovanni Rotondo. His hatred of all priests consumed him, and Michele was convinced that Pio was a liar and a fake. Michele owned a gigantic oven that he used to bake clay goods, and the only thing fierier than the furnace that heated the oven was Michele's hot temper. Every hour of the day he spouted angry blasphemies.

Michele worked diligently and stored straw that fueled his furnace in two rooms alongside the oven. But there came a time when Michele was having a very bad week; a windstorm had been blowing so constantly that he had not been able to light the fire. Cursing with rage, Michele in his desperation finally decided to put Pio's intercession to the test. "Dear Padre Pio," he bargained, "I will believe in you if you can put an end to this windstorm that keeps me from lighting my oven and from working."[246]

At that very minute, a man dressed like a humble farmer walked into Michele's yard and asked the laborer if he could help him light his pipe. At this, Michele flew into a rage, grabbed a pitchfork, and charged at the man, shouting, "I cannot even light my own furnace — what do I care of your pipe? Are you making fun of me? Are you like that #&*@ Padre Pio who makes miracles for the simpletons?" Calmly, the stranger said simply, "I am Padre Pio."[247]

At that very instant, a huge burst of fire leapt from the oven. Michele fainted, but he had a locution telling him, "Don't be afraid. Learn to trust in the Lord and stop blaspheming Him!"[248] When Michele awakened, he saw Pio smiling at him. Pio carried Michele away from the smoldering fire and then left by walking through a wall that surrounded the property. The fire Pio had ignited blazed like a bonfire and spread to the rooms that stored the straw, but the straw did not burn. Michele's neighbors gathered and tried to put out the raging fire but couldn't. No human effort could extinguish it, a phenomenon witnessed by many people.

The sea of flames danced all that night, finally dying down at eleven the following morning. Inside the oven, there had been many pots and vases that were ready to be baked, and Michele was certain the incandescent fire had reduced them to dust. But when he examined them, they were baked to perfection, and his straw was as good as though fire had never licked it. All Michele's friends saw that the fantastic fire had baked the goods perfectly, yet it had not consumed the straw. Then they were shocked to hear Michele praise Pio for lifting him away from the path of the flames. The priest whom Michele had cursed had bravely saved him.

After the miraculous fire, Michele turned his energies from hating to loving the Church and he became a loyal spiritual child of Pio's. He never blasphemed again.

The First House of Healing

During this heady time, Pio was amassing friends, spiritual children, disciples — and energetic enemies. But in 1920 he also started work on founding a hospital in San Giovanni. Up until then, in the environs of the Gargano Mountain health care had mostly been a privilege of the rich. Pio nursed in his heart a dream to give urgent medical attention to everyone, especially the old and the destitute. With the help of a benefactress and a cadre of doctors, Pio began converting an old, abandoned convent into a compact hospital of twenty beds, two wards, and an operating theater. It took nearly five years to turn the dilapidated building into a functioning clinic, and it opened its doors in January 1925. It was given the name Hospital of St. Francis and a group of nuns nursed the patients. But Pio was not able to keep tabs on the running of the hospital as much as he would have liked; he was too busy with his own ministry. It lasted a full twelve years.

Around this same time, someone came into Pio's life who would prove to be his most implacable enemy. A Franciscan priest and doctor, Fr. Agostino Gemelli became Pio's most influential persecutor and almost singlehandedly led the charge to have Pio defrocked. He had the face of an eagle, with round spectacles framing his beady eyes. His thin lips spread across his face in a deadly serious line. He was a highly distinguished man of the cloth with prestigious qualifications: a medical doctor, a psychologist, and a theology scholar. Most of all, however, he had the talents of a master politician and social climber. He went on to become the most powerful man in the Vatican, though he worked in the shadow of the papal throne.

On Sunday, April 18, 1920, Fr. Gemelli rolled into San Giovanni. It was a relaxed day at the friary, two weeks into the Easter season, when Gemelli marched in and boldly claimed to the superior that he had been dispatched by the Vatican's Holy Office to examine Pio's wounds. Because he had no written authorization such as had been given the others who had examined Pio, Gemelli was refused. But he successfully pressed to meet Pio. He was taken to the sacristy, where he found Pio as well as Emanuele Brunatto and Padre Benedetto.

Fr. Gemelli had a hostile demeanor toward the stigmatist, and he pressured Pio to let him see and touch his wounds. When Pio found out that Gemelli had no written permission from the Vatican, he said simply, "I'm not authorized to show the wounds to you."[249] Padre Benedetto with his gigantic beard also stood in the way and did not let Gemelli put his grasping fingers on Pio. Emanuele was unnerved when he saw Gemelli's attempts to strongarm Pio, and he instantly took a strong dislike to this cocky fellow.

Insolently, Gemelli said to Pio, "I want to suggest you cure yourself of your wounds."[250] Then, with an ominous warning, "Padre Pio, we will meet again,"[251] he left the friary in a rage. Gemelli had only been in Pio's company for a few minutes, but he went on to tell many falsehoods based on this one visit.

Gemelli's Assault

On the heels of this visit, Gemelli bombarded the Vatican with letters falsely claiming that he had performed a psychiatric and physical examination of Pio. He made a devastating claim: "Padre Pio is a psychopath."[252] He concluded that the wounds were the product of Pio's mind. In the same way someone who has psychopathy wants to inflict dire harm on another person and cause their death, Gemelli argued, Pio wanted to be wounded with the wounds that caused Jesus' death.

Gemelli concluded that the stigmata were psychosomatic, that Pio's imagination had caused him to develop the wounds of Jesus' Crucifixion. The fact that Gemelli was a medical doctor lent legitimacy to this dire assertion that sounded like a diagnosis. He further denigrated Pio as being of "very limited intelligence"[253] and asserted that he was controlled by Fr. Benedetto, going so far as to make a sick claim that spiritual son and spiritual father had an "incubus succubus relationship,"[254] whereby Benedetto brainwashed Pio, inducing him to produce the wounds on his body.

Gemelli lobbied the Vatican to deny Benedetto all contact with Pio. We'll recall that Benedetto explicitly forbade him from examining Pio, and Gemelli may have felt he could have more access to Pio without Benedetto there for Pio's protection.

A single question preoccupied Gemelli's thoughts concerning Pio: How could a gift so extraordinary as the stigmata be accompanied by such spiritual poverty?[255] Gemelli was a Franciscan priest of the Friars Minor, the oldest branch of the order founded by the stigmatist St. Francis. So it was odd that Gemelli belonged to an order founded by a stigmatist and yet denounced Pio as a fake.

We need to bear in mind that Fr. Gemelli had not been raised as a Catholic. He'd been born into a wealthy family in Milan and had been brought up agnostic with contempt for the Faith. In the early 1900s, when Gemelli was in his early twenties, he was a militant Marxist, and had been arrested several times by the Milanese police for anti-Catholic activism.[256] At that time Dr. Gemelli was working three jobs, as a medical doctor, as a psychologist, and as the editor of the Communist newspaper. Then, at age twenty-five, he read about St. Francis and had a dramatic conversion.

Gemelli entered the Franciscan seminary, but his father was so enraged that he paid men to kidnap his son and bring him home! The men who tried to bundle him into a horse and buggy and abduct him were unsuccessful, but the attempt speaks to his family's disdain for his Franciscan vocation. When he was still young, Gemelli's life changed forever when he became close to another priest in Milan, Achille Ratti, who would become the archbishop of Milan and a cardinal in 1921. They had been best friends for two decades when Gemelli started his campaign against Pio, and as they were close confidants, Gemelli poisoned Cardinal Ratti against the stigmatist. Ratti held Gemelli in the highest esteem and trusted him implicitly. He allowed Gemelli's judgment to sway him in many matters. But for two years, Gemelli waged a campaign against Pio without much success — that is, until Cardinal Ratti was elected pope.

16

PADRE PIO AND THE POPES

From 1919 to 1922 was a time of testing for Padre Pio. He adjusted to the harrowing humiliation he felt with his wounds being on display and the fact that his enemies were mainly men of the cloth who were uniting against him. Yet Pio enjoyed wonderful freedom to practice his ministry. This owed squarely to the fact that the pope at the time, Benedict XV, was a true friend to Pio.

Benedict radiated both authority and tenderness. He was petite, his large head sitting on a thin body with slim, sloping shoulders. His eyes were heavily hooded, and he had a prominent Roman nose and a cap of black hair. Kindness radiated from his face and gentle smile.

Benedict XV would not entertain those who told him Pio was a fraud, mentally ill, or in league with the devil. His Holiness did not come to this conclusion on his own. In early 1920 he sent Dr. Giuseppe Bastianelli, his personal physician, to San Giovanni to examine the stigmata, and the medic was accompanied by two archbishops. No medical report survives of the doctor's examination, but we may speculate that Bastianelli thought the stigmata were not self-inflicted, given Benedict XV's unwavering support for Pio.

Furthermore, Benedict sent his most trusted Vatican officials, men he trusted with his life, to San Giovanni to spend time with Pio so as form detailed impressions of his character, and in turn they reported back to the pope. One of these prelates was Cardinal Augusto Silj. Silj had a shock of white hair, a handsome face with a strong jaw, and serious eyes so dark they looked black. Silj became a very important friend to Pio, and some years later he personally witnessed an apparition of Pio in the inner sanctum of the Vatican, an event that would save Pio's priesthood and ministry.

Another prelate who was to become a powerful friend to Pio, Bishop Alberto Valbonesi, came to see Pio in 1920. Valbonesi had borne much personal suffering, and during the time he spent with Pio he enjoyed a healing of his spirit. He was a mighty prince of the Church and yet he said that his visit with the humble Pio had made up for "years of pain"[257] he had suffered. Sometime later, Bishop Valbonesi was at a meeting with Archbishop Gagliardi and caught him in the act of calumniating Pio.

A Temporary Reprieve

Gemelli sought to sully Pio in the eyes of Pope Benedict XV but had no success. Benedict clipped the wings of Gemelli and said he didn't need to doubt Pio so much. The pope also gave an audience to Cesare Festa, the former Freemason who became a spiritual son of Pio's, and His Holiness encouraged Cesare to do his best to make Pio better known.

We are encountering a major theme of Padre Pio's biography: His life was powerfully influenced by whoever the reigning pontiff happened to be. If the pope held Pio in high esteem, times were good for Pio, but if the pope held Pio in low esteem, then times were bad for him. Pope Benedict XV, who had brought the Church through the cataclysm of World War I, had the highest regard for Padre Pio. He said to Cesare Festa, "Truly Padre Pio is an extraordinary man, the like of whom God sends to earth from time to time for the purpose of converting men."[258] He had a great personal fondness for Pio, and no matter how much Pio's enemies hissed hatred against him, they had little influence while Benedict reigned. The pope with heavy eyelids even objected to Archbishop Gagliardi's letter-writing campaign, whereby the archbishop was ordering priests to write scurrilous letters to the Vatican.

Pope Benedict XV did, however, order a thorough investigation of Pio, which was primarily prompted by Gemelli's loud campaign. Three years after Pio received the bloody stigmata, in June 1921, the pope allowed for a forensic inspection of Pio to be carried out by Bishop Raffaelle Carlo Rossi. Rossi acted as an inquisitor, and he deposed Pio, the friars who lived with him, and the priests who were Pio's persecutors. He made friends and foes alike swear to tell the truth, and to vow total secrecy. Rossi also searched Pio's cell and read all the letters to and from Fr. Benedetto.

Bishop Rossi tried to get out of the assignment, but when the Vatican leaned on him, he accepted the reconnaissance mission with some trepidation.

He arrived at San Giovanni Rotondo as discretely as humanly possible, knowing he had to find evidence that either backed up Gemelli's claims or disproved them.

It says a great deal for Pope Benedict's objectivity that, even though he was enamored with Pio, he sent someone as detached as Rossi, who was more against Pio than in favor of him. Rossi admitted initially feeling hostility toward Pio, even writing in his final report that before meeting Pio, he was "unfavorably prejudiced"[259] against the stigmatist. Rossi was not a mystic, but was genuinely holy, remarkably smart, and scrupulously honest. He was a statuesque man in his mid-forties, a devoutly serious priest who rarely smiled. Perhaps what made him the most suitable candidate to do intense interviews with Pio and write a report on a victim soul was that Rossi had known true sorrow, although of a variety different from the agonies visited on Pio.

Rossi nursed a mother wound. His family belonged to the wealthy class in the city of Pisa. But when he was a boy, his mama had an extramarital affair. When his father learned his wife had been unfaithful, he ordered her to leave and never spoke to her again. As a youth, Rossi had to comfort his mother at having been thrown out of the family home. His suffering was compounded by the fact that, as a young man in the late 1800s, he had to live with the stigma of being from a broken home. He yearned to become a priest so that he could offer Mass for his mother. Rossi bore a cross, and when he asked Pio about the pains of crucifixion, he did it as someone who knew pain.

Bishop Rossi's Report

The investigation of Pio hinged on whether Rossi found grounds to assert that the stigmata were a gift from God. Had he found reason to believe the stigmata were the product of Pio's mind, self-inflicted, or from the devil, then regardless of how much Pio impressed him, Rossi's report would have been damning. On the contrary, Rossi disputed Gemelli's assertions and he arrived with great caution at the conclusion that the wounds were of divine origin.

Pio lamented to Bishop Rossi the publicity his wounds were causing: "Why do they make so much noise about this!"[260] Pio even said he'd been "terrified"[261] of the crowds and that the friars had been forced to call the police to curtail them. Rossi ruled out the notion that Pio was lying under oath, because "imposture and perjury would be in too stark a contrast with the life and the virtues of the Padre himself."[262]

Rossi couldn't help growing fond of Pio, like the many others who loved being in his company. In his report, Rossi praised the "lively, sweet look in his eyes"[263] and said Pio was "serious … distinguished, dignified"[264] but that he also had a humorous side. He underscored Pio's humility, goodness, and truthfulness. Although Rossi found Pio's cell to be somewhat messy — he went so far as to call the drawers "disordered"[265] — yet he was impressed that Pio lived so simply and that Pio's ego was not enlarged by his celebrity.

Bishop Rossi was troubled by the sensationalized stories and publicity that Pio's stigmata had generated, and he was angry with Fr. Paolino, who was still being blamed for Romanelli's report being leaked to the press. But the mystery of how the report reached the newsroom was never solved, and Pio conceded to Rossi that he had no idea how Romanelli's findings were published. Rossi, like the doctors, did a probing manual examination of the wounds. Using his fingers like a pair of calipers, he pressed the wounds and saw Pio wince. Pio submitted, but later he exclaimed, "How much I have felt the burden of obedience today! But the Lord made me feel it all at the beginning: Afterward, things went better!"[266]

Mindful of the doctors' reports, Rossi sided with Giorgio Festa over Luigi Romanelli. Festa, he said, had characterized the wounds as being deep, but Romanelli had described them as "holes."[267] Rossi argued that had Romanelli been correct and had the tissues been torn apart, Pio could not have closed his hand at all, but he witnessed that Pio was almost able to close it. (Of course, when Rossi probed them, the wounds may have been shallower than when Romanelli measured them, due to the stigmata's changing nature.) Rossi said that on occasion the wounds were "more noticeable" but "at times less so,"[268] and astoundingly, "They look like they are about to disappear and they come back, flourishing again."[269]

The biggest differences between the anatomical reports and Rossi's observations concerned Pio's side wound. The doctors had said the wound on Pio's chest was like an upside-down cross, but Rossi found it to be a red triangle. The consistent fact was that it was the side wound that emitted the most blood. According to Pio's account, when Jesus plunged the instrument into his heart,

Our Lord did not then remove it; perhaps for this reason, the wound assumed different shapes: a cross and then a triangle, symbolic of the Trinity.

Romanelli had observed the side wound as being a much more deeply cut sore that injured Pio's ribs. He described it as a "lacerated wound, linear, with definite, slightly wrinkled edges, involving soft tissue."[270] If we rely on Romanelli's finding, it is as though Pio had been pierced with a pointed lance, which is how Our Lord received His side wound. A Roman soldier pierced Jesus's side to ascertain if He was dead. When the soldier's spear reached His Heart and he saw blood and water flow it, he knew He was dead. Jesus' side wound was His death certificate writ on His Flesh. Pio's side wound united him with the wound that cut into Jesus's Sacred Heart.

Rossi established that the wounds caused Pio excruciating pain: "Sometimes I cannot bear it," the stigmatist said.[271] Pio did not, however, tell Rossi that in his body he suffered the entire pains of Jesus' Crucifixion when he offered Mass. This may explain why Rossi made little or no allowance for how the wounds in Pio's hands may have made it harder for Pio to execute certain rubrics at Mass, and in his report, he criticized Pio's "liturgical flaws,"[272] which included that he didn't open and close his hands well.

Unlike Gemelli and the other examiners, Rossi was not a medical doctor. He was, however, the first to do a thorough theological analysis of the stigmata and dispel the idea that Pio had made a pact with the devil in order to receive the continuously bleeding wounds that made him famous. A key reason Rossi utterly dismissed this idea was that he questioned Pio about the devil coming as savage animals and blessedly Rossi believed everything Pio told him.

We will recall that the devil came as a vicious dog, which was witnessed by Fr. Anastasio and as a fierce cat, something recorded by Fr. Agostino in the diary he wrote about that string of demonic apparitions. When Rossi learned of Satan stalking Pio as an abusive animal, he thought it incongruous that the devil would attack Pio because of his holiness while also having control over him. "Padre Pio's most righteous life, his virtue, his piety," Rossi wrote, "are arguments too powerful to believe that the devil, if he fights Padre Pio, as it seems he does, has over him a power that only the subject, for diabolical ends, can give him."[273] Here we may see that the Lord allowed the devil to victimize Pio so that He could bring good from it. The demonic harassment visited on

Pio was hideous, but because it became well-known it was obvious the devil was Pio's enemy.

Bishop Rossi humbly acknowledged that only time would tell the full truth: "The future will reveal what today cannot be read in the life of Padre Pio."[274] This was especially prophetic regarding Pio's stigmata. Their truly miraculous nature was only seen after Pio had borne them for fifty years. Rossi observed that they remained open and bled continuously, but Rossi could not have imagined that they would heal completely before Pio's death, leaving no scars and with the prints on his palms perfectly intact. Pio, when he lay in his coffin, had hands like a newborn baby. This would refute the accusations that Pio had self-mutilated with something like carbolic acid, because criminals use acid to destroy their fingerprints so they can evade being identified. But at that time, in the summer of 1921, Rossi had no way of knowing that Pio's hands and feet would recover completely before the Capuchin priest died.

So why had Pio sent someone secretly to a pharmacy to get carbolic acid and veratridine? Under oath, Pio explained he had requested these corrosive substances to sterilize the needles used to give the boys of the college their inoculations. It had to be kept confidential because he did not have a doctor's prescription. As for the veratridine, he had asked for this so that he could mix it in the other friars' tobacco, which would provoke them to sneeze! The veratridine was meant for a prank, and Rossi found further evidence to support this when he discovered that Pio had only asked for three grams, a tenth of an ounce, essentially a few pinches of the irritating powder, which was enough for a joke but not enough to cause a serious lesion in the skin. Rossi found commonsense reasons to support the sacred nature of the stigmata, and he answered the accusation that Pio's obsession with Jesus' Crucifixion had caused the wounds and were a product of Pio's mental illness. Rossi found no such obsessive or neurotic traits in Pio, and he declared, "He is absolutely normal."[275]

Rossi Reviews Letters of Padre Benedetto

On one subject Bishop Rossi and Padre Pio's nemesis, Fr. Gemelli, were in a kind of agreement: Fr. Benedetto. Fr. Gemelli had leveled very serious charges against Benedetto and had stated categorically that Pio's beloved spiritual father was dominating Pio's imagination and bringing about the stigmata by way of making Pio's mind provoke the wounds on his body. Rossi utterly refuted this, and he questioned how Pio's imagination could cause his body to break out in wounds which had lasted for three years. He begged to know how the imagination could sustain wounds continuously.

On the other hand, Bishop Rossi declared it was Pio who led Benedetto, rather than the other way around! When Rossi reviewed all Benedetto's letters — which Pio provided without hesitation — Rossi found that Benedetto sought Pio's mystical knowledge on many questions. The bishop felt it wasn't right for a spiritual director to seek the advice of his spiritual son. Rossi made his assessment without knowing the full extent of Pio's gift of reading souls. He thought Benedetto was questioning Pio to satisfy "mystical cravings,"[276] when in fact, as we saw when Benedetto asked Pio about the lady who had stopped practicing her faith and was in danger of Hell, Benedetto wanted Pio's insight into souls for the purpose of saving them.

In his final dossier some months later, Bishop Rossi recommended regarding Benedetto that he "limit his activities"[277] with Padre Pio. This meant intense heartbreak for Padre Pio, for Benedetto was the only priest he felt had directed him properly in the mystical life. But Benedetto had few supporters in Rome, and in time it came down as a Vatican order that Benedetto be denied all contact with Pio. Pio and Benedetto were barred from meeting or writing to each other ever again.

Rumors and Results

In the meantime, Pio enjoyed the esteem of his spiritual director and of the friars who lived with him. As we will see, in the decades to come, Pio's fellow friars would turn on him, but in 1921, it was the local clergy who had it in for Pio, and they were not shy about accusing Pio of improprieties with his spiritual daughters. Bishop Rossi sorted truth from salacious gossip.

In one instance, a bitter youth who had stood outside a window and spied on Pio as he counseled a young woman in the parlor claimed that Pio had acted inappropriately toward her. After one of the priests in the area eagerly took the report to Rossi, the bishop investigated and ascertained that the man who stood outside the window had been none other than the young woman's ex-fiancé!

He seemed so resentful at having been jilted that he had resorted to sowing scandal. The bishop discerned that Padre Pio had been a victim of jealousy.

Now in his thirties, Padre Pio garnered the attention of many people who wanted to shower him with money. This provoked priests of a similar age to send letters denouncing him to the Vatican. Rossi did an exhaustive analysis of Pio's commitment to poverty, chastity, and obedience. He learned that Pio did not personally handle the many donations that were sent to him, and that Pio didn't know that his own parents were being helped financially. Grazio and Giuseppa were in their sixties and they had slaved to put their son through school. The many times Giuseppa had to run the farm on her own so his father could earn money for Pio's education were exacting their price on her health. She did not tell her son that her financial shortages were being met by his fellow Franciscans.

Bishop Rossi did find fault with Pio's observance of poverty when he saw that the cross swinging from his waist had a figure of Jesus crucified, because the Franciscan Constitution mandated a plain wooden cross. However, Pio's superior concluded that Pio's chastity was "angelic,"[278] and that there were no grounds for even suggesting that Pio was guilty of the most minor sexual misconduct with his spiritual daughters. In the end, Rossi did recommend that the daughters visit less frequently, and that Pio be "more assertive"[279] with them.

Dr. Festa's Medical Report

Bishop Rossi also did a painstaking evaluation of the reports that had come to him regarding Pio's peculiar diet, the high temperatures he sometimes had, and the delightful floral scent that was said to radiate from him. It had been reported to him that Pio never ate, and that he lived and performed his ministry on absolutely no calories. This, the bishop found out, was a pious misconception, and he saw that Pio ate a little of everything, albeit in such tiny amounts it was a wonder Pio was a healthy weight and an even bigger mystery how Pio put in nineteen-hour days. Rossi saw Pio drink beer and hot chocolate regularly, drinking more beer during the hottest days of summer.

Rossi was uncertain how to verify Pio's body temperature, which was purportedly extremely high — at times as though Pio was burning alive, on fire with love for Jesus. Previously, when thermometers had been put on Pio when he was in such a fiery state, the mercury had exploded inside the glass, causing the instrument to shatter. Then the Vatican inquisitor discovered that Dr. Festa — whom he credited with having done the best examination of Pio — had a thermometer that went up to 130 Fahrenheit, and the bishop borrowed it to measure Pio's temperature, which reached 118.4. Yet Rossi resisted concluding that this was a mystical phenomenon, and simply said that time would tell.

The single greatest factor that caused Rossi's heart to soften toward Pio was the heavenly perfume of violets that emanated from Pio's wounds and his body and which Rossi inhaled. Despite himself, Rossi was delighted by the gorgeous bouquet, and he described it as a "very intense and pleasant fragrance."[280] Rossi took pains to verify that the scent was the odor of sanctity, and he observed that Pio's hair, which had been cut two years prior, still smelled strongly of the scent. Rossi did a thorough search of Pio's room and found no liquid fragrance; all he found was soap.

It was this sacred scent (or "odor of sanctity") that caused the Vatican representative to give full credence to the stigmata being of divine origin, and to utterly reject the idea that Pio himself had inflicted the wounds, because "such morbid conditions cannot produce smells."[281] Rossi even had Fr. Prencipe admit under oath that a person who had been close to Pio had absorbed the scent and had come to Mass smelling the same as the stigmatist. This undercut Prencipe's assertions that Pio's gifts weren't genuine, and Bishop Rossi found the scent so extraordinary as to be miraculous.

Even today, there are those who pray to Pio and are greeted with a heavenly scent of roses or violets or both. They are inhaling Pio's presence. In the epilogue of this book, I will share the time that Pio filled my room with a floral scent like an English garden. For Bishop Rossi, the sacred scent softened him, and he found it impossible to retrain his bias against Pio. In the face of such a marvelous and mystical odor, he wrote, "I could not retain my personal unfavorable prejudice." In the end, he had to concede, "Padre Pio made a rather favorable impression on me."[282]

Papal Tides Turn

In his dossier, in which he formally presented his findings to the Vatican in January 1922, Bishop Rossi wisely and firmly stated that it was unthinkable to move

Pio from San Giovanni. He knew in his bones that a violent revolt would meet any attempt to take Pio away, and there was something prophetic in this insight.

Rossi's defense of the stigmata might have had more impact had the pope who commissioned the report not died that same month. Pope Benedict XV got a bad flu and soon was laid low with deadly pneumonia. As he lay dying, his heavy eyelids about to close for the last time, he called Cardinal Pietro Gasparri and entrusted him with his last wishes and his will. Cardinal Gasparri had become a good friend of the zealous Emanuele Brunatto, the layman and spiritual son of Padre Pio, who was then able to mix at the highest echelons of the Church hierarchy. Although the winds began to turn against Pio with the election of the next pope, Gasparri remained as loyal as Pope Benedict and even had a role in stopping a criminal plan hatched by Fr. Miscio to cheat Pio's family.

When Cardinal Achille Ratti became pope, for two decades he had cherished Agostino Gemelli, the doctor and priest who had been Padre Pio's nemesis, as his most trusted friend and confidant. Ratti took the name Pius XI, and he would be pope for seventeen years, during which time Gemelli had great access to him and many restrictions were placed on Pio's ministry. Pius XI had a stern and deathly serious personality, but his hard expression hid a soft heart. He had certain sympathies that were exploited so Gemelli could move against Pio.

Both Gemelli and Pope Pius XI were atypical Italians in that they were not close to their families. Gemelli's father had certainly not given him his blessing when he was ordained a priest. Pope Pius XI treated his siblings like strangers, and he did not let them visit him spontaneously in the Vatican. It was said that he wanted to give an example of the proper distance every priest needs from his family. During Pius's pontificate, however, Fr. Gemelli visited him in his personal apartment and cooked traditional Milan dishes such as yellow saffron risotto for him. Gemelli had more privileges even than Pius's own family, and their close bond lasted for years. However, from the earliest days of Pius XI's papacy, Gemelli's was not the lone voice against Pio.

Just after Pope Pius XI ascended the Throne of Peter, Archbishop Gagliardi sped to the Vatican for a face-to-face meeting with the new pope, in which he denounced Pio's "horrible means of hearing confessions," which put souls "in a state of agitation."[283] These carefully chosen words were intended to suggest that a demonic influence was present as people were confessing to Pio, because "agitation" is a sign in Catholic teaching of the demonic being given power — as opposed to peace, which is a sign of the working of the Holy Spirit.

Pius XI had a strong personal dread of demonic intrusion. His Holiness was very sensitive to suggestions about satanic subterfuge, where Satan gives powers to someone who is believed to have acquired these powers from God and so presents as a holy person but is in fact an instrument of the devil. Of course, Gagliardi had been the one to give Pio the faculties to hear Confessions in the first place! He made known to Pius XI that he regretted this.

Speaking with melodramatic contrition, the archbishop said, "I have to answer to God for having authorized Padre Pio to hear confessions."[284] Then Gagliardi condemned Padre Pio during a gathering full of Church leaders, the bishops and archbishops of the Vatican's consistorial congregation. Pio had a friend there at the meeting, Bishop Alberto Valbonesi, and he took pen to paper and wrote up an account, which included Gagliardi's dramatic charge that "Padre Pio is demon-possessed. I declare to you that he has a devil and the friars of San Giovanni Rotondo are a band of thieves." According to Valbonesi's record, Gagliardo then claimed, "With my own eyes I saw Padre Pio perfume himself and put makeup on his face!" Before all these princes of the Church, Gagliardi perjured his office when he sealed his lies with an oath, "All this I swear on my pectoral cross!"[285]

Most galling was Gagliardi's charge that Padre Pio was debauched and that he slept in the guest room of the friary, where he satisfied his lusts with young girls. Gagliardi held that the friars were bribing journalists to write surreal stories about Pio and making up miracles which drew a sea of people to San Giovanni. He said the friars were pocketing the donations and were beating each other up as they fought over the cash! And they were using the lire to live luxuriously. A thread in Gagliardi's fabrications was the way the friars supposedly slicked their hair with pomade, as though they were putting on a show.

All the while, Bishop Valbonesi was listening to this, appalled by the crass claims made by Gagliardi. He documented everything and sent the minutes to Pio's provincial, Fr. Pietro. Blessedly, Pietro was not taken in by a word of it, and never for a moment did he hold Pio in suspicion; instead, he called Gagliardi a "malevolent liar."[286] But the newly elected Pope Pius XI believed Gagliardi — he was singing from the same hymn sheet as his most trusted friend, and Pius found himself inundated with reports that the friars were making a display out of the demon-possessed Pio for financial gain. These fed into the pope's worst nightmares of gullible pilgrims being cheated because of their devotion to a priest they thought holy. Pius had a soft spot in his heart for pious peasants, and he was horrified when he thought these poor people were being played.

Why would Archbishop Gagliardi perjure himself like this? Perhaps he wanted to distract and deflect attention from the shambles he had created in his home diocese by bringing lurid tales to the Holy Father. By pretending to regret giving Pio the faculties to hear Confession, he was painting himself as a faithful shepherd, trying to rid his pasture of a "servant of Satan" who was wreaking havoc in his archdiocese.

As Gagliardi was vigorously whipping up a campaign against Padre Pio, Frs. Miscio, Prencipe, and Palladino became emboldened by the fact that they finally had a pope who believed them. Gagliardi became the mailman for the anti-Pio faction, passing their correspondence on to the Vatican. Padre Pio's spiritual father, Fr. Agostino, came to know of the contents of these letters and said they were "full of accusations, exaggerations, libels." Agostino leveled the blame at the father of lies and called the campaign to have Pio's ministry stopped "a true satanic war."[287]

A common theme in the letters was that the friars of San Giovanni were money-grubbers who exploited the crowds who congregated around Pio. Perhaps this was nothing short of projection on the part of Gagliardi, who was fond of costly gifts.

Of all those in the anti-Pio faction, Miscio worked most closely with Gagliardi. The archbishop handed over Miscio's letters directly to the Vatican officials. Miscio alleged that Pio used his spiritual daughters sexually, and that Pio had venereal disease and epilepsy. Epilepsy was a bar to ordination, and in lying that Pio was epileptic, he was essentially saying Pio ought never have been ordained. Pope Pius XI, however, took the matter so seriously that he ordered that all the letters disparaging Pio be given to the prelates of the Holy Office and analyzed for their veracity.

The Vatican Directs Pio's Removal

The director of the Holy Office, Cardinal Rafael Merry del Val, heard testimony from both the anti-Pio faction and Pio's supporters, which included princes of the Church, Cardinals Gasparri and Silj, as well as Bishop Valbonesi, so that he could draw up a list of solutions. Unfortunately, Cardinal Merry del Val was about to make an error of judgment that nearly caused blood to drench the streets of San Giovanni Rotondo.

The cardinal, a cool-headed Brit, had been born to Spanish parents in the Spanish Embassy in London. Educated in some of the best schools of London, he spoke like a royal. Although he looked Latin, with his sallow skin and large brown eyes, his etiquette and intellectual training were those of a highborn Englishman. His calm nature meant he bore any duress with great grace, whereas his intelligence and noble bearing left others in awe.

And so, when the cardinal issued a directive that Pio be moved from San Giovanni Rotondo, he did not foresee how this decision would impact Pio's neighbors and followers, the majority of whom were hot-blooded Italians. The mere suggestion that their saint be taken from them was rejected violently by the San Giovanni Rotondo natives.

The local mayor, Francesco Morcaldi, fought alongside his people to keep Pio. Only a few years younger than Pio, Mayor Morcaldi had a reverence and loyalty to Pio that was on par with that of Emanuele Brunatto. Morcaldi was a quintessential Italian statesman, and he would be mayor intermittently for the next forty years. Some accused him of talking out of both sides of his mouth because he knew what to say to both left-wing and right-wing people to make them think he was their ally. He was squat, thickset with a face like a chubby baby. He wore a formal black suit and silk tie. He wore round spectacles and had jug ears. Morcaldi wasn't brutish, but he had an air of authority and a command over the natives of San Giovanni Rotondo that few ever equaled except Pio.

The Vatican directive contained other provisions that added fuel to the fire, creating a cataclysmic war of wills. Until Pio was taken away, the hour of his Mass was to be at a different time each day and was not to be advertised, with the suggestion that the Mass be offered at an early hour of the morning. Pio was to stop blessing crowds from the window and was never to show his stigmata to people or talk of them. The people's response was immediate and unequivocal, and the Vatican learned the hard way that it was no match for the people who wanted Pio for themselves at any cost.

17

The People Fight for Pio

Mere months after Pope Pius XI was elevated to the papacy, the natives of San Giovanni knew that the Vatican was ordering that their saint be taken from them. The Lord had put Pio among a people who were astute and assertive, who risked even bloodshed to keep Padre Pio in their midst. They loved Pio with a volcanic intensity. Pio had received the visible stigmata in San Giovanni, and it was here he was destined to stay, but it was the local people who ensured this happened.

First, they exhausted civil protest, organizing a petition against Pio's transfer. In the summer of 1922, Mayor Morcaldi, dressed in his formal, tight-fitting suit, presented the friary with a petition that had just shy of three thousand names on it. Both Pio and Morcaldi held sway over the people of San Giovanni, who trusted their sanctity to Pio and their politics to Morcaldi. These were not easily led people, nor were they docile as sheep, but friar and mayor commanded their loyalty.

Pio's superiors quaked in their brown sandals at the idea of the violence that would erupt during and after Pio's transfer. They used the strategy of delay. They didn't obey the Vatican immediately, but neither did they refuse. They just held out and gave Pius XI the impression they were open to Pio's departure. Then the Holy Office published a strict declaration which stated that it had carried out "an inquiry on the phenomena attributed to Padre Pio" but could not uphold "the supernatural character of these phenomena and exhorts the faithful to conform their practices to this declaration."[288]

The months passed, with more people coming to the friary than ever before. The Vatican's plans to curb the crowds had backfired! Padre Pio may have been held in suspicion by many priests and prelates, but what made this ordeal bearable was that Padre Ignazio, the friary's Father Guardian, was very fond of Pio, and Ignazio bore the brunt of the pressure from the Vatican with grace and patience.

Scenes of bedlam ensued. Small-time con artists conned people into buying cuttings of cloth daubed in animal blood, which they said had mopped the blood from Pio's wounds. The scammers were making a fortune as gullible people snapped up blood-splattered cloth to venerate. Others peddled poorly painted pictures of Pio. Once, Pio heard a street hawker outside peddling his wares: "Padre Pio for two cents! Padre Pio for two cents!" Pio quipped to another friar, "The Guardian might hold me in great esteem, but instead — look at this! Padre Pio is worth two cents!"[289]

Reports of this reached Vatican officials, giving them the excuse to increase the pressure on the friars. Wouldn't it be better, they said, to remove Pio from the easy reach of credulous, zealously pious Southern Italians and send him to live among the more businesslike and cynical Northern Italians? Would taking him out of Italy and sending him to Spain or America be the better option?

A Holy Standoff

Pio's superiors were caught between the will of the Vatican and that of the local people. On August 10, 1922 — the anniversary of Padre Pio's ordination — a chilling incident confirmed in the minds of everyone who was making decisions about Pio that real danger surrounded his transfer.

Pio was at the altar during Vespers, about to turn and bless the crowds, when a local man by the name of Donato jumped toward Pio and pointed a gun at his head, saying, "Either dead or alive, you're going to stay with us."[290] The other people and the police manhandled Donato and seized the gun, holding him on the floor. True to his forgiving nature, Pio asked that Donato be treated leniently, but the near assassination illustrated the bloodbath that could result from the standoff.

To placate the Holy Office, which would not back down from ordering Pio's transfer, Pio's superiors decided that Pio was to celebrate an entirely private Mass without a congregation present. The locals were hotly offended when they discovered they could not assist at Pio's Mass. Emanuele Brunatto, who had nerves of steel, was seen weeping in public when he learned he could not go to Pio's Mass.

The order requiring that Pio's Mass be secret and hidden led to Mayor Morcaldi and the local people founding a "People's Association." They organized a huge protest in which thousands of people took part, making known their displeasure that Pio was going to be taken from them. A night of high drama followed, during which the people formed a mob and took out their frustration on the house of Fr. Palladino, who was known to them as being a member of the anti-Pio faction because he had criticized Padre Pio in his sermons.

Morcaldi had to hold the crowds back from setting fire to Palladino's home as the priest slept. Several shouted that they wanted to beat Palladino to a pulp. The townspeople also wanted to burn down Fr. Prencipe's house. This was considered a condign punishment for Prencipe's fickleness in being both Pio's spiritual son and his enemy.

On that same night, upward of five thousand people took torches and marched to the friary as the town band played. In the black of night, the road looked like it was ablaze with dazzling stars. At the helm of this sea of souls was Mayor Morcaldi, and everyone fell silent as he knocked on the door and was met by Fr. Ignazio. Morcaldi then demanded that Ignazio allow Pio to celebrate Mass in public, warning that if he didn't, "I will resign as mayor and fight as an ordinary citizen in the riot that will ensue."[291]

Ignazio let himself be strong-armed by Morcaldi and once again let Pio celebrate Mass in public. The People's Association was appeased in that it did not instigate a riot, but it continued its guerrilla tactics by bombarding Church and government authorities with telegrams protesting the restrictions placed on Pio's ministry. When the Association sent a few representatives to Archbishop Gagliardi, he was glibly charming to them, and acted as though he were on their side, going so far as to promise, "I will do everything possible to prevent the removal of Padre Pio."[292] Yet he was the most influential player in the campaign to have Pio's ministry ground to a halt! Gagliardi was a coward, afraid of incurring the people's wrath. But the locals saw through him, and they became his worst enemies.

All the while, Emanuele Brunatto kept close tabs on the Vatican's decision-making process, to ascertain where and when they wanted to move Pio. He even went to Rome and confronted Gemelli regarding the untruth he was spreading that he had seen Pio's stigmata, when Emanuele knew Gemelli had never been given permission to do so. Gemelli tried to put the fear of God in him and made dire threats that he would ruin him, but he could not cow Emanuele, who facetiously retorted, "Thank you for your Franciscan advice."[293]

Through it all, however, Pio was open to being moved wherever his superiors wanted him to go, at any time. Pio's docility speaks to his absolute devotion to keeping his vow of obedience. He even took issue with Emanuele's handling of Gemelli. Pio upbraided him, "You did a wicked thing! We must respect the decrees of the Church. We must be silent and suffer."[294] And all during this time, Pio suffered immensely, something he confided in his dear friend Bishop Alberto Costa: "I am passing through a period of continuous mortification." Then he asked Costa to pray to the Lord for him, "That He might free me immediately from this harsh prison."[295] Pio expressed many times to various people that he thought of his life as a prison.

A Dramatic Turn of Events

Although Pio often had the gift of foretelling future events, he did not know his own immediate destiny. Pio could often offer deep analysis of the future of other people, but he was in the dark as to the plan God had for him. He even wrote Mayor Morcaldi urging him to cooperate and assist in transferring him: "I beg you use every means to ensure compliance with the will of the superiors, which is the will of God, and to which I will blindly obey."[296] Pio was prepared to leave San Giovanni, but instead the Lord allowed him to bilocate to the inner sanctum of the Vatican and change Pius XI's mind.

Longtime supporter and admirer Cardinal Silj was witness to an extraordinary turn of events that put an end to the Vatican's pressure campaign. One day, Silj traversed the hallowed halls of the Vatican for a very serious meeting at the Holy Office. At the meeting Pius XI was surrounded by high-ranking Vatican officials, the members of the hierarchy in their red and purple skullcaps. They listened as Pius told them he was willing to suspend Pio from all priestly duties — essentially to impose on Pio the same suspension given those who are under suspicion of serious crimes.

Suddenly, Pio appeared out of nowhere and limped toward the gathered prelates, his hands buried in his brown habit. They did not instantly recognize him as Pio. He went to his knees, kissed the feet of Pius XI, and said to him, "Your Holiness, for the good of the Church, do not take this course of action."[297] Promptly Pio asked for Pius's blessing, kissed the pontiff's feet again, stood up, and disappeared.

Puzzled, Pius asked who had let the friar in. The Vatican officials had no clue, so they went out to the Swiss guards and scolded them for letting a friar trespass. The guards protested that they had seen no friar come or go. The pope instructed Cardinal Silj to find out where Pio had been on the day and time the friar had knelt before him. They suspected Pio had made the trip to Rome, which was ridiculous considering how much the locals were determined to keep him.

Silj learned that at that precise time, Pio had been in the choir of Our Lady of Grace Friary, praying the Office. Perhaps they asked themselves if this was a case of Padre Pio bilocating, simultaneously offering the Office and appearing in the Vatican. The experience of the friar coming and kissing his feet dissuaded Pius XI from suspending Pio from all priestly duties. Pius never again voiced a desire to punish Pio in this way, and the Holy Office swiftly informed the friars of San Giovanni that the order to transfer Pio was suspended indefinitely.

18

PIO'S SPIRITUAL DAUGHTERS

As we've just seen, Pio's ability to be in two places at once allowed him to be in San Giovanni Rotondo and simultaneously at the Vatican, where he pleaded his case and saved his ministry. In 1925, Padre Pio was again seen at the Vatican for the canonization of "the Little Flower," St. Thérèse of Lisieux, to whom he was especially devoted. All during these years of the roaring 1920s that we've just covered, Pio was bilocating.

It was this mystical gift that also allowed Pio to travel long distances in order to be with spiritual children in times when they needed him most. In 1922 he went to St. Peter's Basilica — just as Our Blessed Mother had predicted in 1905 — to meet Giovanna Rizzani, the girl who was born the first time he bilocated and who was his very first daughter in spirit, the first he loved as his child. Pio hailed her the firstborn of his heart, and it was to her that he confided some of his most profound insights.

In 1922, Giovanna was on the cusp of adulthood. After her father died, her mother left the countryside for Rome, where she raised her youngest girl. At seventeen, Giovanna had a heart-shaped face, thick brown hair, and dark, round eyes. Her serious expression warned others she was no fool, and her lips were drawn in a solemn, straight line. She was not one for insincere smiles. Beautiful and clever, Giovanna was also the "rough gem," as Our Lady had described her to Pio, because she had inherited doubts from her atheistic schoolteachers. Most especially she had a hard time understanding the Most Holy Trinity.

One summer's day, Giovanna decided to go to Confession in St. Peter's Basilica, but as she arrived it was closing. An obliging sacristan bade her look around and see if any priest was available. At that moment Pio bilocated to be there and Giovanna saw him enter a wooden confessional, though she did not see his face. She seized her opportunity, went in and confessed, and then unburdened herself to Pio regarding her doubts about the Holy Trinity.

Padre Pio addressed her question directly, but with loving tenderness. "My daughter," he began,

> who can understand and explain the mysteries of God? They are called mysteries because they cannot be comprehended by our small intelligence. We can have a faint idea of them by simile. Have you ever seen the dough to make bread? What does the housewife do? She takes flour, leaven, and water. They are three distinct elements: the flour is not leaven, nor water, the leaven is not flour, nor water, the water is not flour, nor leaven. She gathers them together and from the three elements she forms one sole substance. Therefore, three distinct elements, gathered together, give one sole substance. With this dough three loaves are made, that have the same identical substance, but are distinct in form, one from the other, but only one substance.[298]

Giovanna listened on the other side of the confession grill as Pio elaborated:

> From this simile, let us go on to God. God is one in nature, triune in persons, equal and distinct, one from the other. The Father is not the Son, nor the Holy Spirit, the Son is not the Father, nor the Holy Spirit, the Holy Spirit is not the Father, nor the Son. The Father begets the Son, the Son is begotten from the Father, the Holy Spirit proceeds from the Father and the Son. They are three Persons, equal and distinct and only one God.

That moment in the dark confessional, Giovanna's doubts were dispelled and she felt great relief. Pio gave her his blessing and she bounced out of the wooden box. She lingered, wishing to kiss her confessor's hand. The obliging sacristan approached her and whispered that she had to leave; the basilica was about to be locked up. Giovanna said she was just waiting for the friar to come out of the confessional. The sacristan feared he might lock the friar in and so searched the confessional, but he found it empty. They could not find the friar anywhere! Giovanna was baffled and blurted, "Where did he go? We did not move from here and we saw no one leave! It is a mystery."

Pio and Giovanna Meet Again

The following summer Giovanna went with her aunt to San Giovanni. She had not the faintest idea the confessor she had encountered in St. Peter's had been Pio. To her knowledge, she had never encountered Padre Pio. But when she went to Confession to him again in San Giovanni, he said to her, "My daughter, you have finally come! How many years have I waited for you."

Giovanna was incredulous and said to him that he must have gotten her confused with another girl. Pio revealed that he had been her confessor that day in St. Peter's. Then he told her the stunning news that Our Lady had placed her in his care, seventeen years prior, so that one day she might adorn the Queen of Heaven as a stunning diamond, and added, "My daughter, you belong to me. You have been entrusted to my care by Our Lady.... It is time for me to care for your soul, as our Heavenly Mother desires."

Giovanna burst into tears, and she asked Pio, "Padre, since I belong to you, take care of me.... Should I become a nun?" Pio responded, "Nothing like that. You will come often to San Giovanni Rotondo, I will have care of your soul, and you will know the will of God." Giovanna had the awesome privilege of knowing the Lord's will for her. A priest in Rome perplexed her when he practically commanded her to become a nun, so she made an urgent trip to see Pio, and he corrected this notion: "My daughter, Christ does not want you on Mount Tabor, but on Calvary. Religious life is Tabor. Matrimony is Calvary. On Tabor one seeks, one finds, and one lives united with God in prayer and in contemplation. On Calvary one finds suffering in crucifixion with Jesus."

Giovanna was very cheerful — even though she knew she would be united with the Lord in crucifixion — and she returned to Rome with a heart at rest. A little later Giovanna was discerning a marriage proposal. A pious young man of noble birth and good looks had asked her hand. Pio would not consent. "He is not the young man Our Lord has destined for you," he advised. "Wait and pray. Another will come, one who has need of you, of your affection, of your apostolate and of your sacrifice."

In time another young man, a marquis, went to her on bended knee. Before she answered him, she went to see Pio, who edified her with his response: "My daughter if you feel like embracing the cross, take this step, for this is the youth entrusted to you by Divine Providence. Otherwise, do not think about it anymore." Giovanna married the nobleman and together they had a lovely brood of children.

Pio invited Giovanna to become a Third Order Franciscan. Giovanna readily agreed and Pio did her initiation and gave her the new name of Sr. Jacopa. Giovanna protested hotly, "Padre! What an ugly name!" But Pio insisted, "No. You will be called Sister Jacopa." He explained:

> Have you read the life of Saint Francis? In one of the chapters, we read of a noble Roman matron, Jacopa de'Settesoli, named by Saint Francis "Dearest Mother of Our Order" and "our brother Jacopa" for her great charity and generosity towards the friars.... Well, this lady had the privilege of assisting at the death of the Seraphic Father Saint Francis. Remember this, one day you will assist at my death.

Pio's words came true, as we will see later.

Pio's "American Daughter," Mary Pyle

During the jazz age of the 1920s, Pio met an American lady named Mary Pyle, who became one of the most important spiritual daughters during his life — one who may become a saint in her own right. Just as Benedetto left, Mary entered.

May we believe God gives us signs in our dreams? Mary Pyle had a dream that foretold how Pio would change her life forever. At the time, she was in her thirties, traveling and working closely with the education theorist Maria Montessori. In the dream, she and Montessori were traveling in a horse and buggy of old, going at breakneck speed, when a mysterious figure stepped out onto the road, seized the reins, and halted the horses. When the coach had come to a stop, a new road came into view, and the mysterious figure commented to Mary Pyle, "Blessed are those who take the right road, for they will be saved."[299]

The dream held a scary implication: Was the dream implying that young Mary was not on the way to Heaven? In time, Mary Pyle would become known as the "strong right arm of Padre Pio,"[300] but how had she lived before the dream?

In 1888 she was born in Manhattan with a silver spoon in her mouth. Her parents, James and Adelaide Pyle, lived lavishly on Fifth Avenue while they operated a soap factory in New Jersey. James and Adelaide named her "Adelia," but later she was only ever called by the name of Jesus' Mother. Mary, their third child and eldest daughter, was baptized a Presbyterian; her mother esteemed this branch of Protestantism as the best place to situate her children so they could rise in society. Their home had eight servants, and her mother employed nannies and governesses from several European countries. Mary was allowed to speak to each of the governesses only in their native language. As a result, Mary spoke French, Spanish, German, and Italian fluently.

Her upbringing, however comfortable, did not do much to encourage her toward married life. Mary's mother, although highly intelligent, was often hysterically angry. She was prone to leaving her husband, issuing orders to her servants to pack her belongings so they could be sent on and absconding to Europe with Sara, her favorite child, while Mary and the four boys were left behind in New York. Mary's two older brothers became lawyers, because Adelaide felt having sons who practiced law was a good reflection on her as a parent. Mary's mother was determined her children would attain social prominence, so their success would reflect well on her.

As a social climber, Adelaide slavishly adhered to snobbish sensibilities, and tried to mold Mary into the woman she wanted her to become. She sent Mary to two finishing schools, not university like her brothers, because Adelaide thought it was unsuited to a woman of her daughter's birth. At these schools Mary learned music, dancing, and singing, as well as the art of teaching. In both her appearance and manner, Mary was well-suited to the life for which she was being raised. She had a strong face with prominent cheekbones and a round, sharp chin. Honey-brown hair crowned a wide forehead, and her eyes were Celtic blue. A natural smile lit her fair complexion. It would be some time before she discovered her calling. It all began with a quest for truth.

Mary and Maria Montesorri

Adelaide was open to moving around to various Presbyterian communities, but her daughter craved something with more spiritual substance. Adelaide dismissed Catholicism, considering it the religion of the lower classes. However, she employed Catholic servants and had an Irish maid who surreptitiously took Mary to Mass. When Adelaide found out, she forbade Mary from ever going to Mass again. If only she had known that her little girl would one day become a devotee of Padre Pio, assisting at his Mass every day!

Mary found genteel Protestantism unsatisfying, so Adelaide tried to change Mary's mind by having a Protestant pastor talk to Mary. During the conversation, Mary showed spunk, questioning the pastor until he conceded he did not believe fully in the tenets of his religion. Mary replied, "Why then, do you want to impose it on me?"[301]

Mary's honesty and independence became defining qualities that prepared her for her radical departure from the life she had been brought up to lead. In New York, Mary was something of a socialite, her witty repartee and stunning looks winning her admirers, and she was a big hit at balls and banquets, where she danced the night away. To her mother's consternation, instead of meeting a suitable husband, Mary was still single in 1912, at the age of twenty-four.

Around that time Mary met the famous educator Dr. Maria Montessori, who was hugely impressed with Mary and especially Mary's command of languages. Montessori invited her to become her trusted colleague and translate her talks as she went from place to place, holding forth to large audiences on the teaching methods she had used to such success among the slum children in Rome. Mary wrote a letter to her mother, who was away, telling her of her desire to work with Montessori; when Adelaide wrote back condemning this decision, Mary was already on her way to Europe as Dr. Montessori's interpreter.

Maria Montessori became a substitute mother for Mary; she valued Mary's qualities in a way her own mother never had. When she became aware of Montesorri's growing influence on her daughter, Adelaide lashed out and stopped Mary's allowance, declaring she never wanted to see her again. This was an attempt to emotionally blackmail Mary into following the plan Adelaide had for her to become a high-society matron. Instead of taking steps to reconcile with Adelaide, Mary leaned on her companion to such a degree that in biographies of Montessori, Mary is described as her adopted daughter.

Mary Pyle Meets Pio

As Mary voyaged around Europe, she developed a new perspective on Catholicism. Mary realized that her mother's practice of keeping away from Catholicism lest she be tainted with the lower classes was ignorant. When she beheld the grandeur of gorgeous cathedrals that were centuries old and that were the focal point of every major city, she revered the Catholic Faith as having an ancient heritage which had bequeathed a beautiful legacy.

In 1913 Mary sought out conditional Catholic Baptism, taking the name Mary for good. She was given the Sacrament by a friar at the Church of Our Lady of Montserrat in Barcelona. All the same, Mary felt lost, wanting a spiritual director who would be the Sherpa for her soul. On a trip to London, Mary first heard of Pio. From the start, she believed him to be a true man of God. Finally returning to Italy in the autumn of 1923, Dr. Montessori encouraged Mary to accompany her friend Rina to San Giovanni to meet Padre Pio. Little did Montessori know she had put in motion a chain of events that would end with Mary leaving her!

Mary arrived on October 4, the feast of St. Francis. She described San Giovanni as "a small town, poor, dirty but full of hearts that loved Padre Pio," and the hinterland as "a combination of mountains and desert." On the morning she was to confess to Pio for the first time, she arrived early at the church and found herself in a company of farmers in overalls. Suddenly she glimpsed Pio: "A simple little friar, … black bands on his hands from which one could only see the white fingers, passed through the crowd, limping a bit and everyone kissed his hand as he passed."[302]

Pio went into the confessional and Mary took her place in the queue, where she waited for hours. Finally, she knelt before Pio and tried to kiss his hand, but he pulled it away. When she unburdened herself of her sins, she thought she heard Pio tell her he wasn't going to absolve her, but she protested and he seemed to relent. Pio was exhausted from spending long hours in the confessional, and he mumbled something Mary couldn't quite hear. Mary thought she'd been absolved, so she left the confessional, but Pio called her back saying, "Do you want me to give you absolution or not?"[303]

After she had received absolution and her soul was in a state of grace, Pio extended his hand for Mary to kiss. Mary could see Pio through the grill of the confessional, and she thought his eyes "innocent and beautiful" and saw "laughter from Heaven" in them. Mary then assisted at Pio's Mass, and made deeply moving observations. "His hands during Mass were without mittens," she wrote, "and even though he keeps the sleeves pulled down as much as possible we can see the holy stigmata when he raises his hands to say, 'Dominus

Vobiscum.'" She saw an awe-inspiring beauty in Pio's bearing: "His hands during Mass seem to be made of ivory, white and transparent of a supernatural beauty … with dark pink nails almost red as if the tips of those white fingers had been put in the chalice, as if they had touched the Divine Blood." Mary noted, "Padre Pio is not with us during that time, he is with God.… During Mass Padre Pio has the door to Heaven opened and one can almost feel the grace of God coming down over him."[304]

After Mass, Mary went to the sacristy for Pio's blessing. She fell to her knees and called him her father. Putting his punctured hands on her head, Pio told her, "My child, stop traveling around. Stay here."[305] They both recognized each other as father and daughter instantly. Mary, however, did not obey straightaway; she at first returned to Dr. Montessori's side. But she could not resist her irrepressible urge to be with Pio, and the second time she went to San Giovanni, she brought Montessori with her.

During her second meeting with Pio, Mary let slip her strong desire to live near him. She'd been with Montessori for over ten years, and they had grown very attached to one another. Yet Mary found herself torn between her adoptive mother and her spiritual father. Pio passionately wanted Mary to make San Giovanni her permanent home and become his collaborator. He spoke to Mary in a way that betrayed his deep knowledge of her past and moved her to stay with him. He told her to obey her mother, which called to Mary's mind the fact that Adelaide had forbidden her from working with Montessori, but Mary had never told Padre Pio this. And when Pio said, "I will put a chain around you and I will bridle you,"[306] he prompted Mary to remember the dream she had of being in the horse and buggy traveling at breakneck speed when a mysterious figure grabbed the reins.

That day in San Giovanni, Mary parted ways with Dr. Montessori, never to see her again. Instead, Mary become a fixture in San Giovanni. Montessori took the loss badly, and some say she resented Pio for "stealing" Mary. Nevertheless, Mary settled in and found a room in the house of a local family. This was modest accommodation for one used to luxury. From the start, however, Mary never regretted her decision. She declared, "When you find a precious pearl, with what joy you discard all earthly goods in order to acquire it!"[307] Mary forsook the fine silks and furs of her youth, and after becoming a Third Order Franciscan, she donned the brown habit of St Francis. As for her jewelry, she decided to sell it to raise money for Pio's charitable works. She held onto a gold watch speckled with diamonds because she needed it to tell the time. Nevertheless, Padre Pio asked her about it one day in a tone of reprimand, "So, you still have the gold watch with the diamonds?"[308] Impulsively, Mary took the watch outside and slapped it against a wall until the diamonds rained out of it. Gathering them up, she went back to Pio and deposited the gold and diamonds into his punctured hands.

Pio did not ask all his spiritual daughters to part with their adornments, and he made no such requests of Raffaelina or Giovanna, who both wore jewelry after becoming his daughter. However, Mary wholly embraced the ideals of poverty, chastity, and obedience in the form of doing what Pio asked of her, from handing over her possessions to using her talent for music to play the reed organ. Mary quickly fell in beside the other pious souls who trudged up the steep road each day to assist at Pio's Mass at an early hour of the morning, and then she would spend the entire day at Our Lady of Grace Friary. But Mary spent very little time in actual conversation with Pio outside of Confession. She credited her spiritual development to being in his company: "For me his presence teaches more than a library full of books."[309]

She read the letters that came for Pio, and even when he was forbidden from writing letters in reply, Mary wasn't, and on his behalf she replied to those letters. Mary was fluent in five languages, and she replied in the language of the letter writer.

She did not have the best memories of family life, and she didn't feel the loss of a husband or biological children. The years of estrangement from her family had prepared her for the necessary separation from family that is required by religious life, so that no parent or sibling competes with Christ.

One might ask, since she was living like a religious, why did she not become a sister or a nun? Pio directed her on this point, telling her sharply that the convent was not a place for her, but when he spoke of her to others, he always maintained she had been a good religious, meaning she did have a vocation, which she lived out by keeping the vows she'd made when she joined the Third Order, wearing her brown wool habit and covering her hair with a mantilla.

If you have ever felt a calling to religious life but do not feel called to be in a convent or monastery, you may have recourse to Mary Pyle for her example and you may ask her prayers in Heaven. Possibly you will realize your destiny in a similarly unique way, perhaps even with Pio as your director.

Mary Sees Her Brother

In time Mary Pyle's brother David journeyed to San Giovanni and was appalled to see her humble existence, which he thought no place for a person of Mary's privileged birth. David described Mary to their mother as having lowered herself to peasantry, encouraging her to make peace with Mary and reinstate her allowance.

David had influence over his mother. A graduate of Harvard Law, he became a celebrated attorney who also had inherited his mother's domineering character and was able to bend her to his will. Adelaide was soon marching into San Giovanni Rotondo, on a mission to deliver her daughter from the lower classes.

The first encounter she had with Pio did not bode well. Adelaide came to Mass with her yapping lap dog, and when the dog trotted into Pio's path, Pio swept the dog out of his way with his foot, which offended Adelaide, who stormed out of the church. Pio, however, endeavored to win Adelaide over and became her friend. Mary showed mercy to her mother, and they were reconciled, although the relationship always remained cold. Adelaide reinstated Mary's generous allowance, which was an average of six thousand dollars a month, a great fortune in those days.

Although never entirely understanding of Mary's vocation, Adelaide did relinquish the life plan she'd had in mind for Mary and accepted that she was to live a life serving the poor and sick. All the same, when Adelaide returned to America, she sent elegant dresses to Mary that Mary refused to wear, preferring her earth-colored habit (unlike Raffaelina, who always dressed in fine Victorian dresses). Mary had such charisma that she attracted people to her and had a good word to say about everyone. She gave so much to so many in need that she was often out of pocket at the end of the month. Mary had legendary charity, which Padre Pio praised effusively: "The axis of perfection is charity; who lives centered in charity lives in God, because God is charity."[310]

Mary had had a first-rate, expensive education and used her talents for the good of others. She was the nexus between pilgrims and Pio, and between Pio and the people who could not travel but who received replies to their most urgent letters in their own language. Mary was blessed with a lovely voice that had been trained to melodic perfection, and she took over the running of the choir. She became beloved for her visits to the sick and used some of her family's money to build her own house, but she went against Pio's advice to build it in a specific place alongside the friary. Instead, she built it at the bottom of a hill so steep it was practically vertical. Mary regretted this in old age when she struggled to climb the hill to Pio's Mass. Whenever Mary was asked about Pio, she would hail him as "the greatest Saint since St. Francis."[311]

The Pink Castle

Mary's abode became known as "the pink castle" because it had rooftop turrets and was painted pink. At the time it was ready to be occupied in 1927, Mary opened the doors of her pink castle to the poor and the sick, and the house became a hive of activity. Orphans and young people congregated in her cozy kitchen. Throughout the years ahead this would be home to a community of women and serve as a guesthouse for priests visiting San Giovanni. The local youngsters had a catechetical group that met in Mary's house, where she made them dinner. Pio's parents, Giuseppa and Grazio, came to live in Mary's house and be in her care, as she lavished them with attention and catered to their every need. She was born into affluence, yet her empathy for those in dire straits meant she shared her allowance with anyone who needed it. She was also generous to herself, eating and enjoying large quantities of Italian food, which meant she grew portly over the years. But she never considered that she had the inside track on Pio's inner life, and she warned someone writing a book on Pio, "You mustn't deceive yourself. No one knows him except God. No one has access to his inner life except naturally his confessor, whose lips are sealed. We can only gather up the crumbs that fall from the rich man's table."[312]

One day, out of the blue, Mary was inspired to ask Padre Pio, "Can I build a friary at Pietrelcina?" Her question touched on an ardent desire of his — remember that Pio prophesized to Fr. Pannullo that he saw a friary that would send up the incense of prayers and be a place where the angels would sing. Pio instantly responded to Mary, "Do it at once and let it be dedicated to the Holy Family."[313]

Mary received financial help from her mother, and the Pyles paid for the building of a friary, a seminary, and a boys' boarding school in Pietrelcina. Emanuele oversaw the construction, and he even had Pannullo — who was nearly blind at the time — point out the exact location where Pio had seen the new church. Then Emanuele sought out the best of the best to work on building it. All the villagers lent their arms to making Pio's dream a reality and they carried the sanctified stones from the extremely old ruins of the Church of Purgatory to the field where the friary was being constructed. On the day the cornerstone was put in place and blessed, a cross of dazzling light was seen to rise over the site, surely a sign of the Lord's blessing. Emanuele lost favor with some people because, while he was supervising the construction, he could not be silent and openly criticized the Vatican for its treatment of Pio. Soon, we will see more of Emanuele's strenuous efforts to defend Pio, and how he showed extraordinary élan in evading even the most powerful of Pio's enemies.

19

FORGIVING DON MISCIO

In the wild and daring 1920s, Pio was amassing not only spiritual daughters but spiritual sons as well. He captured the most reluctant souls for Christ, even though at the same time the anti-Pio faction did everything it could to harm his reputation. But Pio was self-forgetting and involved himself totally with the soul he was converting, notably in the following two cases.

The Conversion of the Lawyer Di Maggio

In 1926 an arrogant young lawyer of thirty traveled to San Giovanni. His name was Di Maggio and his only purpose for being there was to pass on a letter to Pio on behalf of someone else. Di Maggio strutted into the church just in time for Pio's first Mass and behaved in a loutish, disrespectful way. So irreverent was his posture that he became the focal point of attention. He drew many stares from people, which was unusual because people's attention was normally so riveted by Pio at the altar that they could not be distracted. But the young man's behavior was so impish that the others gaped at him. A radical change came over Di Maggio, however, as he observed Pio offer Mass, and he became gripped with a strange determination to have Pio hear his Confession. After Mass he went to the sacristy to confess, and he surprised himself when he bared the full contents of his soul to the stigmatist.

When he'd been absolved, he and Pio had a spirited discussion. A few days before coming to San Giovanni, Di Maggio had been thinking of becoming an actor. This plan fled from him, and he now wanted to study Sacred Scripture intensely. Before he left San Giovanni, he called a friend of his in Rome, another legal eagle, and invited him to swoop into San Giovanni. The friend thought Di Maggio was in trouble and hurried to the mountain-encircled town only to find that Di Maggio had asked him there so he could meet Pio and have a conversion to Christ. Di Maggio's friend was not pleased and thought Di Maggio was having a nervous breakdown, yet despite his better judgment, and even though he thought his friend was crazy, he spent time in San Giovanni Rotondo and, to his total surprise, did convert.

When it came time for Di Maggio to leave for Rome, he had a conversation with Pio which is of utmost relevance to us today. Di Maggio begged Pio, "Father, I am now returning to Rome, the old occasions of sin. What shall I do … please help me!"[314] Pio answered him, "My son, pray, don't ever leave off praying, and be assured that when I have raised a soul, I never let it fall."[315] If your soul has indeed been raised by Pio, rest assured that he will do for you what he did for Di Maggio, and "never let it fall."

The Conversion of Friedrich Abresch

Then there was the astounding conversion of Friedrich Abresch, who Pio said had sung praises to Satan. Pio even informed him, "Jesus was more compassionate with you than with Judas."[316] Why did Friedrich need so much compassion from Our Lord? He had been raised a Protestant in Germany, in a family which was, to use his words, "violently anti-Catholic." When he married an Italian lady, however, he became Catholic for social convenience, yet he candidly admitted, "The dogma meant nothing to me and I was enthralled by the occult." A friend of his led him into spiritualism, and they contacted the dead, which may have meant conversing with demons posing as departed souls. Friedrich was left disappointed: "The messages from beyond the tomb seemed to me very inconclusive."

Next, Friedrich embraced practices of magic and became a believer in reincarnation. Bit by bit, he was giving away his will and having his intellect informed by demons in disguise. All the while he was receiving Holy Communion every so often to please his wife. When Friedrich heard of Pio, he was "highly suspicious" but decided to go to meet him out of idle curiosity. He traveled a long way from Bologna and after arriving in San Giovanni Rotondo sought out Pio in the sacristy, but Pio was abrupt with him. Friedrich's vanity was wounded: "I had expected a warmer reception after my long and tiring journey."

Pio told him point-blank that in previous Confessions Friedrich had neglected to reveal many grave sins, and he demanded of Friedrich a commitment to be honest. Friedrich said he had not believed in the supernatural character of

Confession, but at that moment in the sacristy, Pio's eyes staring into his, Friedrich was compelled to exclaim, "But now, Padre, I believe in it." Pio went quiet and an expression of dire pain came over his face, before he educated Friedrich concerning his sacrilegious Communions: "Each time you took Communion it was a sacrilege. You must make a genuine confession." Pio instructed him to search his memory for the last time he made a good confession, and with that Pio left the sacristy to hear the women's Confessions. Friedrich trawled his mind but could not remember it.

A while later Pio returned and, finding Friedrich flummoxed as to the last occasion he had given an honest account of his sins, he said, "All right. You made a good confession when you were returning from your wedding trip — leave out the rest and begin from there." Friedrich was amazed that Pio knew this — it was indeed true, and this precise knowledge led him to believe Pio was a genuine mystic. Pio started to enumerate all of Friedrich's sins, including the exact number of times he had missed Mass. He specified Friedrich's mortal sins, making him understand their gravity, then broached his homage to Satan. "You sang the praises of Satan," he reproached the penitent, "while Jesus in the infinite tenderness of His love broke his neck for you." Friedrich asked himself, "Who could have had any knowledge of these things other than Padre Pio, who has the gift of reading our most intimate thoughts and can scrutinize our conscience?"[317]

Pio did not flinch from telling Friedrich he had paid tribute to Satan through his participation in rousing the dead and practicing a combination of magic and theosophy. You may be aware that a debate currently rages as to whether these practices are really portals for collaborating with demons, some saying they are just about "being enlightened" — the question is which creatures are doing the enlightening. We need to ask ourselves if we would do as Pio and dare tell someone we know or love that their belief in magic and theosophy makes them members of a choir that sings praises to Satan.

Friedrich made a firm purpose of amendment not to practice the occult anymore, and was given absolution by Pio, after which Friedrich said, "I felt as light as though borne on wings. On my return to the village with the other pilgrims I behaved like a boisterous child."

All this happened on a chilly day in November 1928, only a few years before Pio was to enter a time of even greater persecution that was to prevent him from doing for others as he had done for Friedrich. Friedrich felt he had to talk openly about his conversion: "One has no right to be silent when one has received such grace." Pio played a massive role in Friedrich's life, so much so that Friedrich would declare that "I owe my life's happiness" to Padre Pio, for "without him I should have had no son." When he met Pio, Friedrich and his wife, Amalia, were childless. Amalia was a lovely woman in her late thirties; she craved a baby but was devastated when doctors discovered a tumor in her womb that caused huge blood loss.

Three specialists insisted she have a hysterectomy, but Amalia resisted, feeling her heart breaking because she wanted a baby so badly. She took time to go to San Giovanni. When she knelt in Pio's confessional, she made known to him her intense longing to have a baby. Pio advised against the operation, saying, "No instruments. The rest of your life would be ruined." When Amalia returned home a miracle happened: "My hemorrhages stopped, and all the symptoms of my malady vanished without trace."

Furthermore, Pio predicted she would bear a baby boy! He even told her when she was pregnant by sending her a telegram which read, "More happy than ever. Start the layette." On the verge of turning forty, Amalia gave birth to a little boy she named Pio. This may be one of the greatest examples of Pio's intercession. His prayers for Amalia meant she bore a son.

There may be an Amalia in our lives who longs for a little one. If so, let's ask Pio's intercession. Amalia and Friedrich decided to raise their little boy in San Giovanni, and they made a home near Padre Pio. Friedrich opened a photography studio and Pio gave him a very privileged role — that of being his personal photographer.

Pio Frustrates Photographers

For many years photographers hounded Pio on all sides for photos, but they would always discover later that the negatives were blank. Professional photographers, reporters, pilgrims, and tourists found that when they took photos of Pio, the roll of film was later shown to have no images whatsoever. Pio prayed for the images contained in the film to disappear! This happened even when his close friends took photos that Pio did not want taken. A beloved friend of Pio's, Dr. Willi Sanguinetti, took two rolls of film of Pio, but every photo turned out blank. On other occasions cameras were pointed at Pio, but the cameras would not work; the shutters would not move when Pio was the object. If the camera was not pointed at Pio, the camera would work. This speaks to the degree of trust Pio had in Friedrich in allowing him to take photos of him, which in turn were developed, and then sold in Friedrich's shop, with Pio's blessing. But most of all, the phenomenon of the "photos that came up blank" challenges us as to how much we believe in the power of prayer and calls us to revisit the prayer intentions we think are "impossible."

Miscio Repents

Although we may find the details of Pio's persecution at the hands of the local priests to be galling, something beautiful happened when one of Pio's most energetic persecutors underwent a dramatic change and went from hating Pio to loving him. This was the mischievous Don Miscio, who was so driven that he wrote a whole book condemning Pio and the entire Forgione family, which he tried to use in a bid to blackmail Padre Pio's brother, Michele. Michele was a farmer who loved a glass of beer and cigarettes, and he had an earthy way of speaking. He was not a bully, but he did not suffer fools.

One December, when Michele was getting ready for Christmas, he was greeted by Miscio, who had traveled to Pietrelcina with a proposition. The cleric brandished the book he'd written in Michele's face and claimed to have gotten an advance of five thousand lire. He said he'd stop the book from being published if Michele would give him the advance instead, after which he would give the five thousand lire back to the publishing company.

To buy himself time, Michele agreed to pay Miscio but said he would have to sell some of his land first. He was willing to do so because he didn't want his younger brother Pio to suffer anymore. When Michele told Emanuele Brunatto, Emanuele did not assent to such a scheme and sped to Rome, where he gained an audience with Pio's fan, Cardinal Gasparri, and told him of Miscio's mischief. Cardinal Gasparri cried out, "Have that canon put in jail!"[318]

Back in Southern Italy, Michele hatched a plan that would lead the police to Miscio. He gave Miscio four thousand lire, having taken down the serial numbers of the banknotes, which he gave to the police who were apprised of Miscio's attempted extortion. Miscio had a promise from Michele that he would get another thousand lire after the sale of some land had gone through. The cops caught up with Miscio and arrested him at his home.

When Pio heard about it, he was beside himself that a priest was being held in police custody and he practically begged Michele not to cooperate with the authorities any further. Michele was headstrong and he refused Pio's request. He felt compelled to defend his brother and stop the calumny contained in Miscio's book from being published.

When brought before the judge, Miscio received a suspended sentence, with the judge making known that he was appalled by the book's content. The news of Fr. Miscio's conviction reduced Pio to tears, and he wailed in the third person, "A priest in jail! And all because of Padre Pio."[319] Miscio was not imprisoned, but he was fired from his job as a teacher. Even though Miscio had maligned Pio for some years and even nastily bullied his brother, Pio wrote to the government making a case for Miscio to get his job back. After Pio's defense, Miscio did get his job back and felt so completely contrite he expressed sorrow to Michele and Pio and pleaded with them for forgiveness.

The Forgione brothers — farmer and friar — forgave Miscio fully. In return Miscio remained devoted to Pio for the rest of his life and never again calumniated the stigmatist. There was a completeness in the way Pio forgave someone which made real the truism "to err human, to forgive divine," and it was Pio's Christ-like forgiveness that earned him Miscio's respect. Miscio had a conversion from nefarious to holy. For the rest of his days, he visited Pio and asked his prayers.

Another Journalist Repents

Don Miscio was not the only one who wrote horrible things about Pio and then converted. Alberto Del Fante was a respected author who had been so nasty to Pio in the newspapers of that time that it seemed impossible he would ever convert, and yet he did — we'll do a deep dive into his conversion later. There was also the conversion of Dr. Francesco Ricciardi, a medical doctor by profession and a passionate atheist. A vocal denier of God's existence, Francesco loudly made known his views in public. He wasn't a benign atheist; Francesco lived inches from the friary and maligned it as a "factory of charlatans."[320]

Dr. Ricciardi was the medic whom Fr. Prencipe was trying to convert, and Prencipe had even demanded that Pio perform some sort of miracle in the center of town so that Ricciardi would believe. The doctor was something of an exceptional figure in San Giovanni because, even though he held Pio in contempt and was on the side of those who wanted Pio's ministry stopped, he was also beloved by his fellow people because he was most generous in treating people who couldn't pay him and never sent a bill to a poor person. He was the only member of the anti-Pio faction that the locals loved and respected. Truly, he had exhibited extraordinary charity in his care of the sick.

Ricciardi was an old friend of fickle Prencipe, while also aligning himself with Pio's foremost enemy, Archbishop Gagliardi. He backed Gagliardi to the hilt, ignorantly, because there is no way he could have been properly informed of all the archbishop's misdeeds. Late in the year 1928, Dr. Ricciardi learned that cancer of the stomach was laying his body to waste, and that there was no hope of a cure. He was only sixty-seven, but soon he was at death's door. Fr. Prencipe visited the physician to try his hand at converting his old chum. When Prencipe arrogantly marched into his friend's sick chamber, Ricciardi threw a slipper at his head and Prencipe had to scuttle away. The doctor informed the cleric, "I intend to die as I have lived." The grim reaper was approaching, but Ricciardi was not going to become a believer to please Prencipe. He revealed a hidden desire to clear his conscience, however, in another outburst directed at Fr. Prencipe. "Only Padre Pio could hear my confession," he roared. "But I've insulted him too greatly for him to come."

All the same Pio was called on to see if he might assist the atheist doctor. Snow was falling heavily and powdering the town white when Padre Pio hastened on his pierced feet to Ricciardi's home, outside of which in the street there was a group of local people on their knees praying for the doctor to convert. Snow settled on their heads and shoulders as Pio shuffled into Ricciardi's dwelling. Snow dusted Pio's brown habit as he greeted the dying man with the warmest of smiles. His heart melted by Pio's compassion, he said, "Forgive me, Padre Pio."

Then he gladly confessed his sins and was granted absolution. Dr. Ricciardi then received Holy Communion from Pio and, when his loved ones were allowed into his bedroom again, they saw his face glistening with tears. The doctor's family were stupefied. Then Pio gave the doctor the happy news that his soul was healed and his body, too! This was a harbinger of the healing awaiting the doctor. Three days later his cancer began receding, and Ricciardi hastened to the friary, where he made profound thanksgiving to Almighty God. He left the anti-Pio faction and became Pio's stalwart supporter.

Although this was an occasion for a double celebration of the doctor's conversion and his miraculous cure, we should bear in mind that Pio offered remarkable and complete forgiveness and showed the doctor who had smeared him such a level of goodness as to prove his saintliness to everyone who witnessed the chain of events. It is the better part to choose Pio's example, but Pio could also read the doctor's soul and had certain knowledge as to his genuine contrition, which enabled Pio to give him absolution. We who are not graced with Pio's gift of knowing souls work more by trial and error, hopefully forgiving someone totally as Christ commands us, but ascertaining through experience whether they are properly contrite. As we will see a little later, Pio always forgave, but he did not always give absolution on the same occasion. There were those Pio made wait.

20

Persecution and Imprisonment

Don Prencipe survived Dr. Ricciardi's throwing a slipper at his head. To be fair, Prencipe had wanted the doctor's conversion for many years. When Dr. Ricciardi returned to the Faith, the anti-Pio faction lost an influential member. Their numbers, however, were swelled when the priests of the neighboring city of Manfredonia joined them. These men of the cloth were resentful for the same reasons; their churches were emptying and people trusted Pio with their money. But Fr. Prencipe had a new quarrel with Pio, one which gave Gagliardi further grounds to excoriate Pio as a "horrible" confessor.

For over two decades, Prencipe satisfied his lusts with a live-in mistress, Maria Di Maggio. Prencipe lured her into bed, falsely assuring her that Sacred Scripture allowed for a priest to be with a woman once a month. When Maria confessed to Pio, she was denied absolution, because she was still sleeping with Prencipe. And until she stopped, Pio would not absolve her.

Wanting to be in a state of grace, Maria started refusing Prencipe's advances, at which point, according to her sworn testimony, Prencipe tried to rape her. (She later retracted her statement, saying instead that Prencipe threatened to murder her if she didn't accede to his advance.) Archbishop Gagliardi flew to Prencipe's defense and used the example of Maria being denied absolution to further his claim that Pio left souls in distress. No censure was brought to bear on Prencipe for attempting to rape Maria or threating to kill her.

Then Gagliardi tried a new tactic: He told more plausible lies. He orchestrated anonymous letters littered with these falsehoods: that Pio demanded that all his spiritual children were not to let eight days pass between Confessions and that Pio was loitering around the confessional to chat with female penitents.

Things became much more problematic for Pio when the provincial, Padre Pietro, fell dead from cardiac arrest. Only forty-four when he died, Pietro's was a great loss because he was very understanding of Pio and had a delicate way of dealing with both supporters and detractors. Pio's new superior was Padre Bernardo, a much more unyielding and authoritarian figure, who suspected Pio was guilty of infractions and wanted Pio removed from San Giovanni Rotondo.

Working with Vatican officials, Bernardo devised strategies to bring about Pio's removal, and he sought the help of the police force in San Giovanni Rotondo and Italy at large, though they were reluctant to cooperate. The Holy Office wanted Pio to be sequestered and to live anonymously in a monastery where the local people would never see him or even know he was there. Although Bernardo was a gifted administrator, he showed hardheartedness toward Pio, and he seemed to harbor hostility toward his fellow friar. Bernardo assiduously enacted the stringent measures from the Vatican, and around the time of Miscio's attempted blackmail of Michele, Bernardo commanded Pio not to allow his pierced hands to be kissed by the faithful. This, however, put Pio under a lot of pressure, because the pilgrims were determined to press their lips to the wounds of Christ. The way penitents, especially women, knelt to kiss Pio's hands bothered Bernardo. Bernardo began to wonder if some of the allegations made in the anonymous letters were indeed true.

Pio was offended that his superior thought he was commanding Confessions. We may ask, Wouldn't Bernardo have known that Pio wasn't ordering his spiritual children to confess? Yet, Confession is a private affair between penitent and priest, the words that pass between them are secret, and if Pio had been ordering his spiritual sons and daughters to confess at least every eight days, Bernardo would not have heard it. None of Padre Pio's spiritual children were spreading the lie that Pio compelled them to confess their sins within a time frame — because he was not doing so. He was *advising* them to confess weekly, but it was never a demand.

While Bernardo doubted him, Pio fell into a deep depression and passed through a new phase of a dark night of the soul, which was his spiritual preparation for his upcoming imprisonment. Pio tried to soften Bernardo's heart by writing to him and confiding in him. The Lord had distanced Himself from the stigmatist, so much so that his soul was entirely bereft of Jesus' presence, and Pio told Bernardo, "My spirit has felt alone — totally alone." Pio lamented that he felt "abandoned by everybody." Pio sorely doubted himself, and although he was converting enemies such as Fr. Miscio and Dr. Ricciardi and bringing into the fold those who had sung to Satan such as Friedrich Abresch, he made known that he was unhappy with his own state and wanted to turn from his sin, and he cried out to Bernardo, "Here is what I constantly ask of Jesus: my conversion."[321]

Pio was in a tight spot. He could not agree to the lies about him, yet he held himself in the lowest repute and wanted to assure his provincial that he was making every effort toward sanctity. But Pio's attempts to win Bernardo's empathy were not successful, and Bernardo thought Pio was flouting his authority by allowing people, especially women, to kiss his hand, even after he had told Pio not to let them. This made Bernardo feel that Pio was defying him behind his back.

To be fair, this was a regular sight, for people compulsively kissed Pio's hands over and over, and it fed the rumors that Gagliardi was spreading. When Bernardo presented Pio with these same allegations, Pio was so devastated that he said to Bernardo, "I feel my very soul ripped up." He stated unequivocally that he was the victim of malevolent mendacity: "My Father, what infamy they have written, knowing that they were lying and that they wanted to lie in a slanderous way."[322]

Pio admitted that he had yelled at penitents to stop them from grabbing his hands and smothering them with kisses, but it had not deterred them. The public saw the gruff, angry Pio, but in private he was being castigated for the passionate piety of his followers. People saw Pio react crossly and heard him shouting in church when they grasped at his pierced palms, but they did not know that Pio had been solemnly forbidden from allowing his hands to be caressed and kissed. This molded Pio's reputation as one who had pent-up rage. Pio was being pulled in two directions, torn between the wants of the pilgrims and the demands of his superiors. This persecution made him long for death, and he prayed before Bernardo, "My God, cut short my exile, as I can't take it anymore!"[323] Instead of having sympathy with Pio, Bernardo demanded that Pio hide from visitors, not greeting them but only nodding at them. He directed Pio to avoid women as much as possible and to use the threat of denying them absolution to keep them at bay. Bernardo took a dim view of the local people and thought of them as fanatics. And he threatened Pio that if he did not keep his spiritual daughters in line, he would be denied permission to hear their confessions.

Subtle Strategies

These more subtle strategies of Gagliardi meant he was successfully maligning Pio, but the people of his archdiocese hated him more than ever and the air was filled with vile stories about the controversial archbishop. There was a wicked irony in that although Gagliardi was persecuting Pio, he was also making things worse for himself and even hastening his removal as archbishop, but his hate for the stigmatist ruled his actions. Over the more than ten years from the time he first gave Pio the faculties to hear Confession in 1917, Gagliardi had engaged fewer and fewer good priests in his archdiocese, and as he had always done, he allowed nefarious, abusive priests to stay in their positions as long as they had similar proclivities to him and were against Pio, and he accepted bribes from bad priests so that they could get lucrative assignments. But Gagliardi punished decent, holy priests if they showed favor to Pio and went so far as to suspend two priests who had visited Pio on his name day, the feast of Pope St. Pius V, so that they could wish him a happy feast. Any priest who had the pluck to speak up against Gagliardi was swiftly chastised.

One person who did not support Gagliardi but who also did not want to see the archbishop castigated was Pio's mother, Giuseppa. When she was in earshot of those who criticized the bishop, she put an abrupt end to any gossip against Gagliardi and asked, "Who are we to permit criticism of the ministers of God?"[324] It's not that Giuseppa defended her son's detractors; rather, she felt that if she criticized Gagliardi, she was engaging in the same behavior as he was, because he was criticizing her son.

Pio's Mother Grows Ill

Giuseppa came to live at San Giovanni Rotondo in the same month that Dr. Ricciardi was converted and cured. Mary Pyle brought her from Pietrelcina, settled her into the pink castle, and lovingly tended to her every need. Giuseppa looked gaunt and was on the verge of death. Ensconced in Mary's home, she coughed constantly, and she warmed the air with the fever that raged through her body. She had come to be near her son during her last days on earth. Her health and strength were greatly diminished, but she had not lost her pithy way of speaking or her fierce frankness, and any chatter condemning Gagliardi and the prelates who persecuted her son was brought to a swift end by Giuseppa, who would then reason, "The Lord said that we ought not judge if we do not wish to be judged ourselves, and this means that we should judge neither the good nor the evil, because we can see only the deeds people do, whilst God alone can see into people's hearts the reason why they do them."[325]

She was dying, but every day she went on her hands and knees to kiss the floor of the church that her son had just walked on after giving her Holy Communion. Mary Pyle was a witness to the last time Giuseppa went to her son's Mass, on the feast of Christmas. But Giuseppa was also doing the most forensic examination of her conscience, something that became obvious in a conversation she had with her son. After Christmas Mass ended, Giuseppa sought out her son in the sacristy and asked him a question in response to which he illuminated essential truths which are of infinite value to us. Giuseppa inquired, "Padre Pio, how can we know if before God we are not great sinners?" Pio's attention was consumed by his mama and he said, "If we put into our confessions all our goodwill and we have the intention to confess everything — all that we can know or remember — the mercy of God is so great that He will include and erase even what we cannot remember or know."[326] For us it bears emphasizing that Padre Pio placed importance on having the intention to confess "everything." After receiving this inspired truth from her son, Giuseppa went back to Mary's home and promptly lost all her strength and went to bed for the last time. The same woman who had made a total offering of her little baby to St. Francis and who had slaved to run the farm on her own while her husband was in America earning the money to put their son through school was about to receive her great reward in Heaven. The doctors said her lungs were full of fluid and her death was at hand. The local people waited with bated breath to see if Pio would intercede for his own mother to be miraculously cured, but instead he conformed himself to God's will.

In the early hours of a January morn, Giuseppa kissed the crucifix as the light left her crystal blue eyes. When Pio saw his mama's dead body, he howled and was reduced to weeping for many days. He was so overcome with grief, he could not attend Giuseppa's funeral. Pio, however, had not asked for his mama to get more time, and Giuseppa was spared Pio's imprisonment, a time when she could have been tempted to turn on her son's enemies.

Emanuele Traps Pio's Enemies

Emanuele could not have been more different from Giuseppa, and not only did he engage in open criticism of the clergy who castigated Pio, he went so far as to write a book, *Padre Pio of Pietrelcina*, which detailed exhaustively the misdeeds and immoral lifestyles of the anti-Pio faction, and it was buttressed with so much lurid proof that it was impossible to sue Emanuele without proving him correct in court. Emanuele gave Cardinal Gasparri a copy. Gasparri agreed with its contents and told Emanuele that because of the book, the pope had ordered a thorough investigation into Gagliardi, an "apostolic visitation."

Pius XI ordained this forensic fact-finding mission to assess how fit Gagliardi was to rule his archdiocese. And Emanuele was part of the team! Pius was not as badly disposed toward Pio as he had been, but His Holiness was also giving his blessing to the plans that were being made to take Pio out of San Giovanni. And there was division among the princes of the Church who were Pius's closest advisers. Gagliardi had a blindly loyal friend in a cardinal who also had the ear of the bespeckled pope: He was Cardinal DeLai, and sadly he covered up — perhaps unaware of its extent — Gagliardi's corruption. Although Pio had Gasparri and his old friend Bishop Valbonesi, who spoke of Gagliardi as though he found him repulsive, Pio's enemies also had their friends. There was also the fact that the Holy Office, to save face, bought every copy of Emanuele's book that they could find and even had it banned. To be fair, it was a scandalous book, with pornographic content, and perhaps the Vatican wished to spare the masses from having their purity compromised.

Several months after Giuseppa's sad passing, Pio had a dream on May 5, which was the feast of St. Pius V, the saint after whom Pio was named. In the dream Pope Pius V appeared to Pio and said that Archbishop Gagliardi would be deposed. This came to pass after the investigation which had been caused by Emanuele's book had been concluded. A report was written holding him responsible for destructive mismanagement of his archdiocese. Gagliardi retired to his place of birth and set down his shepherd's staff for good.

Raffaele Replaced?

At this point in the game, Pio's immediate superior at the friary was Padre Raffaele. The Holy Office proposed to the Capuchins that they replace Raffaele with a superior from further away. Raffaele, however, had not done anything wrong, and he had been diligent in following the directives from the Vatican to restrain Pio's ministry. The prelates at the Vatican suspected Raffaele because he was Southern and they felt Southern Italian piety gave rise to the scenes of hysteria and fanaticism at San Giovanni. But Raffaele, only three years younger than Pio, was a rare character in that he combined meekness with authority; he was a good leader and slow to anger.

Bernardo put this idea before Pope Pius XI: If Pio could not be moved up North, where he would be with more cool-blooded Northerners, then he had better be under the control of a superior not from the region. Raffaele was indeed informed that he was to be replaced by a superior from Milan, which was meant to be a closely guarded secret, but Emanuele got wind of it through his Vatican connections. Soon it was an open secret that Raffaele was to be replaced, and this did not go down well with the people of San Giovanni Rotondo! The locals only knew the new superior was likely to be from the North, which they thought of as a foreign country, and they jumped to the conclusion that this was part of an undercover plan to have Pio moved away. The actions they took were drastic but effective. They erected barricades on the streets, so no cars could go in or out of the friary — they feared that if a car got into the friary grounds, it would be the vehicle that would take their saint out of their midst. Panicked as they were, the locals armed themselves and kept the friary surrounded, taking turns keeping watch. Often, a narcissistic, fake "holy man" is loathed by the people near him because they are close enough to see through the disguise. The local people surrounding Pio were so convinced of his sanctity and they loved him so much they made it their full-time occupation to keep him with them. But they went too far and were at least partly responsible for Pio's time of imprisonment.

Things reached a crescendo when a priest traveled to visit Pio. He was Fr. Eugenio and regrettably for him, Mayor Francesco Morcaldi was on the same bus and got it into his head that this priest was the dreaded interloper who would replace Raffaele and then arrange for Pio to be moved far away. Little did Eugenio know he would be the catalyst for a cataclysmic chain of events. When he arrived at the friary, Morcaldi was busy telling the local people that this priest was the new superior. On hearing this, they swiftly became an angry mob and surrounded the friary, screeching that they wanted to tear this "foreigner" to shreds. Demanding that he be handed over to them, they yanked out a light pole and used it as a battering ram to break down the friary door. They rammed the door open and found Raffaele, who stood in their way and used his wide waist and large frame to stem the tide of protesters and then promised them that Pio would come and speak to them.

Pio hastened to the window of the choir and tried to calm the crowd as he cooed, "My blessed children … I implore you to listen to me, as you always do, and return to your homes without harming anyone." He went on to explain that Eugenio had come to see him for "spiritual reasons,"[327] but the crowd didn't buy it; they thought Padre Pio was being forced out of obedience to say this, and when Pio saw his words were having no influence on them, he left the window and withdrew to his room. At around this time Morcaldi was allowed into the friary so he could speak with Pio, who put him right as to Eugenio's true identity. Morcaldi went back out to address the crowd of protesters, who still bayed to taste the foreigner's blood, but he was successful in calming them, and he assured them that Eugenio-the-foreigner would be leaving in a few hours.

When the Vatican prelates heard that a mad mob had smashed in the friary door and had been intent on murdering someone to prevent their saint being taken away, they took immediate action. The pope himself bound Pio with this stringent directive: "Padre Pio is to be stripped of all the faculties of his priestly ministry except the faculty to celebrate the Holy Mass."[328] But he was only to celebrate Mass in private, secluded in the friary, and never publicly in church. No one was to be present at the Mass except one assistant. They were incarcerating Pio in the very friary where he already lived, imprisoning him in much the same way as if they had been able to move him to a faraway monastery. When Raffaele read the Vatican directive, Pio showed total submission, saying, "God's will be done."[329] Covering his brown eyes with his brown mittens, he said meaningfully, "The will of the authorities is the will of God."[330]

Yet, when Fr. Agostino spoke to him three weeks later, he found Pio dejected and his face tearstained. "I never thought this would happen," he said to Agostino, who was no Job's comforter; instead, he reaffirmed what Pio already knew: "Jesus wants it this way. Let His will be done." Agostino gave Pio the best encouragement when he told him that this new phase in his personal crucifixion could go toward the salvation of souls — the most important thing to

Pio. "You must remain hanging on the cross," his brother Capuchin said. "Men will continue to nail you to it, but in the end everything will work out for the glory of God and the good of souls."[331] When Pio heard this, he wept, and he humbly embraced the extreme limitations placed on him, whereby most of his faculties were removed, the same sanction often given to delinquent priests.

Bilocation Adventures

Many of us say we wish we had lived during Padre Pio's lifetime, but had we been alive from 1931 to 1933 and wanted to see Pio face to face, we would have had no chance to do so, unless he bilocated to us. Throughout these years, Pio did bilocate often. These must have been like vacations for Pio. Once, he even bilocated to the glitteringly beautiful Florence. He went there to visit a nun, Sr. Beniamina, who was in a state of anxiety. Without any warning, she was greeted by Pio, who soothed her nerves and blessed her. When he was not offering Holy Mass, Pio prayed and read Sacred Scripture. When he was in a good mood, he played practical jokes. But he was often despondent because he was away from the confessional, his natural habitat. And he endured enforced estrangement from his spiritual children. His spirit was very up and down. At times, he was joyful and said Jesus was appearing to him. But otherwise, he looked depressed; he was experiencing a dark night of the soul and said Jesus was not talking to him.

Pained by hard doubts that he was living up to Our Lord's expectations, he confided in Agostino, "I would prefer a thousand crosses to this ordeal of never feeling certain I'm pleasing the Lord in what I'm doing."[332] What saved him was that he was able to offer Holy Mass every day, and later we will see that he pleaded with the Vatican that it could take everything from him except the Most Holy Eucharist.

21

"You Want to See Jesus?"

Pio's imprisonment lasted two years, from Thursday, June 11, 1931, to Wednesday, July 12, 1933. During these years, Padre Pio was stripped of all his faculties apart from offering Mass privately. In honor of this time, this chapter is devoted to the Mass of Pio, particularly as he offered it during his imprisonment, when there was no enormous congregation or teeming hordes pushing to get into the chapel, when a solitary silence surrounded the stigmatist.

Each morning Pio's alarm clock erupted at 2:30 a.m. for his lengthy Mass preparations; he meditated and prayed as many Rosaries as possible in the hours before he went to the altar. The other friars saw him moving rosary beads between his fingers — as Pio had seen Grazio do constantly when he was a boy — as he walked to the sacristy so he could vest.

As time went on, Pio's face became increasingly pale and a deathly solemnity overcame him. On that altar, Pio was about to experience mystically the Crucifixion and death of Our Lord. Draping the sacred vestments upon his shoulders, Pio walked into the chapel praying the Miserere; in a low voice he begged God for mercy and that he be washed of his sin. The tone of Pio's voice was one of utter self-abasement. With slow, unsteady steps, he climbed to the altar as though he were climbing the rock-road to Calvary. Pio looked weighed down, as though the cross were on his back. The door of the chapel was closed firmly to outsiders. Pio's Mass could last up to four hours. The only two people there were Pio and the altar server.

Although there were only two people bodily present, I invite you to discern: When Pio offered Mass, did he see you? During his life, Pio said that every time he offered Mass, he saw "all" of his children, and by "all" he meant all the souls God had entrusted to his care. If we take Pio strictly at his word, "all" meant that no soul was left out of this vision: all the souls of his spiritual children who were alive then and all the souls of his spiritual children yet to be born. I believe Pio saw my soul and may have seen your soul, too. As he told his beloved Cleonice, "I see all my children who come to the altar, as if in a mirror."[333] Were you to pray to Pio, he might reveal to you whether you are one of the souls entrusted to him and whether he saw you when he offered Holy Mass.

Pio also revealed that Our Lady is present at every single Holy Mass: "How can the mother of Jesus, present on Calvary at the foot of the Cross, who offered her Son as victim for the salvation of souls, be absent at the mystical Calvary of the altar?"[334] Whenever you assist at Holy Mass, Our Lady is also present, and you are in her company. The difference is that we believe this by faith, but Pio could see Our Lady. There was an intimate bond between Pio and Our Lady, which owes to him being the bearer of her Son's wounds. Our Lady never left Pio, who was bleeding from the wounds of her Son's Crucifixion, in the same manner Our Lady never left the foot of the Cross, where she watched her Son's blood rain down from His hands and feet.

Our Lord did not just give Pio His wounds, He gave him His mother to comfort him. Our Lady lavished attention on Pio, and he was known to boast, "She treats me as if I were her only child on the face of the earth."[335] Jesus was Our Lady's only biological child, and there is a parallel with Pio because Our Lady treated him like her only child in the world, her eyes fixed on him as her eyes were fixed on Our Lord hanging from the Cross.

Pio also made it known that at every Mass, "The whole celestial court is present."[336] Pio was privileged to be with all the angels, every saint who has ever lived, the Queen of Heaven, and the sea of souls who were entrusted to him. Truly an enormous number of souls.

The Readings

During every Mass Pio offered, his true character shone through more than at any other time. Pio read the epistle and the Gospel extremely calmly; Christ's peace infused every word that Pio said so delicately. In these moments, no one could accuse him of being angry, as they so often did otherwise. At times his head twitched as though he were being bothered by invisible pests, perhaps a demonic attack. On other occasions, Pio looked like he was trying to avoid being consumed by ecstasy as he sanctified the air with the words of Sacred Scripture. Pio's Mass became the Cross at Calvary. Pio defined the Holy Sacrifice of the

Mass as "Gethsemane, Calvary, the altar! Three places of which the third is the sum of the first and second."[337]

When Pio offered Mass, he suffered all the physical pains Our Lord suffered on the Cross. "I suffer inadequately all that Jesus suffered on the Cross," he said, but he carefully qualified this point by explaining that it only concerned his fallen human nature: "I suffer … as much as is possible for a human creature."[338]

In the Presence of Our Lady

Our Lady suffered more than any human in seeing her Son crucified — she, the Immaculate Conception. No mere human with Original Sin could suffer more than God's mother. Pio was acutely aware of this; at Mass he would often preach about the Immaculate Conception. Our own salvation, like Pio's, began when Our Lady was conceived. As Pio said, "The Immaculate Conception is the first step on the path to salvation."[339]

Now, let us draw a crucial distinction between Our Lord and Pio. Jesus had two natures, human and divine, but Pio had only a human nature. As a human creature, Pio's agony during Mass was limited to the full capacity a son of Adam has for agony. Whereas Pio experienced Christ's Crucifixion in his human nature, Christ experienced the Crucifixion in both His human nature and His divine nature simultaneously. Pio revealed that what sustained Our Lord on the Cross also sustained him. Once, Pio was asked, "You are nailed to the Cross for the whole duration of Mass?" and Pio replied, "Yes." When asked how he did not collapse while he offered Mass and suffered a crucifixion, Pio said, "In the same way as Jesus remained upright on the Cross."[340] Pio always suffered the wounds of crucifixion, and not just at the altar, but he made known that he suffered more intensely when he offered the Holy Sacrifice.

The Offertory and Consecration

At the Offertory, when Pio offered to God the Father the bread and wine that were about to undergo transubstantiation, his eyes were riveted upon the crucifix. Raising the paten and chalice, his sleeves fell and the lesions on his hands could be seen in all their bloodiness; his body contracted painfully, his teeth grinding in agony. Heavy tears fell from his eyes like rainfall. The sacred, shared union between Pio and Christ was consummated as he took in his hands the

Divine Victim. Tears turned to ecstasy when he elevated the Host. Pio was seen smiling with joy on beholding his Savior, who was under the appearance of bread. In that moment, Pio offered his agony in atonement for the sins of mankind. Although Pio was not divine and not the Savior, he was an instrument in the redemption of souls, including your soul and mine.

It was also during the consecration that Pio could be seen wearing three braided crowns of thorns upon his head, like a large hat of thorns, while blood streamed down his face. When Cleonice asked Pio which sins Jesus paid for with the crown of thorns, Pio answered, "All of them, particularly sinful thoughts."[341]

Pio clarified to Cleonice that nothing that happened to him during Mass was of his own doing: "All of it at no merit of my own and only because of His Goodness." While Pio suffered "all" of the sufferings of Christ's Crucifixion proper to his human nature, the graces that came through Pio's agony came from Christ's goodness. Although Pio was given "all" the human sufferings of Our Lord, Pio collaborated by fully accepting all the pain. Pio may have been a mortal man, but he offered up his entire human nature to be filled with pain. This was Pio's gift and the way he assisted in the work of our salvation. But Pio was not the cause of our salvation; Jesus was the cause. Although Pio suffered the same agony in his human flesh as Christ did, Pio was wholly dependent on Our Lord's sacrifice for his own salvation. When Pio offered Mass, his face was wet with tears and had a heavenly glow. "You want to see Jesus?" he once said. "Look at my face during Mass, you will see Jesus."[342]

A Mystical Death

When he offered the Holy Sacrifice of the Mass, Padre Pio experienced the exact process of being crucified, including a mystical death. "I die mystically during Holy Communion," he said. We might readily think he died of pain, but no, he said his death on the altar was from "love rather than pain."[343] Before Pio consumed the Body of Christ, he beat his chest in a self-punishing, violent way and pronounced the words "Lord, I am not worthy" with palpable humility.

After receiving the Body and Blood of Christ, Pio bowed low, remaining a long time in this submissive posture. He went from being a victim to worshipping the Victim; after Pio shared all the agony and the physical death of Our Lord, he went to his knees to adore the Divine Victim. He worshipped Our Lord as you and I are meant to do, for we are invited to have the same disposition as Pio. When he had rendered sufficient thanks to Our Lord, he cleared the paten and chalice with great care. At the end of Mass, when he read the Last Gospel, his voice trembled when he uttered the words "and the Word was made flesh."

A Mass Meditation

Pio said that our encounter with Christ at the Mass is the same as though we were meeting Him at the places of His Passion. This was true of Pio's Mass, but it is also true of every Holy Mass where we may assist: We are at the same time before the altar and at Calvary. Pio spoke of the disposition we need to have: "When you attend Mass, renew your faith. Keep your mind in the high spheres of the mystery which is unfolding before your eyes. Let your mind transport you to the scene on Calvary and meditate on the victim who is offering himself to divine justice, paying the price of your redemption."[344]

We may be tempted to think that it would have been better had we assisted at Pio's Mass than at the Mass we may assist at today, but Pio said, "Every Holy Mass, heard with devotion, produces in our souls marvelous effects, abundant spiritual and material graces which we ourselves do not know."[345] Taking Pio at his word, every time we assist devoutly at Mass, our soul is enriched with marvels and graces. Pio often saying voiced this spectacular insight: "The earth could subsist without the sun, but it could not subsist without the Mass."[346] Pio regularly revealed that were we to know how highly the Almighty esteems the Mass, we would go to great lengths to get there. "If we only knew how God regards this Sacrifice," he declared, "we would risk our lives to be present at a single Mass."[347]

PIO IS FREED BY HIS CHILDREN

Pio's imprisonment was wholly unjust. He was treated like a criminal, though he had never committed a crime. The pope had stripped Pio of all his priestly faculties except offering Mass in private, a punishment that could have gone on for many, many years, had his spiritual children not intervened in dramatic ways.

Throughout it all, Pio's spiritual daughters came together in the church every morning and prayed for Pio's liberation. While they were there, Pio was high above their heads, in the choir. He was in prayer, too, but his daughters were never allowed the briefest glimpse of him because he was prohibited from going near the railing. The only person from the outside world allowed to visit Pio was Pietro Cugino, who ran errands for the stigmatist. Pietro had such a discrete and dutiful nature that he didn't speak of his time with Pio and never bragged about this privilege or gossiped about the goings-on inside the friary.

Pio's Defenders Arise

Others made great sacrifices to intervene on behalf of their dear spiritual father: One daughter offered her life for Pio's liberation, and Emanuele risked being sent to jail. Beloved Mary Pyle became a victim of injustice, and she shared acutely in Pio's plight when the Vatican banned the publication of all books and pamphlets about Pio. Even so, works that argued for Pio as being a man of God came into circulation, including books by seasoned journalist Alberto Del Fante and Dr. Giorgio Festa. Emanuele wrote an incendiary book, *The Anti-Christs in the Church of Christ,* much like the previous one in which he took to task Pio's local enemies, but this time Emanuele aimed to expose the Vatican prelates. Emanuele paid a heavy price, but he may have had the biggest practical role in freeing Pio. Another person who had a colossal role was a future pope, Cardinal Eugenio Pacelli, who worked slavishly to soften the heart of Pius XI toward the stigmatist.

Let us first turn our attention to the daughter who made the highest sacrifice. Earlier we met Lucia Fiorentino. We recall that Jesus favored the raven-haired lady with a vision of Pio's mission; Lucia saw Pio as a gigantic tree and that whoever took shelter under him was rewarded with salvation. Lucia offered her life for Pio's freedom and return to monastic life. She explained her rationale in this way: "My life is not worth as much as his."[348]

Our Lord accepted Lucia's offering, and previously, Jesus had spoken to her about Pio's soul. "I am the one who acts in that soul, I have found all the favorable dispositions and have descended into him," He said to here. "Everything that Padre Pio does is completely permitted by Me.... I will make him great, this son of Mine, who adheres to My will even at a heavy price of horrible pain.... I am very pained by everything that is happening." Then the Lord shared with Lucia, "He is My trumpet, through which my voice passes and announces truth." Throughout the seventeen years that Lucia knew Pio, he had assured her that the messages she received from Jesus were true and not a deception or imagination. As she lay on her deathbed, Lucia did not regret it. She said of Padre Pio, "He can do more good for souls than I."[349] She was only forty-four.

Our old friend Dr. Giorgio Festa penned a fine book on the miraculous nature of the stigmata entitled *The Mysteries of Science in Light of Faith*. But it looked like this book could not be published because of the Vatican ban. Cardinal Gasparri showed himself to be quite the hero: he convinced the Holy Office not to put Festa's book on the Index of Forbidden Books, and an exception was made for its publication. Consequently, the book enjoyed a good reception among the powerful princes of the Church who were pro-Pio. But other books caused panic in the Vatican and became the paper wedges that divided Pio's ardent supporters.

Alberto Del Fante teamed up with an extremely pious lady, Carolina Giovannini, and together they wrote and published, in defiance of the Vatican, the controversial *Padre Pio: Messenger of the Lord*, which contained many miracle stories and sought to enshrine Pio as a true saint. It was seen as Del Fante's way of embarrassing the Vatican prelates who were treating Pio as anything but God's emissary, and as retribution the book was swiftly banned and the Holy Office further curtailed the ministry of the Franciscans in San Giovanni by ordering the closure of the Seraphic College for young men considering a vocation.

While Carolina Giovannini had been writing *Padre Pio: Messenger of the Lord*, Mary Pyle was accused of feeding the author sensationalized stories of her beloved spiritual father. And when the college closed, possibly signaling that Pio's imprisonment was permanent, Mary took the brunt. Even Agostino turned on Mary, and she was roundly rejected by the locals. She received the silent treatment for months on end, and when she knelt to receive Holy Communion people made space around her. Mary suffered even more intensely because she could not get any comfort from her spiritual father.

Intent on forcing the Vatican's hand, Emanuele ruthlessly dug up dirt on the Vatican's financial corruption and the sordid secrets of the "lavender mafia." He had been a successful con man in his youth, and was someone who could distinguish a truth-teller from a liar; he was especially good at smelling cover-ups. When he was done, his book shocked the world.

Mayor Morcaldi took Emanuele to task, insisting that the book not be used to strongarm the Vatican. This only riled Emanuele, who began flashing his book in the faces of the bishops he had the goods on. Had Emanuele not been able to prove all his findings, he would almost certainly have gotten a criminal sentence. It was still a big risk for him to take, because had Pio's enemies found the tiniest glitch in Emanuele's account, perhaps a detail that he could not substantiate, they could have sued for libel.

Emanuele's book also got a strong reaction from a prelate whom we know well. Twelve years had passed since Bishop Raffaello Carlo Rossi had conducted his forensic inspection of Pio. Rossi was now a cardinal, and although he had softened toward Pio because of the celestial scent, he always remained more on the side of his fellow princes of the Church.

Cardinal Rossi dispatched two officials from the Holy Office to speak with Pio, in the hope that Pio would intervene and prevent Emanuele from disseminating his book. Msgr. Pasetto and Msgr. Bevilacqua journeyed to see Pio, and when they reached the friary, they had to pass through the armed guard of local people who surrounded the entrance 24/7 so no one could steal their saint away. When they encountered Pio, they found him willing to defer to them, and he was sweet-tempered and not the least bit bitter. The two monsignors expressed grave concern that Emanuele's scandalous book could destroy the reputations of certain bishops. Like an innocent child, Pio presumed the accounts were false and proposed, "Refute the episodes alleged in the book that could create a scandal."[350]

Tears welled up in Bevilacqua's eyes as he conceded, "Those allegations are true."[351] This gave Pio a shock, as he had not thought it possible for his leaders to be complicit in all sorts of sexual and financial misconduct. In the end an agreement was struck: The bishops would intervene with the Holy Father, and Pio would persuade Emanuele not to publish a book that would unquestionably damage the Church.

When the monsignors returned to Rome, they put before Pius XI's round-spectacled eyes a lovely report on Pio. Pio kept his promise and begged Emanuele to hold back from making the book available, instructing him to burn his book, which he said revealed "what no human being ought know."[352] There is a galling irony here, in that Pio's correspondence was generally stifled — except when it was thought fit for Pio to protect the reputation of the very men who wanted his ministry stopped.

However, Emanuele could not be moved. He intuited that Pio was under obedience to deter him, and he was more gung ho than ever. This meant that Emanuele was roundly hated by Pio's superiors, who banned him from coming near Pio ever again: He was forbidden to enter the friary and treated like an outcast. Even so, Emanuele would not stop pursuing Pio's persecutors. Throughout the first half of 1933 Emanuele continued to hold the book over the heads of the Vatican hierarchy, blackmailing them with the threat that he would make the book available far and wide if they did not liberate Pio. Although this was a dirty tactic, it was effective. It silenced Pio's enemies and allowed the voice of one prince to be heard clear as a bell. This man was Cardinal Eugenio Pacelli, who later became Pope Pius XII.

Pacelli Persuades Pius XI

At the time, Cardinal Pacelli was fifty-seven, two decades younger than Pius XI, who trusted him implicitly and relied on him heavily. Cardinal Pacelli had dove-like eyes framed by round, gold-rimmed spectacles. He was tall and gaunt, with narrow shoulders. Born to a noble family in Rome, Pacelli was an ascetic. His thinness, however, owed more to lifelong serious stomach ailments.

Pacelli had been papal nuncio to Germany, and for three decades had been the protégé of Cardinal Gasparri. Pacelli may have caught a devotion to Pio from

Gasparri, and Pacelli copied his mentor's example in relation to the Franciscan mystic. When Gasparri retired as secretary of state, the role was given to Pacelli. Pacelli had been raised to be a prince of the Church. Many of his relatives held positions at the highest echelons, but they also considered themselves the humble servants of the pope. It was widely presumed that in working so closely with Pacelli, Pius XI was grooming his successor. Pius esteemed his abilities more highly than those of any other cardinal and was fond of him in a way that rivaled his fondness for Gemelli.

This was good news for Padre Pio. Pacelli led the pope to regard Pio more favorably. He could also rely on the positive reports that were arriving in the Vatican. The highly favorable report on Pio from Msgrs. Pasetto and Bevilacqua might never have been written had the two prelates not been compelled to visit Pio to ask him to rein in Emanuele. Added to the chorus of their voices was that of Archbishop Andrea Cesarano, who now held the role that had belonged to the disgraced Gagliardi. Cesarano was as good and virtuous as Gagliardi had been bad and corrupt. Cesarano, with a big nose and flowing beard, had not been in his role as shepherd very long when he took it upon himself to go to the Vatican and meet with Pope Pius XI and tell the granite-faced pope of Pio's goodness.

Pacelli was so keen for Pio's liberation that he convinced Pius XI to garner new intelligence from face-to-face observations of Pio and from those closest to him. Pius was given a file of sworn depositions from Pio's fellow friars, who spoke in defense of their angelic brother. After Pius had processed all the reports on Pio, the pope lifted a portion of the restrictions, allowing Pio to offer Mass in public and to hear the confessions of the other clergy. The pope acknowledged his action in liberating Pio was exceptional: "This is the first time that the Holy Office is retracting its decrees."[353]

Pius XI regretted the times he had relied exclusively on the anti-Pio faction, saying ruefully to Archbishop Cesarano, "I have not been badly disposed towards Padre Pio, but I have been badly informed about him."[354]

Pio's Restrictions Lifted

News of Pio returning to public ministry spread like wildfire on an intensely hot Sunday, on July 16, 1933. The announcement came in a most surprising — and subtle — form. Cleonice Morcaldi was in the church when she saw a friar placing the chalice on the altar, and she immediately understood the significance: Only when Pio celebrated Mass was the chalice set up beforehand.

Her heart was still racing when she saw a sea of people, somehow alerted to this significant development, rush into the church. Several of them kissed the ground with tears in their eyes. Through her own tears of joy, Cleonice saw Pio come out to offer Mass. He, too, was weeping with happiness. The congregation were weeping so many tears of relief that Pio commanded them, "Enough. No more crying!"[355]

As an act of thanksgiving for Pio's release, Cleonice walked on foot a sixteen-mile pilgrimage from San Giovanni to Monte Sant'Angelo. Mary Pyle had further psychological suffering after the imprisonment ended, and she was not immediately welcomed back into the hearts of the locals. The native Italians found it hard to forgive Mary for allegedly fueling the fires of fanatics who had caused the Vatican to keep their saint imprisoned.

Mary had also been a victim of intense jealousy. Of the community of spiritual daughters in the town, there were a couple who were intensely possessive of Pio. These few spiritual daughters would cause significant trouble for Pio in the decades ahead. But in 1934, when at last his faculties as a confessor were fully restored, they waged a dangerous vendetta against Mary.

When, for the first time in years, Mary was able to go to Pio for Confession, she braved the glares of the women who congregated around Pio's confessional. When she went into the box, Pio shouted at her, "Wretched one!"[356] All the other women heard this, but Mary was bewildered that Pio had loudly insulted her. And to us today, it seems unthinkably cruel; hadn't Mary poured her inheritance into building a Franciscan seminary in his home village?

Emerging from the confessional, Mary was greeted by the satisfied smiles of the women who resented her. The next time he had a minute alone with Mary, Pio told her the reason he had loudly scolded her: "Some of these women would have killed you because of the terrible resentment for you they had in their hearts."[357] He wanted to give the possessive women the impression that she had fallen afoul of his affections, to protect her from their jealousy.

Why had Pio not confronted his resentful daughters? He understood that severely jealous people cannot always be reasoned with, and if we take what

Pio said to Mary as being wholly true, perhaps he needed to do it to save her from violence.

As we will see, in the years to come some of these women hatched criminal plans born of their obsessiveness to have Pio all to themselves! At this time, however, these insecure spiritual daughters were made to feel secure that Pio did not esteem Mary more highly than he esteemed them. They were warmed by the knowledge Pio was not going to be taken from them and moved to a distant land. Also, they were able to assist at his Mass every morning, which satisfied their longing to be in his presence.

23

A Mission to Heal the Masses

Pio's imprisonment ended, and his golden era began. This period would last fifteen years, the rest of Eugenio Pacelli's lifetime. When Pius XI was still alive, he was being guided by Pacelli to leave Pio in peace, and he did not take any more punitive actions against the stigmatist. Gemelli still influenced Pius's thoughts, but Pacelli influenced his actions.

Gagliardi's replacement, Archbishop Cesarano, could not have been more favorable toward Pio, and blessedly he was going to be the local archbishop for the rest of Pio's life. We will meet him again in our story, especially during Pio's most savage persecution of the 1960s. At this time, however, Cesarano kept the anti-Pio faction in check, and because they had protested so much in the past, he was loathe to believe them. When in 1939 the hawk-nosed Cardinal Pacelli became Pope Pius XII, he told Cesarano to approach him freely whenever Pio needed anything.

The new minister general, Padre Donatus, was initially dubious about Pio and asked if the friar could be neurotic or fanatical. But he spent much time with Pio and thoroughly examined the stigmata. Donatus came away saying Pio was "a great saint," and he praised Pio's "sane piety."[358] Also, Fr. Bernardo, who had been such a control freak, went to his eternal reward and was replaced by beloved Fr. Agostino.

Fr. Georg Pogany

Another wonderful boon came in the form of Fr. Georg Pogany. Fr. Georg had initially come to Italy for treatment for kidney stones but took shelter in the friary of San Giovanni. Because he had Jewish blood, he was unable to go home — he would have been rounded up and sent to a concentration camp. Georg had a classic semitic face with dark almond eyes framed by round, wire-rimmed spectacles and a crown of black curls. He didn't smile much, but he had an innate solemnity and an almost scrupulous devotion to telling the unvarnished truth.

Pio developed a deep fondness for him, and Fr. Georg became Pio's confessor and secretary. Georg was born into a Jewish family in Hungary and, along with his identical twin brother, was baptized at age eight. His mother, Gabriella, was a most fervent Catholic convert who died in Auschwitz with her fingers wrapped round her crucifix.[359] Fr. Georg was Pio's confidant for seventeen years.

The Home for the Relief of Suffering

Pio was now in his mid-forties, and he used his freedom to make his most ambitious dream a reality: to build a spectacular hospital for San Giovanni Rotondo. The little St. Francis Civil Hospital, which Pio founded in 1925, had been destroyed in an earthquake. Providentially, it was empty, so there was no loss of life. But that hospital had been a few miles away, in the oldest part of town, and Pio wanted to build a brand-new hospital by his monastery, so that clinic for soul and clinic for body could be side by side.

Although it was frustrating not to be able to replace the St. Francis hospital immediately after the earthquake, Pio had a clear vision for the kind of hospital that was needed and understood that it would take time to realize this dream. He wanted to establish the best hospital in the world, where every sickness and disability could be treated by top-flight physicians, the poor and destitute would never pay a bill, and only the highest-quality medical technology would ever be used. There was a dire need for such a facility; thousands of sick pilgrims came on a weekly basis. It seemed a fantasy, and exorbitantly expensive, too. But it is believed that Jesus gave Pio this mission in the light of an ecstasy. Jesus then gave every grace to make it happen.

First Pio needed to raise the money — lots of it! Divine Providence touched the heart of a noblewoman, Countess Oliva Bajocchi, to give Pio the profits from an invention that would revolutionize the railway system. There was a patent for a new diesel engine that could be fitted in trains — previously trains had run on steam engines powered by burning coal fires. This design for an engine that could run on diesel fuel was worth a fortune.

Pio, however, could not go around the world producing these engines and selling them, so he enlisted Emanuele to do it. Some suspected that Emanuele, with his shady past, would bilk Pio, but Pio could see Emanuele's soul and saw his good intentions. Father and son-in-spirit were also totally loyal to each other.

When the patent was in Emanuele's hands, he knew business was very hard to do from inside Italy because the red tape was horrendous, so Pio instructed Emanuele to move to France and make Paris his headquarters, which his spiritual son promptly did. From the City of Lights, Emanuele traveled the world to make the most lucrative deal. He even went to Russia and tried to do a huge deal with the Soviets, but this fell through. Then he went to America and entered tough negotiations with businessmen there. He was demanding too much money, until Pio intervened and told him to be happy with what he was being offered. Pio's trust in Emanuele paid off big, and eventually Emanuele sent three and a half million French francs to lay the foundation of the hospital.

Pio Staffs His Hospital

While the money was coming in, Pio sought out the extraordinarily wonderful people who would build and run the hospital. He had a spiritual son, Guglielmo Sanguinetti, a medical doctor, who besides Pio, was the most important founder. He was bald and squat, and everyone called him "Dr. Willi." He had an air of authority, but also a great deal of personal modesty. He deflected compliments and looked down when he was being photographed. Dr. Willi was an exceptionally hard worker, and he was always active, yet he was always calm. He liked sucking on a cigarette, but never took a break from work.

Before he met Pio, Dr. Willi had been a Mason and had not been to Confession in twenty-five years. He was so opposed to religion that he wouldn't have been seen dead in a church. But his wife, Emilia, was pious, and she asked him that for their wedding anniversary gift if he would accompany her to San Giovanni. Grudgingly Dr. Willi went, and he was awestruck by Pio's presence. He felt compelled to confess to the saint, and he went from being totally against Catholicism to being on fire for the Faith. Dr. Willi confided in Pio that he had money troubles, but Pio mystified him when he said that a ticket would sort everything out.

Then Pio made a startling prophecy: "You are the man who will come here and build my hospital."[360] At the time Dr. Willi had his medical practice, a seven-hour car journey away in Tuscany. He had no spare money to move and set up shop in San Giovanni. Pio also said to the doctor that he was going to drive a certain truck around the local area. Lo and behold, Dr. Willi won a fortune in a lottery — this was the ticket Pio had referred to — and he used the flood of cash to relocate to San Giovanni, where he bought a farm and built a cottage for himself and his wife near the friary. And, while he was overseeing the construction of the hospital, he drove the exact model of truck that Pio had predicted. It must be said that Pio was especially fond of Dr. Willi, this self-effacing, tireless worker who wanted results and not recognition. The doctor's past life at the lodge was no barrier to him being high in Pio's affections, and Pio smiled his brightest smile in his company.

There was also Dr. Carlo Kiswarday, a pharmacist from Yugoslavia who had been led to San Giovanni in a strange turn of events. He and his wife, Mary, had been traveling to Bavaria so they could visit the stigmatist Teresa Neumann, but suddenly they found themselves on their way to San Giovanni without knowing why they were going there. They drove eight hundred miles, and it was like the Holy Spirit was driving their car! When the Kiswardays arrived, Pio came up, hugged Dr. Kiswarday, and immediately asked the couple to make San Giovanni their permanent home. The Kiswardays never left. They moved into Dr. Willi's cottage, which served as a base of operations for the founding of the hospital.

There was also Dr. Mario Sanvico and his wife, Maria Antonietta. Sanvico was a veterinarian and a successful entrepreneur. He ran a hugely profitable beer factory. But he decided to sell his business and move so as to be permanently at Pio's doorstep. These three married couples — the Sanguinettis, the Kiswardays, and the Sanvicos — were the beating heart of what would come to be known as the Casa. They were instructed by Pio to establish a committee and assign the key players their roles.

So, in the deep winter of January 1940, when snow lay all around, they gathered in Dr. Willi's cottage and planned. In fulfillment of Pio's earlier prophecy, Dr. Willi was given the supreme role of medical director. Dr. Kiswarday was made the treasurer and Dr. Sanvico was made secretary. Also present was a lady by the name of Ida Seitz. She is a quiet figure in the life of Pio, but she was nonetheless dynamic. She was appointed the role of director of internal organization. They all agreed unanimously to defer to Pio in all matters, and said, "Anything that has to be done must first be put to Padre Pio and must have his approval."[361]

A Home for the Poor

The men then went to visit Pio in his cell and update him. He encouraged them with this beautiful insight: "The man who overcoming himself bends over the wounds of his unfortunate brother, elevates to the Lord the most beautiful and noble prayer."[362] Pio also made known his wish that the word *hospital* was not to be used; rather, *casa*, which means home. The Casa was to be a home in every sense of the word.

Pio offered them the first donation, when he pulled from the pocket of his brown robe a little gold coin which had been given to him for his charitable causes by a lady who was dirt-poor but who would not let Pio refuse her offering. Pio said of the coin, "This is the handsomest donation I could ever hope to receive."[363] They placed the organizational plan for the Casa into Pio's brown-gloved hands and inquired of him if this scheme met with his expectations. A joyful expression came over Pio's face and he gave the nod of assent to the plan, blessed it, and told them, "This evening is the beginning of my great earthly work. I bless you and all those who donate to my work, which will grow to be more and more beautiful and even greater."[364] Such confidence Pio had! At the time many learned people thought Pio was in the grips of a delusion, that he was ignorant if he thought he could orchestrate for a first-rate hospital to be built on the side of a mountain.

Pio spoke to the select souls seated before him, the very people who would make this great work of charity a reality. Also present was Pio's faithful friend Pietro Cugino, who, blind as he was, was still privileged to hear some of the most remarkable insights Pio ever pronounced. Pio said to his friends, "One single act of love on the part of man, one single act of charity is so great in God's eyes that He could not repay it even with the immense gift of His entire creation!"[365]

The meaning of this statement is so profound. To think that one act of genuine charity done by you or me is so important to God that He cannot sufficiently reward it with all the works of creation — this compels us to acknowledge that there is nothing in this life that can repay true charity. Indeed, it can be painfully futile to look for such reward, which simply cannot be had here on earth. If even all the created works do not and will not suffice as a reward for your true love and true charity, then it seems that this is the role of Heaven, to be *the* place of reward for those who have performed true works of charity. For our time here on earth, we may edify ourselves by remembering that when we give ourselves to doing acts of charity, these acts of love are "so great in God's eyes."

That cold night when Pio was asking some of his closest friends to give of themselves entirely to building the Casa, he was also telling them that their charity and love would be immense in the eyes of God but their reward would not be had in this life. As for the love in their hearts for the patients they would serve, Pio told them, "Love is the spark of God in man's soul and is the essence of God personified in the Holy Spirit!"[366] This was said to an audience in Pio's cell, to motivate his listeners to build an exceptional hospital where love would be lavished on the sick and suffering. Yet applying it to ourselves tells us that all the love we have in our hearts and all the love our loved ones have in their hearts for us are truly sparks from the divine fires of God. The genuine love we have for others in our souls is the action of God "personified in the Holy Spirit" working through us.

In addition to the three and a half million francs sent by Emanuele, little and large bundles of lire poured in, and then there came a boost of a one-million-lire donation. The committee pooled the money and bought a landed estate. But World War II was ripping Europe apart. The plans for the Casa were put on hold, especially after Italy's leader, Benito Mussolini, entered the fray fighting on the side of Hitler, and thus united, they declared war on England and France. The sad realization dawned on Pio that the war would mean massive inflation, so that donations he had received were reduced to paltry amounts. The plan to build the hospital was put on hold for five years, but Pio kept the dream ablaze in his heart.

24

"WE WON'T WIN"

Pio was forced to plan and build his great hospital in two stages — before and after the hellscape of World War II. In the spring of 1940, Mussolini joined forces with Hitler, who was on a spree of violence and destruction unparalleled in the annals of history. Bombs rained from the sky and reduced many parts of gloriously beautiful Europe to dust, and whole streets full of ordinary people exploded with blood and gore.

German troops tore through Europe and took hold of Italy as though the country were its own boot. With arrogant abandon, the German soldiers stormed churches, treating houses of God like frat houses. Many monasteries, including the one in Pietrelcina that Mary Pyle's inheritance had built, were turned into barracks for German soldiers, who promptly wrecked them and scribbled curses on the walls.

Pio warned that the war was not going to end swiftly. "The war will last very long," he lamented. "You will see it pass from town to town like a river in flood, spreading destruction, blood and death! God, help us!"[367] When the local people asked Pio if they ought flee San Giovanni, Pio gave a very confident prophecy — albeit an outlier because it was so positive — and assured them that San Giovanni was not going to be harmed: "Not one bomb will fall on San Giovanni."[368] Pio's words came true to the letter: San Giovanni was never bombed. Rather, it became a sanctuary for all the people who had welcomed Pio with open arms.

Earlier in Mussolini's reign, Pio had been softer toward the jug-faced dictator. "I pray he might convert," he said.[369] Perhaps that meant he had seen that the grace of conversion was on offer for a man who had been raised by the staunchest socialists and as a child had no instruction in the Faith. Later, however, Pio was totally appalled by Mussolini's pact with Hitler. Both had grandiose dreams of leading empires that mimicked the empires of pre-Christian times; Mussolini wanted to make Italy the helm of a new Roman empire, essentially as it had been in the centuries just before and after Christ. Hitler despised Christianity and wanted to make Germany more pagan, as it had been before it became a Christian nation.

Interestingly, Pio disdained Hitler more, because the German commander had been raised by a devout Catholic mother and had more formation in Catholicism than Mussolini. But Hitler's father was a vicious brute who was anti-Catholic and hated his wife's faith. After Hitler left home, he never practiced as a Catholic, and when he came to power, he was happy when sacred sites were vandalized or even obliterated.

Although some of his fellow priests thought it was opportune that Mussolini aligned himself with Hitler, whom they all presumed would win, Pio would not stand for such self-interest. Pio even sparred with a bishop about this, which was most out of character for him, because he was usually at his most deferential when in the company of a prince of the Church. This bishop thought Italy would win, and Pio roundly rebutted this strange notion: "No, we won't win! Hitler goes against the Pope and publicly blasphemes the Madonna." Then Pio reiterated, "We won't win! And if we were to win, victory would be given to us as a punishment."[370]

Pio did not refrain from calling Hitler "evil," and when the battle raged between the Axis powers and the Allies, Pio said, "We lack the means to win, and also the help of God, because Mussolini and especially Hitler are too evil."[371] Pio had a condign punishment in mind for Hitler, which he shared with Fr. Pogany. "Do you know what I would do with Hitler if I could get my hands on him?" the friar began. "I'd put him in a cage and take that cage everywhere throughout the world so that Hitler would know what people were saying about him."[372]

At every turn Pio denounced fantasies of Italy's victory, and he asserted that such a win would only be a win in name only. "To win the war would not mean that we won it, but that Germany won it," he said. "Then we would fall under Nazi slavery, which is the most diabolic slavery that one can imagine."[373] Pio decried Hitler's "religion of blood," as he called it. Most tellingly, Pio declared that "Hitler and Stalin are two devils."[374] If you take to heart Pio's words, this means that to be under the Nazis was to be under "diabolic slavery," to be slaves to the devil. We have all heard of the barbarism of Hitler, but much less is said of Hitler's master: the devil, who rules over all the devils — thus people who were under Hitler-the-devil were ultimately serving the evil one.

Pio was outraged at Hitler's blasphemy against Our Blessed Mother, taking it as a sign of possession. Pio's identification of Hitler as a devil may mean that Hitler had given himself over to a devil and that his body was the base of operations for demonic control. This unveils the true nature of the epoch in history known as World War II as an attempted satanic coup, whereby Satan and his satellites tried to seize control of the world through leaders who worshipped Satan, who were at the evil one's behest and aimed to turn whole nations into serfdoms of Satan; and whereby ordinary people were empowered by their own pride to think themselves superior to other humans and were enlisted into killing frenzies of innocent men, women, and children, mutilating and destroying creatures of God made in His image. This strikes at the heart of why Pio held that Nazism was worse than Russian Communism:

> Nazism attacks all religions, attacks the very idea of God. It would substitute for religion of God the exaltations of the race and the deification of a greater Germany. And that is an idea which could capture the imagination of all, especially the youth. On the contrary, the negative materialism of the Soviets will never succeed in satisfying the mysticism that is part of the Russian soul. Russia will return to religion and to God![375]

Pio also prophesied that Germany would be "destroyed" in words that foreshadowed Hitler's own scorched earth policy, where the führer bombed Germany extensively as a punishment to the people who elected him for failing to win the war. Pio said, "Germany will be destroyed because she is cursed by God!"[376] Although Pio said that to be under the Nazis was to be serfs of Satan and that Germany as a country was "cursed," he did not display any dislike or contempt for people of German ethnicity. We can call to mind Friedrich Abresch, a German who was converted by Pio: Friedrich and his ever-smiling wife, Amelia, were much beloved by Pio, and they named their little boy after him. Pio was happy for Friedrich to photograph him, something that he normally only allowed out of obedience and then under duress. Pio also fasted from bread as a sacrifice on behalf of the millions of people, including Germans, who were starving in the war.

Pio had his own share of losses in the war. His sister Pellegrina, who had been considered the black sheep, died at the age of fifty-one. The family said she'd died in a bomb blast, but that was discovered later not to be true. Her cause of death was not made public, and her family maintained stony silence. Pellegrina may have been an alcoholic. She died estranged from her relatives, she had not reconciled with Pio, and she had not made amends for all the hurt she'd caused others, especially Felicita and her family.

Had Pellegrina wanted to be welcomed into the fold again, she would probably have had to make the first move, but she may have felt unforgiven. In charity, we cannot assume that Pellegrina didn't wish to make things right; perhaps, as she was dying in a hospital, she may have wanted to reach out and apologize. Tragically, the ravages of war may have made it too difficult for her to do so; travel was often impossible as train stations and roads were destroyed, as were phone lines, and the mail system went from unreliable to dysfunctional. It seems she died penniless and alone; she may not have had the money to send word or had someone to act as her intermediary.

We may look with empathy on the circumstances of Pellegrina's death, that she died young at the height of a brutal war. Food was very hard to come by, and she may have been hungry and malnourished for some time before her passing. It is likely she suffered much. She had in Pio, however, a brother who did his best to beseech Heaven to give her grace. When asked about her demise, Pio said simply, "I have prayed. I have made offering. I have suffered."[377]

Pio regretted his sister's life choices, especially her adultery, but he suffered with her and for her at the same time. Pio had insight into her situation that bears careful consideration; reportedly he said of Pellegrina, "It was foreordained that her life was to go this way. It's her destiny. It's God's will."[378] Nevertheless, even though Pio had this mystical insight, he never stopped praying for her.

Wartime Separations

The war also meant that Pio had to be separated from his beloved Mary Pyle. When America entered the war against Italy, as a U.S. citizen Mary was seen as the enemy. The authorities even had the power to put Mary in a concentration camp! Mary was called to Rome for formal interrogation at the Ministry of Internal Affairs. Accompanying her to the Eternal City was Fr. Emilio, and when they entered the stuffy office, they found a disinterested bureaucrat who didn't give a fig for her answers and acted as if her going to a camp was a foregone conclusion.

When the bureaucrat announced that they'd like to search her and her home, Mary collapsed. Emilio promptly opened her tight coat to help her breathe better. As she lay on the floor, the bureaucrat was astounded to see that Mary had on her Capuchin habit, pectoral cross, knotted cord, and big rosary. He was overawed by her holiness and sighed, "She looks like Our Lady of Sorrows."[379] Seizing the opportunity, Emilio asked the bureaucrat to let her spend the war in Pietrelcina under house arrest at Pio's family home. The bowled-over bureaucrat agreed readily.

So Mary moved to Pietrelcina to live with Grazio. The local people grew extremely fond of her. While she was far from her spiritual father and he was without one of his ablest disciples, Mary was able to have a reprieve. Mary was fifty-three and had been in San Giovanni for thirty years with scarcely any time off. This was a time of rest, when she could do spiritual reading, have long, peaceful walks, and be nurtured by the same people who had nurtured Pio. Our old friend, Dr. Cardone, the first medic ever to examine Pio's stigmata, hailed her as the best woman he'd ever met. Mary suffered at seeing the seminary that she had helped to build being used as a den for soldiers who trashed it, when she wanted it filled with young men training for the priesthood. But she kept a stoic silence about this. Mary had been in Pietrelcina for nineteen months when Mussolini was deposed and Italy surrendered, changed sides, and declared war on its old partner, Germany.

America Enters the War

When people called upon Pio to predict when the war would end, he would say direly, "People are hardened. They do not turn to God and the Lord is not moved to compassion."[380] As the Americans invaded Italy, a panicked Mussolini sent emissaries on his behalf to Pio who begged his prayers, but Pio would not coddle the dictator. "So, now you come to me," he scolded, "after you have destroyed Italy!" He gave Mussolini's representatives a verbal reprimand to bring back to Il Duce: "You can tell Mussolini that nothing can save Italy now! Nothing! You have destroyed her!"[381]

American soldiers invaded Italy and moved up the country from Sicily, fighting the Germans on Italian soil and ousting them from the country. The young, fresh-faced American soldiers were welcomed by the Italian people, who'd had their culture and their Faith threatened with obliteration. Mussolini, who had brought Italy into this sordid mess, had overestimated the support of ordinary people, because he came to power partly through stolen elections, and he wanted to be an emperor, using German military might to help him conquer nations.

But whereas Mussolini wanted to be a conqueror of nations, Hitler wanted nations selectively annihilated and whole races wiped out, and many Italians did not want to lend their arms to such diabolic dreams. Thus, more and more they saw Hitler as Pio had always seen him, as "evil," and together with Pio they helped the Americans overthrow the Germans. What ensued was a bloody struggle for Italy, with Germany fighting ferociously not to lose her, while Americans bombed and blasted the country's infrastructure to bits so it could no longer be used by the Germans.

The fact that Italy and America were on the same side meant that Mary Pyle was no longer the enemy, and she could return to San Giovanni. In her last days at Pietrelcina, Mary had the glorious sight of energetic American soldiers coming across the countryside. She traveled back to San Giovanni in a farm wagon that had to traverse the rough terrain of ruined roads and bridges. Together with Pio, she would make San Giovanni a haven for American soldiers, who in turn did their bit to make Padre Pio an international celebrity.

25

THE FLYING FRIAR

There was an American army officer who was determined to bomb San Giovanni — he was utterly convinced that the Germans had a secret store of weapons and ammunition there. General Nathan F. Twining oversaw the military airbase at Bari, some seventy miles away, and he wanted to destroy these alleged arms before they could be deployed by the enemy, even if it meant the destruction of a town.

Twining looked like the quintessential army pilot. He was a Protestant, and he knew nothing about Catholic saints or mystical gifts. So, when he organized a bombing mission and flew the plane leading the squadron, imagine his shock and wonder when, as they approached San Giovanni, they saw Pio appear in the clouds!

The friar was flying at the same speed as their planes, with both arms outstretched, preventing the officer and his men from flying further. Suddenly the hatches of the planes opened without the men touching the controls, and the bombs were released into a field, where they did not explode. The officer was so amazed by this sighting that he ordered his men to turn around. Pio was not famous outside of Italy, so the officer had no idea who he might be, but he risked looking like a coward and a liar who had abruptly aborted a mission because of this flying friar.

The flabbergasted Twining got back to his army base and recounted the story to the others. An Italian officer volunteered that the monk was probably Padre Pio. Curiosity led the officer to make a trip to San Giovanni, where he saw Pio in the flesh and knew beyond doubt that he was the Franciscan who had halted him in the sky that night. Pio greeted him tellingly, "So you are the one that wanted to destroy everything."[382] Twining converted to Catholicism, but he waited until later in his life to be more open about having seen Pio flying that day.

More Bombings Thwarted

Pascal Cataneo was an army pilot who had much the same experience as Twining. Afterward, he decided to visit Pio and verify that he was the one he'd seen. When Pio laid eyes on him, he rebuked him, "Ah! So you are the one who wanted to kill us all!"[383] Pascal was leading a bombing expedition toward San Giovanni when Pio appeared in the sky and the bombs Pascal and his men were carrying dropped spontaneously in the woods. If we take Pio at his word, then Pascal's actions would have resulted in "all" the lives of the men and women of San Giovanni being wiped out, including Pio's, so in this instance Pio saved his own life, too. Pio was also preserving the town where he was going to build his first-class hospital. Pascal had been a non-Catholic, but he promptly converted to Catholicism. The fruits of Pio flying to prevent bombs being dropped and utter destruction from being wrought were not only the saving of many lives but also conversions and vocations. Although these descriptions of Pio flying like an angel seem the stuff of the most fantastical fiction, consider that Pio was seen by many pilots from a variety of countries, and not just by Christians but also by Jews and Muslims.

War Stories

Alfonso D'Artega was born in Mexico, and at thirty-seven he was serving in the U.S. Army Air Forces. He was ruggedly handsome with the face of a movie star, a full head of dark hair, glittering brown eyes, and a pince-nez moustache. He was a brilliant musician and composer, and before joining the army, he'd written a number one hit song. One night at the base, Alfonso and his friends were gathered round, sharing a drink, when a chap piped up, "I saw that phantom fly again."[384] Alfonso was confused as to what "that phantom" could mean. He assumed the drink had gone to their heads, but one fellow who had not had a drop of liquor said he had been in a warplane when out of nowhere a monk flew at the speed of the plane through the air and waved his arms, which caused him to freeze in fear, so much so that he returned to his base without dropping the bombs. But he was met with a tongue-lashing from his superiors for not carrying out the bombing. This episode of random soldiers enjoying a drink and sharing stories as to "that phantom" speaks to the frequency Pio was seen to appear in the sky to prevent a bombing expedition. Alfonso had a friend who was a Protestant, who after discovering the "phantom" was Pio, decided to convert to Catholicism and later became a Catholic priest!

Pio was sighted in the heavens several times during the war. Gaetano Pavone kept the following account to himself for over two decades. During the war, Gaetano had many roles: pilot, gunner, and flight engineer. One time he was in the air, operating the top turret of the plane, with so many windows it was like he was flying in a glass house, affording him an amazing view of the sky. Returning from a bombing mission, he was flying toward the Gargano when the clouds parted before him and he saw Pio, looking like a younger man with brown whiskers that were distinct from the white clouds.[385] In fact, at the time Pio was fifty-seven years old and had a graying beard. But Pio appeared as a still, silent witness to Gaetano, calling him to faith.

Once, a Genoese man asked Pio if Genoa would be war-scarred, and tears gushed down Pio's face as he revealed, "Genoa will be bombed. Oh, how they will bomb that poor city! So many homes, buildings and churches will crumble!" He had, however, good news for this man: "But, be calm. Your house will not be touched."[386] This came to pass in 1944 when the Allies bombed Genoa to bits and the man's house was the only one within a large tract of devastation that was left perfectly intact.

On another occasion, Pio was visited by a spiritual son, Alberto Cordone, who was returning to visit his native Pietrelcina. Alberto and a group of his buddies were in San Giovanni for a mini-retreat. After three days, they worried they'd have to get home because their food was running out. But Pio encouraged them to stay on and said, "Eat together like one family. Don't eat on your own, and there will be enough food for you all."[387] Alberto and his buddies did just that and their food miraculously multiplied.

One day after Mass, they found Pio in the garden and he looked down and announced, "Poor Foggia today!" The boys did not have a clue what Pio meant, but only moments later they saw planes coming from all over, going down to Foggia to drop bombs. Pio's eyes were full of tears, and he told them they had to leave urgently in the morning and get a train home from Foggia, the same place that had just been laid to waste. The stigmatist had gone from bidding them stay to chiding them to get home. Pio said to rush, and gave them this mysterious advice, "You've got to ask somebody how to get to the train."[388]

The next morning, the boys found Foggia in ruins, with dead bodies littering the streets. The living wailed as they walked among the dead. They saw the train station was destroyed, and Alberto knew that had Pio not made them stay in San Giovanni, they'd have been victims of the bombings. But they had no idea how they could find a way to get home. Seemingly out of nowhere, a man in a black suit approached them and asked if they needed any help. The boys explained that they wanted to get a train home. He said he'd show them, but they'd have to hurry, and he ran with them to a field that still had tracks and a train that was just departing. He sprinted with them and they scrambled on board. Then he promptly disappeared.

The Consequences of War

The accounts of Pio's miraculous "flying bilocations," his predictions of the spiritual son's house in Genoa being untouched, and his advice to Alberto and his friends saving them from a horrible death — all these things raise an important question: Why did Pio not save more lives, or indeed why didn't he stop all the bombings during World War II? The question deserves careful discernment, but we may first concede that although Pio had many mystical gifts, awarded to him by the Lord, to put it bluntly, Pio was not the Lord.

Pio did as much as the grace of God allowed him to do. He often said that people's hearts had been hardened and that many had given their will to evil leaders. In the hell of war, man's inhumanity to man was on full display, and Pio did his best to lessen the bloodshed. All the while, he wept over the destruction wrought on his beloved Italy: the bombs that reduced cities to rubble so they could no longer be used by the Germans and the corpses that dotted the land as the streets ran with blood. But he had also foretold that Italy was going to be punished, especially on account of the peninsula's original pact with Germany. He predicted the doom that followed, that "this is something that will lead to punishment!" Pio was never more severe than when he decried "a people chosen of God uniting with the enemy of God."[389]

Of course, God had not turned his back on Germany as a country — it is the homeland of many great saints. Yet, during this time of history, the leaders of that country had come under the influence of the evil one. Italy's allying itself with such a force of evil, even in the interest of self-protection, had dire consequences. Pio's warnings of "punishment" came true to the letter as the Italian people paid dearly for their country's alliance with "the enemy of God." Would it have been possible for Germany's Hitler and Russia's Stalin to convert? On this point, Padre Pio did not mince his words: "Hitler and Stalin are two devils and their public conversion after so much evil, after committing so many massacres, would be a scandal."[390]

Pio had a tremendous source of joy and consolation, however, and that was the great number of American servicemen who became his spiritual children and his disciples. As the war raged, far fewer Italian pilgrims were able to travel to Pio, which meant Pio was able to give these honorable young men much more time and attention. Pio loved Americans dearly anyway, but at this time he nurtured several key American disciples who were to spend the next fifty years making him known back home. We will look at some of the biggest players, and you may wish to review their lives and discern if you may be called to a similar mission. We will note the difference between those who became spiritual children and the few who became disciples, and we may ask ourselves to which vocation we are called.

Pio's American Friends

Let's start with the man who brought the first group of soldiers to meet Pio and who would labor for over fifty years to make Pio known to Americans. William Carrigan hailed from Iowa and was short and slight, with ruddy cheeks and a black cap of hair. He possessed tremendous energy and was very smart. At home in the States, he taught psychology, but during the war he was based in Foggia, where he worked for the Red Cross, looking after the men in the Army's Air Forces.

William had seen the horrors of war, yet he was mentally strong and always wanted to help others rather than himself. He saw the devastation that Pio had predicted, including Foggia being bombed to bits, killing twenty thousand people. Carrigan found it very tough to find a church where he could pray; the local ones had been used as dorm rooms by German soldiers, and the gritty coating of war had obscured the beauty of Italian Catholicism.

Not long after he started his job supporting the airmen, he heard word from the officers about a stigmatist high up in the mountains. The soldiers told red-cheeked William something that sounded straight out of Narnia. They had been climbing the Gargano, hunting for eggs and any food that the wild animals had not yet found along the trails, when they happened upon San Giovanni and met a rosy-faced lady with a halo of white hair — Mary Pyle — who astonished them by talking in perfect English. She welcomed them profusely, told them stories about Pio, and promised to feed them like kings.

When William heard all this, he was intrigued. He, too, wanted to meet the American lady who had a heart of gold and the priest who lived the Crucifixion and read souls. It all sounded like a fairy tale come true, and William wanted to experience it all for himself. And so, when men in uniform asked him to drive them up the mountain using a Red Cross truck, he was only too happy to do it.

Thus, on a bitterly cold winter's day when snow made the mountain look like a wedding cake, he went with twenty soldiers to San Giovanni. The roads were treacherous, but they were guided to Pio's doorstep without a hitch. William walked into the church in the middle of Pio's Mass. He was frozen with the cold and no heat was running, but a supernatural warmth came over him when he felt Pio's presence. When he witnessed the sublime way Pio offered Mass, he was convinced to his marrow that Pio was a genuine mystic. He knew Pio was in dire pain, and he later said, "He jerked his head from one side to the other, as if he were suffering blows to the head and neck."[391]

After Mass, when William and the others met Pio, the stigmatist told William that they were the first American soldiers he had met. William had a premonition that his future and Pio's were intertwined. "I knew we had a destiny together," he recalled. "I sensed that I wanted to make him known in America." Once, when William inquired of Pio how he felt about having the stigmata, Pio spoke with candor, "I find them very embarrassing to have, but I deem it a great privilege to suffer with Christ."[392]

After that, William chauffeured many men to Pio's Mass. The church was always completely packed, but Mary would lead the men in uniform in by the back door to the sacristy and then to the front pew. They were overawed by the priest whose raised hands dripped blood. After Mass they went to the monastery garden and gathered around Pio. Then Mary would always take them to the pink castle for steaming coffee and the most scrumptious meals she could give them.

There they met lively Grazio, who matched Mary's accounts and told stories of the young boy Pio and his guardian angel.

While he was still stationed in Italy, William wrote a letter that was published back home in the States. It was a love letter to his spiritual father, which made known the tender loving care that Pio had lavished on the American soldiers. The letter was printed far and wide in many publications.

Joe Peluso was another American soldier who became Pio's favorite. Far from his native Pennsylvania and his loving wife, Rita, Joe had a mop of rich brown hair, a charismatic smile, and good looks inherited from his Italian forefathers. Joe was a warm soul whose brown eyes shone with innate goodness. He first heard of Pio in a letter from his mother, which he received when he was in the hospital with an injured leg.

Joe's mother, who was home in America, urged Joe to look up the holy friar. His mom was ahead of her time, devoted to Pio before most American Catholics had heard of him. Following his mom's request, Joe asked his military chaplain about Pio's whereabouts and the chaplain looked in the direction of the Gargano and said, "Behind those clouds on that mountain is where you can find this priest, who is called Padre Pio."[393]

Joe and a bunch of his friends piled into a car and went to see Pio, who was overjoyed to meet them, and after that first occasion, Joe went as often as he could to see Pio and brought as many young men to the stigmatist as possible. He became especially close to Mary Pyle and was fed like royalty. One day Joe asked Pio if he could become his spiritual son. Pio agreed. But Pio wanted Joe to be his emissary back home in America and make known his will and his desire to be the spiritual father of every American. "Joe," he said, "when the war is over and you return to the United States, tell the American people, that for those who would like me to be their spiritual father, my answer is yes. I accept all Americans as my spiritual children."[394]

This is as true today as it was then. Pio is open to "all" Americans becoming his spiritual sons and daughters. If you are American and would like to ask Pio to be your spiritual father, you have a great opportunity. During the same conversation with Joe, Pio added, "I only have two requirements, that they lead very good Catholic lives and that they regularly receive the sacraments. And please, tell them never to embarrass me in front of Jesus and Mary. You must tell them, Joe."[395] Pio delivered a message to all Americans — those who were alive then and those who were yet to live — through Joe Peluso.

Joe and Pio delighted in being in each other's company for over ten months. The pair could be seen beaming at each other, and it was beloved Padre Agostino who told Joe, "Padre Pio loves everyone, but he especially loves you!"[396] Joe was given certain privileges. He had a key to the monastery, and when he advised Pio to change the time of his Mass, from 5 a.m. to 9 a.m., so that more soldiers could come, Pio instantly did this. Joe had the rare honor of joining Pio for meals and observed Pio eat like a bird, pecking at his food like the dove in the arms of St. Francis. When fabric became scarce, Pio's habit got very old and threadbare. It looked like he was going to have to wear something other than his Capuchin robe for the first time in over forty years! Joe's father was a tailor, so Joe measured Pio expertly for his new habit and arranged for the brown cloth to be sent from America, so Pio could have a new habit just in time for a bitter winter.

Just before Christmas, Joe was sent on a mission to Rome. Pio's supply of religious medals and rosaries had been dwindling; he loved to give a blessed St. Benedict medal and a rosary to every visitor. So he sent Joe to Rome, but he gave the soldier no instructions. Joe and a friend went to the Eternal City led only by the inspiration of the Holy Spirit.

As they approached the city, they found themselves at the bottom of a huge hill and decided to go up it in their car and see a grand view of all Rome. At the top, gazing down at the beautiful city, they turned around and found themselves facing the motherhouse of the Benedictine nuns. Joe rang the bell and was welcomed in by a smiling nun. He told her of his hunt for medals and rosaries and she promptly produced a large bundle of St. Benedict medals — Pio's favorite! And a mass of rosaries! As a bonus, she gave Joe a relic of St. Rita for his wife Rita, who was waiting for him back home.

The next day, Joe went to a papal audience and Pope Pius XII asked the congregation to hold out their religious goods for him to bless. When Joe got back to San Giovanni, he saw how eager Pio was for his return, and in that moment he received the gift of tongues: He spoke to Pio in English and Pio spoke to him in Italian, but both understood each other perfectly. Pio delighted in the large bag of his favorite medal and the rosaries, and chuckled as he said to Joe, in a familiar Pennsylvanian accent, "You bought out all of Rome!" Joe kept a little share for himself, but Pio asked, "May I have those medals and rosaries back? I want to bless them again. This time I want to place a very special blessing on them for you."[397] Pio then blessed them again and returned them to Joe.

Joe had a video camera his brother sent him, and Pio agreed to allow his American son to take footage of him, something Pio normally found repugnant. When he returned home to America, Joe made an impressive presentation of his spiritual father. The audience could see Pio rejoicing in Joe's company and feel Pio's love for Joe — and for them as well. Over the years Joe showed this video to thousands of people, until the old-fashioned reels got worn out! Joe died in 1996, having spent more than fifty years as Pio's ambassador, giving a sea of souls a warm introduction to the holy friar.

Another favorite of Pio's was Joe Peterson. He was a gentle giant, at six feet four and 230 pounds, with a long face and nose. He had been a mailman in his native New York, in the Bronx. Like General Twining, Joe had been stopped miraculously by Padre Pio in his attempt to bomb San Giovanni.

"Tall Joe" was based in Bari, which was a mere seventy miles from Pio's home but a difficult journey during war. He hitchhiked with three other soldiers to see Pio; when they arrived, Joe had his first meeting with his spiritual father. When he assisted at Pio's Mass, his experience mirrored that of William: "You felt you were at Calvary. You could see the great suffering he went through."[398]

What distinguished Joe's relationship with Pio was the fun they had together. With Tall Joe, Pio was like the little boy who played pranks on Felicita again. Together they did a type of comedy show, and in front of the other friars they put on a mock wrestling match. Pio was tiny compared with Joe, but Joe used to let Pio wrestle him to the ground; Joe would pretend to be so weak he could not get up off the floor. The friars roared with laughter as Pio was hailed the victor.

Pio also thought it very funny when Joe imitated a clucking chicken. Once, when they were in the garden with Pietro and a doctor, Pio prompted Joe to do his chicken act, so Joe obliged. Then the doctor said to Pio, "Padre, Joe's from New York. They don't have any chickens there — only skyscrapers. But you're a farm boy. Let's hear your chicken!" Pio gave a weak performance, and the doctor asked why it was so lackluster. Pio wittily replied, "Joe does a chicken who is well. My chicken is convalescing after paying the doctor bills."[399]

It was a huge compliment to Joe that Pio was so lighthearted around him — not at all stern and strict, as he tended to be with others. Even in offering spiritual insights, Pio often had a jovial tone. Once he said to Joe, "The man who invented refrigeration went to heaven, but the man who invented television …"[400] Pio pointed down without finishing the sentence.

Joe made a hundred slides of Pio, which the stigmatist personally blessed. Like Joe Peluso, when Tall Joe returned to the United States, he gave talks and presentations on Pio. But he went back to San Giovanni for a month every summer for the rest of his life and became much loved by the locals. All the spiritual daughters who lived around the monastery treated him like their own blood brother, which is a great indication of how much Joe impressed them. They were very discerning as to whom they let join their inner circle.

During the war, Pio had the American soldiers come to the aid of his spiritual children in San Giovanni, as though they were all one big, close-knit family. One day Pio asked to speak to William urgently, then ordered him to take Amelia Abresch to the hospital as soon as possible in an army ambulance. The ever-smiling Amelia was deathly ill.

Initially William refused outright, saying an army vehicle could not be used to ferry a civilian. But Pio persisted, and gave this dire warning: "You must take her to Ancona or else she will die." Ancona was 211 miles away, an eight-hour round trip. A battle of wills ensued, until Pio commanded William, "Get an army ambulance and take her there!"[401] William agreed to ask the colonel at the military base, and to his surprise, the colonel agreed. Amelia was spirited to Ancona, and even though she was at death's door, she smiled all the way there and back. She always bore suffering with good cheer. Though there was no miracle, Pio's prayers were answered through William's act of charity.

On another occasion a soldier by the name of Ray Ewen became a hero to a local San Giovanni lady who was on the point of death. It was the dead of night; her condition was so critical that if she didn't get to the hospital in Naples — a two-and-a-half-hour trip each way — she was going to die before morning. There was no gasoline in town for the doctor to drive her, but the military base had plenty of gas to power its trucks.

When Ray heard of her plight, he pinched five gallons of gas and took them to the doctor, who sped to Naples on a full tank of gas. Ray could have been court-martialed for giving away army supplies to a civilian, but the other soldiers covered for him when he went to deliver the fuel and his absence went unnoticed by his superiors.

Pio's Disciples

During the war, Pio garnered many spiritual children, but far fewer were the number who became his disciples — those who created vital connections between him and other spiritual children, his foot soldiers in the battle for souls on American soil.

When he returned to the States, red-cheeked William Carrigan graduated from driving soldiers up the mountain to see Pio. Once he was home, William gave speeches and presentations, bringing tens of thousands of souls into the same spiritual family. William had a wonderful way with words, and keen insight into people owing to his training as a psychologist, and he met people where they were. He brought people into Pio's fold who seemed unlikely converts: outliers who felt like outcasts, people who had troubled pasts, and people who were usually indifferent to faith.

Like William, charismatic Joe Peluso and tall Joe Peterson pursued a calling to do all they could to make Pio known. Though they came from widely different backgrounds, each of them put over fifty years into this apostolate. Mary Pyle, a wealthy heiress, remained in San Giovanni; she was Pio's disciple for forty-five years (from 1923 to her death in 1968), showing tireless hospitality to pilgrims and seekers. These Americans were among the few of Pio's children who rose to the challenge of discipleship, mirroring Pio's time in the trenches.

26

PIO'S PROFOUND PROPHECIES

Only a few of Pio's prophecies are available to us, including a volume of notes housed at the friary in San Giovanni, which is a written log of the predictions Pio made about the future, including events that were to take place after his death in 1968. They are kept secret. Once, when a priest who read the prophecies was asked if they could be published, he replied, "No! It will be given up drop by drop within 100 years, otherwise the world would be upset!"[402]

During the Wold War II, Pio shared with brother priests visions he had received about the future, visions that speak to us now more than ever. Fr. John P. Duggan, a chaplain of the 304th Wing of the 15th Air Force, was stationed at Cerignola, about an hour's drive from Pio's friary. Duggan was a lionhearted priest who at the time was in his thirties, and like William Carrigan, he brought many American servicemen to meet Pio. In this, Fr. Duggan showed himself to be of great faith and deep humility: He was a priest who was introducing soldiers under his spiritual care to another priest, who he knew could lead these men in higher ways.

The Future of America

At the time, there were other chaplains who discouraged young soldiers from going to visit Pio. When Fr. Duggan asked Pio about the future of the of America, the stigmatist said, "The conversion of the United States will be slow but sure." As for Communist Russia, Pio had this startling revelation: "The Russian people will be converted. Their total conversion will happen very fast."[403] If we take Pio at his word, then both America and Russia will be converted, albeit at different speeds, and Russia will have a rapid and "total" turn to God.

On another occasion, Pio reiterated this same insight when he was talking to an American soldier, Leone Fanning. Corporal Fanning, as he was then, had felt a call to the priesthood but could not pursue his vocation because he'd been drafted. No one had breathed a word to Pio that Fanning was hoping to be ordained, but when Pio met him, he said, "Your name is not just Leone. Someday it will be Father Leone."[404] The young corporal was confirmed in his vocation, and he believed in Pio's supernatural gift to read the future.

Pio's words all came to pass: When Fanning was discharged, he returned to America and was ordained in 1954. He was a priest for the next fifty-four years, and like his peers, charismatic Joe Peluso and tall Joe Peterson, he outdid himself to spread devotion to Pio.

While he spent time with Pio, young Fanning asked the Capuchin about the conversion of Russia and received this assurance: "Yes, Russia will be converted as the Blessed Virgin said.... Russia will teach the United States a lesson in conversion."[405] It is both edifying and humbling that the people who have lived under the yoke of Communism will instruct Americans in the Faith.

When we merge the two prophecies, we get the following: Russia, with a current having population of over 144 million, will have a swift metamorphosis. In contrast, the United States will be slower but "sure" and will copy the restored Christian ways of Russia. Our Lady of Fatima foretold on the eve of the Communist Revolution that the errors of Russia would spread, and indeed they did. But the reverse can happen, too, if in the coming times, Russia will give such an example that Americans will copy her.

Prophecy of Penitence

Just as Italy was recovering from the ravages of World War II, a woman told Alberto Cordone (the same chap who with his friends had escaped bombed-to-bits Foggia) all about the time she knelt in Pio's confessional and he gave a kind of "reverse prophecy" about something she had done. Alberto and the woman were neighbors, so they had an easy rapport and knew each other well. She didn't want to share her story directly with others but gave it to Alberto to make it known.

The first time she tried to confess to Pio, he was not satisfied with her account. "Try to remember the other sin," he invited her. She responded, "Padre, I think I gave you all the sins I know." Without absolving her, Pio gave her a harsh penitential exercise: "Go to the cross and say 15 Ave Marias and 15 Our Fathers."

The cross was at the top of the mountain, and it could be reached only by going up a very bad road — a dangerous expedition. But the lady did as Pio asked, and when she went back to him, hoping to get absolution, he said to her, "Do you remember all your sins?" Again, she was adamant that she had previously confessed all of them, "Padre Pio, I've confessed everything." Pio was patient and blamed it on her memory: "No, you still don't remember all." Then he assigned the same penance. "You've got to go to the cross at the top of the mountain again." When she returned from her perilous climb up the mountain, she still claimed not to remember the other sin, and Pio asked her to go to the cross for a third time.

The third time she returned to his confessional, resolute that she did not remember anything else, Pio questioned her more closely. "What do you mean, you don't remember anything? Don't you know he could have been a good priest, a bishop, even a cardinal?" In that instant the woman recalled her abortion from years before. Tears welled up in her eyes and she defended herself: "Padre, I never knew abortion was a sin."

Pio did not soften his stance. "What do you mean, you didn't know this was a sin? That's killing." The lady thought the cloak of secrecy had granted her immunity. "Nobody knows about this," she replied, "only me and my mother, how could you say it could have been a priest or a cardinal?" But Pio knew. The mere fact that Pio said the boy could have been "a good priest" is exceptionally telling, because Pio rarely said that a priest was good; he was harder on priests than he was on anyone else. He even denigrated himself so harshly that it was hard for Pio's enemies to insult him worse than he insulted himself.

This genuine account is not just the story of the mother's tragedy, but ours as well, because it follows that if he had been a good priest as Pio indicated, he'd have been a much-needed good prince of the Church. Pio did not say he'd have been a pope, but as a cardinal, he could have voted in a good pope or even become pope. The priest would also have been from Pietrelcina, so Pietrelcina would have produced not only the first priest with the stigmata but also a good prince of the Church. Pio ended the conversation with the woman by saying solemnly, "[Abortion] is a sin, a very great sin."[406]

This would have been in the mid-1940s. Tragically, during World War II there was a sharp increase of abortions in Italy. Pregnant mothers panicked by the war fell prey to bad doctors who wanted to make easy money by doing illegal abortions; as law and order had broken down, rarely if ever did these abortionists face charges.

This penitent, this post-abortive mother, was not a woman without faith; she was someone who went to Confession at least twice a year, at Christmas and Easter. Had she been away from the sacraments for years, Pio would have sent her away without speaking to her and would have made her wait, or he would have stated her sin without trying to induce her to tell him. The mere fact that he first gave her penance tells us that it was a recent abortion, because otherwise Pio's concern would have been to make her feel how long she had been away from Confession before her actual sins were voiced.

The woman's surprise at hearing of the immorality of abortion indicates that she was among the first generation of Italians that needed to be instructed as to its evil. Before the war, abortion was exceedingly rare and thus there was little spoken catechesis devoted to it. This post-abortion woman — who knew Alberto and seemed quite young — came of age when it was regrettably more accepted. Thus she was aghast when Pio emphasized its evil. But the child she lost was also our loss, because as a decent prince of the Church he could have done a lot of good.

A Family of Disciples

Irene Gaeta was dumbfounded when Fr. Gerardo Di Flumeri, the vice-postulator for Pio's canonization, told her she was a disciple. "The Disciples of Padre Pio are also written in the book of his Prophecies," he informed her.[407] Irene thought that disciples should only be of Jesus, to which Gerardo responded, "In Padre Pio, Jesus lived! The stones of San Giovanni Rotondo are bathed in the blood of Jesus. If it had not been Jesus in him, he would not have lived more than three days for the blood he was shedding!"[408]

By that time, Irene and Pio had a long history. Irene grew up in Lanciano, in central Italy (the site of the first documented and approved eucharistic miracle). One day in 1945, as she was coming home from school, eight-year-old Irene was lured to a house and locked in a room with a man who threw her on a bed and tried to violate her. Irene fell on the floor to get away from him, scrambled to the door, which miraculously opened, and ran away.

Humiliated and fearful, she didn't tell a soul until, a month later, Pio appeared to her and told her he had opened the locked door for her. She was astonished that he knew, and that he had been able to protect her in this way. The stigmatist also gave her a vision of him offering Mass, and she saw the Host become Flesh, as well as the wine become Blood that overflowed from the chalice and rained down Pio's hands. Pio said to her, "The Eternal Father has entrusted you to my hands since the day you were born. I know everything about you. I will always protect you."[409]

From that moment on, Pio helped her with every detail of her life and often came to her in dreams. Sometimes he bilocated to instruct her in prayer, telling her to address a particular prayer to the Eternal Father, another to the Sacred Heart, and still others to the Virgin Mary. The priest with pierced palms gave this young child predictions of future events that always came true, and on occasion, he made requests of her to pray for people who were at risk of calamities, such as bombs and even mine explosions.

As she grew up, Irene came to share in some of Pio's gifts, leading the souls of people around her to holiness and total conversion, and receiving visits from saints and holy souls. St. Anthony of Padua even came to spend time with her. When she visited San Giovanni on a day when it seemed impossible to find Pio, Pio bilocated to the confessional and heard the account of her sins. As she grew older, she did more and more to spread devotion to Pio, and organized coaches of people to make pilgrimages to San Giovanni. Yet, her approach tended to be more one-on-one; she spoke to people individually, whereas disciples such as Joe Peluso and William Carrigan addressed big gatherings. Yet, what she was doing on the ground in Italy was the same mission in which Joe and William were engaged. They were all foot soldiers in the battle for souls by bringing people to Christ through Pio.

Pio gave Irene a twofold vocation. First, he guided her work. She had marvelous talents as a fashion designer and dressmaker. Irene had left school when she was twelve to care for her family, but under Pio's exacting direction, she opened a high-fashion clothing business in the heart of Rome. Here she met celebrities and the very wealthy, whom she led to the Faith and who became Pio's spiritual children. Once Pio asked her to get him a new chalice, an expensive purchase, and Irene wondered how she'd get the lire for it, but Pio assured her she'd get the money in three days. Sure enough, a husband and wife, both celebrated actors, came in and asked her to make a wardrobe of clothes quickly. Irene worked furiously, bought the chalice, and sped to San Giovanni. She arrived on one of the busiest days of the year; as the crowds pressed in on her she had to raise the chalice over her head to keep it from falling. Pio's penetrating eyes sought her out, and he walked to her. When she offered him the chalice, Irene said, "I had the impression that I was in that chalice, [that] my life was being offered, too."[410]

Next, Pio pointed out her future husband to Irene. She had wanted to enter a convent, but Pio said it was God's will that she marry. One Lent, a busload of pilgrims arrived from Rome, and after she assisted at Pio's Mass, Pio directed her to the young man who had driven the bus to San Giovanni and had been sleeping in the coach while the others were at Mass.

This young man had not been to Confession in twelve years, and Pio urged Irene to get him to go to Confession. After many invitations he finally agreed, but when he went to Pio, he fibbed and said he'd not been in three years. Pio sent him away and scolded him, "You unhappy wretch. You leave the other nine years to me. Off with you!"[411]

But that same day, he found another priest and confessed. When they were back in Rome, he asked Irene out and their courtship ensued. Irene was still unsure that she was really meant for marriage. When she went to see Pio, she was determined to ascertain if this young chap was the man for her. She was forthright with Pio, imploring him, "You have to tell me what I must do." Pio's face became bathed in a bright light and he said, "Marry, my daughter, marry. Fulfill God's will."

Irene persevered. "Marry whom?" Pio smiled broadly and gave this witty reply: "The young man in Rome. Who else would you think of marrying? Me?" He gave Irene a lovely, reassuring promise: "I bless your marriage. Your family will be mine."[412]

Marriage was to be Irene's cross. She nearly died in her first pregnancy, and then during her fourth, she was so deadly ill that she lost the ability to speak. She could not move from bed because of heart trouble that developed into septicemia. Her doctor told her she risked dying by continuing the pregnancy and that the baby would more than likely have a disability. Her husband wanted her to abort, and when she refused he stopped speaking to her. Even so, Irene kept entrusting the baby to Our Lady and Pio and was given strength to keep going.

Her condition did not approve, and Irene was taken to the hospital. As she lay dying, she didn't call for her husband. Even after the months of his emotional blackmail, he was hurt, and when he came to her bedside, he said, "You're dying and you haven't even asked for me." Irene answered poignantly, "I wanted to die alone."

Then she told him something that Pio had told her: "My life and your daughter's depend on you. Padre Pio has told me that God holds both of these graces in His hands; my cure and the health of our daughter. You must ask; if I ask for them, they won't be granted. The prayer must be made by you, along with your repentance for having offended and insulted God."[413]

Ah, that this young husband, who had so disregarded the Lord, was the one to win the graces! It speaks to Pio's gift of seeing grace, of knowing who was to ask for them, and the condition on which they would be granted — in this case, if the husband repented. So Irene's husband took this very solemnly, repented, and prayed for his wife and baby. A little girl was born in perfect health, and Irene recovered completely, just as Pio predicted.

27

THE DARK WAR ENDS, AND PROVIDENCE DAWNS

When young men in uniform asked Pio when the war would end, he answered cryptically that Christmas 1944 was to be their last with him. Thinking that they would be leaving in the New Year, they decided to go to Midnight Mass before returning home.

That night was dark — the electricity lines were down — and the roads were so thick with snow that their trucks had to plow their way to the church. Getting into the church was like crossing a wall of snow, and they must have looked like little snowmen as they entered. Only candles lit the scene. The travails of getting there were forgotten as they saw Pio enter, carrying the baby-sized doll of the Christ Child in his hands. We know from our study of his childhood that Pio was at his most joyful at Christmas — his favorite time of the year — and many times people saw in a burst of light a vision of Baby Jesus nestled in Pio's arms. Pio looked so completely in love as he cradled the child.

A last Christmas with Pio was a fitting treat for these fine young men before they resumed civilian life in suburban America. After the Allies won in 1945, Pio said goodbye to them. Few would be able to return to his side often — apart from Joe Peterson, whose discipleship was nurtured when he went on to spend every summer at San Giovanni.

Pio also waved a temporary *arrivederci* to Mary Pyle, who traveled to the States to go on a speaking tour, exhorting the crowds to give money to Pio's next big project, his hospital. While she was there, she contacted the soldiers who had grown so fond of Pio, telling them, "We are members of the same spiritual family."[414]

The reality was that, had the American soldiers stayed in Italy, regularly climbing the mountain to San Giovanni, they would not have had as much time with Pio as during the war. The ravages of war had meant few could travel to Pio.

As Italy healed and roads were rebuilt, pilgrims once again flooded San Giovanni, and they came from many other countries as word about the miracle-worker continued to spread. But back in the States, several of the brilliant young men who had come to Pio during the war were following special orders he had given them: to raise funds for his grand dream, a world-class hospital — though Pio was adamant that it wasn't to be called a hospital; instead, it was "the Casa," a welcome home for all sick and suffering.

This was the time when it was God's will for the Casa to come into existence, and everything started coming together. Land was donated just in time. Maria Basilio, a lady of some means from Turin, made a gift of land near the friary. But it was a hilly highland, so lumpy with rocks that it looked like there were more stones than earth, and some people laughed at the idea of a big hospital being built there.

A Work of Divine Providence

Pio refused to go into debt to pay for the construction of the hospital. He refused all loans and deferred to Divine Providence. "This is the house of Providence," he declared. "When Providence doesn't have any funds available, let work be stopped."[415] The timetable for construction and for buying the necessary furniture, medical equipment, and technology for the Casa was structured around the financial gifts provided by donors.

This prompts us toward a deeper understanding of Divine Providence. We may be wary of pigeonholing Divine Providence as merely collecting money for charitable causes. Pio said, "Beneficence, from wherever it may come, is always the child of the same mother, that is Providence."[416] We may be too proud to think we are beneficiaries of Providence, but *all* giving is, to quote Pio again, "always" Providence.

Providence is more than just money and aid being given to the poor, people on the margins; anytime we perform any type of beneficence — no matter how small — we too are instruments of Providence. To give one example, Pio set up a fund in the name of Mario Gambino, a domestic worker in New York who managed to scrape together and send ten dollars, one dollar in honor of each of his children. This was all Mario could afford, and his generosity warmed Pio's heart. In Mario's name he created the Fund for the Poor, a pot of money to be reserved for the health care of those who had no money or insurance.

In all this talk of Providence, we need to bear in mind that Pio had nurtured certain souls who also turned out to be the agents of Divine Providence. He'd been in San Giovanni for thirty years, and in that time he'd invited several brilliant people to live alongside him, and they all helped make his dream come true.

Cleonice Morcaldi was one such beloved spiritual child. She did a lot on the ground to raise funds and motivate the will of the local people. She organized raffles, produced pieces of theater, and screened wholesome movies; the proceeds of the tickets went into the hat for the Casa. And although Pio gave his consent to all sorts of fundraising enterprises and encouraged others to solicit donations, Pio gave all credit to Divine Providence. Providence did indeed provide for Pio: Little sums and great sums of money arrived in tandem with valuable chalices and vestments, as well as parcels containing all sorts of things people envisioned could be put to good use in a hospital — even food! All this arrived at the friary.

There was a special scheme in place to move the money. The friars laid a white handkerchief on the table, placed all the bills and checks inside, then folded it. Each day the sainted Dr. Sanguinetti, "Dr. Willi," came, collected the white handkerchief, put it inside his jacket, and took it to the home of the faithful Dr. Mario Sanvico, whose house was like a secure safe. Sanvico's home became so filled with packages that he could hardly walk on his own floors and even had to use his own bed to store items! The food was swiftly given to the poor. The chalices and exquisite vestments were carefully stored to be used in the hospital chapel, which was being built. Money came in mostly from America, and such generosity was a reason Pio had such affection for Americans. If you are an American, you can take a measure of delight in that it was predominantly your countrymen who gave the means for the Casa to be built.

The Casa could not function illegally, outside the law. It needed legal backing. The committee, with Dr. Willi at the helm, decided to set up a company of shareholders. Each shareholder signed an individual contract that forfeited their right to any profit. A contract was drawn up, legally founding a company with a capital of one million lire, which broke down into a thousand shares of one thousand lire each. The contract was brought before Pio for his blessing — when he was at the deathbed of his beloved father.

The Death of Pio's Father

Thus, October 1946 was for Pio the happiest of times and the most sorrowful of times. Happy, because on October 5 the Casa had legal standing and the real work of construction could begin. Sorrowful, because two days later Grazio, Pio's beloved father, died. It was October 7, the feast of the Most Holy Rosary. This was a kind of blessing, for Grazio had kept his hand on his rosary beads during every free moment of his life. Before his death, Grazio was being cared for by Mary Pyle in her pink castle.

Some months before he was to die, Grazio was climbing the stairs in Mary's house and had a bad fall, which could have been fatal, but later Pio said that Grazio's guardian angel had cushioned his fall. After his tumble, Grazio was reduced to staying in bed all the time, and when he was in extremis and death darkened the door, our old friend Padre Raffaele gave Pio permission to keep a vigil at Grazio's bedside until the moment came to give Grazio the last rites.

On the feast of the Holy Rosary, Pio held his father in his arms as his last breath left him and Grazio went to be reunited with Giuseppa. Pio was inconsolable. For a week after Grazio was laid to rest, Pio spent most of the time in bed. You may notice a pattern here, thinking that grief was Pio's weakness, which is perfectly understandable. But it was also an anomaly in his life, because Pio's obsession was the salvation of souls and he wanted to devote every moment of his life to this end. Yet, when he lost someone close to him, Pio wept streams of tears and slept for days. According to Pio, his father went to Heaven. Pio and his strong-willed brother Michele wrote a tribute, asking Grazio to remember them before God. Giuseppa, however, according to Pio had not gone to Heaven immediately but to Purgatory first.

God took Grazio with one hand and gave the legal grounding of the Casa with the other. Blueprints for the design of the hospital were submitted to Pio for his approval. Pio found only one to be to his liking, but to their consternation the committee found that the fellow who had drawn up this blueprint was a man of little education; he had only five years of primary school education, and no formal training as an architect. His name was Angelo Lupi, and he was a giant of a man in his early forties, clad in big, paint-stained knickers tied with a black belt, and huge boots. His hair was grubby and he grinned boyishly. He looked more Dennis the Menace than Master of Design. Yet his blueprint was thought the best by Pio. Angelo was a temperamental genius with a profound array of gifts, and after he was chosen by Pio for the job, he went on to design a hospital that trained architects have since hailed as an extraordinary feat; it has even been called a miracle of design.

The Casa Builders

Angelo had his weaknesses; in particular he was prone to rages, had little patience with people who did not share his vision, and was filled with manic energy. Pio, however, did not think this would be disastrous. Angelo was given the role of architect, with the view that he would also supervise construction of the Casa. Angelo did not employ men with formal qualifications exclusively, and he gave jobs to farmers and agricultural laborers whose lives had been spent tilling the soil. Yet, with boundless energy and innate expertise, Angelo instructed them in the ways of carpentry, bricklaying, decorating, and painting.

In Angelo, we see Pio's gift for reading hearts and minds. Ostensibly, Angelo was an unlikely choice, but Pio knew he was the right man for the job. The 350 men who worked under Angelo had been simple laborers, but under his direction they became skilled craftsmen. They learned on the job. Looking out from the window of his monastery, Pio kept a close eye on the construction site as wall by wall it came into shape. A special treat for Pio was when Dr. Willi took him around the site in his car. Dr. Willi's calm temperament was the solid foundation upon which the hospital was built. The gentle Dr. Willi had the right touch with Angelo and was able to work with him despite Angelo's drastic changes in mood. This was no small feat when one considers that in a previous job in a monastery, Angelo had become so mad at the monks that in a fit of rage he tied eight of them to the scaffolding!

In time, Angelo's terrible tantrums took a toll on Dr. Willi's heart. However, he bore it all with tremendous grace because Angelo was ensuring the Casa was the beautiful light-filled haven of luxury corresponding to Pio's dream. Angelo even ran a workshop where the men made artificial marble, and it was arranged for the Casa to have air-conditioning. This earned Pio censure from people who thought he was wasting money. Pio didn't countenance those who begrudged the best being given the sick, and he said, "Nothing is too good or too beautiful for the sick and suffering!"[417]

We need carefully acknowledge that apart from Pio the person who deserved the most credit was unquestionably Dr. Willi. He was seen at all hours of the day in his puffy coat, black beret, and black-rimmed spectacles, doing anything that needed to be done. A highly qualified medic, his amazing array of talents meant he could advise as to where the blood bank needed to be built or how the wards needed to be arranged so doctors could best serve their patients. He took a hammer and chisel and, with his surgeon's hands, etched the title "CASA" on the façade. He worked like a Trojan, seeking out the building materials that were to make the Casa a haven of healing. He drove trucks around the building site, and he even took a donkey schlepping sacks of soil up the mountain, which Dr. Willi used to plant seedlings for trees all over the grounds. He gave himself over without reservation, and his only luxury was his close bonds with his devout wife and his trusty Dr. Sanvico, who kept a diary of all that was said and all that happened and was like a big-eyed puppy before Pio, hanging on every word that came from Pio's mouth.

While Willi and Sanvico had to cope with the temperamental genius, Angelo, they also had their own fairy godmother in the form of Dr. Nora Figna, the chief engineer. She looked like the stereotypical Italian grandmother, diminutive with a silk scarf around her head. Her humble looks belied her extraordinary abilities; she was a math whiz and authority on engineering. Nora worked quietly and found ingenious solutions to make this hospital so far ahead of its time that few could have imagined how great it was going to be. She may even be an intercessor for engineers.

Another extraordinary emissary of Divine Providence was an Englishwoman, Barbara Ward. She was born in North Yorkshire. Her mother had raised her to be devout, and she had lovely etiquette without affectation or snobbishness. Barbara was startlingly beautiful, with a heart-shaped face, large eyes, thick brown hair, and a look of Our Lady. She was also brilliant: She'd graduated from Oxford University and gone on to be a correspondent for *The Economist*. She had been tasked with visiting war-ravaged countries and reporting on how they were recovering. When she heard of Pio, she was intrigued and visited him the first chance she got.

Barbara saw the Casa as the foundations were being laid, and because her heart burned with love for the poor, she wanted to do all in her power to raise money so that the destitute could have decent health care without monstrous bills. Barbara was every bit the English rose, but also the true Yorkshire lass, and she showed great pluck in approaching her contacts in the United States and arranging for 400 million lire to be allocated for the Casa. But when the money arrived in Italy, the government pocketed 150 million lire, with the result that only 250 million reached the coffers of the Casa. Pio was most hurt by this and considered the missing money to be an act of theft that could never be pardoned. Nevertheless, Barbara was hailed a heroine, and Angelo Lupi was so especially fond of her that he prepared a special surprise for her in the chapel of the Casa. Barbara got another gift as well: She'd asked Pio to pray that her fiancé, who was a Protestant when they became engaged, become Catholic. After Pio prayed, her fellow swam the Tiber and they were married.

28

DR. WILLI GOES TO GOD

The Casa was to be not just a corporal work of mercy but a spiritual work as well. Pio established prayer groups as powerhouses of grace behind the working of the Casa. "It is time to unite both intentions and actions," he said, "to offer Our Lord collective prayers imploring His mercy for a humanity that appears to have forgotten Him."[418]

Dr. Willi was Pio's ambassador in setting up the prayer groups in well over twenty Italian cities. A key condition for a group was that every single one be under the direction of a priest because, as Pio sagely prescribed, it was the only way to ensure unity with Mother Church. (Something to consider for those thinking of setting up a Padre Pio prayer group: A priest at the helm can ensure sound leadership and ward off infighting.)

Pio was enjoying the sight of the Casa being built and the proliferation of the prayer groups all over Italy, but then tragedy struck. Dr. Willi took a day off and went mountain climbing. His heart stopped and he went to God. He was only sixty.

Pio was crushed by the loss and was also in shock, having had no warning of his close friend's death. Tears sprang from his eyes whenever Dr. Willi's name came up in conversation.

Pio was not omniscient. That Our Lord had kept Pio in the dark about his beloved friend's impending exit galled Pio greatly. "You took him without first telling me!" Pio moaned. "If You had told me that You were going to take him, I wouldn't have given him to You. I would have snatched him out of Your hands!"[419]

In these bitter words of Pio we hear the pain of grief but also Pio unwittingly disclosing his human weakness. Pio was bound to follow the will of God as much as you or me. God's will to take Dr. Willi had trumped Pio's will to have him stay on earth. And yet, Pio let slip that he did indeed have the power to move the hand of God to allow someone to live, if Pio knew God wanted to take that person.

Mr. Bianchi

Grief reduced Pio to his most unsaintly, and we may find it disturbing that he took issue with Our Lord's will. But trouble ensued which most likely would not have, had Dr. Willi been alive. New directors came on board to replace Dr. Willi, but they did not have the same steel hand in a velvet glove approach to Angelo, and one director resigned because of Angelo's angry impetuousness. The next director fired Angelo. The temperamental genius sued for unfair dismissal but didn't get his job back. A few years later, Pio seized an opportunity to intervene to have Angelo reinstated, but in the meantime, Pio was without Angelo and Dr. Willi, the two men he'd relied on most.

The director who ousted Angelo went against Pio's vision for the doctors who would work in the Casa. Whereas Pio wanted the doctors to be chosen mainly from among his spiritual children, the new director disregarded this, and headhunted the best of the best doctors, regardless of whether they were spiritual sons or daughters of Pio's.

All during this time, Pio was as busy as ever converting souls for Christ. And in at least one case he drew from this pool of souls one who helped build the hospital. There was a fellow by the name of Mr. Bianchi, who had a past that for some time had kept him away from the sacraments. However, this Lothario left lustfulness behind once he met a woman who attracted him more than all the others, even though she was devout. They married quickly and he gave up his "sinful attachments,"[420] as he called them.

While Bianchi occasionally kept his wife company at Mass, he never gave his will to assisting at the Holy Sacrifice. His wife was devoted to Pio, and when she made trips to San Giovanni, her husband would come with her; but when she went to Confession to Pio, he made himself scarce.

During the war, the couple was deterred from traveling to San Giovanni, but in the late 1940s they took a bus trip to the monastery. On the coach, one of the other passengers told them how his little boy had been deaf but was cured by Pio's intercession. When he heard this, Mr. Bianchi said he felt extremely uncomfortable because of his "sinful state" and he resolved to seek out Pio and make a good Confession.

When he met Pio in the sacristy and recounted the life he had led, Mr. Bianchi saw Pio's face contract and grimace in pain. Nonetheless, Pio recognized the man was sincerely contrite, so he absolved him and agreed to be his spiritual father, warning, "If you dare to do any of those things again ..." as he raised his hand in a threatening gesture.

And so, after many years away from the sacraments, Mr. Bianchi's soul was returned to a state of grace, a state of bliss. "After confession I felt as if I were literally walking on air," he marveled, "a distinct physical sensation as though a huge weight had been removed from my body, as if I were floating rather than walking." That lightness, the feeling of being filled with helium, is something echoed by many penitents who confessed to Pio.

Mr. Bianchi certainly amended his life —"I turned my back on my sinful habits" — and became a daily communicant and moved to San Giovanni permanently. He was also someone who received a cure without asking for one — for severe back trouble. He had been wearing an orthopedic device when he decided to move to San Giovanni. When he had settled into his new home, out of the blue Pio commanded him to take off the device supporting his spine and do his share of manual labor in building the Casa, even though this seemed to be dangerous advice! But Mr. Bianchi did exactly as Pio asked, and he never had any back pain again.

Pio Rebukes the Archbishop

These precious postwar years, through the 1950s, were the era when Pio enjoyed the most freedom, which he used to establish his hospital and to bring souls such as Mr. Bianchi out of sin and into the light of salvation. The biggest reason for this was that Pope Pius XII was so unwaveringly supportive of the stigmatist that he never allowed Pio's enemies to move against him. But there was an episcopal thorn in Pio's side: The Franciscan seminary back in Pietrelcina was empty because a certain archbishop was blocking it.

Mary Pyle had poured money into the building of Holy Family Monastery, but before it could welcome young men seeking to follow in St. Francis's bare footsteps, it needed the authorization of Archbishop Agostino Marcinelli of Benevento. Years after its completion, it remained completely out of use, and Archbishop Marcinelli absolutely refused to confer on the Capuchin campus the vital permission to function. It also needed restoration; the friary had been requisitioned for the billeting of soldiers, who vandalized the premises and used the walls as a canvas for curse words.

Sternly rebuking Marcinelli, Pio wrote perhaps the most strongly worded letter of his life. Pio upbraided this prince of the Church for being "truly hard of heart."[421] At age fifty-nine, Pio was no longer as docile to bishops as he had been as a youth. Now Pio was unflinchingly assertive, saying that "souls are being lost and the enemies of God are wreaking havoc."[422]

At that time Jehovah's Witnesses were making a lot of converts in Pietrelcina, and people were leaving the Church. The leader of this cult was brash and even wanted to buy the Franciscan seminary to hold ceremonies! Even more disturbing, Pio said that Marcinelli bore blame for the bombing visited on his archdiocese: "Benevento was bombed … as a punishment for the Archbishop." If we take Pio at his word, this means the Lord punished Benevento for the archbishop's hardness of heart, which harks back to Pio's insight that the war was going to last a long time because people were "hardened." Pio told the stubborn prelate that "my heart bleeds to say this, but it's true."[423]

Peppino Saves the Seminary

Pio's letter did not persuade Marcinelli to give permission to the seminary to function. But Pio also saw mystically that it was not his role; another priest was meant to play a game of diplomatic chess and win the authorization for Holy Family Monastery to welcome young Franciscans at Pietrelcina.

Pio had a close friend and cousin, Don Giuseppe Orlando, whom he fondly called "Peppino." Peppino had classic Roman good looks, dark deep-set eyes, a long nose, and a big dimple in his chin. He always had impeccable priestly dress and was a born diplomat. Pio asked Peppino to uncover the cause of the archbishop's refusal. Peppino found out that Marcinelli's denial of authorization to the friary was actually not totally bad. The archbishop feared that if the seminary became a thriving friary, filled with young seminarians and the friars who instructed them, the people of Pietrelcina would give all their financial offerings to the friary because of their fondness for their native son Pio and neglect to support the secular clergy. He was thinking of the other priests, who perhaps would go penniless.

Ultimately, the archbishop wanted to prevent a conflict of clergy against clergy, the like of which had motivated envious priests such as Fr. Prencipe to attack Pio in the 1920s. Peppino had a meeting with Marcinelli, where he brokered a compromise. Marcinelli said he'd be willing to change his mind were ways found to make sure financial offerings to the diocesan clergy continued, even after the seminary was up and running.

Next Peppino went to Rome, where he had several providential meetings until he reached the prince of the Church who was going to change it all. He met with Cardinal Luigi Lavitrano, who was moved to intervene. After Lavitrano dialogued with Marcinelli, the archbishop of Benevento was suddenly of a mind to grant permission to the friary. This was all thanks to Peppino, who had run interference on behalf of Pio and had brought Lavitrano to the table with Marcinelli. Pio was extremely proud of his friend, saying, "See, Peppino, God chose you to accomplish this work!"[424] This is telling in that the Lord appointed Peppino by way of Pio.

Peppino had a question for Pio, because he'd experienced a lot of coincidences, and wondered if they were just that — that he'd randomly been in the right place at the right time to meet the right cardinal in the form of Lavitrano. Pio set him right: "There is Somebody up there who arranged those coincidences."[425]

April 1947 was a most happy time for Pio. The friary opened and there was a hungry hope among his own people that he would be moved back there. Pio had been away from them for thirty-one years, and he hoped to attend the consecration of the new friary, but when the people of San Giovanni got wind of his travel plans, they armed themselves and guarded the monastery day and night, in much the same way they had prevented his transfer during his persecution of the 1930s. Much as it was a bitter penance, Pio agreed to stay away from Pietrelcina. This possessiveness on the part of the people of San Giovanni was a recurring theme in the life of Pio, and as we will see was to become a bigger catalyst in Pio's last and most painful persecution.

29

ON HEALING

After the Casa received its legal standing in 1946, it would be another decade before it opened its doors. The auspicious opening took place on May 5, 1956. A massive crowd of some fifteen thousand people came, including prelates from the highest echelons of the Vatican, prominent politicians, and other dignitaries. Pope Pius XII lauded the Casa as a "a magnificent success."[426] The *New York Times* hailed the Casa as "one of the most beautiful as well as one of the most modern and fully equipped hospitals in the world."[427]

When Barbara Ward saw the hospital chapel, she got a great surprise: Angelo had used her face as the model for the Blessed Mother's face on a stained-glass window. Barbara was beautiful in body and soul, and Angelo had so admired her work of charity in getting funds from America that he'd had Barbara's exact likeness painted in glass.

Pio had some heartache at this time: His beloved confessor, Fr. Georg Pogany, was transferred to America so he could help Hungarian immigrants. Hungarian was Georg's mother tongue, and he became a great asset to the Catholics of Irvington, New Jersey.

The Casa Opens Its Doors

In the beginning there were only a few patients, and the Casa was mostly empty. Some scoffed that the stigmatist had been misguided, but then Pio led a eucharistic procession, with the Blessed Sacrament exposed, to every part of the Casa, and suddenly every room was filled. The entire "Work" was said to belong to Pio, but he corrected this with, "God's work, just as He shows me."[428]

Inviting the Lord's presence into an apostolate — or any work He gives us to do — is so important. Asking a priest to lead a procession with the Blessed Sacrament is an especially powerful way to extend that invitation. When we ask for the Lord's blessing in this way, according to the Lord's will, the fruit of our faith is sure to follow.

Pio made a practice of carrying a monstrance with the Blessed Sacrament through the Casa. Pio was adamant that those who could not pay for their treatment were to be treated anyway, and generous offerings came from his followers continuously. Even the poorest patients were never turned away. Throughout his life, Pio recited one whole Rosary a day for the sick. For Pio, the active role of encouraging charity in the form of donations was always accompanied by beseeching Heaven on behalf of the sick, as well as teaching the doctors how to love their patients.

Pio shaped the Casa's Christian ethos, and although he had no medical training, he instructed the doctors, "Bring God to the sick. It will be more valuable than any other treatment." He also gave them a treatise on the importance of their love in healing the sick: "You have the mission of curing the sick, but if at the patient's bedside you do not bring the warmth of loving care, I fear that medicine will not be of much use."[429] Pio was, however, unequivocal that patients and doctors alike could only give love if they had love. "Here," had declared, "patients, doctors and priests shall be reservoirs of love which will communicate itself to others in proportion to the extent it is found in them."[430]

To the patients who were suffering, Pio had a different message. Their love of God could be demonstrated by accepting their suffering: "The suffering patient must have in himself the love of God by a wise acceptance of his pains."[431] Furthermore, Pio said, "The love of God must be strengthened in the spirit of every patient through his love of Jesus Crucified."[432]

For Pio, the healing of a patient's bodily afflictions was no more important than the saving of their souls. Pio revealed his game plan for saving souls: "The goal of the Work is namely to care for the bodies to arrive at the souls."[433] On that note, Pio described the true motivation behind the Casa as being a "clinic for souls."[434] The patients, even those who were seriously ill, were being given a golden opportunity to orient their souls toward Heaven.

Padre Pio on Suffering

Now that we've covered how the Casa came to be, let us explore Pio's mystical insights on suffering as well as the healing of body and mind, to glean insights that will inform our own understanding of these matters.

For example, why did Pio, a miracle worker, need to build a hospital? Could he not have interceded for every sick person to be given a miraculous cure? Pio knew he could not always intercede for a miracle, saying, "Miracles only occur when human intervention cannot achieve the purpose."[435] When Our Lord deigned to give grace for a miracle through Pio's intercession, then a sick person was healed miraculously. But if there was no miraculous grace on offer, that person needed grace in the form of medical attention. That is why the Casa was needed.

From the earliest days of his fame, Pio saw crowds of sick or disabled people who had made arduous journeys to his monastery in the hope that he would intercede for a miracle cure. Pio's heart ached to help everyone who came to him, and he possessed a profound willingness to take on himself the sufferings of other people: "If I knew that someone were suffering whether in body or soul, I would ask God to free that person from whatever their problem is. And I would willingly accept that person's suffering on myself if that would save the person and allow the person to share in the fruits of that suffering."[436]

This was a great irony at the heart of Pio's life. He founded a hospital to relieve suffering, yet he himself embraced it and knew souls could be paid for with offerings of pain. Pio was ready and willing to be a servant to suffering, offering it up to the Lord in exchange for salvific grace. When it was suggested to Pio that he share his suffering by giving parts of his pain away, his curt reply was, "I do not share my precious jewels with anyone."[437]

Pio's Hernia and Redemptive Suffering

In an earlier chapter, it was mentioned that Pio had a hernia that left normal scar tissue. At thirty-eight he had surgery to treat the adhesions that had anchored themselves to his body, and from this account we can gain extraordinary insights as to the value of pain.

As he was about to undergo an operation, he refused all anesthesia. Dr. Giorgio tried to ply him with Benedictine (a strong glass of grog), but Pio declined to drink it, joking, "There must be no quarrel between Capuchins and Benedictines." The operation took longer than expected, and Pio cried out to the surgeons, "Hurry! I can't stand it any longer." Restraining himself, he trained his eyes on the crucifix and uttered in agony, "Forgive me, my Lord. I have never offered thee anything of value, and now that thou givest me this simple chance I complain unreasonably."[438]

Have you ever had the opportunity to make such an offering as Pio did? We may not be stigmatists or living saints, but we are presented with a process whereby our soul may become more akin to that of Pio —by offering up our suffering. In doing so, any human soul might have much more in common with Pio than is commonly thought.

As he suffered on that operating table, Pio spoke to Our Lord saying, "It is nought compared with Thy sufferings on the Cross,"[439] and asked the Lord to forgive him after complaining. Such suffering can help to purify our own souls or be given to other souls to help them in their salvation; this is known as "redemptive suffering."

When Pio beheld his beloved Jesus on the Cross as the scalpel scored his skin, he recalled that Our Lord's Passion on the Cross was the price of our entrance into Heaven. On that day, Pio offered his surgery for a soul and afterward was heard to ask a fellow Capuchin, "Do you think that the Lord has accepted my sacrifice for X?"[440]

We must be good stewards of our health and take care of our bodies. We should not purposely inflict unnecessary pain or suffering on ourselves. Pio had much more mystical insight than most and saw through this needed surgery an opportunity to offer up his necessary suffering for the good of others.

For those of us who do not have his gifts, when to seek medical help can be a tricky decision — as well as what kind of help and from which doctor. If we are sick, are we solely meant to pray and do nothing else? Should we wait to see if Our Lord will miraculously alleviate our pain, or does the Lord want us to get treatment from doctors and/or other health professionals?

We have but to turn to Pio's example to answer these questions, recalling his efforts to alleviate suffering through the Casa. Let us also consider the advice Pio gave Raffaelina, who became a victim soul and offered her life for Pio's return to monastery life. When she had a tumor in her breast, she did not get medical attention because she did not want a male doctor seeing her unclothed. Learning this, Pio was not impressed. "Do you know that anyone who refuses human remedies exposes himself to the danger of offending the Lord?" he asked. He scolded her for ducking the doctor, saying, "And do you not know that God tells us through Sacred Scriptures to love the physician for love of Himself?"[441]

Faith and Healing

Sometimes one who has been seriously ill may find it hard to accept the miracle, thereby losing the attention and sympathy they had received in their illness. One young girl who had been seriously ill became the beneficiary of a miraculous cure. She went to visit Pio and pretended to still be sick, in a bid to test Pio, to determine whether he could see through her playacting. "Go away, child," he told her. "You are quite cured. Be careful that you never the tempt the mercy of the Lord."[442] Although this may seem a childish tactic, have we ever been tempted to stay in our comfort zone, even if it meant holding on to what made us unwell?

Whether or not Our Lord will grant us a cure may be dependent on our faith. Filippo de Capua was a learned professor whose wife was expecting a baby. When doctors gave him the devastating news that either his wife or child would die, Filippo consulted Pio. The stigmatist contradicted the medical experts. "Neither the mother nor the child will die," he promised. But Filippo pestered Pio anxiously, and in a pithy rebuke, Pio informed Filippo his anxiety was symptomatic of lack of faith. "It is not yet written in the decrees of God," he declared, "but if anything happens, it will be because of your lack of faith."[443]

What an extraordinary revelation, that lack of faith might diminish or cancel a grace of healing! Indulging excessive anxiety amounts to doubting God, and such anxiety may replace trust in our minds. The remedy here is to pray for the gift of faith and pray for hope and trust in the Lord, which will supplant the room occupied by anxiety in the human mind. It is also demonstrative of one of Pio's unidentified charisms, being able to read "the decrees of God" and knowing what was written and what was yet unwritten. This explains his certainty in predicting future events.

When We Don't Get a Miracle

But what if it is not God's will for a person to be cured? What if neither medical intervention nor a miracle relieves a person's suffering? There is another way of approaching illness: a radical imitation of Christ, where the person embraces incurable illness visited on them as their cross and, relieved of the desire for a medical cure or a miracle, makes an offering of their pain.

Pio had a spiritual son, Giacomo Gaglione, who was almost completely paralyzed but was given the grace to surrender himself to his condition and thus enjoyed the accolade of resembling Pio closely because he shared Pio's surrender to suffering. Giacomo was in his twenties and almost totally paralyzed when he was rolled in to meet Pio for the first time on a flat wheelchair tilted at a forty-five-degree angle. Giacomo could not move and could not talk, but he could use his fingers. He had not always been paralyzed; he was born healthy and into privilege. His mama was of Italian nobility and his papa was a celebrated lawyer. As an assertive firstborn, Giacomo had a competitive streak; as a teenager he entered sports races and won, and he vied for the attention of young ladies.

At the tender age of sixteen Giacomo felt an acute ache in the heel of his foot; soon after his legs and feet swelled until he could no longer move any of his limbs, and he was diagnosed with a rare form of polyarthritis. Giacomo's mama had to feed him like a baby. All the medical treatments and surgery did nothing. He lived in pain but got some relief when he lay in a flat-bed wheelchair made of iron bars, which relieved the pressure his body weight put on his joints. He had been in love with a young lady, but the mother of his girl broke them up and the heartbroken Giacomo became suicidal. He steeped himself in bitterness and habitually uttered blasphemies. He had been paralyzed for seven years and was always in a sour mood, until a taste of sweet hope came.

Giacomo read newspaper reports about Padre Pio and heard of sick people who were awarded miraculous cures that defied scientific explanation. Giacomo determined that he would visit Pio — he hoped to be able to get back the girl he loved. His family took him to San Giovanni, and the long-awaited moment arrived when Giacomo was with Pio. Giacomo recalled that "Padre Pio looked at me with his eyes so deep and so beautiful and smiled at me with a smile of an innocent child. To see Padre Pio and to forget the reason for my journey was one and the same event."[444]

Giacomo realized that he was not to ask for a release from the prison of polyarthritis, but he was to imitate Pio in accepting his cross and the extreme limits his lack of functioning limbs placed on him. He heard a call from God to stay as he was, and an even better miracle took place. Giacomo had this precious insight, "If it is a miracle to make a paralyzed man walk again, it is even more of a miracle to make him welcome with joy, for his entire life, the will of God." Consequently, Pio never asked Our Lord for Giacomo's healing. The desire to be a victim soul supplanted Giacomo's desire to walk again, and the will to be free of pain was replaced with the will to have a lifelong Calvary. So Giacomo was seen to be "crucified with a smile."

The Apostolate of Suffering

Giacomo founded "The Apostolate of Suffering," a movement of people who recognize their role in offering their pain to God in atonement. Giacomo further graduated spiritually when he decided to use all the Lord had given him for the good of others; he saw that the Lord had left him with an intact mind, keen intelligence, and a gift for writing. Giacomo went on to author several books, and every year he responded to an average of 3,500 letters from people afflicted with illness, empathizing with them and encouraging them to make a beautiful sacrifice of their sufferings. Giacomo wrote, "The infirm person has the mission to glorify the Lord and help sustain creatures in His grace." Padre Pio often bilocated to Giacomo, and Pio's heavenly scent could be inhaled in all its delightfulness in Giacomo's home. As Padre Pio had the visible stigmata for fifty years, so too was Giacomo paralyzed for fifty years. He died in 1962.

At his funeral, Pio promised that Giacomo was in Heaven, "With Jesus on the cross, with Jesus in Holy Paradise." When Pio was asked if Giacomo was a saint, Pio was adamant: "A Saint? Giacomo is a great Saint!" Previously Pio had reserved the honor of the title "a great saint" for St. Thérèse of Lisieux and St. Philomena.

Perhaps you might invite the intercession of Giacomo for people with disabilities, and especially for people with debilitating arthritis, but also for men and women who cannot marry the person they love. But perhaps the bravest move is to ask Giacomo's intercession for someone who is sick beyond cure, to ask for the grace of radical acceptance of the Lord's will.

In April 2009 Giacomo was declared venerable by Pope Benedict XVI.

A Husband's Faith

There is an astounding case of a man who gave his will so entirely to God that when his wife fell deathly ill, he didn't pray for her to be miraculously cured. He prayed only that God's will be done.

Vincenzo Mercurio was born blind. He was raised agnostic, but he had a brilliant mind and was a first-class academic, earning degrees in philosophy and science. He became Professor Mercurio, but he had no faith. Some relatives of his went to Pio and asked him to pray for Vincenzo. Pio said they should have a contest, that whoever could pray the most for Vincenzo would win!

Sure enough, after many had interceded on his behalf, Vincenzo went to Pio for counsel. The blind professor was so impressed by Pio's humanity that he decided to confess. He made it known to Pio that he was not seeking a miraculous cure for his blindness; rather, he wanted to know if Catholicism was the true religion, and the stigmatist convinced him this was the case. Soon, he moved to San Giovanni for good, but found living alone hard, so Pio advised him to marry.

When a lovely obstetrician came to work at the Casa, Vincenzo fell for her, and Pio told him that she'd been sent by God to him. They married, Pio blessed their union, and in the short years that followed they quickly had five babies. Not long after the fifth was born, Vincenzo's wife was diagnosed with an incurable disease. In the event of her death, he would be left to cope with five little ones, and he could not even see them.

When a priest, who was a spiritual son of Pio's, encouraged Vincenzo to pray insistently for her recovery, the blind father replied, "Day and night I pray that the will of God be fulfilled in my family. He knows what He is doing. If He wants my beloved wife as a victim, let Him take her for the greater glory of His most holy Name."[445]

Another priest pressed him to pray as taught in the Gospels, that we may pray in Jesus's Name for everything, and that he could pray specifically that his lovely wife be spared from imminent death. Vincenzo, however, wanted instead to pray in Jesus' Name only for the intention that His most holy will be done. Vincenzo's response shows remarkable spiritual maturity. "These words of the Gospel are for souls who were recently converted, vacillating before trials," he suggested. "Jesus, to help them, invites them to ask, to knock, to pray in order to receive graces. Those souls already formed by the teachings of Christ have no need to ask. They know they are totally possessed by the Lord and have no desire other than to be conformed to the will of God."

Instead, Vincenzo asked the Lord to allow him to take the place of his wife. "Lord, if you want a victim in my family, take me, for I am a poor blind man; save my wife, for she is needed by the children." When Vincenzo did not become the victim, he conformed himself ever more to God's will and explained, "I will not rebel against His will, instead I pray that it be fulfilled in all its fullness in my family for the greater glory of God."

At the funeral, the five little ones crowded round their mama's coffin, but Vincenzo resolutely gave thanksgiving: "Let us thank God. His Most Holy Name has been glorified in my family. May His Divine will always be done."

30

THE DEATH OF THE POPE WHO LOVED PIO

Let us once again pick up the thread of Pio's life story. In 1957 Pio wrote to Pope Pius XII and unburdened himself as to a dilemma he faced: He had taken a vow of poverty, yet he was getting financial donations of all sorts for the Casa. This sometimes caused pernicious problems. For example, when someone left Pio something in their will, the other heirs sometimes challenged this, arguing Pio could not receive an inheritance since he had taken a vow of poverty.

Pius XII held the Casa in the highest esteem and admired Pio even more than in the days when he urged his predecessor Pius XI to free Pio from the imprisonment of the early 1930s. Pius liked Pio's pluck and perseverance in making the Casa a functioning and flourishing institution. Now, he gave Pio the freedom he needed to operate the Casa while remaining faithful to his vows: he granted Pio a dispensation from his vow of poverty for the sole purpose of transferring money from his brown-gloved hands to the Casa's coffers. Pio was no longer under the control of his superiors as to how he used the donations for the Casa, but he had to defer to them in every other matter. These donations were going to cause serious division later between Pio and his superiors and foment the greatest persecution of Pio's life, but for a time Pio was the main middleman for the donations for the Casa.

Pius XII was on the throne of Peter for two decades, and these were the most fruitful years for Pio because the pope had such high regard for the stigmatist and completely believed in him. Pius XII was a public advocate for Pio, openly encouraging the faithful who came to his general audiences at the Vatican to visit the stigmatist. Pius's sister, Maria Teresa, took her brother's suggestion and visited San Giovanni to be close to Pio. The affection Pius XII had for Pio was returned by Pio, who hailed him as "Sweet Christ on earth."[446]

This all changed, however, upon the death of Pope Pius XII on Thursday, October 9, 1958. It meant that Pio no longer had an admirer and stalwart defender on the throne of Peter to watch out for him. Pio felt crushing grief, as he had felt at the deaths of his father and Dr. Willi. Yet when he was asked about the eternal destination of Pius XII, Pio wore a face of radiant joy and said, "I have seen him in Paradise."[447] We may carefully note that during this same year of 1958, when Pius XII became a citizen of Heaven, Pio prophesied the election of Pope St. Paul VI, then Archbishop Montini of Milan, through a messenger.[448] "Tell the Archbishop that he will one day be Pope, and to be prepared. Mind you, tell him this."[449]

Five years later, Montini did become Pope Paul VI, but when Pio prophesied his future, Montini was incredulous, saying, "These saints do get some strange ideas!"[450] Archbishop Montini had great affection for Pio, and when Pio celebrated fifty years of priesthood, Montini sent a warmly worded letter of congratulations.

In the five years between Pius XII and Paul VI was the papacy of Pope St. John XXIII, which turned out to be Pio's worst years on earth. It would seem that Pio did not know about the persecution that was fast approaching. It would be a long five years until his liberation.

Some would argue that, had Pio wanted to curry favor with the future pope, he would have omitted the advice to "be prepared" — as though he was not ready at present. However, Pio was actually being thoughtful in sending this message to Montini, whose pontificate lasted many years after Pio died. Our Lord gave this precise knowledge to Pio, who conveyed it to Montini to give him time to strengthen himself spiritually. At the time it is said that Montini had something of an unhealthy prayer life, including an aversion to the Rosary, and that he had a brittle personality. As it was, the Lord gave the future pope a reprieve, for he had an inkling he was going to be pope five years before the 1963 conclave.

The Papacy of John XXIII

Pope John's first introduction to Pio came through our zealous friend, Emanuele Brunatto, who spoke of Pio to the portly prelate in glowing terms. He may have protested Pio's sanctity too much, for all his gabbing didn't succeed in influencing Pope John to be favorably disposed toward Pio. Instead, Pope John was troubled by Pio's ministry and deplored "the mythomania created around his name."[451]

Pope John never met Pio, nor did he spend any time with him. When Pope John was in Pio's region of Italy, he strictly avoided going to visit Pio on at least two occasions. As we are about to learn, Pope John did not nurse hatred against Pio personally, but he did hold his ministry in contempt. It is likely that, had Pio not been famous, Pope John would never have had any quarrel with him. But in the years before he became pope, John seemed to have developed a personal loathing for the stories about Pio's mystical gifts, which he took to be a mix of lies and legends.

When a reporter wrote a sensationalized story claiming that Pio had prophesied to Cardinal Roncalli that he would be pope, and that following his election Pope John had given Pio his blessing, the pope sent the following to Archbishop Cesarano: "What is reported is completely invented. I never had any relations with Padre Pio, nor have I ever seen or written him, nor has it ever passed through my mind to send benedictions." In reply Cesarano defended Pio as "a religious of great virtue and great wisdom, a priest tireless in doing good."[452]

Then, in the early 1960s when Pope John was presented with false evidence and perjured testimony that Pio was promiscuous with a spiritual daughter, Pope John said he worried for Pio's soul. If all he heard was in fact true, it would have dire consequences and entail "a terrible calamity of souls, a calamity diabolically capable of discrediting the Holy Church in the world."[453] Thus Pope John worried that the reputation of the Church could suffer. Amid the Vatican's investigation of Pio's ministry in those years, Pope John was presented with a negative report from an ambitious priest who wanted to make his name by bringing Pio to heel. Pope John wrote in his diary, "Padre Pio is revealed as an idol of straw."[454]

Before we cover the last and most brutal persecution of Pio, let us first turn our attention to Pio's miraculous cure procured by Our Lady of Fatima, his love for Our Lady, and how it may inform our love of Our Lady, and the role this miracle may have had in provoking Pope John to read the third secret of Fatima before Our Lady had stipulated it was to be read.

31

PADRE PIO AND OUR LADY OF FATIMA

For several months in 1959, before John XXIII became pope, Pio was bedridden. A cancerous tumor had sprouted deep in his lungs, and he was plagued by pleurisy: His chest was so heavy with fluid that he was pinned to his bed. He didn't have the strength to offer Holy Mass or hear Confessions. Then, from May to August, as the Pilgrim Statue of Our Lady of Fatima toured Italy, Pio was deathly ill. During Our Lady's three-month visit to Italy, the Pilgrim Statue was brought to San Giovanni by helicopter, and when she graced the presence of the blessed town, the people came in droves to venerate her.

Pio had to be carried down in a chair to see Our Lady of Fatima. Tears rained from his eyes and he mustered the strength to kiss her feet, then he placed a golden rosary around Our Lady. He was in such severe pain that he was carried back to bed promptly. When the time came to leave, she was taken back in the helicopter. Pio was still confined to bed while the flying machine flew over the friary, and the ailing saint felt forlorn. Later Pio recounted,

> Our Lady was leaving without having healed me, I was upset, and I turned to her, praying with tears in my eyes: "My mother! You came to Italy and you brought me this problem, you came to San Giovanni Rotondo and you found me still sick, now you are departing and leaving me in this condition, without even giving me your blessing!" In that moment I had a feeling of warmth and well-being.... I was healed.[455]

A close friend of Pio's, Padre Alberto D'Apolito, heard Pio describe his illness as a "problem," and he asked, "Spiritual Father, you said that Our Lady brought you a problem. What did you mean by a problem?" Pio replied, "The illness. Was that not a problem for me?" Alberto answered with a piece of wisdom Pio had previously given him, "Padre, you have taught us that illnesses are gifts from God. Now, if Our Lady brought you this illness, it is not a problem, it is a gift."

Pio explained that debilitating illness can be both a gift and a problem simultaneously. "Yes, a gift, but a problem, too," he acknowledged. "I was no longer able to celebrate Holy Mass, I was no longer able to hear Confessions of so many people who came from afar. Tell me, was this not a problem?"[456] This time Alberto agreed with him, and his outlook was broadened to see that illness may be two things simultaneously, and that we may bear it as Pio did in atonement, for a time, but then ask to be relieved of it so we may continue our mission.

Padre Pio and Our Lady

Not long after this, Pio was restored to health. On August 10, the forty-ninth anniversary of his ordination to the priesthood, Pio was able to resume offering Mass, and on the twenty-first of that month he was able to hear Confessions once more. Had Our Lady heard his plaintive cry as she flew over the friary in the helicopter? Not quite.

Notice that Pio said he *turned* to her. Our Lady of Fatima must have been in the same room as Pio. The truth was that Our Lady was with him almost constantly. Once, when another friar asked Pio if Our Lady ever came into his room, Pio's reply was ironic: "Ask me, instead, if she ever leaves my cell."[457] They were together always. Our Lady kept vigil in the life of Pio because he shared the wounds of her Son's Passion. Our Lady had the same role of bearing witness in Pio's life, this time to a twentieth-century Franciscan friar who bore the wounds for the same reason her Son did: for the salvation of sinners.

Throughout his life, Pio thought it nothing out of the ordinary that he saw Our Lady and that she kept him company constantly. He was surprised that others did not see her. Once Pio asked his beloved Agostino in an incredulous tone, "Don't you see the Blessed Mother?" Agostino said truthfully that he never saw the Blessed Mother, but Pio was skeptical, "You say this out of holy humility."[458]

You may have heard Our Lady referred to as "God's masterpiece." Pio went a little further; he hailed Our Lady as "the greatest of all the masterpieces created by His hands"[459] and the "incomparable masterpiece of the Creator."[460] This tells us that not only is she a masterpiece but she is "incomparable." Thus, as God's masterpiece she has no peers among fallen humanity, and is the greatest masterpiece among all creation, human and angelic as Pio emphatically affirmed: "No creature surpasses her."[461] As for her relationship with the Divine Being, "she participates in His perfection."[462] Her Son was the Messiah: He had a human and a divine nature, and although Our Lady was not divine, still among all creation she has no equal and was God's most perfect creature absolutely. When he beheld her, Pio was rewarded by the sublime sight of Our Lady's supreme beauty.

On another occasion Agostino overheard Pio speaking to Our Lady: "Your hair is magnificent.... You are beautiful.... Your eyes are more splendid than the sun." Pio said that Our Lady was more stunning than the sun, which is why one evening he got irritated when a group of pilgrims were outside in an open field singing a song to Our Lady with the refrain "You are as beautiful as the sun." Pio was not impressed and griped, "If this were so, I would refuse to go to Paradise."[463]

Once, Fr. Alberto gave Pio a holy card of Our Lady which Agostino thought a beautiful portrait of her. He was shocked by Pio's reaction to the holy card: "They could not have made her any uglier than this." Alberto deferred to Pio: "You have seen Our Lady, that is why this holy card looks so ugly. How does Our Lady look?" Pio was at a loss, and had to answer with a rhetorical question, "Who can portray the beauty of the Blessed Mother?"[464] But in his epithets to her, Pio gave insights as to Our Lady's loveliness when he saluted her as "Woman bathed in light" and "Exquisite Dove."[465]

Pio's Prayer to Our Lady

Pio prayed in his own words to Our Lady:

> *Oh, gentle Mother, make me to love Him.*
> *Fill my heart with the love that burned in thine,*
> *purify my heart that I may know*
> *how to love my God and thy God!*[466]

Will you allow this prayer to become yours as well? This prayer is designed to allow us to win the grace so we may love God with all our hearts, all our minds, and all our souls, and thus fulfill the first commandment.

Pio said of Our Lady, "She shines like the morning star over the whole of creation," which tells us simply but spectacularly that light from Our Lady falls on us, human creations made by the Creator. Pio's assertion that "all things revert to Her, all grace passes through Her hands"[467] makes it known to us that every time we are the recipient of a special grace, we can know it passed through Our Lady's hands before it came to us. Even more spectacularly, if we merit the grace of salvation which makes our place in Heaven possible, this grace, too, was handed to us by Our Lady.

We may avail ourselves of a treasure trove of graces through offering the Rosary, which Pio called the "crown of graces."[468] Pio had such a dynamic devotion to the Rosary that he kept his rosary beads in his hands as much as humanly possible, a reflex he had learned from his father. He would pass his beads between finger and thumb, offering the Rosary with his right hand and left, often until he had said dozens of Rosaries a day. A friar who lived with Pio recounted how he had to help Pio wash his hands one at a time — not both hands at once — because he would pray on his left hand while the right was being washed.

We may find it very enlightening that Pio said, "Mary is present in every mystery and she participated in everything with pain and love."[469] We, too, may invite Our Lady's presence into our life when we offer a decade of the Rosary. Pio offered the Rosary during his every spare minute, and this was his way of staying in constant contact with Our Lady. We know she was with him constantly, but this was his way of being actively in touch with her, of returning her communication with the set of sacred salutations that is the Hail Mary.

Padre Pio and the Rosary

Just how constant was Pio's recitation of the Rosary? Once, late at night, a very young friar named Eusebio sought to learn from Pio how many Rosaries he had offered that day and prompted Pio by telling him he had offered three Rosaries of five decades. He then asked, "How about you? Forty?" Without any fuss, Pio said, "I have said sixty of fifteen decades but keep it to yourself."[470]

What Pio prayed in one day, some of us would need six months to pray! Although we may marvel at the many Rosaries Pio offered, he was not known to regularly command others to go beyond offering one five-decade Rosary a day, which is what Our Lady asked us to do at Fatima. Those of us who offer one five-decade Rosary every single day need not feel inadequate that there were days in his life when Pio offered 179 more. We may even ask Pio to help us say the Rosary once a day and to intercede for us to have a greater love of Our Lady. Pio said Our Lady is "the only worthy repository of His secrets,"[471] which evinces her most privileged place as one who God confides in. And to think the means are in our hands — when we move the rosary beads between our finger and thumb — to make the Lady in whom God confides present in our daily lives.

Do You Love Our Lady?

Pio expressed his passionate desire to call as many people as possible to love Our Lady: "I would like to have a voice loud enough to invite the sinners of the whole world to love Our Lady." We may feel the lack in our love for Our Lady when we contemplate the love Padre Pio had for her, which made him offer the Angelus with a rare reverence, investing with great devotion the prayer that honors Our Lady for giving her will to become the Mother of God. Even when Pio held Our Lady on high as his great lady, he was of a mind to cultivate within himself Our Lady's humility. A fellow priest wrote of Pio, "His imitation of Mary meant, in the first place, imitation of her humility."[472]

It was Pio's humility, like the Mother of God's humility, which allowed him to accept with the silence of a sacrificial lamb the piercing physical pain, but also the calumnies against him which resulted in the imprisonment of 1931 to 1933, and the last most dreadful chastisement of 1960 to 1964. For Pio, Our Lady was the ultimate example to himself and others as to how to bear persecution. He used say, "Rest like the Virgin on the Cross of Jesus and you will not be deprived of comfort."[473]

Our Lady rested on the Cross, but was she free from terror? No, Padre Pio told us, "Mary stood petrified before her Son crucified." But then he added, "But it cannot be said she was abandoned."[474] God allowed for her to feel great dread, as she was human with normal emotions, but He never deserted her. There is a fine lesson for us here, in that when we are at the mercy of human emotions, feeling scared because of hardship, this does not mean we have been left stranded by God. Although we may feel as though this has happened, it is not actually be the case.

Pio uncovered something else that may help when we are in the throes of torments. He said God's love for Mary grew because she bore suffering: "He loved her so much more for her suffering."[475] This makes perfect sense when we consider that Our Lady gave herself up to suffering for the fulfillment of

God's plan for the salvation of our souls: She saw her Son die on a Cross, the life draining from Him before her eyes, so that He could pay for the sins of mankind. Pio deftly explained how this proves her love for us: "She loves us so much that she offered her only natural Son to God the Father in order to save the adopted children."[476] It is conceivable that God may love us more for giving ourselves to His plan, which may mean, as in Our Lady's case, swords of sorrow stabbing our hearts, essentially embracing pain if it is part of completing God's will for our life. Quite the incentive, I proffer, to take to heart the idea that God may love us more if we suffer for His purposes, because if we sacrifice ourselves for His sake, we actively love God and keep the law of love by offering ourselves as He offered Himself on the Cross.

Our Lady, Tabernacle of the Most High

"Tabernacle of the Most High"[477] is how Pio described Our Lady, to convey that by carrying Our Lord in her womb Our Lady became a living tabernacle. When we kneel before a tabernacle in a church, we may consider that Our Lady was a tabernacle of flesh and blood. "May the Blessed Mother of God reign supreme over your hearts"[478] was an invocation often on the lips of Pio when someone came to him. We may take Pio up on his invitation to make Our Lady queen of our hearts.

Pio also hailed her as an "abyss of grace and purity,"[479] meaning our human minds may never measure her grace or purity, and so we must not ever say anything that undermines Our Lady's nature as one who is "full of grace," because to do so is to be in contradiction with how God created the woman who bore His Son. Pio said of Our Lady, "She was the first to practice the Gospel in all its perfection before it was written."[480] Here is the insight given by Pio that inspires the most urgency to seek ever greater closeness to Our Lady: "We must make every effort to walk close to her, since there is no other path leading to life except the path followed by our Mother."[481] That there is "no other path" to eternal life should chivy us along the same route as the Blessed Virgin Mary.

Devotion and Confession

But what of practical devotion to Our Lady? That is, are we to venerate publicly, in procession with crowds of other people, as a picture of Our Lady is held aloft on a banner? As the following story will demonstrate — urgently — these means of cultivating devotion to Our Lady are essential to our ongoing personal conversion.

Padre Pellegrino was a strong young friar with big, round eyes, bushy eyebrows, and brown hair and beard as full as a sheep's coat. Pellegrino was always in robust health, and for decades he stayed by Pio's side when Pio was ailing and getting weaker. Pellegrino was thick-skinned, and Pio used to tease him, "You have an ugly face. Only when you recite the Rosary can you say you have ruby lips."[482]

On one occasion, Pellegrino insulted Pio when he deliberately stayed away from a Marian procession. The people of the town were holding a procession with the picture of Our Lady of Grace, Pio's favorite image of Our Lady, in which the Christ Child sits on her lap and offers His mother to us. Pellegrino could have gone, but instead he rested under some pine trees. Pio knew he had done this, and when next they saw each other, he demanded in a thunderous voice why Pellegrino had missed the procession. Pellegrino defended himself; he said that he considered such public displays of people praying out loud and singing to be "harmful" to true devotion and even a waste of time. When Pellegrino realized he had offended Pio very much, he asked Pio to hear his Confession, only to have Pio order him, "Leave my room immediately."

Pellegrino replied, "I believe that without banners and processions, devotion to Our Lady is more sincere and beautiful." Pio gave this telling response: "In manifesting your disdain for exterior practices, you are showing you haven't even a little of that devotion which you call essential." Pellegrino told Pio he knew that he needed Our Lady's help so that his soul wouldn't go to Hell, but Pio countered by saying that Pellegrino's devotion to her was cold as ice, and he further said, "If you have the opportunity of offering outward and public homage to the Madonna, you could even break your legs in order to do so."

Pellegrino was still keen for Pio to hear his Confession, but Pio refused; he sought to lead his friend to true devotion to Our Lady. "Our Blessed Lady is the channel of grace always at your disposal. If you want to make a good confession, you need not even make an effort to discover this rich and precious channel, you need only come closer."

We don't need to go on a difficult voyage of exploration to find Our Lady, we need only move nearer and our closer proximity to the Mother of God will allow us make good Confessions. Let us have the strength of character to understand that in the absence of coming as close as we can to Our Blessed Mother, we may not make good Confessions. We would do well to hold dear what Pio told Pellegrino, that "the sacrament of penance was instituted for man [and] only through tender devotion to Our Lady will you find the way to make good use of it."

At the time Pio said this, he was still making Pellegrino wait to make his Confession, and Pellegrino still thought it "useless" to ask Our Lady's help in making a good account of his sins, but Pio was again uncompromising in his explication of Our Lady's unique role. "You must recommend yourself to the Blessed Virgin. Only she will tear asunder your ropes and chains." Pio revealed that "Our Lady furnishes the confessional with the clothing of mercy."

In this same string of conversations, Pellegrino became manipulative. He offered Mass for Pio's mother, Giuseppa, and hoped this would move Pio to hear his Confession. But no. Pio told him that he needed Our Lady to assist him in putting his conscience in order: "What kind of confessions do you make, if you don't ask Our Lady for the grace to know how to separate good from evil in an orderly manner?" It was only when Pellegrino showed that he was coming closer to trusting and loving Our Lady that Pio relented by saying, "I hear myself being begged for love of Our Blessed Lady, I can confess you." Pio gave Pellegrino this lovely assurance: "You will become an angel if you are devoted to Our Blessed Lady."

We may follow to the letter all that Pio told Pellegrino: By venerating Our Lady in public we will show our peers the very real love that is in our hearts; by just moving closer to her we may get the grace to make good Confessions; and by merely ask her help in enlightening our sin-stained minds we may order our conscience by sifting the good from the bad. The most important jewel in these insights is to cherish and uphold Our Lady's uniqueness. Pio repeated that she is the only one who can free us and intercede for us. She is singular for a reason, and our eyes need be on her, because she alone can bring us to the Lord.

A Miracle Cure for Pio

Padre Pio was seventy-two when he was afflicted by the tumor and bedridden with pleurisy. At the time, the average Italian man lived to be only sixty-three, and so before his miraculous healing, the faithful all over Italy had been anticipating his imminent death. This was the high point of Pio's life in terms of reputation and good standing; the scandalous rumors that were to haunt him in the 1960s and give rise to his persecution had yet to happen.

When the best doctors surrounded the stigmatist and pronounced that he was going to die because of a malignant tumor embedded deep in his lungs, millions of Pio's devoted followers around Italy were in shock. Many Italian Catholics each year spent their vacation time taking a pilgrimage to see Pio. The nation of Italy eagerly awaited news about their favorite friar.

In the early months of John XXIII's pontificate, the new pope was not quite garnering the same attention as Pio. Although he was very popular, something he courted, he was not held up as high as this wonder-working saint whom people were already openly grieving.

The following summer, in August 1959, Pio experienced his miraculous cure through the intercession of Our Lady of Fatima. John had been pope for a full nine months, and he had not yet opened the third secret of Fatima (which was to be opened in 1960). But rather than wait, Pope St. John XXIII opened the letter in the latter part of August 1959 and read it during that stiflingly sticky summer.

The question of why Pope John opened the secret early has long baffled commentators. The seer who was given the secret, Sr. Lucia, had placed it in a sealed envelope with the instruction that it was to be opened by the pope of 1960, which had been the express instruction given Lucia by Our Lady. Could he not have waited four more months?

Some have suggested that the fact he did not wait for the specified time to read the third secret could have indicated his mistrust of the Fatima apparitions.

And yet, how could the pope ask the masses to follow Our Lady of Fatima when he did not? The apparitions had been ratified twenty-nine years earlier by Pope Pius XI, and Pope John was as free as any Catholic to doubt private revelation. Yet we may well ask, why did he want to read it so suddenly? One thing is certain: He did so later in the same month that Pio received his miraculous healing.

When Pio was cured, he resumed his usual fifteen-to-nineteen hour day to the delight of the faithful, who were ecstatic that their "Second St. Francis" had defied death and that Our Lady of Fatima had cured him!

The miracle happened on August 5, and people made plans to go to San Giovanni in droves. Those who had regretted not going sooner were not going to waste their opportunity to see the sainted stigmatist. Two weeks after Pio's cure, Pope John opened the third secret of Fatima.

Did Pio Know the Secret?

Pio's miraculous healing surely had crossed the mind of John XXIII, and maybe it dominated his thoughts as it dominated the news. It is likely that it was already known in papal circles that Pio had been told the third secret by Our Lady. Reportedly, Pio told the amazing Vatican exorcist, Fr. Gabriele Amorth, that he knew the contents of the third secret.[483] It is within the bounds of possibility that John XXIII felt himself on the back foot and wished to remedy his lack of knowledge sooner rather than later. It is possible that John felt there was something of a competition between his Catholicism and that of Pio. This is not about whether we are a foe or a fan of Pope John. Even those who love John XXIII and hail him as a saintly reformer admit that objectively his view of the Church was at odds with that of the more traditional stripe of Pio and his followers. Only one vision could win out, and John knew it. He may have wanted the message of Fatima to be further in the future and, egged on by the recent explosion of interest in Our Lady of Fatima in Italy, he opened the third secret ahead of time, so that he could put it to bed as soon as possible.

John XXIII had a pattern of rejecting negative predictions about the future. In his speech that opened the Second Vatican Council, he decried the "prophets of doom"[484] who made unwelcome portentous warnings about the Church and the world. He made known that negativity and words of caution were not going to influence him or his trusted ministers, and this was irrespective of whether they could be true. Thus, doubt surrounding the truthfulness of the messages the seers at Fatima claimed came from Our Lady were the reason the Church made this statement in February 1960: "Although the Church recognizes the Fatima apparitions, she does not desire to take the responsibility of guaranteeing the veracity of the words the three shepherd children said that the Virgin Mary had addressed to them."[485] Essentially, Sr. Lucia's witness was thrown in doubt, and as we'll see, Pope John had very serious doubts about Pio as well, which led to the last and worst persecution of the stigmatist. But before damning reports about Pio reached Pope John, Pio was betrayed by his own friars.

33

DARK TIMES AND SORDID ACCUSATIONS

A strange series of events led to the draconian restrictions placed on Pio when he was old and infirm. Pio was in his seventies, crowned with a wreath of snow-white hair while frazzled, white whiskers trimmed his face. Dark circles shadowed his brow and sometimes the bags under his eyes looked bulging. He looked constantly weary. His stare was still piercing, and life experience had leant a twinkle to his eyes.

Yet old age had been cruel to him. He had declined in health to the point that he had a constant runny rose, ear infections, and asthma. Kidney stones caused him severe internal pain, and arthritis hobbled him so much he couldn't stand for very long on his pierced feet. He couldn't distribute Holy Communion on Sundays and feast days, when there even bigger crowds than usual. It was on top of all this that Our Lord sent the most stringent test to Pio.

This may be a strange comfort to us: Our Lord does not spare even souls gifted with many mystical charisms from such torturous trials when they are at their weakest. The nature of the persecution visited on Pio in old age was unlike anything else he had ever endured. Even the suppression of his ministry in the 1920s and "the imprisonment" of the early 1930s did not have the nasty intensity of Pio's persecution from 1960 to 1964. The reason was that his persecutions of decades prior were caused by two chief orchestrators, dark-eyed Archbishop Gagliardi and eagle-faced Fr. Gemelli, both of whom had never been trusted by Pio and certainly never been friends of his, and therefore there was no bond between them. Gemelli had died in 1959, and so he had no hand in the last persecution when Pio was thrown to the wolves — first by a coterie of his fellow friars, then by a spiritual daughter who appeared to have narcissistic personality disorder. Pio was betrayed by those closest to him, and throughout it all he bitterly resisted. Here we see the two sides to Pio: He was one who made himself a voluntary victim, but he was also victimized by others against his will.

Betrayal from Within

During the year Pio was laid low with his tumor and then miraculously cured, his Capuchin superiors assigned Padre Giustino Gaballo as Pio's personal assistant. Giustino was forty and impressively devout and passionate about executing his duties. And yet it turned out to be an error in judgment: Gaballo appeared to be grappling with some painful issues; namely, envy and sexual neuroticism. He bore himself with haughty self-importance and acted as though he could mind-read the sexual thoughts of others. He would point at his brothers and claim he knew they were consenting to impure thoughts and acts (which may have been his way of initiating a conversation on sex). As one priest observed, Giustino was "very serious and rigorous, but sick on the subject of sex."[486]

Although his issues may have occasioned suffering for him, Giustino was regrettably typical of the lower caliber of priests who were then being given a place in the Capuchins — unlike the days when Pio's novice master, Fr. Tomaso, had eyes like a guard dog and was tough on the young men aspiring to be friars. He would never have allowed someone like Giustino to be ordained.

At this point, we need to remember a priest we've met twice already: Fr. Georg Pogany, whose parents converted from Judaism to Catholicism when he was a young lad. Fr. Georg was a very strict chap, unerringly direct and earnest to a fault. He didn't curry favor, which is why his assessment of Pio's soul has weight. After hearing Pio's Confessions for seventeen years, he had this to say: "I don't believe he ever committed sin, not even a venial one. No, I don't think so. I heard his confession."[487]

Unlike Georg, Giustino openly ruminated on the sexual sins of others, and had a dangerous tendency to confuse his suspicions with facts. And here is where he became Pio's enemy: He became convinced that Pio was breaking his vow of chastity. Giustino had already allowed himself to be poisoned against Pio by Sr. Lucina, a local nun who had set herself up as a seer and claimed to have a divine revelation that Pio was possessed and also "in constant peril of damnation"[488] because, she claimed, he was sexually involved with women. Giustino revered Sr. Lucina as a true mystic, whereas he held Pio in suspicion, and he was determined to find proof to back up Sr. Lucina's claims. Giustino was hell-bent on gathering hard evidence that Pio was sexually active with his female disciples, and poor Giustino lacked the humility to question his own premise. He was totally convinced he was right, and this self-righteousness and certainty in his assumptions led him to conduct a witch hunt.

Using his privilege as Pio's assistant to sneak into the stigmatist's cell when Pio was not there, Giustino would pick through the trash can and pull out the notes that Cleonice Morcaldi had sent to Pio, which had been hand-delivered by Pietro. When Giustino read the notes, in which Cleonice declared her filial love for Padre Pio, Giustino jumped to the conclusion that Pio and Cleonice were intimate. He furtively fitted recording devices in the guest room where Pio met spiritual daughters and recorded a conversation in order to build a case that Pio kissed women romantically and behaved as a lover.

The idea that Pio could have been having a physical relationship with any woman in this "room" was preposterous. The guest room was of the old-fashioned variety that used to be common in monasteries. Pio sat in a tiny locker behind a wall that had a small window in the center. The wall between him and a spiritual daughter was over three feet thick, and they spoke through the window. And yet, the fact that these women loved their spiritual father so much seems to have given rise to extreme envy in Giustino, and he nursed a toxic hate for Pio. Giustino aggressively plotted against him, and hastily appealed to the highest echelons of the Franciscans and the Vatican to have Pio shamed and disgraced.

Giustino Makes His Case

After Giustino made a faint, largely incoherent recording of Pio talking to a spiritual daughter, he took it to the superior of the friary, Padre Emilio, and convinced him that Pio was romantically involved with at least one spiritual daughter. He had a pile of "love notes" that he claimed added further credence to his suspicions.

Fr. Emilio had already been allowing Giustino to gossip about other friars' impurity. Giustino was certain of his claims, yet Emilio may have had his own reasons for wanting Pio controlled — reasons that had to do more with money given for the running of the Casa than with sex. Emilio let his ears be bent by Giustino, and together they plotted. They seized their opportunity when the provincial, Padre Amedeo, the highest-ranking Franciscan in the land, came to visit San Giovanni, and they forced a meeting with him.

Fr. Amedeo found himself confronted by two intensely earnest Franciscans claiming that their recording contained the smacking sounds of lips kissing (considering the three-foot wall, a more likely scenario might have been a spiritual daughter kissing Pio's hand). It is strong custom among Italians that a penitent kiss the hand of the priest, who holds the Body and Blood of Christ during the Sacrifice of the Mass. In Pio's case, to kiss his hand was like kissing the wounds of Christ and venerating the marks of their salvation.

To make a case that such veneration of Pio's wounds was in fact a sign of sexually illicit relationships is the stuff of satanic subterfuge. In the same way Our Lord was betrayed by Judas giving him a kiss on the cheek, Pio was betrayed by friars engaged in a search for a romantic kiss that never happened.

Intent on proving their suspicions, Giustino and Emilio demanded that Amedeo order further recordings to be made of Pio's exchanges with women so that "evidence" could accrue. Flustered, Amedeo refused, so Giustino browbeat him. "We repeat, we came for you to authorize us to continue to tape the confidential conversations of Padre Pio. It's absolutely necessary." When the leading Franciscan in all Italy would not give permission, Giustino pressured Amedeo sanctimoniously: "Then, know for certain that, because Padre Pio's name is renowned everywhere, extremely grave consequences will come of your failure to give authorization."[489] At last Amedeo gave in, and soon the guest room and Pio's cell were fitted with listening devices —without Pio's consent or knowledge. Later it was claimed that they also bugged Pio's confessional, and this point is still a matter of intense debate. If it happened, then they committed sacrilege.

Pope John XXIII Is Informed

Giustino had a well-positioned and well-respected friend in the Vatican by the name of Umberto Terenzi, whose laughing face and boyish appearance belied the power he wielded. Don Terenzi had a heart-shaped, smiling face. He had narrow shoulders and was slightly chubby. Dark strands of hair peeped out under his biretta, which looked huge on his small head. His eyes had a deep intensity of rarest empathy, and truly Fr. Terenzi had a heart of gold. He had worked tirelessly to help poor, starving people get regular food until they got decent employment. He had earned a reputation as a hero who lifted people up after they had fallen on hard times.

Yet Terenzi had a grievance against Pio, because he'd come to Pio looking for money and had been refused. Terenzi had wanted Pio to give him money donated to the Casa to help the poor in Rome. Pio refused, because the donors had not given money for that purpose. It was Terenzi, as Giustino's friend, who arranged for Giustino to get the faint, largely inaudible recordings of Pio to Pope John.

Terenzi got permission from the Holy Office for the tapes to be made, then forced the hand of the dithering Fr. Amedeo, saying, "Do not prohibit Padre Giustino and his collaborators from recording the private conversations of Padre Pio."[490] Then, in the blazing hot summer of 1960 — one year after he had opened the third secret of Fatima — Pope John was apprised of the tapes and given an account of a conversation between Pio and Cleonice, in which she said, "I feel all hot,"[491] and her spiritual father passed his glove through the little window, so she could comfort herself with something that belonged to him.

Pope John committed his reaction to the pages of his diary. "Extremely serious information about Padre Pio," he began.

> Thanks to the Lord's grace I feel calm and almost indifferent, in dealing with a troubling religious mania.... I am sorry about Padre Pio, who does have a soul to save, and for whom I pray intensely.... The discovery by means of tapes, if what they imply is true, of his intimate and improper relations with the women who make up the impenetrable praetorian guard around his person, point to a terrible calamity of souls.[492]

All in all, twenty-three tapes were made between October 1960 and March 1961. The conversations, which had been clearly recorded, were usually of a totally innocent nature, but Terenzi and Giustino continuously beat their drums and protested to Vatican officials that the tapes had noises of smacking sounds that suggested loud kisses!

Although it is true that kissing sounds would have been picked up each time Pio offered his hand through the tiny window for Cleonice to kiss, Giustino and Terenzi were obsessed with the notion that Pio was engaged in intimate kisses, part of an intimate relationship. At the time, Cleonice was in her sixties, stout with a large, round face that had thick brown hair crowning it. Had she tried to climb through the window, she would have gotten stuck!

Friar Envy

Some of the friars began calling Pio names because of his relationship with the local women. Back to the 1920s, Gagliardi had reported to Pope Pius XI that Pio was lascivious. But it is curious that Pio's friars suddenly started vilifying Pio, since these local women had been under his spiritual protection for many years — some, such as Cleonice, for over forty years!

It is very likely that the friars resented the spiritual daughters because they gave money to the Casa and less to the Franciscans. But Pio had given Cleonice a privileged role in soliciting large amounts of money for the Casa — she raised money for the poor people who could not pay for their health care — and this may have earned her more resentment from the other friars. Earlier we touched on something: that Pio may have fallen foul of his superior Fr. Emilio because of money. Other friars in the friary and around Italy may have shared this bitterness.

The great success of the Casa meant Pio was renowned as a sainted philanthropist, but this same magnificent work of charity may have been the catalyst for intense infighting among the Capuchins. Why?

As money flowed into the friary for the upkeep of the Casa, the Capuchins were trying to raise money for the restoration of churches and friaries that had been scarred by bomb blasts during World War II. The Franciscans had been so eager to make money quickly, they decided to take part in a Ponzi scheme run by a shady character by the name of Giambattista Giuffre, who went by the nickname "God's Banker." Greedy Giuffre attracted other greedy souls because he promised interest rates as high as 90 percent, in advance, on money consigned to him.

Pio was pressured by his Franciscan superiors to give them some of the donations arriving for the Casa so these funds could be invested with Giuffre. Pio refused because he said the money had been given by donors for the sick, and when Pio reviewed the promises made by Giuffre, he had doubt about the fraudulent nature of the scheme. At the time Pio was entitled to withhold the donations from his superiors because he had total administrative control of the Casa.

Before long, Pio was proved right: Giuffre's game failed. After he declared bankruptcy in 1958, the Vatican ordered that the religious orders that had borrowed money from laypeople and given it to Giuffre had to pay back the money.

But the Capuchins were devastated financially. With the heavy burden of debt on their shoulders, Pio's superiors tried to lean on him once again for money meant for the Casa. To their chagrin, Pio refused again, telling them simply that the money was not his to give but rightfully belonged to the patients.

Pio's superiors found this second refusal most galling because it showed them up as foolish: They were in debt for trusting Giuffre while Pio was allowing for money from all over the world to flow into a most noble institution, the Casa. They became more determined to have a say in how the donations for the Casa were used, but first they would have to seize control of the Casa from Pio, and at the height of his most painful persecution they succeeded in terminating Pio's control of the hospital.

Pio Finds the Wire

One day, Pio had an alarming discovery. "Look here, son," Pio called to his young personal assistant, Fr. Eusebio. He held up the wire that ran from Giustino's room to his. "They put a microphone to spy on me, and I cut it myself with this knife."[493]

Pio could easily read the motives of his fellow friars. When his dear old friend, Don Giuseppe Orlando (or "Peppino," as we came to know him when he back-channeled with Vatican officials to persuade them to allow the functioning of the friary at Pietrelcina), came to see him, Pio showed him the bugging devices and exclaimed in horror, "Look at what my brothers are doing!"

"Father forgive them, for they know not what they're doing," Peppino intoned, but Pio gestured impatiently and replied, "They know what they're doing!"[494]

34

AN APOSTOLIC VISITATION

Pio was the most famous Franciscan in the world; the most powerful was Fr. Clement Neubauer. With his flowing white beard, Clement looked like he was in the winter of life. He was an American, and as minister general he led a religious order that had monasteries all over the world. Fr. Clement had a good heart, but he was very indecisive and could stall when urgent action was needed.

The choleric Italians did not warm to the unemotional Clement, and they mocked him behind his back when he made them wait for a resolution. He delayed making big decisions, and effectively he asked the Vatican officials to fill his role as superior — with unfortunate consequences for Pio as well as the souls under his care. Many of the Italian Franciscans distrusted him fiercely, and certainly the hot Italian temperament conflicted with his cool demeanor. Consequently, the powerful superior was marginalized. He genuinely didn't share the bad intentions toward Pio, but the smear campaign was conducted energetically, and Pio's enemies were able to force Clement's hand.

There are credible reports that Fr. Clement revered Pio's sanctity. And the whole business of bugging Pio's cell and the guest room was done behind Clement's back. Had Giustino and Emilio wanted to tell Clement, they were prevented from doing so by the officials at the Vatican, who directly forbade Amedeo from notifying Clement, his superior. Later, when Terenzi informed Clement of the tapes, one can imagine he might have felt deeply betrayed that he had been locked out of a plot operated by a cabal of friars and Vatican officials. This exclusion gives credence to the notion that Fr. Clement was a supporter of Pio's, because had Giustino and his helpers thought Clement was on their side, they would have hastened to enlist him.

Pio's Spiritual Daughters Raise Concerns

After Fr. Clement learned that Pio's cell was being bugged, he was provoked into unusually swift action. He appealed to Pope John for an apostolic visit to happen as quickly as it could be arranged and said such a drastic course of action was needed to prevent disaster, because he foresaw "a dangerous situation emerging in San Giovanni Rotondo around the venerated person of Padre Pio." Clement listed some of the issues he felt warranted scrutiny during the high-level Vatican inspection that is an apostolic visit. One was that the Casa had no manager accountable for its running, and the board of administrators was rarely assembled. Clement was also concerned that Pio's spiritual daughters were making management decisions for the Casa, and opening Pio's mail, which often had highly personal content and "many delicate cases of conscience." Finally, donations and offerings were apparently being mishandled, and the friars in charge of Our Lady of Grace Friary were being stymied in their attempts to address "discipline, ethics and finance." Rumor had it that the spiritual daughters had waged a campaign to make anyone who opposed them leave town, and Clement even referenced a plot to take Padre Pio out the friary and have him live in the Casa. Clement lamented to Pope John that the spiritual daughters were fomenting fanaticism and "an ambience of false mysticism."[495]

The group of spiritual daughters derogatively called "the pious women" feature many times on the list of issues that Clement gave Pope John, and these spiritual daughters were intensely disliked by some friars close to Pio, whereas Pio loved them with all his heart and trusted them implicitly. This is the crux: Pio distrusted many of his own friars about money, whereas he placed his trust in his spiritual daughters, especially Cleonice, who worked tirelessly to solicit donations for the Casa, which had a policy of giving free health care to the poorest, sickest people and of never, ever turning anyone away.

The local spiritual daughters had known Pio all their lives and had been cherished by Pio since they were little girls, so their emotional attachment to Pio was strong. They had been born into humble homes nearby, and raised as strong, hardworking Italian women, but as they lived inches from the friary, they had been witnesses to great scenes of mysticism and miraculous cures and had seen on a daily basis a sea of souls rush at Pio. They had seen Italian celebrities come to Pio as hardened sinners, only to become so contrite that they wept before the friar with the stigmata. And it was this friar who drew them to him as his daughters! This made these Italian ladies feel very special, and for a few of them it became a type of drug, where they needed more and more attention from Pio to feel as special as they had in the past.

Yes, there were a few narcissists among them, which was at its most obvious to outsiders in the way they behaved before Mass. At break of day, when the doors of the church opened, some of them barged their way in, sharply jabbing their elbows at anyone who dared go into the church ahead of them and aggressively fighting for the pews with the best views of the altar. They even put chains and locks on the pews closest to the altar to protect the best seats. As a result, all the local spiritual daughters were maligned because of a few bad actors.

Giustino was allegedly scandalized by a spiritual daughter who confided in him that she had gone to a witch to bind Pio to herself; she wanted his spiritual aid in making reparation for the evil she had committed. This, however, speaks more to the daughter's possessiveness than it does to Pio's rumored misconduct. Had Pio been willing to "bind" himself to her, she would not have had need of a witch to do it for her. Also, Giustino was impervious to the pains Pio took to make sure his spiritual daughters did not worship him. This following example is instructive of Pio's way of showing his children that they should obey the Lord first.

A local spiritual daughter was confessing to Pio when she divulged, "Father, I fear lest I love you more than Jesus." Pio stayed silent and absolved her. A few days later, when she came back to see Padre Pio, he instructed her authoritatively to go and say something blatantly wrong to a certain person. She was flabbergasted, "Father, I would never do such a thing." Pio persisted, "I command you, do it under obedience." This pious woman refused to obey, and Pio declared, "You see now you do love Jesus more than me. Don't you see that when I order a thing obviously contrary to the will of God that you do not obey? Are you convinced now?"[496]

We must be wary of an attempt to throw all the spiritual daughters under the bus. There has been a tendency to tar the more humble and saintly daughters with the same brush as the aggressive ones, who seemed addicted to feeling special. It is to the humble daughters that so many in Pio's lifetime owed a debt. And today we owe them a debt of gratitude — certainly to Cleonice Morcaldi, whose diary contains profound truths that are inherited by us today and will be the inheritance of future generations of spiritual children.

Pio confided the holiest of holy revelations to Cleonice, including that he saw every one of his spiritual children when he offered Mass. On the practical level, Pio trusted Cleonice with many sensitive tasks. Pio trusted her to do his laundry — this was no small responsibility because there was great demand for Pio's bloodstained linen — and Cleonice was never tempted to make a small fortune by cutting up the cloth and selling it. Instead, while she scrubbed blood from cloth, she learned intimate facts about his stigmata, including Pio's flagellation wounds. Once, during a boiling hot August, Cleonice sent Pio a white linen tunic, because Pio always wore a tunic and she thought linen could keep him cool. Pio kept and used this tunic for three days, and when he returned it to Cleonice, she saw it was covered in blood: "I saw that there were scabs of clotted blood, and inside the scabs were marks of wounds on top of each other." When she next saw Pio, she exclaimed, "Father, you are all one big wound from head to foot." And Pio said to her, "Isn't this for our glory? If there would not be any more room on my body to put another wound, we will make wound upon wound."[497]

Cleonice became a victim of a few spiritual daughters who were jealous of her standing with Pio. Two sisters in particular, Elvira and Angela Seritelli, appeared to be obsessed with Pio. They resorted to the worst catfighting with women they felt got more time and attention. Elvira and Angela were so aggressive to Cleonice that she would hide whenever they came into the church.

Elvira had much less self-control than Angela. Elvira had the role of flower-arranger in the church. One day, when Elvira was carrying a vase of fresh flowers, she saw Pio deep in prayer, and when he opened his eyes to gaze at the tabernacle, she thought he was looking at the cleaning ladies, which she took to mean he had more affection for them than for her. She flew into a hysterical rage. A while later Pio tried to placate her by having her mend his habit in full view of everyone else. This remedy failed to lessen Elvira's jealousy, which was building to a violent crescendo.

On the eve of the Vatican investigation, the jealousy of the spiritual daughters was at its worst, and they spread sordid rumors that Pio and Cleonice were intimate. They no doubt wanted Pio to distance himself from Cleonice. But during the Vatican investigation there was a perfect storm: the friars funneling tapes to the Vatican just as Elvira stirred up trouble, even if it meant betraying Pio.

In May 1960 Giustino and Emilio had strong-armed their provincial, Amedeo, into giving his blessing to the spy operation which was already underway. Two months later, a Vatican investigation was to happen. Pio made no secret of the fact that he was dreading it, and he foretold that they were going to mar his reputation and force him to submit in obedience to decisions that would impede his outreach to souls.

Msgr. Maccari Investigates

In July 1960 the Vatican sent Msgr. Carlo Maccari to San Giovanni as apostolic visitor. Maccari was forty-seven and had a soft face with full cheeks, round ears, and a strong nose. His eyes had a driven, ruthless stare. Maccari strode forcefully into town, and his black soutane cut a dash in the dusty streets. He was possessed of an uptight, dynamic energy, which he needed, because this expedition involved staying up all night so he could watch how the crowds behaved as they waited for the church doors to open for Pio's Mass, and then having enough stamina to act as a trial lawyer during the day when he cross-examined Pio and his followers.

Maccari made a temporary home for himself in the Casa, where he slept whenever he was not staying up all night. Although Pio wanted to be totally obedient, he was not quite the meek lamb he had been during his first persecution three decades prior, and here we see a tougher, battle-hardened Pio, who did not suffer ambitious monsignors. Pio had supernatural insight into Maccari's meaner motives, and knew he was ambitious to the point that he would throw Pio under the bus to make a name for himself. Pio even said of Maccari, "We've got to be a little wary of this monsignor. He's sick with 'cardinalitis' and wants to crucify me." Pio meant that Maccari longed for a red cap. Pio, however, wanted the best for Maccari's soul, and in spite of the danger Maccari posed, Pio said, "Nevertheless, I want him with me in paradise."[498]

Clergy Questioned

As in years gone by, there was a pro-Pio faction and an anti-Pio faction, even in the highest echelons of the Vatican, but Maccari clearly felt he had better chances if he aligned with the anti-Pio faction. In view of the Vatican investigation, the anti-Pio faction that had fomented trouble against Pio in the 1920s regrouped as a bunch of embittered old clerics. Maccari met them and gave ear to their issues with Pio. After more than thirty years they resented that people gave money to Pio for his hospital but were not so willing to give lire to them. When Maccari strode into Pio's friary, he ordered the provincial, Fr. Amedeo, to bring together the entire community of friars as an assembly so he could address them. Maccari told his brown-robed audience of his plans to investigate the functioning of their friary as well as the person of Pio. After Maccari concluded his comments, Amedeo tried to speak to the assembled friars, but he was prevented by Maccari, who undermined him in callow fashion when he snapped, "Remember that it is I who am to be the last to speak — not you!"[499]

Maccari arranged his first meeting with Pio. But when Maccari canceled at the last minute, it upset Pio because he could have used the time to hear Confessions. When Maccari did show up for a meeting, Pio said to the self-important monsignor, "I don't have time to waste." Padre Pellegrino, who was by now an old friend of Pio's (and who will become highly important in our story at Pio's death), overheard the conversation and later scolded the stigmatist: "That wasn't right to give an answer like that to an envoy from the Pope, to whom you owe allegiance." Pio replied, "But I haven't acknowledged him, and therefore, I'm not obligated to speak to him out of obedience, because his authority over me is zero!"[500]

Soon Pellegrino discerned that Maccari's chief area of interest was to discover any evidence, however superficial, to substantiate the rumors that Pio was in intimate relationships with his spiritual daughters. When Maccari questioned Pellegrino, he prompted Pellegrino that Pio had red cheeks after meeting with the spiritual daughters, and that this was suggestive of kissing. Pellegrino defended Pio and excused his red cheeks as being from his habit of resting his face in his hands.

Maccari was aided by one Msgr. Giovanni Barberini, who started supervising the opening of the letters that came for Pio (even those marked "confidential"), so he could see if the donations for the Casa were in fact being given to the hospital. He trailed the receptionist and checked to see that there was no meddling with the huge sacks of mail while they were en route to the mail room. He also made the rounds of restaurants and pubs at night to question natives about Pio while they were imbibing liquor. Pio was disheartened by Barberini's presence, and his face took on a sickly look whenever he saw him, but nonetheless Pio cracked jokes with him as a way of diffusing the tension.

Spiritual Daughters Questioned

Maccari called the spiritual daughters for interviews and imposed questions designed to ascertain if Pio was sexually active. Such questions shocked most of the daughters. One spiritual daughter, scandalized, exclaimed to a friar, "Only a devil from hell would ask the questions that he did!"[501]

Cleonice Morcaldi was called three times by Maccari, and she came the first two times. While Maccari questioned and Cleonice answered, Barberini made recordings of the interview. When asked if she knew Pio was in open rebellion against the Catholic Church, Cleonice hotly defended her spiritual father: "The Church perhaps has never had a son more holy and more obedient than Padre Pio!"[502] She was mortified at Maccari's other questions, which were designed to make her confess that she was in a sexual relationship with Pio. Cleonice thought Msgr. Barberini positively simian, calling him "an ape in priest's clothing."[503] On the third occasion Cleonice was called, she refused, insulted and unwilling to legitimize their scheme. "By now I understood what they wanted me to confess. . . . I refused to go along with them."[504]

Unfortunately, not all Pio's spiritual daughters protected his reputation. The narcissist Elvira, consumed with jealousy for Cleonice and unhappy that Pio did not make her his favorite, swore on the Gospels that she had been sleeping with Pio until he had rejected her for Cleonice. She sealed her testimony with an oath that Pio and Cleonice were intimate in the guest room twice a week![505]

When Maccari confronted Pio with Elvira's deposition, Pio denied it all and swore he had always been chaste. Using the notes from Cleonice that Giustino had picked out of the trash bin, Maccari tried to provoke a confession from Pio, but he would not admit to such a thing. Maccari later said that Pio put up a front of meekness and used deception. Essentially, Maccari thought Pio a liar, and he reported, "Reticence, mental reservations, lies: these were his weapons to evade my questions."[506]

In fact, Pio was very elderly and dogged by health problems, and the investigation became more and more nerve-racking for Pio, who complained bitterly,

"I'm watched constantly, like somebody who has committed … many crimes!"[507] Pio was deeply hurt by Maccari's mean criticisms of the Casa. Maccari said it had been a mistake to build it on the side of a mountain and that it ought to have been built in a large city like Rome. Maccari cruelly said to Pio, "A month after you are dead, your hospital will have to close its doors."[508]

The Golden Jubilee

The summer of 1960 was meant to be a time of immense celebration — there was a big party planned to mark the fiftieth anniversary of Pio's ordination — but the golden jubilee fell on August 10, right in the middle of the Maccari investigation. Maccari ordered that the party be much curtailed, but he could not inhibit the exuberant local people who held many private parties in celebration of the anniversary of their saint's ordination.

Maccari did not celebrate Pio; rather, he found ways to hold him in contempt, saying, "There is a real industry that lives and prospers with propaganda about the 'sanctity' of 'the first stigmatized priest.'" Like Archbishop Gagliardi in the 1920s, Maccari felt the cult of Pio grew out of the ignorance of the local people; he damned devotion to Pio as the "myth of the wonder-working saint" that gave rise "to superstition and magic, the idolatrous cult of an individual."[509]

Although we may take Pio at his word that Maccari was acting out of personal ambition, he was not without evidence. Recall that one narcissistic spiritual daughter had reportedly gone to a witch. And Giustino was in constant touch with Sr. Lucina, who claimed she had revelations from God that Pio was sexually active. We do not know what motivated Lucina — her revelations may have come from the devil, or perhaps she was lying or mentally ill. On the other hand, Pio's enemies and critics, then and now, were only too eager to give credence to her falsehoods.

Maccari also interrogated Padre Raffaele as to Pio's alleged sexual activity. Raffaele was meek and patiently answered at first, having known Pio for many decades. Finally, he roundly rebuffed Maccari: "All I can say is that if all priests had the baptismal purity and innocence of Padre Pio, the Church would be truly holy in all her members."[510] When Maccari took issue with the sale of fake relics made from cloth daubed with the blood of beasts, Raffaele pointed out the hypocrisy of a Vatican official making such a fuss of fake relics, since in

Rome, inches from the Vatican, there has always been a similar trade in such merchandise.

Confessional Queries

Maccari had heard of issues surrounding the confessional. He'd learned that accommodations were being made for Pio's comfort — the door of the confessional left open and the screen drawn so that Pio got more air — which could compromise the seal of the sacrament and the privacy of the penitent. People were poking their hands in to touch Pio's hand and kiss it. Some spiritual daughters loitered with the intent of knowing when Pio withheld absolution. Pilgrims and visitors also loitered and misbehaved around the confessional without censure.

Maccari told Pio that he was recommending to the Vatican that they put in place an injunction that would allow the local women to confess to Pio once a month, as opposed to once a week as Pio usually advised. The friar objected strenuously. "Don't do this! You can't do it! Why deprive these poor souls of a spiritual guide?"[511] Maccari could not induce Pio to criticize even mildly his spiritual daughters. "He defended them from every accusation and described them as generous souls, completely dedicated to doing good."[512] When Maccari brought up the belligerent conduct of the spiritual daughters who sharply elbowed others away so they could claim the front rows of the church for themselves, Pio defended them still: "They get up early to have this right."[513]

Maccari's qualms about the spiritual daughters were not assuaged, and he banned Pio indefinitely from writing certain spiritual daughters and from meeting them or having any contact. Later Pio grumbled that those who led the Vatican inquiry were causing undeserved pain to the spiritual daughters. "They have isolated and prohibited those poor creatures, who are so good and generous, from having contact with me," he lamented. "These poor creatures have sacrificed so much to help me in my charitable work, without asking anything."[514] Pio had been unable to convince Maccari that he needed their assistance in managing the money for the Casa — that they were among the few who could be trusted not to pinch and pocket the donations for themselves.

Maccari's endless interrogation — accusing Pio of lying, unchastity, and all sorts of wickedness —took a great toll on Pio's health. There came a point when he broke down in front of Maccari and exclaimed, "I can't go on!" He raised his voice, "I hardly sleep anymore! I have little appetite! I can hardly eat anything! I feel weak, sad and alone." Being forcibly separated from his spiritual daughters, Pio was heartbroken, like a parent whose child has been forcibly ripped from his arms. "You've given my heart a wound that's too painful," he mourned. "I, too, have need of some people who love me ... with whom I can spend a few minutes like family.... I fervently pray to the Lord to call me to Himself.... I'm an old man and I suffer too much!"[515]

He conceded to Maccari that he needed the filial love of his daughters-in-spirit. Pio was desperate to convince Maccari that this love was not erotic but rather the stuff of a pure father-daughter relationship — not unlike the love Our Lord received from Mary Magdalene.

Maccari demanded of Pio why he had lavished so much time on the mentally ill. "Why waste time, so much precious time, with people who are little deserving of your attention and spiritual concern?" The irony was that it was Maccari who had lavished time on the mentally unbalanced when he went to the trouble of getting sworn testimony from Elvira, who was known to be unstable.

Pio smiled patiently at Maccari. "Even crazy people can have need for our care to be able to go to Paradise," he replied. "My system is to take souls as the Lord sends them.... Some have more need for a piece of sweet candy and to be treated with gentleness, to wean them gradually from worldly things."[516]

Maccari Concludes His Visit

The idea that Our Lord entrusted souls to Pio led Maccari to think Pio was delusional, as though God "conferred on him a type of power so vast as to be on a par with that of the Pope." There came a brief ceasefire when the Vatican official asked the stigmatist if there was any message he would like to convey to the Holy Father. Pio was glad of the opportunity. "Say that I would like to be able to perform my ministry in behalf of souls with the necessary liberty."[517] The meeting ended with Pio and Maccari giving each other a fraternal hug.

In the end, Maccari found it mind-boggling that God gave a ministry to so "small and petty a person" as Pio. "Why does the loving providence of God," he wondered, "permit such deception and concede to such a deficient instrument the ability to accomplish so vast and great a work of good?"[518] Some threads of Maccari's assessment revealed his prejudice against Southern Italians; Pope

John also had a long history of looking down his nose on the piety of the Southerners, saying, "The ignorant devotion of the faithful is stirred up to exploit their faith and their money."[519] When he delivered his negative account to the Vatican, Maccari leveled the blame at Pio's "southern origins" as the cause for his theological ignorance — an assessment that aligned conveniently with Pope John's prejudices.

In the decades after Pio had gone to God, when the Polish Pope St. John Paul II speedily moved the cause for Pio's canonization ahead, Maccari seems to have had a change of heart to align his beliefs with those of the ruling pope. Padre Pio became a saint, and Maccari, as much he had yearned to be a cardinal, never did get his red cap.

35

THE FINAL PERSECUTION

After Maccari returned to the hallowed halls of the Vatican and conveyed his unfavorable impressions to Pope John, the portly pope lamented in his diary, "What to think of this religious [Padre Pio] who certainly does good, yet one can't succeed in dissipating shadows and doubts concerning his alleged sanctity?"[520]

During this most painful persecution of the 1960s, Pio was under attack on three fronts: first, from his own friars; secondly, from his own spiritual daughters; and then from the Vatican authorities. When the persecution was at its worst, Pio was under attack from all of them. This was the 1960s, the time of the early stirrings of the sexual revolution, and some younger friars were much more sexualized than the friars of older generations. Some young friars were not respectful toward Pio and gave him the impression they thought the dirty rumors about him were true. One shamelessly asked Pio, "Is it true you had affairs with women?" Pio meekly replied, "I never did these things even when I was young. Now, even if I wished to do them ... I'm an old man."[521]

Maccari's Report Is Read

Pope John XXIII read Elvira's testimony and believed her. After Maccari met with the pope and delivered his unfavorable report, it was entrusted to Cardinal Alfredo Ottaviani, who read the contents and drew up a list of directives and practical solutions for Pio's superiors. It said, in summary: "Stop the repetitions of acts that have the character of a cult directed towards the person of Padre Pio."[522]

Cardinal Ottaviani had the reputation as an astute and holy man. He was also fair. He did not imprison Pio, as had happened in the early 1930s. He struck a decent balance in his directives which were designed to afford Pio a lower profile. He ordered that priests and bishops were forbidden from serving at the Mass of Pio, that the Mass was to be at a different time each day, that the faithful were never to congregate around the confessional or try to talk with Pio as he came and went, and that no one was to gain entrance into the church without a ticket when Pio was in the confessional, thereby limiting the number of curious bystanders. Furthermore, the practice of female visitors meeting with Pio alone was completely forbidden, laymen and women were not allowed to hang around the sacristy or friary garden, and railings were to be put up around the wooden confessional. The last directive was of benefit to penitents, because it meant people could not go near enough to the confessional to eavesdrop.

In his wisdom, Cardinal Ottaviani did not limit the spiritual daughters to confessing to Pio once a month, the prospect of which had reduced Pio to begging. What is more, the proverbial swamp was drained: Fr. Giustino was exiled to Malta, and Fr. Emilio (who had backed Giustino in his plot to spy on Pio) was removed from his post. Emilio was replaced by Padre Rosario, a skeletal Sicilian with a deathly serious temperament. Rosario began to run the friary as if it were a military base, which gave Pio more protection.

Fr. Rosario Protects Pio

Perhaps in response to these measures, the narcissistic spiritual daughters hatched plans to break into the friary in the middle of the night, kidnap Pio, and take him away, so he could be all theirs. Hearing of this plan, the newly appointed Rosario decided to lock Pio in his cell every evening, treating Pio like a criminal. For this, Rosario was soon despised by many of Pio's followers, because locking Pio in his cell every night was not a directive from the Vatican. Rosario earned a few harsh critics who saw him as one who visited unfair punishments on Pio, but we may consider that many people did not fully appreciate how fanatical a few of the spiritual daughters were, and it is more the case that Rosario simply wanted to prevent Pio's abduction.

To keep relations as peaceful as possible between the Franciscans and the Vatican, Rosario put up signs in the church instructing people not to talk to Pio outside of the confessional. Fearing that his daughters would forcibly move Pio to the Casa, Rosario refused to grant Pio permission to visit the sick in the Casa. It sounds outlandish, but Pio really could have been abducted — his maniacal daughters, such as Elvira, would not stop at anything to have Pio to themselves.

For all Pio's miracles, it seems that his daughters-in-spirit — including those who had full-blown narcissism — were not known to be recipients of miraculous psychological healings. Instead, their jealousies were both a cross to Pio and an ongoing source of their own temptation. Although he did not blame Fr. Rosario or resent his spiritual daughters, Pio did say he felt incarcerated.

There was harmony between Pio and Rosario. In Rosario's emaciated body beat a heart full of love for Pio. A touching case in point is that when Pio persisted in going on his knees before Rosario each night to kiss his hand, Rosario told him to stop because of the stigmatist's advanced age. Rosario did not want to put Pio under any more physical duress than necessary. Nevertheless, Pio persisted in going on his knees every evening and kissing Rosario's hand.

One of the worst aspects of Pio's persecution was how intensely he was isolated. The friary became an unfamiliar place, as many of his friends were reassigned or moved away and strangers took their place. Pio's heart was wounded when Pietro Cugino, the blind man who was beloved by Pio, was told to leave. He had lived at the friary for thirty years and was trusted by Pio. But when he was asked to leave, Pietro left without making a fuss and Pio wept silently.

Pio's New Helper

A grace came in the form of Padre Eusebio, who was appointed as Giustino's replacement and had the solemn duty of caring for Pio's person and his cell. Eusebio was a twenty-seven-year-old friar who was loving and charismatic, while also being an honest and straight-talking chap.

At first Eusebio was not a devotee of Pio's. In the years after Pio died, Eusebio forthrightly reminisced, "Before coming to San Giovanni Rotondo, I didn't believe in him. My skepticism was not about his stigmata but about his sanctity.... I wasn't sure about his holiness. At that time, he was under restrictions.... Many people were against him, and I didn't know whom to believe."[523] Although he was doubtful of Pio, Eusebio set about caring lovingly for Pio as though he were his own father.

When Pio was in the throes of harrowing psychological pain, Eusebio could cheer him up. Once, Eusebio came into Pio's cell and found him with his head between his hands in a state of depression. "Help me, son! I can't deal with it anymore! I'm losing my faith!" Pio cried out. Eusebio told Pio he was under demonic attack. "The devil is coming to torment you with these doubts, but don't give them a thought," he said. "Be calm. Soon we'll go to say Mass and he will be defeated."[524] Then Eusebio gave Pio a blessing and noted that then "Padre Pio seemed to calm down."

Fr. Eusebio had spent time in England and Ireland and spoke English fluently. He took care of the correspondence from English speakers, which amounted to a thousand letters a week. On occasion a letter gave him and Pio cause for mirth. A girl sent Pio a letter asking him for prayers that she become prettier and for the intention that her facial features change miraculously. She enclosed an array of pictures, cutouts from magazines of the facial features she wanted. When Eusebio brought the pile of clippings to Pio's attention, Pio quipped, "Did she say anything about a brain?"[525]

Eusebio came to believe in Pio totally. The young friar was afforded a privileged view of the stigmata. Eusebio found the crusts from Pio's wounds in the washroom every morning and later explained, "He cleaned his wounds in the morning. It was painful for him. He had to push the crusts aside." When he was changing the bed linen, Eusebio would find that the sheets were covered in blood. He remarked, "At those times he was compelled to renew his bandages twice a day, especially the bandage on the wound of his heart." This echoed the doctors' observations as well as that of the inquisitor, Rossi, who said the wound on his heart, "the side wound," gave out the most blood. Eusebio saw it as cross-shaped. "The long part of the wound of his heart, which was horizontal, was about four inches long," he observed. "Across that was a shorter one, about two or three inches long, crossing at an angle, left to right.... It was an open wound."[526] Eusebio attended to Pio with great tender loving care and was at Pio's side throughout the rest of the persecution, which entailed many humiliations.

The Inquiry of 1961

In February 1961 the Vatican sent a French priest named Paul-Pierre Philippe to interview Pio. Philippe hectored Pio as though he were an errant priest. "The Church fears and trembles for you. The Holy Father wants you to be sure that you think about the salvation of your own soul!" Then he tried to extract a promise from Pio, "I can't return to Rome without your promise to do everything to put in order not only your soul, but also your priestly ministry, especially concerning your favored women." When he heard this, Pio did not protest his innocence but swiftly stood up for himself. "Thank the Holy Father for his interest in my soul, but also ask him to allow me to exercise my ministry freely, especially concerning the women of the town. Let me have my freedom!"[527]

Like Pope John, Fr. Philippe was inclined to believe the testimony of Elvira; when Philippe reproached Pio for kissing women, Pio raised his hand to Heaven and refuted this claim. "I never kissed any woman, Father. Moreover, I say before the Lord, I didn't even want to kiss my Mamma. I made her weep because I didn't return her kisses."

Fr. Philippe also took issue with Pio's way of hearing Confessions, especially for his refusing absolution to certain penitents. Did his inquisitor not consider that it would be dishonest for Pio to go through the motions of giving them absolution when they did not merit it? As hard as Philippe was on Pio for his rumored sins, he expected Pio not to be hard on sinners in the confessional. Pio said he followed his conscience by occasionally refusing absolution.

When he returned to Rome, Philippe wrote a report that was perhaps the most condemnatory ever written on Pio. "Padre Pio appears to me to be a man of limited intelligence," he concluded. "He is not nor can be a saint. . . . He is not even a worthy priest. . . . Padre Pio is not only a false mystic who knows his stigmata are not from God but also allows all his fame of sanctity to be built around him." With a final flourish, Philippe signed his name to the statement, "The case of Padre Pio is the most colossal fraud that can be discovered in the history of the Church."[528]

Philippe advocated that Pio be banished from San Giovanni and sequestered in a remote convent, and that he be forbidden from hearing confessions or offering Mass ever again. Philippe wanted Pio's ministry ground to a halt and for Pio to be made a recluse. Philippe later became a cardinal under Paul VI. However, Pope John XXIII did not put Philippe's recommendations into effect. Esteemed members of the pro-Pio faction spoke to Pope John in Pio's defense, including Cardinal Giuseppe Siri, who had in previous years benefited from Pio's gift for telling the future. Some years prior, Cardinal Siri had been in some trouble and didn't know what to do. He had told no one of his dilemma, but a telegram arrived from Pio with precise instructions, and when red-capped Siri followed Pio's advice, he got himself out of a terrible mess.

Pio's Defenders Come to His Aid

From that day forward, Siri had been fiercely devoted to Pio and used the time he met with Pope John to come to Pio's rescue. "For months I defended Padre Pio to Pope John XXIII," he recounted. "We spoke about him at every meeting we had. I had many responsibilities at the time, and I would often meet with the Pope. Each time we met we ended up talking about Padre Pio." Siri said that Pope John "was worried and confused."[529]

Courageously Siri tried to convince the pope that much of what he had heard was slander. Siri's was not a lone voice. Pope John placed a lot of trust in our friend, the gaunt Archbishop Cesarano. When Cesarano went to the hallowed hall of the Vatican to meet with Pope John, he seconded Cardinal Siri and boldly told the pope that the nasty reports he'd been given on Pio were "all slander." Cesarano emphasized that he had known Pio for twenty-eight years, and he hailed him as "an apostle who does immense good for souls."

Pope John objected, "Those women, those recordings. They even recorded kisses." Cesarano's eyes filled with tears as he said, "For charity's sake, it's not the case of sinful kisses."[530] The purple-capped Cesarano admitted that his own sister went to Pio and that she kissed Pio's hand repeatedly. Cesarano pointed out to the pope that he had been given false evidence — that photos he'd been given of Pio with women had been doctored to make them look scandalous and that Elvira's sworn testimony that she'd been Pio's lover was most dubious because of her mental state, which was common knowledge among everyone who knew her. In the end, Pope John let the restrictions from Cardinal Ottaviani stay in place and did not replace them with the severe sanctions about which Fr. Phillipe had been so adamant.

Around this same time Mary Pyle was writing letters home to her friends in America about the effects of the strictures imposed by Rome. "We can only approach Padre Pio when we go every ten days to confession." Mary saw that Pio became even more "similar to our crucified Lord."[531] In private, Pio was keenly aware of how much his spiritual sons and daughters suffered because of the pain of separation, and Eusebio would see him weep and lament, "My poor children … how much they have to suffer — because of me!"[532]

Pio's life was so controlled by strictures that there could be no question of inappropriate conduct with women. Yet it was still believed that Pio's superiors were pressuring him to hand over money so they could pay their debts. The officials at the Holy Office were genuinely concerned that the huge sums of money arriving for the upkeep of the Casa, which had caused such division between Pio and his superiors, could cause even more explosive internecine fighting. Finally, the Vatican ruled that the Casa would become its property, a remedy that Cardinal Ottaviani defended as being "in Padre Pio's best interest, so that the Capuchin Order could not touch Padre Pio's work."[533]

Pio Signs Over the Casa

In 1962 the minister general, the indecisive Clement Neubauer, journeyed to meet Padre Pio and instructed him to sign over the title deeds of the Casa to the Vatican. Pio meekly took a pen and signed the papers in complete obedience. When the ink of his signature dried, the Casa became the property of the Holy See.

This development brought peace between Pio and his superiors, who could no longer try to tap him for lire. It would have been wonderful had Pio's last years not been compromised by conflict between him and his superiors over money. When Pio signed over the deeds to the Vatican, it was a great mortification for him, a type of practical admission of his ineptitude. Had he foreseen from the beginning that this was the best course of action, no doubt he would have volunteered to sign over the title deeds to the Holy See. Instead, he was being ordered to relinquish all control of the Casa, as though he were unfit, and this was a galling humiliation. He had pioneered every essential aspect of the Casa; now he had to let it go completely. Yet Pio accepted this insult with grace and resignation.

This may seem to us an injustice. Why didn't the Vatican simply forbid the higher-ups in the Franciscans from pressuring Pio for money? Here we need to revisit the essence of Pio's own words on charity: that it is so great in God's eyes He cannot repay it even with all the works of His creation. True charity cannot be adequately rewarded in this life, but although there is no reward, that does not mean there is no earthly humiliation for those who do charity. If all earthly reward is stripped from someone, then we may have faith that Our Lord will make the heavenly reward all the greater.

When Emanuele Brunatto heard that Pio had given up control of the Casa, he was enraged. Since the donations for the Casa had come from people who wanted their money to go directly to Pio, Emanuele considered it illegal for the Vatican to seize control of an institution run on money sent for Pio. Emanuele hot-footed it from his home in Paris to Rome and had a meeting with Cardinal Ottaviani, who tried to placate Pio's friend by telling him that they had taken over the Casa so that Pio would not fall victim to his fellow Franciscans.

If anything, Ottaviani's words inflamed Emanuele, who was no fan of the Vatican authorities. With his quick mind and white-hot love for his spiritual father, he prepared a "white paper" to be sent to the United Nations, documenting the violations to Pio's human rights, and organized a conference in Geneva in the spring of 1964 to mark the occasion of the white paper being made public. Then he called off the conference in a blaze of publicity, when Pio got in touch with him, saying, "If truly you love me as a father, don't continue doing what they say that you are doing for me.... It will mortify people in Holy Mother Church and the Capuchin Order.... You can't love the Son by mortifying the mother." Pio gently consoled Emanuele, "Rest assured, everything will return to the way it was before. It will not remain for us to eat the fruits of our actions because these belong to the Lord."[534]

This must have been embarrassing for Emanuele — he had put in two years working to bring the United Nations in to side with Pio. And although he obeyed Pio out of love, he refused to back down from the hierarchy, who continued to put pressure on his beloved spiritual father. It would be difficult to overstate the frustration Pio felt from 1960 to 1964 while he underwent this most painful persecution. Pio lived and breathed so he could free souls from Satan's shackles, and he was being treated like a miscreant, severely limiting his contact with souls.

A year before the most painful persecution ended, Pio's beloved confessor and spiritual father, Agostino, died. In his last years, Agostino was confined to bed with ulcerated legs and distemper, lovingly nursed by the scrupulous and skeletal Fr. Rosario. The many sacrifices that Rosario made for Agostino endeared Pio to him. Pio was at Agostino's side when his beloved spiritual father breathed his last. The same friar who had been among the first to learn that Pio had received the wounds of Christ went to the next world. Pio had a vision of Agostino in Heaven.

If you have need of finding a spiritual father who is of kind heart, perhaps you may ask Agostino's help. As he was the kindliest father in spirit for Padre Pio, he will find the right man of the cloth for you. If you have need of an intensely intellectual father in spirit, then maybe pray to Fr. Benedetto, who, while less tender and loving than Agostino, was his intellectual better. Although Pio knew it would not be long before he would be reunited with Agostino, his grief for Agostino was immense and he wept every time he walked by his confessor's old room.

The Death of Pope John XXIII

On June 3, 1963, Pope St. John XXIII died, the inner lining of his stomach fatally inflamed. Pio had never harbored any bitterness toward Pope John, insisting that the pope made his assessment based on what others told him. In the last days of his life, Pope John was heard repeating, "On Padre Pio, they deceived me!"[535]

Pope John did strike a balance between Philippe's virulently anti-Pio stance and Siri's supremely pro-Pio stance when he allowed for Ottaviani's list of restrictions to be kept in place. But John was never a big supporter of Pio's and there are those who question whether John was genuinely poisoned against Pio based on false evidence or instead used the false evidence as justification to support his prejudices. What we do know for sure is that, when Pio was alive, every time a new pope was elected, some of the hearts of those closest to the ruling pope were laid bare, especially when they sought to use Pio for their own purposes — such as when Gemelli lied about examining the stigmata and when Maccari held up Elvira's deposition as credible testimony.

While the conclave was taking place, Fr. Eusebio pestered Pio to predict the next pope, and Pio revealed, "It's going to be Montini."[536] On June 21, 1963, Cardinal Montini became the new pope, Paul VI. No doubt the newly elected pope often thought of that moment, five years before, when Pio had prophesied this moment.

Pope Paul VI believed with all his heart in Pio's sanctity and goodness, and he used the power of his office to remove the restrictions which had been placed on him. Paul VI ordered, "Liberate him from those restrictions. Make the work of Padre Pio easy so that he can fulfill his apostolate."[537] Paul VI declared frankly that it was unacceptable that Pio was being treated "like a criminal" and that this was to end. The new pope instructed Cardinal Ottaviani to announce, "It is the will of the Holy Father that Padre Pio exercise his ministry in full liberty."[538]

As the sixties wore on, there were reportedly strained relations between Paul VI and Cardinal Ottaviani; perhaps Ottaviani's list of restrictions that he had drawn up at the behest of Pope John played a minor role in this. Paul VI held Pio in such high esteem that it may have affected his judgment of Ottaviani, though on the whole the cardinal's measures had tried to strike a fair balance.

In 1964 Paul VI removed the sanction that forced Pio to offer Mass at a different time every day, and Pio was once again given freedom to talk to people after he heard Confessions. Laymen were given leave to congregate in the sacristy and talk with him. Pio's dear old friend Pietro was welcomed back into the friary, and once again he came to live there and resumed his post as Pio's loyal servant.

At all times Fr. Eusebio shepherded Pio as he came and went from his cell, and protected him from the crush of crowds. Men, women, and children pushed in on Pio and shouted all sorts of questions and petitions. And now that the persecution had ended, he was allowed to answer them freely. Pio would say to Eusebio, "Son, you've seen everybody asking Padre Pio to help them with this and that. I wish somebody would say, 'Padre Pio, pray that the Lord might help me to bear the cross.' "[539] Whatever our most pressing need, let us consider asking Pio for that grace.

It is often said that there cannot be an Easter Sunday without a Good Friday. After his liberation, Pio lived four more years, a time of freedom. These four years allowed the stain of the lies that led to the persecution to be wiped clean. In a certain sense, the persecution had purified his reputation, putting an end once and for all to the rumors of sexual impropriety. Now those restrictions, too, were lifted that had barred him from having any meetings with women. Had Pio died while under restrictions from the Vatican, a shadow may have fallen over his name, but Pio died after four years of freedom, and he died during the pontificate of Pope VI, who was very fond of him.

36

CONVERTED HEARTS

In the same year that Pio was liberated, there was a dramatic change in the heart of Elvira Serritelli, the narcissist whose jealousy had caused so much harm to Pio. She was sent to the Casa, where she lay dying. While Sister Death hovered, she felt compelled to ask for a priest and she made her Confession. The next day she confessed again and received Holy Communion. Not long after, she died. When he was asked as to whether Elvira was saved, Pio was magnanimously positive: "An act of perfect love cancels all sins." Some days after this pronouncement, he said that she had gone to Heaven. Even though Elvira had defamed Pio, he wrote charitably of her, "In life she constantly aspired toward Heaven, and death found her prepared for her encounter with Jesus. Now from on high she watches over those she left to mourn her on earth."[540]

Elvira's conversion was quite a stunning affair, as was Pio's revelation that she went to Heaven. Pio's greatest victories were the conversion of sinners, and he used his many charisms to convert a huge variety of souls. We saw earlier how Pio converted Di Maggio, a raffish young lawyer who after his conversion praised Pio to Pope Benedict XV. We met the Freemason, Cesare Festa, who became Pio's spiritual son and then threw away his white apron and went back to the lodge to convert the others, even as they made dire threats against him. We met Friedrich Abresch, who had converted to Christ in Pio's confessional and later became his personal photographer. Emanuele Brunatto, who had made a killing as a con man and was living among prostitutes, also converted and then battled the Vatican on Pio's behalf. "Mischievous Miscio" went from blackmailing Pio's brother to being Pio's devoted follower. The atheist doctor Ricciardi, who slandered Pio savagely, later became a faithful Catholic. The Manhattan heiress, Mary Pyle, despite her mother's prejudices, became so passionately committed a Catholic that she slept in her brown habit and gave her inheritance away to the same sort of people her mother had scorned. What might we glean from such spectacular conversions?

In the chapters that follow, I have curated conversion stories from different parts of Pio's life. They have been picked for the value they offer us in saving our souls. Among them is the prostitute in London, the post-abortion woman who knew healing from her psychological pain only when she developed true contrition, the Freemason who converted many other Freemasons and a distinguished atheist materialist, and the woman who had decided to have an abortion but was brought to a full conversion of heart by Pio's promptings. Each one is unique, and yet they can all speak to our hearts. Each has something to teach us.

The Power of Prayer

Pio had an array of mystical gifts, but the most effective was his devotion to prayer. He prayed for souls with all his heart, and this must be our primary way of converting loved ones, too. Sometimes, the only means through which Pio brought a soul out of sin was prayer. He often reminded people, "One does not win the battle without prayer," as the following case demonstrates.

A desperate woman in London wrote to Pio, "Padre, I'm a prostitute. Every evening, at nine, I'm dragged out onto the street. I am ashamed. I'm writing to you so that you might help me overcome this shame." When Eusebio gave him the letter, Pio said, "Answer her I will pray for her with all my heart." In time the woman wrote Pio that she had gotten free of her pimp. "Dear Padre, thanks to God after receiving your letter, nine o'clock comes, but I no longer go down on the street. I succeeded in ridding myself of the one who dragged me there." Pio lifted his heart in thanksgiving and exhaled, "Deo gratias."[541]

The Necessity of Confession

The primary site where Pio converted sinners was his confessional, his hospital for sick souls. We can also learn a great deal from how Pio acted when he made an account of his own sins.

One day Pio asked Eusebio if he would hear his Confession. Eusebio listened while Pio listed his sins. Pio was a very old man, but he cried like a baby the whole time, and Eusebio said to him that he did not see how Pio's small sins merited such sorrow. Pio gently corrected Eusebio's idea of sin: "Son, you think sin is the breaking of law. No, son, sin is the betrayal of love."[542] Pio earned a reputation for being hard on people for their sins, but he was harder on himself than anyone, and his words to Eusebio paint a picture of one who was profoundly sorry for his sins. No absolution is possible for the one who is not genuinely contrite, as this next story shows us.

Pio would refuse absolution to those who were not truly penitent. Carlo Campanini, a famous actor who was converted to the Faith through Pio, once challenged Pio about the fact that he sent so many people away without giving them absolution. "You're taking a big responsibility on your shoulders by sending them away without absolution. What happens if they die after they leave church?" Pio threw up his arms and defended his actions: "If I've made a mistake, do you think God would make a mistake? God will take care of things."[543]

Here Pio clarified the realities of his ministry: He was not divine, and there were limits to his powers. Only through God's grace could a soul in sin be eligible for absolution in the future. Pio did not see fit to cooperate with people who were "keeping in place a dirty cloth" between them and God, or to condone their actions by going through the motions of giving them "absolution."

Carlo then asked a question that bothered people then and still bothers people today: Were the people refused absolution by Pio condemned to walk the earth in mortal sin for the rest of their lives, and even die in that sin? This story answers that question.

I obtained the following account from a spiritual son of Pio's, Irishman Dónal Enright, who was one of Pio's most humble and devoted servants. Dónal traveled to San Giovanni whenever he had time off work, so he could lend a hand to Pio and to the penitents coming and going from Pio's Confession box. I asked Dónal whether he knew anyone who confessed involvement with an abortion and had been refused absolution by Pio.

Dónal's watery blue Irish eyes shone with the memory of a time he had been praying in church outside Pio's confessional and saw a lady leave the box in a state of great distress. She was shaking and crying, and not a little angry. Pio signalled to Dónal, whereby Dónal understood he was to talk to this lady and comfort her. When he approached the wailing woman, Dónal invited her to have a coffee. She agreed, and while they were in a café nearby, she told him that years earlier she had had an illegal abortion. She had hoped she could confess it now and be restored to a state of grace, but to her chagrin Pio had refused her absolution. "You are not truly sorry," Pio said to her.[544]

How dare he say such a thing! Could the saint not see she was wracked with guilt as well as being extremely agitated and anxious? She told Dónal she had various psychological problems; her regret had given way to depression. It had been many years since her abortion, she was married and had children, but she could not stop thinking about it. She winced whenever she referred to her "eldest child," who was not really her eldest child. Even such normal, everyday occurrences as someone asking how many children she had provoked hysterical responses that her husband and children found difficult to understand. Her children walked on eggshells around her. Didn't the psychological pain and obsession with her abortion mean she was "truly sorry"?

She had been born to a family with a wealthy background, nominally Catholic, and enjoyed an expensive education. She was not raised to be devout, however, and after experimenting with promiscuity, quickly became pregnant. Knowing that her parents would have been embarrassed by a pregnant, unmarried daughter and would have asked her to put the child up for adoption, she decided that abortion would cause her less suffering. So she'd had an illegal abortion, as she told Dónal, so she could save face. Although she'd regretted it bitterly, she still felt her reasons justified her action, but ruminating on these reasons gave her dire anxiety.

She had only just met him, but she readily bared her soul to Dónal. He was a gentle and genial Irishman with the softest brogue. That day in the café with Dónal, she was ready to listen to him explain why Pio had refused her absolution. Dónal told her in his lilting voice that Padre Pio could see her soul and was right when he said she was not "truly sorry" and that she would have to undergo a process of becoming genuinely contrite before she would be validly absolved of her sin. She was sorry for herself, but she was not sorry to God. After they parted that day, they stayed in touch. She gave her heart to cultivating true contrition and she felt more at peace than she had in years, and her psychological problems diminished.

What Is Genuine Contrition?

Serious consideration is owed to Pio's explanations as to what is genuine contrition and what is in fact false contrition — one state is from God, the other inspired by Satan. When a man told Pio that memories of his past sins caused him distress, Pio said, "That which you feel is pride; it is the demon which inspires you with this sentiment, it is not true sorrow."[545]

How does pride play a role here? When we think so much of our sins that we allow them to overpopulate our mind, maybe even falling into a state of despair where we think it is beyond God to forgive them. Or when we think, "I'm so much better than that, how could I have let myself do that?" This is preoccupation with the self, how our own self has failed. When we offer a genuine apology to God, the sorrow for our sins leaves us and goes to God, and thus there is a release.

Pio delineated how we may know the spirit of God when he said,

> The spirit of God is a spirit of peace, and also in the case of grave sin, it makes us feel a tranquil sorrow, humble, confident and this is due precisely to His mercy. The spirit of the demon, on the contrary, excites, exasperates, and makes us in our sorrow feel something like anger against ourselves, whereas our first charity must be to ourselves, and so if certain thoughts agitate you, this agitation never comes from God, who gives you tranquility, being the Spirit of Peace.[546]

We might ask, Why agitation? This exasperating agitation is to inspire thoughts that you will never recover from your sins, and if you succumb to forming your will around this deception, then you may abandon the sacraments and not make reparation for your sins. This bold dishonesty clouds the mind badly, and if we entertain it, we may fail to see Our Lord's Sacrifice on the Cross, His Precious Blood spilled so our sins may be washed away. Redemption means we need never let ourselves wallow in the filth of our sins. The devil wants us to fixate on our evildoing, but God wants us to experience the peace that comes with trusting that Our Lord's Passion will redeem us.

When we hold the mirror up to ourselves or obsess at the sight of our sin so much that we don't see beyond the smoke of Satan surrounding us, then we may fail to go to Confession, kneel before the crucifix, tell our sins for which Jesus died, and be absolved. Pio assured us that we will "always" know the Spirit of God by the "tranquil sorrow" that fills us. When we embrace the tranquil sorrow, we may also offer the decade of the Rosary the Scourging at the Pillar, which is dedicated to the intention of asking for true contrition. Also, let us reiterate that Pio said "Our first charity must be to ourselves" and that we do a charity to ourselves by rejecting the spirit of the demon.

If we have confessed and been absolved yet are still bothered by a kaleidoscope of images of old sins, we may wish to take heart from Pio's words:

> In our thoughts and at confession we must not dwell on sins that have been already confessed. Because of our contrition Jesus has forgiven them.... With a gesture of infinite generosity he tore up and destroyed the bills we signed with our sins.... To go back to these sins, to bring them up again ... because of doubt that they were really and abundantly remitted, would this not be a lack of trust in the goodness which he proved by tearing up every document of debt contracted through sin?[547]

According to Dónal, that post-abortion woman took one whole year to become truly contrite. When the tranquil ache of true sorrow pierced her soul, she returned to San Giovanni, where she met up with Dónal and then went to Confession. Pio told her simply, "Now, you are truly sorry," and he absolved her of all her sins. A beautiful fruit of being in a state of genuine contrition was that she no longer had constant psychological pain but was free from distress and was at peace. "I never saw anyone happier in my life," is how Dónal described her when he saw her leaving the church after Confession.[548]

If we need to go on a journey similar to the post-abortion lady — whether we were involved in abortion or another serious sin — it may take time and patience. On our knees we may ask Our Lord to bless our cultivation of contrition and pray for strength and support. Prepare to be amazed at Our Lord's generosity in providing the people and the means to help you. When the woman who'd had the abortion first went to Pio, she was hoping that he would heal her miraculously of her depression and anxiety. Instead, he led her along a longer, more healing path — and gave her Dónal to walk with her until she could be truly freed from her burden. If you ask, God will do the same for you.

Dónal also knew a woman who had been prevented from having an abortion; Pio bilocated to her while she was lying on the table in a dirty den. "Get out of here now! Get out of that bed and get away from here!" commanded

Pio as she was waiting for the doctor to come in. She was covered neck to toe in some grubby sheets, having given a large sum of money to a greasy man to pay for an abortion. No one knew she was pregnant, not her boyfriend or her parents, and she was determined to keep the abortion a secret. The pregnant lady's boyfriend wanted to marry her, but she was of the mind they could have another baby once they were married. She didn't want to walk down the aisle with a baby bump under her white satin.

She was shocked to see Pio appear out of nowhere. How had he known she was here? She'd grown up thinking that people who said Pio appeared to them in bilocation were holy, and that this could never happen to her. But here he was, right in front of her, fixing her with his piercing stare that could split marble as he said sharply, "If you stay here your child will be killed and your life will be ruined. Once you've allowed the killing of your baby, everything else you hold dear will be as nothing to you."

Thoughts of the money she had spent, however, kept her pinned to the bed. She had withstood the sleazy doctor's hands abusing her when he "examined" her; had she gone through all that not to have the abortion? Reading her mind, Padre Pio exclaimed, "Yes, that dirty man abused you with his hands. But you must get out of this evil place now! My appearing here is a very special grace and if you forfeit it, you will regret the loss of your baby for the rest of your life." She was so stunned that Pio could read her mind that she could hardly move. Then he said it again: "Get out of here now! The blood of your son will be on your hands!" At that instant Pio disappeared into thin air. She scrambled off the bed, threw on her clothes, and ran away, never looking back. She went to Confession, then quickly married the father of her child. Months later she gave birth to a baby, who as Pio had predicted was a boy.

The young mother was happier than she had ever been. She went to San Giovanni to thank Pio for preventing her child's death. When she knelt before Pio in his confessional, he greeted her like an old friend while she wept tears of joy and gratitude. "Thanks to you, my son is alive today!"[549] she said to Pio, and admitted "The reasons I had for going for the abortion were very selfish." But she was startled when Pio gave her a piercing stare and reminded her of how upset she was at the time because of the money paid to the greasy doctor. The memory that she had been more concerned with money horrified her, and with a contrite heart she said to Pio, "At the time I put a price on my son's life. I am very sorry."

She was supremely sorrowful to God for nearly allowing the mutilation of His creation, her child. Just before granting her absolution Pio said, "Now you have a great horror of abortion, never lose it. You do not owe me thanks, but you must thank God; He saved you from committing a very grave sin." The woman left the church and while she milled around outside, she met Dónal, who befriended her. The young mother decided to tell Dónal how it came to pass that she avoided an abortion, and then said, "I am ecstatic to have my son, but also just as grateful that I threw away my old self which was egotistical and childish and thinking only of what I wanted, but now I follow God's plan for my life. When He saved me from myself —I didn't kill my son — it was the best thing that ever happened to me." She asked Dónal to share her story with a wider audience when he saw fit.

Dónal told me of three other cases that were very similar to the one above, when Pio through bilocation appeared to women who were about to have abortions and stopped them in their tracks. We must resist losing the horror that Pio asked the young mother never to lose. This chimes with that which Pio told Fr. Pellegrino: "It will be a terrible day for humanity when men lose their horror for abortion.... Abortion is not only murder, but it is also suicide." Suicide? Pio explained, "Understand this suicide of the race ... the earth populated by dribbling and toothless old people, devoid of children.... By limiting our offspring, the lives of the parents are also mutilated."[550] This has surely come to pass as birth rates have plummeted and the world longs for the gurgling of babies, who have tragically been snuffed out in the womb.

A Terrible Sacrilege!

One of the most serious sins Pio would refuse to grant absolution was for the sin of sacrilege, for receiving Holy Communion while in a state of mortal sin. According to Pio, only when they are in receipt of "a very special grace obtained by souls who stand very close to God" can a soul who has committed sacrilege hope to be absolved.[551] This special grace could be seen by Pio.

An English lady once knelt in Pio's confessional, but when she came into Pio's view he savagely slid the door shut and sniped at her, "I have no time for you." She persevered, and for twenty days she came back and was refused in the same severe way. On the twenty-first day, Padre Pio consented to hear her Confession, telling her she was a "poor, blind creature" and instructing her, "Instead of complaining of my severity, you should ask yourself how the Divine Compassion can receive you after so many years of sacrilege. Do you realise you have done a terrible thing? To keep up appearances of respectability, you have taken Communion for years at the side of your mother and husband *in a state of mortal sin*."[552]

She was obviously someone conscious of her appearance, and so it must have been humbling for her to go again and again for three whole weeks to Pio's confessional. The mere act of her telling her testimony is indicative of a real conversion, because it shows she was putting appearances in second place. Pio had informed her, "He who commits a sacrilege brings about his own damnation."[553] And to be cleansed of this most sordid of sordid sins, a special grace must be awarded after souls who "stand very close to God" have offered prayer.

Let us stress the specifics: It is not the prayer of one soul, but of *souls*, meaning more than one person's prayers. Let's devoutly consider this as a strategy for saving souls. If we have a friend or a loved one who has committed sacrilege, enlist holy people to pray for them. There were twenty-one days between when the lady first sought Confession and when she was granted it, time which Pio likely used to pray for her. And when he did consent to hearing her Confession, he granted her absolution. The English lady's soul was restored to a state of grace and she utterly rejected her past ways and committed herself to making atonement.

37

More Spectacular Conversions

Of all converts that Padre Pio counts among his beloved spiritual children, Alberto Del Fante may be the one whose grand legacy offers the maximum benefit to us in today's world. Alberto was a bald man with an oval face and eyes that were espresso-black; his cynical stare suggested he was overly skeptical. Before his conversion, he claimed to be an honest man, though he had a habit of lying.

Alberto was a prolific journalist and author based in Bologna. During Pio's persecution of the 1930s, Alberto wrote a book defending Pio that the Vatican put on the Index of Forbidden Books. But he wrote this book *after* his conversion, before which Alberto was vehemently anti-Catholic. "I was a Mason, I was an atheist, I believed in nothing," he acknowledged.[554] Also prior to his conversion, Alberto was an aggressive opponent of Pio who wrote the harshest stories, excoriating Pio as a charlatan. He laid the charge that Pio "abused the ignorance of the naïve and credulous masses."[555]

One day Alberto's life turned upside down. His beloved nephew Enrico was stricken with kidney disease and tuberculosis, and he was at death's door. No doctor could offer a cure. Someone got in touch with Pio and invited his prayers for the boy. A day later the young nephew made a miraculous recovery that baffled the medics. Alberto was in a painful quandary, because the same priest he had denounced as an "imposter"[556] in popular newspapers was the one whose prayers had moved God to give a total healing to the person who was the apple of his eye. Alberto halted his campaign to discredit Pio, and he journeyed to meet Pio face-to-face. But he said he still had aggressive animosity toward Pio.

When Alberto met Pio, Pio had no bitterness and had already forgiven him totally, just as he had forgiven Dr. Ricciardi and Fr. Miscio. Pio never allowed himself to be soured in his quest for the salvation of a soul. Astoundingly, when

Alberto was before Pio, he started confessing his sins, even though he did not respect the stigmatist and later said, "I confessed without faith, without enthusiasm as to any ordinary priest." Alberto was unnerved when Pio read his soul and saw that he was still a Mason. "He said I belonged to a class which recognized God but did not like the clergy."[557]

Del Fante told Pio he took pride in being a truthful man. But Pio bluntly disabused him of this self-conceit. "Honest?" asked Pio, and he proceeded to give Alberto a precise account of times he had lied. Alberto was astonished: "He told me things he could not possibly have known." After he had confessed, Alberto did something that previously nauseated him: He asked Pio to pray for his pregnant wife. Pio warmly agreed, "Of course, of course. God has said, 'increase and multiply.' He loves him who creates." Pio then read Alberto's heart and told him the exact reason he had asked for prayer for his wife: She had wanted to breastfeed their other children but had not been able and she longed to feed the new baby herself. Alberto was shocked and he blurted to Pio that this very personal intention was what he'd yearned to tell him. "It is right that the mother should suckle her child," said Pio, and then he read the future, promising Alberto that his wife was going to have no problem breastfeeding their new baby. Everything happened as Pio said.[558]

Alberto became a faithful Catholic who took special delight in his children offering grace before meals. He became a devoted spiritual son of Pio's. He burned his white apron and repented, saying, "I have done evil by having been a Mason." Alberto daringly converted other Masons, and he said that bringing Masons out of the lodge and into the Church was "a real joy" for him. Yet, he didn't flinch from describing it as penance. "The penance I do today … is to persuade my former associates to return to the bosom of Mother Church."[559] The methods Alberto used are very insightful for us, and he made an account of them when he recorded the conversion stories of Masons who forsook the lodge so they could save their souls.

Alberto's story may inspire us to ask Pio's intercession that the legions of Masons may be converted to Christ. As Pio led Alberto out of the lodge, and as Alberto led many others out, we may consider Alberto as an intercessor worthy of praying to, so that his intercession might cause men to leave the Masonic lodges nowadays. Here is where our lives intersect with Alberto's "penance":

We may use his methods. They are the stuff of basic human decency, friendship, and politeness, as well as a reliance on Pio.

One day Alberto met up with an old friend whom he called a former associate. Alberto had left Masonry dramatically, whereas the friend had stayed. Alberto did not do a hard sell but instead told him that he was about to have a story published about Pio, and he instructed his friend, "Buy the newspaper *La Settimana*. In it is published one of my articles." Days later Alberto met up with him again and the Mason said, "I have read your article. Tell me more." Alberto was delighted but was inspired to tell him to wait. "I told him that I would see him about it at some other time."[560]

When next they saw each other, Alberto told him he was about to visit Pio. Alberto's friend asked something astonishing: for Alberto to take to Pio a picture of St. Francis which he always kept in his pocket so that the stigmatist could bless it with his pierced palms. Alberto's friend gave him a message for Pio: "Tell him that whenever I can, I shall visit him." When Alberto went to Pio, he told him of his friend's desire to meet him and presented him with his holy card of St. Francis. Pio knew (without having been told by Alberto) that the man was a Mason, and he said of the card, "It belongs to a Mason, but a Mason who keeps St. Francis in his pocket has already the spirit of faith."[561]

Pio's insight is illuminating because it shows there may be hope for someone with small seeds of faith, such as one who carries holy items, even if his heart has not yet turned wholly toward the light of Christ. Soon the Mason traveled to see Pio, and shortly afterward stopped being a Mason. He knew a new happiness and was profoundly grateful to Alberto. Alberto had already left the Masons, but had stayed friends with this chap, and had used the normal circumstance of a meetup to tell him about his conversion at the hands of Pio. He pointed him toward the story he had written, which allowed the friend to discern in private and without pressure. Alberto allowed himself to be inspired as to the timing of how he would lead this soul to Pio, and when the time was right the man presented himself to Pio and rapidly decided to ditch his white apron. If we have a friend who is like Alberto's friend, we may do as Alberto did and show them the milk of human kindness by socializing normally with them and then inviting them to read something about Pio in their own time.

Guarding the Will

We have focused on people who radically changed their lives, but they, like all of us, cannot rest on their laurels, and at any stage of conversion, but perhaps especially after coming to Christ, there needs to be a guard against the demonic. Pio placed utmost importance on guarding your will: "The demon has only one doorway by which to enter your soul: your will. There are no secret or hidden doors."[562] Perhaps too many Catholics put too much emphasis on the demonic being wholly responsible for their personal sin (as though the demon who tempted them will be the one to stand before Jesus and answer for their sin). Although a soul may be subject to furious temptations, it is only in letting the demon come into the will that he may goad the soul to sin. To keep a guard on our will is our responsibility, yet there is a crucial difference between sin and human weakness, which Pio described. "When there is no action of the will there is no sin, but only human weakness," he said, and "No sin is a sin if not committed with the will."[563] There is also a need to keep a safe distance, as Pio cautioned. "The demon is like a dog on a chain, beyond the range of the chain it cannot bite anyone. And you, therefore, keep your distance. If you get too near it will get you."[564]

Cultivate Humility

Many fall prey to demonic forces because of their personal hubris, thinking they are so superior they can veer closer than others to a demon and not be harmed. Pio is best known for his saying, "Pray, hope and don't worry." But he also said that among other things, worries can come from Satan: "Temptations, discomforts, worries are merchandise offered for sale by the enemy."[565]

We may buy these goods with a part of our will. The devil calls out loudly to attract us to his wares for sale. Demonic noise created in a soul may be troubling, but according to Pio this is a good sign: "If the demon makes a lot of noise, it is a sign he is still outside, and not inside. What should frighten us is when he is at peace and in harmony with our human soul."[566] Often it is the very people who do not hear the devil because his voice is "in harmony" with theirs, who look on holy people as being crazy when they complain they are being pestered by predatory demons. Pio pointed to deception as a sin that allows a demon to reproduce: "The lie is the child of the demon."[567] Pio gave some highly specific warnings and tips, which cause some people to react defensively. For example, he said, "The devil is in the cinema."[568] He advised his spiritual children not to watch television, and when Mary Pyle pondered getting a television for her pink castle, he told her not to.

There is a definite dividing line between temptation and suffering, which is useful to know. Many souls feel that the trials they undergo are caused directly by devils, but this is not the case, Pio said. "Your temptations come from the devil and Hell, but your sufferings come from God and Paradise.... Despise temptations and embrace tribulations."[569] Perhaps there have been times when we have withstood the pressure of temptation to sin, did not give in, but nonetheless felt depleted afterward, even depressed. This was a question posed to Pio: "How is it that when the temptation is past there is a sensation of suffering?" Pio answered, "Have you ever felt the tremor of an earthquake? While everything trembled, you trembled too, but you didn't get caught under the wreckage."[570] The "wreckage" is a metaphor for sin. The "trembling" may cause us to feel shaken, but when we resist temptation and avoid sin, this exact process is a cleansing for the soul.

If thoughts of past sins cause heartache, even tears, then we may have recourse to the words Pio spoke to Luisa Vairo, who was a beautiful actress but had a horrible past. When Pio found her weeping in the church, he said to her, "Calm yourself, my child, Divine Compassion knows no bounds and the blood of Christ washes away the sins of the world."[571] But how did Pio counsel that such sin can be avoided in the first place? Our Lord Himself enlightened us that pride is the root of all sin, and for this reason, Pio's insights on how pride may be remedied are of paramount importance.

Pio had a blunt conversation with another priest, a certain Padre Giovanni, whom Pio admonished, "Pride oozes from every pore of your body."[572] Giovanni was a natural-born leader and a gifted public speaker, but because he was such a great preacher, he was prone to arrogance. When Pio told Giovanni he was full of pride, Giovanni laughed, but he asked how Pio stayed humble. First Pio illuminated the true value of humility — "Humility is truth"[573] — and then he explained how he kept pride at bay: "I don't know how the Lord made me, but I feel I should have to try much harder to make an act of pride than an act of humility. Because humility is truth and the truth is that I am nothing and all that is good in me is of God."[574]

This line of Pio's spoken to a fellow friar ought tell us that who we are — all that is good in us — comes from God. But Pio went on to say that his being surrounded by thirsty souls was the process by which he remained humble. "When I see so many people coming to me with requests, I don't think about what I am able to give but what I am unable to give, so that many souls remain parched with thirst because I have not been able to give them the gift of God." To imitate Pio and his humility, we may think of what we cannot give others, while being grateful not to ourselves but to God for the good we are able to give, because all the goodness which we may share comes from Him. Pio admonished Fr. Giovanni because he was too tough on other friars, and Pio instructed him, "Even in reprimanding you could combine reproof with politeness and mildness."[575] And Pio recommended to Giovanni that he grace his sermons with more love.

Elsewhere Pio said, "Man is so full of pride that when he has everything he needs and good health, he believes himself a god and superior to God Himself." Pride may take root because of perfect independence, when human needs are met by human endeavor. When we have admirable autonomy, we may start to adore ourselves, our own prowess. The self may see itself as being wholly responsible for its survival, which may induce the self to thinking that it is the source of its salvation. Pio enlightened us as to the awakening that awaits the person who is so full of pride but finds himself helpless. "But when something happens and he can do nothing, and others can't do anything about it either, only then he will remember there is a Supreme Being."[576]

Cultivating humility not only will mean greater freedom from sin, but the more humility, the more the Lord will speak, Pio affirmed. "According to the measure that you empty yourself, that is love of your senses and of your own will, and make progress in rooting yourself in holy humility, to that extent the Lord will speak to your heart." [577]

Pio used to say succinctly, "God enriches the soul which empties itself of everything."[578] Many of us yearn to have the Lord illuminate our calling in life, as we feel lost, but we may be somewhat responsible. There is an onus on us to take our part in stripping ourselves of love of our senses and attachment to our own will. We should strive to uproot our own will and replace it with the will of God. We may ask why the Lord speaks more to those who are grounded in "holy humility," which was the term Pio used. Were Our Lord to speak to a heart not rooted in holy humility and who wanted to follow their own will and not Our Lord's will for them, that person would only do their own will anyway, and thus Our Lord's words would be wasted. The mystery of the Rosary in which we especially pray for humility is the Annunciation — meditating on Our Lady's yes to the plan God had for her, to let His will be done even though it meant forgoing the usual life of a woman of her time and knowing her Son was to die a hideous death.

Search for Love

Before we discern our state in life—for example, to get married or stay single — there is first a need to have the humility to accept that God loves us more than we love ourselves and to let Him make this decision for us. As Pio said, "The Lord loves you more than you love yourself. If he wants you to get married, he knows where you live, and he will come and look for you."[579] There are some cases where Pio, as Our Lord's instrument, played matchmaker. We know from the life of Giovanna Rizzani that Pio told her the man destined to be her husband. And a disciple, Irene Gaeta, was told by Pio that she was to marry the chap who drove the bus to San Giovanni, even though at the time he'd been away from Confession for twelve years.

God Is Captive to Our Prayers

Pio used say unequivocally that "Prayer is the oxygen of the soul."[580] Taken literally, this means that without prayer, the soul dies, and if we neglect prayer, we deprive our souls of oxygen. Pio exclaimed, "Let us pour out our whole soul to God in prayer. God is captivated by our prayers and will come to our aid" — which rather contradicts the idea of God the Father being removed from our prayers. Instead, He has made Himself captive to them.

We may ask which of our prayers are good, and Pio counseled, "All prayers are good when they are accompanied by good intentions and good will." These are the two sides of the same coin — good intentions and good will — and if both are there, then our prayers are good. Even in the direst circumstances, perhaps especially so, we can hold fast to Pio's saying, "God is merciful and will hear your prayer."

Here are some other good thoughts on prayer from Padre Pio:

He who prays much is saved. He who prays little damns himself.

Scruples are like shoes you can't walk in because they are too tight — despise them.

If we can have true patience amid the trials of this life, we will be martyrs even without the executioner's sword.

Always have the heart of a judge for yourself, the heart of a son for God, and the heart of a mother for your neighbor.

When a lady asked how she could keep in touch with him when they would be separated by thousands of miles, Pio replied, "Kneel in front of Jesus in the Tabernacle and you will always find me there."[581]

Prayer as a Spiritual Mirror

Padre Giovanni spent a great deal of time preaching, but when he admitted to Pio that sometimes he didn't leave time for meditation, Pio's response was uncompromising: "If that's how things are, just go away. I don't intend to pray for you anymore."[582] Giovanni then defended himself and Pio softened, but his initial retort tells us the importance Pio placed on meditation. Why was Pio so high-handed with Giovanni concerning meditation? Pio said, "Whoever does not meditate is like someone who never looks in the mirror before going out ... and doesn't bother to see if he is tidy and may go out dirty without knowing it."[583]

Meditation allows us to see ourselves and review our soul's appearance, so we know what we need to keep and what we need to clean or change. How does meditation allow us this facility of self-inspection? As Pio revealed, "The person who meditates turns his mind to God, who is the mirror of his soul, seeks to know his faults, tries to correct them, moderates his impulses and puts his conscience in order." When we give our minds to God in meditation and concentrate our thoughts on God, who is all good, we become aware of the aspects of us that are not of goodness: We see things in us that need to change. Without meditation and taking time to be before the mirror that is God, we do not have clear perspective. Yet what a thrilling list of benefits lies in store for us in meditation; namely, being able to regulate our impulses and our conscience.

Honor the Sabbath

When Fr. Giovanni asked Pio for a succinct strategy for sanctification, Pio said, "Two things are necessary, a right intention and self-control." Let's pray that we have good intentions and can regulate ourselves. One way of doing this is taking the time to honor the Sabbath. According to Pio, labor must be avoided on Sundays at all costs, as the following example dramatically shows.

During the time he was a young priest living back home in Pietrelcina, one Sunday he passed the house of fellow villager, Mariandreana Montella, and saw her sitting on her front steps sewing a ribbon onto a dress. Pio took issue with her. "Today is Sunday. Today no one must work,"[584] he said to her. Mariandreana carried on sewing, not letting Pio's words impede her. Pio was, however, so perturbed he took off home, fetched a scissors, and then returned to Mariandreana's house. Grabbing the ribbon, he snipped it to smithereens, which made her furious. She chased Pio down the street! But Pio was impervious to her fury because she had been laboring on the day God asked us to keep as a day of worship and rest. There came a time later when Mariandreana became of the same mind as Pio and came to see all unnecessary work done on Sunday as wrong.

Not just content with stopping older matrons like Mariandreana from toiling on Sunday, Pio prevented his own father from doing so. Grazio wanted to be out in the field, checking for ripe wheat to gather it swiftly lest sunshine or rain damage it. When his priest-son made it known to Grazio that he was vehemently against this practice, his quick-witted father said he felt God would not see it as an infraction because it was done with the intention of safeguarding their food and livelihood. His son would not accept his reasonable explanation and refuted it with reference to Holy Scripture, which bids us, "Remember the sabbath day, to keep it holy. Six days you shall labor, and do all your work. But the seventh day is the sabbath to the LORD your God; in it you shall not do any work" (Exod. 20:8–10).

I can give you many sweetly sociological arguments in favor of not doing unnecessary work on a Sunday —for instance, it is good for family life and it stops society from becoming work-obsessed —but I think it is best to hold purely to Padre Pio's example of abiding by God's law. Embracing toil on a Sunday is a recommitment to our fallen natures and to the fallout of Original Sin. When we work on Sunday, we turn our backs on what God has asked us to do; a rejection of His timetable for us. The inheritance of Adam and Eve's Fall has been the work of a slave. But Sunday rest is designed to give us a break from such work.

By working on Sunday, or by forcing others to work, we are in fact burdening ourselves with one of the negative consequences of Original Sin — toil and strife — by making drudgery a constant feature of life. So, when we do not escape from labor, we make drudges of ourselves and deny God's law. Instead of languishing in our labor, we might take a page from Padre Pio's book and simply rest — or play. On Sundays Padre Pio organized games to be played outdoors for the villagers in his native Pietrelcina.

Cultivate Fear of the Lord

According to Pio, fear of the Lord is a good thing! Pio used say, "As long as you have fear of the Lord, you will not sin." But Pio also warned us not to have "the fear of Judas." How do we arrive at healthy fear of God, avoiding that of Judas and avoiding the state where fear has usurped love? It is a balancing act in each human person between the right amount of fear and the right amount of confidence. As Pio was wont to say, "Too much fear makes us act without love, too much confidence prevents us from reckoning with and fearing with intelligent caution the danger we must overcome. The one must help the other."[585]

For Pio, it is a matter of seeking the one which is lacking: "If we are too confident, we must seek to have fear" and "If we are aware of being overly frightened we must then run to confidence." How do we know holy fear? Pio told us that "holy fear gives light."[586] This light guides our steps and shows us the way.

Does fear blot out love? No, they have a symbiotic relationship; to quote Pio, "Love and fear must go united together, fear without love becomes cowardice. Love without fear becomes presumption." What about when there is only love? "When there is love without fear, love runs without prudence and without restraint, without taking care where it is going."[587]

Carry Your Cross with Joy

According to Pio, those of us who make being happy our life's mission are on a wasted journey. A Sicilian schoolteacher moved to Bologna and settled into a good life. He heard talk about Pio but was reluctant to believe it, thinking those who spoke of Pio's mystical gifts were psychologically unwell. He was, however, open to learning more about Pio because he read the story of Alberto Del Fante's conversion from Mason to fervent Catholic.

The night he finished it, he went to sleep while thinking of Pio. He woke in the middle of the night to see in his room a Capuchin friar who said to him, "I am Padre Pio. Do not be astonished at my visit. My mission is precisely to console the afflicted, especially those in spirit. I know you are frantically seeking happiness and truth that is God." Padre Pio would then go on to answer the question that troubles most people: "The first thing you are seeking is not possible for you or for anyone on this earth which is a valley of tears where everybody must carry his cross. Happiness is, in fact, not of this world."[588]

Many times in the course of writing this book, the question was posed to me whether Pio had said anything about happiness in this life. It is possible to have peace in our hearts, if we do as Pio instructed the schoolteacher: "Purify your heart of every human passion, humble yourself to the earth and pray. In this way you will certainly find God Who will give you serenity and peace in this world and eternal beatitude in the next." This echoed Our Lord's promise that He can give a peace that the world cannot. Pio finished his message to the schoolteacher with "May Jesus Christ be praised"[589] and then he disappeared. The teacher had just had a mystical vision and had become one of the people he used to disparage. Immediately, he wrote up an account of Padre Pio appearing to him. His pen flew along the page, and he was given special prompting when he could not remember a word.

38

THE DEVIL'S LAST ASSAULT

We return to the mid-1960s and pick up the straight thread of Pio's life story. At the height of the sixties, one evening Pio went to say a few words to a massive assembly of pilgrims outside the window of the old church. The microphone was near him as he surveyed all the faces of the people who looked up at him. He let slip into the microphone as if talking to himself, "If all the devils that are here were to take bodily form, they would blot out the light of the sun."[590]

For the final four years of Padre Pio's life, after the last persecution, demonic attacks intensified and were of a similar savageness to those he experienced as a young priest. This was Satan's last stand: the final attempt of Satan and his minions to sabotage Pio's mission to sanctify souls.

One regular occurrence was visits from demons who disturbed Pio with their ugliness. When Pio went to the veranda of the friary to spend a little time relaxing with the other friars, he would frequently stare fixedly at something that was invisible to everyone else, and when asked what it was, he gave the chilling reply, "I see a face."[591] The devil also continued to haunt Pio under other guises. At this time in his life, the devil adopted a more simple and cunning disguise than that of a fierce dog; he came as a little mouse approaching Pio and then changed into a claw that tried to gouge out Pio's eyes.

One dramatic episode occurred when a possessed young woman was brought from Bergamo to San Giovanni. She was only eighteen, and it was hoped Pio could free her from the devil occupying her. But Pio was seventy-seven, too frail to undertake the exorcism himself. When she was in Pio's presence, she shouted abuse, littered with curses. Pio raised his hand and made the Sign of the Cross over her. A few days later a group of Capuchins obtained permission from the local bishop and began an exorcism of the teenager, but it was no good; the devil used the body of the girl, causing her to laugh and sneer at them relentlessly. The priests had not prayed enough, nor fasted enough, and the demon threw this in their faces.

When Pio heard of the failed exorcism, he devoted one whole night to praying for the girl. But simultaneously he was punished by the devil who was holding the girl captive. The evil one snuck into Pio's cell and delivered such a deathly blow to Pio's spine that he fell face down. His forehead struck the ground, where it earned a nasty gash, his cheeks were battered, his nose leaked blood, and his eyes were black with bruises. Pio was so beat up that it was impossible for him to offer Holy Mass the next morning.

The devil, however, boasted about this attack. There was a throng of people waiting in the square for the church to open and in their company was the possessed teenage girl. Instead of hearing the shuffling of Pio's heavily bandaged feet as he made his way to the altar, the crowd heard a brag come from the possessed teenager: "Did you hear? ... The old man will not come down to say Mass! I beat him up last night!"[592] This betrayed the fact that it had been the devil inhabiting the girl who had attacked Pio.

Mary Pyle was there, too, and heard from the lips of the possessed young woman, "Pio, I've known you since you were small." Mary also witnessed a priest who had tried to exorcise the girl ask the evil one, "Where were you last night?" Mary and the priest heard the reply, "I was upstairs to see the old man I hate so much, because he is a source of faith. I would have done more only the White Lady stopped me."[593] The night before, just after Pio had been thrown to the floor, he had cried out and the other friars ran to his aid, but to their bafflement they saw a cushion under Pio's head. Pio informed them that Our Lady had put the cushion there.

Today, the cushion that Our Lady put under Padre Pio, stained with his blood, is on display in his cell. A difficult teaching is that demons may only carry out acts of violence when they are given permission by God. That poor young woman was being used to do the devil's thuggery.

A few days after the attack, Pio mustered the strength to hear the Confessions of the women. One woman grumbled to Pio, "Everything's going wrong, just as if the devil were causing it ... except I don't believe in the devil." Pio retorted, "You don't believe in the devil! Can't you see the marks he put on my face?"[594] When Pio was well enough, he was able to offer Mass, and on the day he returned to the church, the possessed young woman was in the congregation again. The moment she saw Pio come in, she screamed and fainted. Some minutes later she came out of her fainting spell. She was calm and free from the devil. This may go some way to explaining why the demon who had possessed her was so determined to prevent Pio from coming to the church to offer Holy Mass. Pio coming into the church with *the intention* to offer Mass was the event that caused the devil in her to flee.

39

PIO'S LAST HEARTACHE

After the Second Vatican Council had been in session for three years, Pope Paul VI sought out Pio's advice as to how to proceed with the council, sending Cardinal Antonio Bacci to talk with Pio. After Bacci left, Fr. Eusebio eagerly asked Pio about his visit. Pio replied, "The Pope sent him. He wanted to know what I think of the Council. I said, 'Tell the Pope, what he had to do, he has done. Close it.' "[595]

Pope Paul VI appeared to do as he was advised by Pio and closed the council later that same year. Whereas Christ's Vicar sought Pio's direction, Pio was fiercely resisted by his own sister, who had been a nun for almost fifty years before fleeing her convent.

Sr. Pia was cloistered in the Brigittine Convent in Rome. People who admired Pio used to flock to her to seek her advice and honor the sister of the sainted stigmatist. But Pio was not so well disposed toward her. A man who had gone to visit Sr. Pia and who had been very impressed by her outward appearance of loveliness and holiness praised her to her famous brother, only to be met with a rebuke by Pio: "Don't come talking this rubbish."[596] Rubbish? Pio thought assumptions as to Sr. Pia's piety did not accord with reality.

The reputation Sr. Pia had for sanctity clashed with the reality Pio saw in her soul. Although there were also rumors that Sr. Pia shared some of her brother's charisms, such as invisible stigmata and the aroma of flowers, Pio never affirmed the truth of this. Was this simple sibling rivalry? It seems unlikely that Pio would merely be downplaying Sr. Pia's piety as a way of making himself stand out. On the contrary, Pio once told the same person who talked up Pia's piety, "Listen. I am the best one in my family. Only one surpassed me, but she [Felicita] is no more."[597]

As it turned out, Sr. Pia left the Brigittine Order under a cloud, and she did not heed Pio when he told her to return. In 1965 Sr. Pia's convent became unrecognizable from the days before Vatican II. Sr. Pia, ostensibly offended by the changes, took leave of the convent and found an apartment in Rome. Later, Sr. Pia traveled to San Giovanni to meet with her brother and plead her case as to why she had forsaken the convent.

When Pio saw that she had traded in her full black habit for a dark suit and taken off her veil to expose her shock of white hair, he was apoplectic with anger. "Just look at what you've become," he lamented.

Sr. Pia defiantly yelled back at him, "And you ... what would you do?" She told him why she left, and Pio acknowledged she had good reasons to be upset with the liberalization of convent life. He said, "They are wrong and you are right, but still you must obey, you must return."[598] How could she hold in contempt the nuns in her old convent for failing to keep their vows strictly, when she herself was breaking her vows entirely by running away from the convent?

Much as Pio tried to persuade her to return to religious life, she refused. A battle of wills ensued, and the brother-sister relationship was torn asunder. Pio may have been uncharitable in his speech and tone, making her dig in her heels. But we may wonder, too, if Pio pressed Pia to return so that she could save her soul. When Sr. Pia refused to go back to religious life, Pio fell into a dark depression, pointing to a very real loss. So many obeyed his every word, even when it posed great challenges to them. But his own sister in religious life would not be led by him.

Things ended badly between brother and sister. Sr. Pia went back to Rome and never spoke to Pio again. And although it could be argued that Pio would have done better to make up with his stubborn sister, for the sake of his own salvation, this could have leant legitimacy to her leaving religious life.

This incident in the life of Padre Pio can speak to those who have stormy relations with family members. Pio was known to pray ardently for his sister to return to the convent enclosure, but his many prayers went unanswered. You may have prayed for a family member and not have seen these prayers answered. Well, Pio was a wonder-worker and yet he was known to moan bitterly in these last years, "The Lord doesn't listen to my prayers anymore."[599]

It can be a difficult test of our love for God when He denies our prayers for a loved one. Pio knew the excruciating pain of having a loved one forsake her vocation. Are we, however, to take the same tone as Pio? Not necessarily. In his acrimonious meeting with Pia, Pio spoke as one who had taken vows to another who had taken vows. He treated her like an equal — and he held priests and nuns to much higher standards than laypeople. To the modern mind it is baffling why Pio was in pain after his sister abandoned religious life. But Pio would have seen his sister as a bride of Christ and he felt this as a betrayal of Christ Himself. It bears emphasizing how highly Pio esteemed religious sisters and their role in the war against the devil. Pio once told a fellow friar, "My son, Satan has his headquarters here!" Then, "to counterbalance this dark presence,"[600] Pio spearheaded the building of a convent for cloistered Capuchin sisters.

Dressing for Confession

During a summer vacation in Italy, I spent two weeks with nuns who had known Pio very well. Before they were nuns, they had first been spiritual daughters of Pio's, and along with telling me of his loyal devotion to St. Philomena, they helped me see the standards Pio expected of brides of Christ. Before she entered the convent, the mother superior had held a prestigious post in academia, but when she went to meet Pio, he told her simply, "You are meant to be a nun,"[601] and as soon as possible she entered religious life.

When I was with these extremely prayerful sisters, I saw they wore the traditional habit with black stockings, but they did not tell me as a spiritual daughter of Pio to wear black stockings, even though I had brought them just in case. I have heard it said that Pio asked *all* his spiritual daughters to wear black stockings, but this directive was meant strictly for women who were destined for religious life. This is an example of how Pio's views on women's clothing have sometimes been misunderstood.

We will recall that Pio teased Mary Pyle, who was a Third Order Franciscan (religious laywoman), when she wore elegant dresses, but when laywomen in similarly stylish and fashionable (but modest) dresses came to him in Confession, such as Barbara Ward or his first spiritual daughter, Giovanna, he said nothing to them about their elegant clothes, most likely because they were laywomen and did not have vocations to religious life.

This applied to skirt length, too. Pio was not shy about vocally reprimanding people who came in revealing dress, but I have amassed multiple examples of laywomen who did not have vocations who came in skirts that were a little below the knee or even on the knee and Pio didn't say anything. There was a sign in the church that stated women who were going to confess to Pio were to wear skirts eight inches below the knee. This was directed to all women, because there were those who did not know they were called to convent life, and Pio was always fastidious in preparing women destined for the cloister to live — and dress — in a way that prepared them for life in a full habit. The sign ensured that women who were unaware of their calling came already dressed in a way that was especially for brides of Christ and was not rigorously applied to women who might date and marry.

It is sometimes said that Pio was angry to the point of shouting when someone was dressed modestly yet not according to standards he is said to have had for those who entered his confessional. However, looking at Pio's life and ministry over his fifty-eight years of priesthood, he was not as exacting with laywomen, including his own mother, who did not stringently follow the dress code Pio is said to have enforced for everyone, as the following shows.

A young Indian lady came and urgently wanted to confess to Pio; she had traveled over four thousand miles to do so. But in the crowds her sari got disheveled, and she was, to quote Fr. Pellegrino, "half naked."[602] Yet she persevered in going into Pio's confessional, whereupon he ordered her to leave and come back. Mary Pyle gave her a dress to replace the sari she had lost, and when she returned clothed in it, Pio heard her Confession.

The fashions of the 1960s did cause Pio to feel dejected. At times women and men came in clothes he thought inappropriate or lacking in modesty, and he asked them to go home and rectify their dress. Girls in short skirts and boys in short shorts could come under Pio's censure, but his pattern seemed to be that if the person *knew* they were dressing scantily or in a way that did not befit their vocation, he told them to go home. But if they did not know, as in boys or girls dressed by their parents, then he tended to hear their Confession and then instructed them how to dress more appropriately.

Pio was also hard on men about their choice of clothes, including priests. Once a Dominican priest came to visit Pio, and he had taken off his white cowl and dressed in trousers in a deliberate attempt to disguise himself as a layman. The Dominican had never met Pio before, but when he was in the sacristy with Pio, Pio saw the indelible mark on the priest's soul, and in front of a large group of other men Pio demanded of him why he was not wearing the cowl of St. Dominic. The priest was embarrassed and rushed away. Notably, Pio felt that it was often hopeless to influence his fellow priests and nuns, and he was fond of saying wittily that preaching to religious was as useless as washing a donkey's head.

A Prank on Pio

As colossal changes were being wrought in the 1960s, there was a lot of talk that the friars would throw off the brown robe of St. Francis and wear civvies —that is, jeans and T-shirts — to be more like the common man. Pio was distraught that this was even up for discussion. Pio was traumatized, to the point of breaking down in tears, at the mere suggestion that he would have to wear jeans.

One day, one of the friars approached the elderly Pio with a tape measure and told him he needed to measure him for trousers. It was a prank, but Pio began to sob forlornly and cried out, "Have you lost your senses? I have lived and I will die with this blessed habit on! Do you understand?"[603]

Pio was increasingly dismayed as Italian society underwent more and more extreme changes and the sexual revolution was getting underway. He lamented to Cleonice, "My daughter, don't you see that the world and the human race are going to rack and ruin?"[604] And to another priest he exclaimed, "Don't you see the world is catching on fire?"[605] The "fire" may well be a direct metaphor for the flames of Hell, licking at the world. He was often seen to be horrified when the discussion turned to current affairs.

Pio Loses Padre Eusebio

As the sixties wore on, it became a common sight for nuns to leave their convents in droves, but Pio never could accept his own sister breaking her vows, and he never recovered from the grief that Pia was no longer a bride of Christ. So much so, it was said to be one of the worst hardships he ever endured. This blow to his heart was made all the worse because two months after the fierce fight he had with her, he was struck by another loss: Fr. Eusebio was ordered to leave his post as Pio's assistant.

When his superiors broke the news to Pio that Eusebio was leaving, Pio implored them, "No, don't take that boy away, I need him too much, especially now!" They were deaf to Pio's pleas, and Eusebio asked Pio to pray that they might change their minds, but Pio responded that he couldn't. "I can't, because I made a vow to the Lord never to pray for myself, never to ask for anything, but to pray only for others."[606]

On the morning that Eusebio had to go, Pio said he wanted to die rather than be parted from him; he had been badly hurt by his previous assistant, the devious Giustino, and he may have dreaded that the new assistant might be like him. Pio was given no supernatural insight as to the character of his new assistant, and this meant Eusebio's departure pained him even more.

Pio's Final Decline

Soon, however, Pio was being tailed around the friary by a young friar, Padre Alessio. Pio questioned Alessio as to why he lingered in his shadow. Alessio admitted that he was his new assistant, and Pio welcomed him into his life without reservation. Alessio was softer-spoken than Eusebio, whose way of talking had been more in line with Pio's parents and thus more natural to his ear.

In time Pio praised Alessio as being like a faithful dog. Alessio nursed Pio with an exquisite tenderness, which was so badly needed by Pio because in these last years, his health declined so much that he endured a total bodily agony simultaneous to the pains of crucifixion. He said he'd never suffered so much in his life. He was wracked with the pain of arthritis, and he could barely stagger about if he leant on Alessio. He took more tumbles and admitted, "I feel completely paralyzed from head to foot, and I fall."[607]

Soon Pio had to be brought from his cell to the church in a wheelchair, and he had to offer Holy Mass while sitting in a chair because he could not stand. Something he had never done much in his younger years was complain about physical pain, but now he had such extreme aches in his ears, gums, and teeth that he complained irritably. His bladder bled, small kidney stones rattled in his urinary tract, nasty sores erupted in his stomach lining, and his head throbbed with migraines. He was often seen to be crestfallen. Yet, amid the darkness and depression, he had times of ecstasy. Alessio later recalled, "I saw Pio in ecstasy, completely absorbed. He was in a different world. His face was beautiful."[608]

It was not only depression that caused him to retreat into himself and stay quiet; he was plagued by a severe cough. "He could not talk…. His breathing was heavy because of asthma and bronchitis and he coughed all the time, like a horse. At night he would be more tired than if he'd been working all day, because of the coughing."[609] How silent Pio was in his last years may also be due to fear of sinning with his words. He took to imploring his superior every night for permission to die. He slept little and he made this offering throughout the nights: "My Jesus, my mother Mary, I offer up to you the groaning of my poor soul!"[610] There were nights when Pio got no sleep at all because he said inside him there was "an internal sword . . . moving up and down my left side."[611] Here we need to return to the time, fifty-seven years earlier, when Pio asked the Lord to let the sword reserved for bad priests fall on him. It could well have been the same blade.

Sleeping only ten minutes at a time, Pio heard fifty Confessions every day. This may be a prime example of grace strengthening him, giving him the energy supernaturally when he was so deprived of sleep the normal physical response would have been to collapse for want of rest. Grace enables us to rise above the limits of the human condition, and if we find we cannot get adequate levels of sleep, we may ask the Lord for the same grace He gave Pio, to be as productive on so little rest.

His holiness, goodness, and sanctity did not mean he would not suffer the ravages of old age, and this serves to impress upon us Padre Pio's humanity. His flesh and bones gave him the same grief it gives most other elderly people. If you have ever felt that a physical illness visited upon you was a sign of being out of favor with the Lord (perhaps the thought crossed your mind that if you were in His favor, He would relieve you of the sickness), then take consolation in the fact of the sicknesses that beset Padre Pio throughout his life and especially bothered him so badly when he was an old man.

Pio was too old to do exorcisms, yet demons continued to pay visits, and Pio did not have the stamina to dodge the blows. More than ever, Pio needed the physically robust Alessio to help him fend off the demons. One night Padre Pio called on Alessio so many times in the dead of night that Alessio lost his temper, demanding of Pio, "Why don't you let me sleep at least a half hour?" Pio pleaded with him, "Stay with me! The devils won't let me alone for one minute."[612] Alessio remained in Pio's cell for the night and was witness to devils flaunting their presence and threatening Pio. But at least Pio was calmed and comforted by Alessio's company.

As Alessio said of the times he kept Pio company in his cell throughout the nights, "Once I would be there, he wouldn't be scared." Alessio was a young friar then and would live for decades after Pio had gone to God, but he is no longer in the land of the living. Possibly he is a citizen of Heaven and an ideal intercessor for those who are afflicted by demonic oppression and in need of the same comfort Alessio gave Pio in the last three years of the stigmatist's life.

"Never Have I Suffered So"

The pains in his chest intensified, and Pio was informed he had cardiac arrhythmia. The accumulated aches, sicknesses, and sorrows meant that this was the worst period of suffering of his entire life, which Pio confirmed. He often pronounced, "Never in my life have I suffered so!" This latter part of his life meant that the pilgrims who flooded the friary of San Giovanni met Pio when he was in the most physical and mental pain, and quite a few of them described him as a curmudgeon, a ratty old man. Although this could be true, they may have been taking his bad mood too personally, thinking they were the cause of his irritation, when in fact Pio was not usually annoyed at anyone in particular. Alessio noted, "He was irritable sometimes for no reason.... But he was never irritable with me." Pio was, however, embarrassed that he needed help getting out of bed, as well as bathing and dressing. And he was also heavy with guilt, as Alessio related: "He asked forgiveness for the trouble he was causing. He used to cry because he was a burden to me and to the community."[613] You may feel a sadness reading these words of Pio's, because there is poignancy in his lack of regard for himself and his lack of awareness of how much he meant to others.

Time did not heal. A year after Sr. Pia abandoned the convent for good, his superior described the complete change in Pio that owed to his dire depression. "He is completely withdrawn into himself. He very rarely behaves as he once did: telling stories, jokes and using witticisms and lively words from which he opened conversations on spiritual matters."[614] Pio was repeatedly known to say, "Thank God I am old and near death."[615]

In his last years, death separated him naturally from those closest to his heart. The complex-yet-contrite Emanuele Brunatto died in suspicious circumstances. He was said to have died of heart failure, merely one year after he had nearly pitted the United Nations against the Vatican. There were those among his friends who suspected he had been done away with, that perhaps his death was not really from natural causes. As we saw repeatedly, Emanuele was relentless at uncovering the dark deeds of Pio's enemies.

Pio's older brother, the strong-willed Michele, had bad dementia. The sad sight of seeing his brother slowly die, his mind and memory failing, instilled in Pio the fear that he, too, might go the same way, and this became Pio's worst fear. By the time Michele died, most souls that Pio had loved best had gone to God.

Pio saw the decline in Mary Pyle, whose reddening cheeks bespoke blood pressure going higher. As Sister Death approached Mary, she fretted about the separation this would impose from her beloved spiritual father, but Pio assured his most generous collaborator that she would go to God first and he would join her soon after. Mary showed her stubborn streak when she persisted in going to daily Mass even when she was shaken after a series of strokes. She would leave her pink castle and journey up the steep hill. Pio had to direct her only to go to Mass on Sundays and feast days, because she was often so ill, and then she went by taxi. She received Holy Communion every day in her home, which fulfilled Pio's exhortation to his spiritual children that they try to receive the Sacred Species once a day.

A little while after her eightieth birthday, Mary was sent to the Casa, where her nurse was her good friend Maria Salvatori. Pio was not at Mary's side when she left this life. However, Mary died in the Casa after experiencing perhaps her most profound mystical experience on her deathbed.

On that day Mary was lying in bed, and Nurse Maria was cajoling her with conversation about an upcoming visit from her American relatives. Mary suddenly collapsed. A priest was called, and he came with his purple stole dangling from his neck, but when he arrived at Mary's side, she had taken on the white pallor of a corpse. Thinking Mary had expired, the priest began reciting the prayers of Extreme Unction. As he intoned the prayers, Mary came back to life! Her lips opened, they were once again suffused with color, and her pulse could once again be felt. While the priest prayed over her, Mary said, "Even this is needed."[616] The last rites administered, Mary's soul left, this time for good.

After her death, many of her papers were destroyed, per her expressed wishes, including records of people who owed her money. She did not want people to be shamed were it to come to light they were in her debt. Perhaps Mary Pyle is an able intercessor for people who are in debt and we may ask her to intercede for someone who is grappling with burdensome debt, that their debtors may be as kind to them as Mary was to those who owed her money.

A few days after her passing, Alessio asked Pio as to the destination of Mary's soul, and Pio answered that Mary was in Purgatory. Alessio was a bit stunned and so spoke of Mary's good works, but Pio said by way of explanation for Mary's time in the purging flames, "Yes … but that which she failed to do before."[617] Mary was not to be afflicted for long in Purgatory; she spent about eleven days there. Another spiritual daughter of Pio's had a dream where Mary appeared to her and told her she was in Heaven, having been released on Pio's name day, the feast of Pius V, May 5.

40

HEAVEN CALLING

When in 1918 Pio was given the mission of bearing the stigmata, the wounds of Christ, Our Lord told had told him that he'd bear them for the next fifty years and then go to Him. The meeting with Christ that awaited Pio is the same meeting that awaits us. Our death will precede our meeting with Christ as our judge. In 1968, Pio was to meet Christ three days after the fiftieth anniversary of him becoming a stigmatist.

According to Alessio, only a few years before Pio died, his stigmata wounds had not healed; they looked "scary" and "were like those of a leper."[618] The wounds were "covered with a crust of dried blood." When this crust broke, "it would form sharp projections that pointed into his flesh and would be very painful."[619] The dried shards of blood which penetrated Pio's palms were part of his agony. Both Alessio and Eusebio noted that Pio's bed linen was usually covered with blood.

Whereas Pio carried the bleeding wounds, the other incisions on his body from surgeries and injuries healed normally according to the usual time needed for skin to restore itself, and they left normal scars. There were times when Pio bore the stigmata while also having surgery. The skin that had been cut by the surgeon's scalpel healed normally, leaving scars, but the stigmata went through no such healing process until the very end of Pio's life, when gradually they began to close and heal. On the eve of Pio's death, the wounds had disappeared without the faintest scar, and when he lay in the coffin, his hands were without a scratch. But the scars from other times in his life when he underwent surgery or was injured were still on his body.

A Letter of Farewell

Eleven days before he was to die, Pio was very weak, but he wrote a letter to Pope Paul VI, who was being pilloried for his encyclical *Humanae Vitae*, which condemned contraception. Pio wrote, "I know that your heart is suffering much these days" and gently touched on the cause of Paul's pain, "the lack of obedience of some, even Catholics, to the high teachings that you, assisted by the Holy Spirit and in the name of God, are giving us."

When we read this letter today, it still edifies us that Pio, as a mystic, affirmed that Pope Paul, when he classified contraception as mortally sinful, was being aided by the Holy Spirit and was giving such teachings "in the name of God." Pio's letter continued, "I offer you my prayers and my daily sufferings as a small but sincere contribution." These sorrows and prayerful supplications on the part of Pio were being done, he said, "in order that God may give you comfort with His grace to follow the straight and painful way in the defense of eternal truth."[620]

If we have ever questioned whether Pope Paul VI made a mistake in writing this encyclical, then perhaps we should trust in Pio's insight that the Holy Spirit had "assisted" the pope.

A deeper analysis is that Pio wrote the letter to keep Pope Paul from wavering and from conferring consent to contraception. We will never know whether Pio's letter changed the course of history. What if Pio had never written this letter, and Paul had decided to go back on *Humanae Vitae*'s core message? It is quite possible that Pio's "small contribution" won the graces Paul needed to stay strong, so he would "follow" the way of "truth."

Pio's message to Paul VI offers succinct refutations of the argument being made at the time in favor of contraception: that the Church has to move with the changing times. To this, Pio countered that the "truth" Paul taught "never changes." Pio went on to thank Paul profusely for *Humanae Vitae* and to pledge his "unconditional obedience" to Paul, praising his "illuminated direction."[621]

The Last Station

As Pio's health problems rapidly multiplied and the end was nigh, Cleonice Morcaldi was pained to see her beloved Pio in such total bodily agony, and she cried out to him, "My Father, I'm tired of seeing you suffer and suffer. At least tell me if this is the last station of your way of the cross." Pio concurred, "Yes, it's the last. But remember that it's the longest, most painful and torturous. It's agonizing."[622]

During this last station, Pio went into deeper and deeper silence. He retreated into himself, as though doing the most meticulous examination of conscience ever. He made it known that Our Lord was giving him very little light into his own soul. His deep introspection and quietude were those of a man eking out any sin in his soul with only the dimmest of light and at times, no light at all. Pio was also in the dark as to his sanctity. He pressed his friend Pietro, "Do you think I'll be saved?"[623] In old age Pio had developed a holy fear of his own death. He had longed for death for decades — remember his letters to Raffaelina in which he did his utmost to wheedle prayers from her so that he could die then, when he was only in his twenties. The irony was that when he about to die, his holy fear made him hesitant about death. "Pray for me," he was known to say, "I am afraid to meet Christ. I have not corresponded to his love and to his infinite graces."[624] His fear of judgment did not lessen his desire to die, and when another friar told Pio he wished him a further fifty years, Pio bitterly snapped back, "What harm have I ever done you?"[625]

There were quite a few occasions when Pio foretold his own death. To his cherished Pietro, Pio confided he would die when he was eighty-one. The most stunning prediction was made to his own niece, Pia, Michele's only child. When Pia asked Uncle Pio about a few sensitive family issues, Pio answered with great certainty that they would be resolved within two years but added somberly that he'd be dead by then. Pio did not see fit to be secretive about his upcoming death with Cleonice, and he exclaimed, "I'm dying! I'm dying! I'm preparing myself for the great passage."[626]

At this point, we'll recall a prophecy that Pio made to his first spiritual daughter, Giovanni. In the 1920s, when he was in his thirties, he had told her she was going to be present at his death. Giovanna was now sixty-three; she'd had a happy albeit stressful marriage. She'd married the Marchese Braschi of Cesena, and his work meant they had to do a great deal of traveling, and this somewhat peripatetic lifestyle was hard on Giovanna's nerves. But she'd been able to go to San Giovanni several times a year and had enjoyed Pio's rich counsel over the decades.

In September 1968, Pio gave her an audible locution: "Come quickly to San Giovanni Rotondo, because I'm leaving. If you delay, you'll never see me again." Giovanna made haste to San Giovanni, and on September 19, four days before Pio died, Giovanna confessed to him, and he informed her, "This is the last confession you will have with me. Now I give you absolution for all the sins you committed from the age of reason until now." Giovanna was in denial, but Pio reiterated that he was about to go to God. "My hour has arrived. Jesus is coming to meet me."[627] Then his words came true to the letter, and she assisted at Pio's death, in the same way that the noble Roman matron Jacopa had assisted at St. Francis's death. As Pio was the Second St. Francis, Giovanna was the second Jacopa.

The First Prayer Convention

The weekend before Pio died was the first day of a gigantic convention in San Giovanni, the International Convention of the Prayer Groups. People from all over the world who were members of a prayer group organized in Pio's name had traveled to San Giovanni to take part in the convention. San Giovanni was like the Bethlehem where Mary and Joseph tried to find shelter: Every room at every type of inn was booked as a flood of fans and followers of Pio came to town. No venue was big enough for a gathering of this size, so they listened to the speakers hold forth from a platform in front of the church.

September 20 marked the fifty-year anniversary of Pio receiving the visible wounds of Christ's Crucifixion, and gifts of roses from all his spiritual children filled the church. It was fitting that it fell on a Friday, the day of Our Lord's Passion. When night fell, a sea of souls made their way in a candlelit procession to a spot under the window of Pio's cell. cheering, "Viva Padre Pio!" Their beloved Capuchin did not share their wish for him to live on this earth much longer. Pio's will to die soon was not their will. Their faces were lit by candlelight as they kept their eyes on the cold glass of the window in the hope Pio would open it and give them his blessing while waving his white handkerchief. Alas, they waited in vain, for their dear Pio lay in bed, too weak to greet the tens of thousands of spiritual children who were outside, and too fatigued to get out of bed to see the fireworks that zipped across the night sky in a celebration of him.

Now in the winter of his life, having spent fifty-eight years offering the Holy Sacrifice of the Mass in a standing position — albeit treading on pillows while he offered Mass to ease the searing pain in his stigmatized feet — he was given permission to offer Holy Mass while seated. There may have been some who were troubled by this, feeling it is not a respectful enough posture in which to offer Holy Mass. But, in charity, we may acknowledge that Pio's legs were so weak he could have stumbled during the Mass, with the Eucharist tumbling tragically to the floor. Such havoc was prevented by Pio being in a seated position. This is not entirely conjecture, because when Pio celebrated the very last Holy Mass the day before he was to die, while the friars assisted him going from the altar to the wheelchair, his legs failed him, and the congregation gasped in shock as he collapsed into the arms of his helpers before he was placed into his wheelchair.

Pio's Last Mass

Pio had wanted his last Mass to be a Low Mass — a simpler, quieter Mass — but when his superior insisted that he sing a High Mass, Pio agreed. Pio came into the church in a wheelchair and the sea of people erupted in ecstatic cheering, which gave way to eerie quiet when Pio began celebrating the Mass. Pio's skin was like white marble. The most shocking spectacle was that Pio did not even try to cover his hands to hide his wounds, for there were no wounds, no scabs, and no scars. His hands were perfectly smooth, like those of a child. The marks on the feet had disappeared a year before, in 1967. Whether the wounds on his feet were still there invisibly remains a subject of debate, because Pio was seen to suffer excruciating agony whenever one of the young friars put on Pio's socks and sandals.

Under the summer sunshine of 1968 the wounds on Pio's hands were swiftly disappearing; they then became scabs and finally blotches of red. Just before death, he was relieved of the worst part of the stigmata: the humiliation of the visible wounds being seen by curious eyes. Throughout his life he had changed a lot as a person, but one thing remained the same: Pio did not like curiosity. Insatiable nosiness was a trait he loathed. He frequently claimed, "The habit of asking why has ruined the world."[628]

When he offered this last Mass, Pio's voice faltered, and when he could not lift his voice to chant, he had to speak the sacred words. As he was wheeled through the church, he called out in a tone of great affection, "My children, my children!"[629]

Later that morning at ten thirty, Pio made a surprise visit to the choir window of the old church, the same place where Our Lord had appeared to him with the blazing blade and given Pio His wounds. From this vantage point, Pio waved his white handkerchief to the throng of thousands below and bestowed his blessing on them.

Final Moments

The evening of the twenty-second, Padre Pio wept profuse tears in his cell. Big-eyed Pellegrino was beside Pio and was wiping away Pio's tears. Pio asked Pellegrino the time while he grabbed at Pellegrino's fingers. In those anxious moments, Pellegrino thought Pio seemed like a nervous child who had a big appointment ahead of him. A little after midnight, dogs in the town were heard howling as they sensed Pio's death was at hand. In the early hours, Pio asked Pellegrino to hear his last Confession, something that was witnessed by none other than Giovanna. Unbeknownst to Pellegrino, she had bilocated to Pio's cell and was with Pio in his last agony. Until that time, no woman had ever been in Pio's cell and no photograph had ever been taken, but Giovanna could see every detail of her spiritual father's bedroom and where he breathed his last. She was distraught and in shock at seeing the life drain from Pio and that he was so excruciatingly ill. Giovanna worried how she could cope after his death, but then she remembered that Pio had told her to emulate the strong women of Sacred Scripture.

Pellegrino shivered with shock when Pio asked him to be witness as he renewed his vows, which is customarily done by a monk on his deathbed. It informed him Pio's death was really at hand. Giovanna saw him make the same vows he had made fifty-eight years before, and she became hysterical with grief. Pio asked Pellegrino to offer Holy Mass for him the next morning and made a specific request: "My son, if the Lord calls me today, ask pardon for me from the confreres for all the bother I have given them and ask my spiritual children to pray for my soul."[630]

Pio's next movements confused and startled Pellegrino. Pio asked Pellegrino to lend him a hand getting out of his bed and, once out of his cot, Pio dressed and washed his face and said he wished to lay his eyes on the starry heavens, soon to be his destination. Amazingly, Pio stood straight and walked quickly like he was a young friar; not needing any help at all, Pio strode to the veranda. Joining him, Pellegrino shared his view of the star-speckled sky. Pio's eyes then became fixed on a part of the veranda which in a matter of hours would be the precise spot his dead body would rest, until the time came for him to be laid out in the church.

Out on the veranda Pio's face turned ashen white and he could hardly stay on his feet. Pellegrino got the wheelchair and took him back to his cell, where Pio slumped in his armchair while chanting over and over, "Jesus … Mary." He was on the edge of eternity when he said in a low voice, "I see two mothers,"[631] as he beheld the Virgin Mary and his biological mother, Giuseppa. In years gone by, Pio had remarked that Our Blessed Mother never left his cell; now she was accompanied by the mother from whom he had taken his flesh.

Pio's face turned whiter, the same color as his snowy beard. His lips became violet and his breathing began to fail, which disturbed Pellegrino so much that he started to leave the room for help, but Pio used his remaining strength to restrain the young friar, saying he did not want to cause a disturbance. But Pellegrino bolted from the cell, called Dr. Sala on the phone, and went to rouse the other friars. Minutes later the doctor was by Pio's side while Pio kept intoning, "Jesus … Mary." Pio was given oxygen and his skin was pierced with injections to chemically stimulate his heart. Pio was surrounded by a brown-frocked friars who started praying the prayers of extreme unction over him. Pio sighed the sigh of a soul who was about to soar to his Savior, and died that instant at 2:30 a.m., Monday, September 23, 1968. The cause of death was a heart attack caused by asthma.

Final Preparations

Moments after Pio had passed, black-and-white photographs were taken of his body, showing that the skin on his hands, feet, and side was like a that newborn baby. If we had been there then looking at Pio's hands and feet and had no prior knowledge of the stigmata, we would have had no clue that he had borne the wounds of Christ. In the hours after Pio died, Pellegrino offered Mass for him, as Pio had requested. As Pio was lowered into a wooden coffin, the purple stole around his neck matched his lips. He was clad in his brown gloves to cover his hands, which were smooth and scarless. This was done lest the many miles of people who were going to file past his body and venerate him be shocked at his lack of stigmata.

His body was placed at the foot of the altar in the church. Even in death, Pio had to be protected from those who wanted to desecrate his body by cutting off a body part and selling it or keeping it as a relic, so his body was moved from the wooden coffin into a steel one with a glass top. Police officers stood about the church to keep order among the faithful, many of whom were in the throes of grief. For the entirety of September 23 mourners filed past the coffin. Over one hundred thousand people came to the town on the top of the mountain to attend Pio's funeral. Among the mourners was Pia, Pio's last surviving sibling, who had never reconciled with her brother. Only a matter of months after Pio's death, Pia herself died, and we may hope that, if and when she reached Heaven, she met her brother and they were reconciled.

The Funeral Procession

Miles of mourners filed past Pio day and night, all Tuesday and Wednesday and until noon on Thursday, when the friars had to close the coffin, to the chagrin of the crowds, so they could prepare for the funeral procession. Pio's coffin was put on top of an open hearse. Later in the afternoon, in the gentle, golden sun of September, the procession was ready to make its way through the streets of the town. Soldiers in full military dress met the coffin, and as they banged their drums the procession began to move through the town. Everywhere it went the body of Pio was greeted with rapturous applause.

Assembled on the streets were the same locals of San Giovanni who had fought tooth and nail to keep Pio in their midst when attempts were made down through the years to have him moved away. Tears flowed down their faces and they called out to Pio to remember them before God. The procession went as far as the town graveyard, greeting the deceased who were buried there: Pio's parents, Mary Pyle, and many of the townspeople, such as Dr. Francesco, who had converted to Christ at the hands of Pio. Like a funeral for a king, a squadron of military planes flew over the procession and showers of flowers fell from them onto the people below. Then the procession turned around and Pio's remains were brought back to the church for an early evening funeral.

Pope Paul VI was not there in person but sent a deeply felt telegram conveying an "Apostolic Blessing and condolences to the religious community in their sorrow, to the doctors, staff and patients of the Home for the Relief of Suffering and to the entire population of San Giovanni Rotondo."[632]

Let's meditate on the fact that a funeral Mass was offered for the repose of Pio's soul. Was it necessary? Well, yes, it was. The fact that Mass was offered for Pio's soul days after he died reminds us all of the importance of having Masses offered for a departed soul rather than assuming they are already in Heaven. The fact that Mass was offered for one of Pio's sanctity ought to inspire us to have Mass offered for our departed loved ones.

Let it warn and warm us that Masses were offered for Pio, a saint universally renowned even in his lifetime. Let it edify us to think there is no shame or humiliation in arranging for Masses to be offered for dead loved ones.

The Burial

After the funeral Mass, Pio's coffin was taken to the lower level of the church, to the crypt, where a seven-ton block of blue Labrador granite was placed on top of the burial plot. This was to prevent what happened after St. Francis died, when many people in a frenzy dug up the ground to find his body. Finally, the ardent desire of the people of San Giovanni was fulfilled: Pio was never to leave them and would be with them for all time.

When he was still alive, Pio used reply to people who were in anticipatory grief at the thought of losing him, "Come to my tomb and you will receive more than you did before." Pio used give the invitation twice, "Come visit my tomb. Before, to speak to me, you had to wait. Then, it is I who will be waiting there."[633] We have it from Pio's lips that he will be "waiting" for us in his tomb. For us there is an implicit promise of "more," and for us there may even be greater merit in visiting him now than when he was still alive. Had we been alive when Pio was alive, we would have had to wait, maybe even for days, to reach him. Now he waits for us. At the moment you are reading this, he waits for us.

What does "more" mean? For us it means ever more graces and blessings of healing of mind and body, as well as conversion of soul and the graces for a richer, more beautiful life, which we may lead with Pio's intercession. There is no sadness to be entertained because Pio may no longer be found sitting in his confessional, but only joy to be experienced in Pio's ability to do "more" for us.

We might think that because so many people pray to Pio, we will get lost in a big crowd of souls. Again, Pio answered this concern in a spirited conversation that foreshadowed the individual attention he would give each soul. A collaborator who had done much to help Pio said to him that, with the great number of people Pio had to pray for, he would have to put them all in one big cauldron. Pio replied feistily, "In a cauldron is where I am going to throw you!" Pio then corrected the notion that all the recipients of his prayers are one large, anonymous group by saying, "I remember them and I call them one by one, and count their hairs, and then some."[634] Likewise, Pio assured his faithful disciple Cleonice, "When the Lord calls me I will stay closer to you, I will assist you more."[635] This is be our guarantee, too, that Pio is closer and can "assist" us more.

EPILOGUE

In death as in life, Pio's reputation for sanctity depended quite a lot on the ruling pope. In the years and decades after his death, millions came to pray at his tomb, and many of them already held Pio in their hearts as a saint. His tomb quickly became one of the most popular shrines in the world, and this occurred under the auspices of Pope Paul VI, who remained pope for ten years after Pio went to his eternal reward. Paul, the pope with the worried face and troubled gray eyes, never seemed to waver in his admiration for the stigmatist, and nearly three years after Pio's death, Pope Paul kept his memory and his good name alive when he spoke so well of Pio to the superiors of the Capuchin Order. The pope who followed Pio's advice and closed Vatican II was heard to say,

> Look what fame he had, what a worldwide following gathered around him! But why? Perhaps because he was a philosopher? Because he was wise? Because he had resources at his disposal? Because he said Mass humbly, heard confessions from dawn to dusk and was —it is not easy to say it — one who bore the wounds of our Lord. He was a man of prayer and suffering.[636]

Padre Pio's Cause

The official process to make Pio a saint was not started right away. The Vatican did not grant permission for the local cause to be opened in the Archdiocese of Manfredonia, where Pio practiced his ministry, until the papacy of John Paul II. There has been speculation that this delay could have been due to politics, or to prejudice from Pio's surviving enemies, or even that Rome wanted to see if the passionate love that Pio's followers had for him was going to survive the test of time. Despite the delay, it can be said confidently that Pope Paul continued until his death to hold Pio in high esteem. There may have been a feeling among the authorities, however, that Pio's Catholic practice, especially that he only ever offered the Traditional Latin Mass, was at odds with the changes promulgated in the 1970s, and that a gap of time allowed for the changes to be wrought without the potential tension of a stigmatist whose formation happened before the council becoming a celebrated saint. This could have been the mindset of the pope who immediately replaced Pope Paul.

When Pope Paul went to God, his successor was Pope John Paul I, the pope with boyish charm and laughing face. When he was Bishop Albino Luciani, he'd been a powerful critic of Pio. He is often described as genial, cheerful, and generous in his assessments. We may, however, bear in mind that in the same year as the stringent Vatican investigation into Pio, 1960, the future Pope John Paul I wrote an article which meanly dismissed Pio's ministry as an "indigestible dainty" and cast aspersions on Pio's followers as people with an "exaggerated craving for the supernatural." He opined that "the faithful need solid bread (the Mass, catechism, the Holy Sacraments) to nourish them, not chocolates, pastries and sweetmeats."[637]

The future pope made known that the many pilgrimages people made to San Giovanni bothered him, and he even banned his priests from leading or taking part in such pilgrimages. At the time, had he checked with Pio, he would have known Pio often felt the same way. As we saw throughout this book, Pio disliked crowds of curious people who rudely pressed on him from all sides, who asked self-centered questions and treated him like a spectacle: They took time that he needed to hear Confessions. In any case, Pope John Paul I's opinions on Pio did not have a substantial bearing on the process by which Pio became a saint. He was pope for only thirty-three days in the fall of 1978. Then the Polish Cardinal Karol Wojtyla, an old friend of Pio's who had a rich history with the friar, was elected to the throne of Peter. For a long time before he became pope, Wojtyla had nurtured a personal devotion to the stigmatist.

The Papacy of Pope John Paul II

Two years after World War II, and thirty-one years before becoming pope, the young, dashing Fr. Karol Wojtyla visited Pio. He was newly ordained and was doing further study in Rome. He journeyed to San Giovanni and spent a week in the company of Pio. Because the roads had been bombed, there were far fewer pilgrims at the time, and so the young Fr. Wojtyla had the opportunity to speak at length with Pio.

Decades later, in the 1970s, when Wojtyla became the Holy Father, people speculated as to whether Pio had told him he was going to be the pope. But Pope St. John Paul II clarified that Pio did not verbally tell him that he would be pope. There is, however, a case to be made that Pio treated him as if he was already a pope. Fr. Wojtyla asked Padre Pio which one of his wounds caused him the most suffering, and — without asking the Pole for his letter of permission — Pio divulged, "It is my shoulder wound, which no one knows about and has never been cured or treated."[638]

We'll recall that Fr. Gemelli had pushed to interrogate Pio about his stigmata, only to have Pio gruffly refuse him because he didn't have the necessary documentation, the letter granting him permission. The only person who could have asked about the stigmata and examined them without authorization was the pope. Had Pio not been certain he was talking to a future pope, he'd have been disobedient in answering. And, after the most diligent analysis of Pio's life, it was revealed that Fr. Wojtyla was the only person Pio ever told about his most painful wound. Pio bore the wounds of Christ, and deliberately confided in the priest who was destined to be the Vicar of Christ.

In 1962, at the height of Pio's worst persecution, Wojtyla wrote a letter in Latin to Pio, asking for urgent prayer for Dr. Wanda Poltawska, a wife and mother of four little girls. She was a psychiatrist who was expert in family issues, and her scholarship influenced Wojtyla very much. Wanda had a kindly face and looked so like Wojtyla that she could have been his sister, but they were not blood relatives, only good friends. Wanda had been diagnosed with incurable cancer; she had a tough, round ulcer in her intestines. She was no stranger to suffering, having been imprisoned by the Nazis in a concentration camp for six years. Her mind was at peace when she was told that if she had an operation to remove the cancerous growth, she'd have three years maximum left to live. She was only forty.

When Wojtyla sought prayer for her, he did not tell her. Yet, when Pio received Wojtyla's letter, he said tellingly, "It's not possible to say no!"[639] Sure enough, in the same month Pio prayed for her, Wanda's doctor discovered that the cancer had vanished without a trace. Wanda, however, did not discover that Pio's prayers had been invited until five years later. She made a pilgrimage to see Pio, and when he saw her, without being introduced, Pio inquired, "Now, are you all right?"[640]

Wojtyla's belief in Pio's intercession continued after Pio had died. He went as archbishop of Krakow on a personal pilgrimage to Pio's tomb in 1974. Then, in 1982, as Pope John Paul II, he gave permission for the local cause to be opened in Manfredonia. The Polish pope with cornflower blue eyes made it known to his friends that although he prayed for and was eager for Pio to be beatified, he did not want to push, because he did not want his efforts to be seen as the reason Pio was a saint. He wanted Pio to be seen as an intercessor in his own right, not merely as a holy friar who had a fan in the pope. The miracles that happened when Pio's prayers were invoked demonstrated ably that Pio was powerful with God in Heaven.

A Beatification Miracle

Consiglia De Martino was a pretty brunette with a lovely smile and bubbly personality. She was a wife and mother of three children, and a member of a Padre Pio prayer group. Consiglia had been devoted to Pio for a long time when she had a devastating health crisis. The thoracic duct in her neck burst and two liters of lymphatic fluid flooded into a huge swelling that bulged like a balloon. She called the friary of San Giovanni and requested prayer. Pio's help was asked at his tomb, and in her hospital room, 177 miles away, Consiglia was greeted with a celestial fragrance. Then the fluid reversed course, seemingly against gravity, and was reabsorbed. Consiglia recovered completely.

Only a few years later, five medical experts were assigned to pore over her medical notes and assess the veracity of the claim that she'd been cured miraculously. They concluded she had, and this was followed by the Vatican's Congregation for the Causes of Saints approving her case as a canonical miracle: Pio was going to be beatified. The happy day came, May 2, 1999, and three hundred thousand people packed Rome so they could personally witness the Polish pope announce, "Pio of Pietrelcina will from now on be called Blessed."[641]

Pope John Paul II's homily shone with his tender love for the new blessed. He said poetically that people who had known Pio "saw in him a living image of Christ suffering and risen. The face of Padre Pio reflected the light of the Resurrection."[642] These words resonated with those (including me) who had seen Pio appear to them in the years after he went to Heaven — his face had something of the glow of the Resurrected Christ. John Paul II's sermon was both theologically deep and very personal, because he shared with the multitude gathered that he'd confessed to the same stigmatist whom he was declaring a saint, and that it was a "privilege" to do so.[643] John Paul also extolled Pio's magnificent charity: "His charity was poured out like balm on the weaknesses and sufferings of his brothers and sisters. Padre Pio thus united zeal for souls with a concern for human suffering, working to build at San Giovanni Rotondo a hospital complex."[644]

The Canonization Miracle

The first time Padre Pio appeared to me, in 1998, he was a year away from being beatified. When he appeared to me for the second time, in 2001, he was a year away from being made a saint. Consiglia had recovered without any treatment, but the miracle that led to Pio's canonization was wrought after medical intervention had been exhausted. Matteo Pio Colella, the son of very committed Catholics who had an ardent devotion to Pio, was stricken with meningitis.

Matteo was only eight when he fell ill with severe flu symptoms, including shaking. When frightening purple spots multiplied on his skin, his parents rushed him to the Casa. This was an emergency, and Matteo's own father, who was a doctor, had to admit that his efforts at home to make him well had not worked. The medical staff did their level best, but Matteo fell into septic shock. He was getting so little oxygen that he was put on a respirator, and his heart stopped. They were able to restart it, but he fell into a coma. The doctors related the grave news that the little boy was at death's door.

The distraught parents, Antonio and Maria Lucia, watched while their son, with thick, jet-black hair and a chubby baby-like face, wrestled for his life. Matteo's mother got permission to pray in Pio's old room, and she knelt in front of his bed and begged unashamedly for her son to be restored to health. Then, that night, she prayed the Rosary at Pio's tomb, and had a vision. In her words, "While praying with my face on the cold granite, I saw with closed eyes, in black and white, a friar with a beard who advanced resolutely to a bed and picked up with both hands the small rigid body of a child and put him on his feet."[645] It was a harbinger of the miracle that awaited her when, five days later, Matteo started to escape his coma.

The miracles that led to Pio's beatification and canonization concerned miraculous healings of the body. But for many of us, the most extraordinary examples of Pio's intercession are the conversions of souls, and I think it most miraculous that I am a practicing Catholic. Now that I am ending this book, I ask myself if, when he said solemnly to me, "I am waiting for you," is this the small project that he wanted me to do for him?

I was greeted with five key celestial perfumes when writing this. Once, after a long night of working on conversion stories, I retired to my bedroom and was met with the delightful fragrance of many flowers, like an English garden, each flower perhaps representing a soul that Pio had rescued. When I was writing about how Pio offered Holy Mass, there was a sweet baking smell of an almond cake, which soothed my stress because I was only barely paying my bills at the time. On several occasions there was a sharp aroma of tobacco, always signifying danger, which I was able to avoid. A strong vanilla scent gave me encouragement that I'd make it through heartbreak. Then, when I finished the manuscript of this book, the smell of incense wafted all around me, and reminded me to embrace more and more prayer.

Helping Friends

Pio led other souls to me who gave me the help I needed to write this, even when I had no plans whatsoever to write a book about him. One such person, Dónal Enright, was the one who made the single greatest contribution to this book. At the time I met Dónal, I was home in Ireland from London for a brief holiday and I heard he had a brown glove that had been worn by Pio. Dónal was known for bringing the glove to the sick. Astounding miracles always happened, especially among babies and children who were thought to be dying, until the glove was placed on them and they made complete recoveries. I was interested in being blessed by the glove because I was being checked for a serious illness. Only my doctor in England and I knew. My physician in London was planning to have it checked and I didn't want to worry anyone by telling them. I was so young that I couldn't understand the pain I was frequently in, and I wondered if I was just a hysteric, but the doctor took it seriously enough to nod her head when I asked if an illness was really a possibility.

I rang Dónal Enright and asked if he had a spare moment to see me, and he invited me round straightaway to his home, appropriately named "Villa Pio." It was as warm and welcoming as the coziest, most Catholic Irish home, yet it was sparsely furnished with hard, iron chairs. Dónal's gaze turned deathly serious for a moment when he assessed me and I was flummoxed when he struck my collar bone with a bony index finger and pronounced, "Pio will ask you to do something for him." He paused and said, "You're a writer; you'll use your pen to make him known and bring more spiritual children into the fold." I had not told Dónal I was a journalist. Dónal swiftly assured me, "I'll give you what you need." Then he commented regarding his own work, "I've nearly completed my mission, just a few more jobs for Pio left in this life." He smiled ecstatically as he told me he would die in two years. That night, he seemed full of vigor, but he was extremely thin. His peachy skin covered a gaunt face which had a radiance of holiness.

For several hours, Dónal recounted that Pio had given him the role of helping tough cases, people who needed someone to pull them out of the mire. As we know from earlier in this book, Dónal had helped women who were post-abortion and could confide in him without fear that he would sell their story to the press because he was entirely uninterested in money or personal notoriety. He had worked hard to avoid fame that had been offered him on a plate. But he had worked quietly and so exceedingly hard that he put me and most others to shame.

Several of the women had, however, asked him to share their testimonies anonymously so that others might learn to have that "horror of abortion" which Pio had stressed was so necessary. The women also wanted their journey back to a state of grace to be known, as well as how recovery from sin had been their route to total healing and peace. Dónal had done his utmost by these women, and he had never asked anything in return.

Pio had, however, rewarded Dónal by treating him as though he were a close family member. Pio revealed to Dónal the precise details of the offering that his mother, Giuseppa, had made of his life to St. Francis when he was just a newborn, still slick with womb grease. St. Francis took her at her word, and the book you have just read has been written ever mindful of Giuseppa's sacrifice of her son. After Dónal had spoken at length for hours, he seized the brown glove that had blood stains on it and reminded me that I'd asked to be blessed with it. I had never said a word as to my reason, but Dónal abruptly specified the exact illness the doctor was planning to search for — though I had not said a word to anyone — and this convinced me that Dónal had mystical abilities of his own. Without my saying a word, he placed the glove on the exact spot of my body that was under scrutiny. When I later returned to London, the doctor found nothing, and the symptoms disappeared.

After he blessed me with the glove, Dónal exclaimed, "You have a great devotion to St. Philomena!" and he bowled me over for the umpteenth time when he said, "Eileen introduced you to her!" He knew, though his mystical gaze, the beautiful old lady who had first told me that St. Philomena was a wonder-worker. But that's not all he knew: Dónal was the person who had been informed by Pio that St. Philomena is the princess of Heaven, and Pio was born on the day her relics were discovered, ordained on the anniversary of her martyrdom, and he made known his love for her many times.

There was a golden thread that tied everything Dónal said together. He had helped women who'd lost their unborn children. He had saved many children from early death when he brought the glove of Pio to them, which meant their deadly diseases were washed away with the blood on the brown mitt that Pio had worn. And he had been given a glimpse of Heaven's royalty when Pio told him that St. Philomena is the princess of Heaven. Our Lady is the queen, and as the highest virgin-martyr, Philomena is a sovereign saint. Later I learned that Philomena is the patroness of babies and infertility. Dónal was a husband and father of five children, and a disciple to parents. Pio's own parents were his first and most important disciples.

This is a book about a big saint who has an even bigger future role than we know. It is left for us to discern our own role: as someone who takes inspiration from Pio concerning how to grow in holiness; as a spiritual child; as a disciple in the mold of so many of the characters we've met during our review of Pio's life; or as a more exact replica of Pio, a victim soul. Whichever role we assume, we can be confident that Pio, as our spiritual father, will lead us expertly and intercede for us. He promised, "I will stay at the door of paradise and I will tell Him: 'Lord, I will not enter before I see that all my children have entered.' "[646] In closing, I ask that we hold this image uppermost — that he is stationed at the threshold of eternal life, waiting for us.

ACKNOWLEDGMENTS

With all my soul, I thank the Immaculate Heart of Mary and the Sacred Heart of Jesus. Thank you, Pio, for teaching me to pray to Our Lady and Our Lord. It is a great honor that Sophia Institute Press has deigned to publish this work, and I thank its staff for their generosity to me. Sophia's thirst for the salvation of souls is the most noble endeavor of all. It is to be commended for having the bravery to publish a book that may not make us popular with the denizens of Hell. May everyone at this hallowed publishing house be rewarded for giving greater recognition to Pio and the choir of saintly souls who graced his life and whom we have met in the pages of this book.

Dear readers, of your love, I ask that you pray for all these dear souls that I'm about to list, and for their loved ones. I'd like to give a special thank-you to Patrick O'Hearn who, as a true friend, nobly shepherded this book to publication. Patrick combines fortitude and integrity as well as a remarkable zeal for his fellow Catholic authors to thrive. He is truly selfless. Patrick, may you get every blessing and may all your books become bestsellers. With all my soul, I thank Anna Maria Dube and Caleb Selecter, who work tirelessly to bring forth new treasures of Catholic thought and theology. God bless them and may they enjoy every grace in this most exalted mission. Thank God for Heidi Hess Saxton, who as my editor took such care and sensitivity in pruning the manuscript. Heidi transformed it into a plant that will bear much more fruit than it ever would have had she not done such a remarkable job . Heidi has a fine poetic sensibility that elevates an author's prose to new heights and enthuses souls to sanctity. A huge thank-you to Kevin Shmiesing, who expertly and excellently copyedited the manuscript. Kevin brought such a thorough and thoughtful approach that he treated every sentence like it were fine china; a gift to me especially after eight years of hard work. A most heartfelt thank-you to Claire Lejeune who took my author photo and made me look much more attractive than I am in real life. Claire is my Friedrich Abresch and just as brilliant.

With a grateful heart, I'd like to thank the following with every fiber of my being: Archbishop Charles John Brown; Keith Berube; Sally Collins; John Hammett Carmichael Sr. and John Hammett Carmichael Jr.; Fr. Ambrose Criste and all the priests at St. Michael's Abbey, Orange County, California; The Norbertine Canonesses of Tehachapi, California; Dónal Enright; Elizabeth; Daniel Harrington; Olivia Jennings; Tom, and Barbara and Gus Leopold; The Religious of Mary Immaculate, London, England, James Ignatius McAuley, Esq.; Mark Mulrooney; and Dr. John Newton; Catherine Pearson; Frank Rega; Danny Risdon; Bruce Roe; Jeanette Salerno.

Thank you also to everyone who decided not to be mentioned by name for fear of reprisals from secularists who resent figures such as Pio. Like everyone named here, there would be no book without them. There might be no need for such a book as this were there no one to convert; a plea from my heart to yours, please pray in union with me for all the souls I'm hoping will come to Christ through Padre Pio.

ENDNOTES

1.   Agostino of San Marco in Lamis, *Diario* (Edizioni Padre Pio da Pietrelcina, 1975), 269.

2.   Author's interview with Dónal Enright of County Cork, Ireland, as reported in Mary O'Regan, "When Absolution Was Refused," *Mass of Ages*, Autumn 2016, 12, https://issuu.com/latinmasssociety/docs/final_moa-_issue_190_-_winter_2016_.

3.   Padre Pio of Pietrelcina, *Letters*, vol. 1, *Correspondence with his Spiritual Directors (1910–1922)* (Edizioni Padre Pio da Pietrelcina, 1980), 234.

4.   Maria Winowska, *The True Face of Padre Pio* (Catholic Book Club, 1961), 182.

5.   Pellegrino Funicelli, *Padre Pio's Jack of All Trades* (Our Lady of Grace Capuchin Friary, 1991), 267.

6.   Ibid., 362.

7.   Fr. Charles Mortimer Carty, *Padre Pio, The Stigmatist* (TAN Books, 2010), 243.

8.   Ibid., 232.

9.   Morcaldi, *La mia vita vicino a Padre Pio*, 50
As quoted in Kathy Andre Eames, "The Mass of St. Padre Pio", Soul Food Ministries, 2017, https://soulfoodministries.wordpress.com/2017/02/14/the-mass-of-st-padre-pio/

10.   Acts of the First Congress of Studies on Padre Pio's Spirituality, 1972, 253.

11.   Morcaldi, *La mia vita vicino a Padre Pio*, 55–56.

12.   Gennaro Preziuso, *I Genitori di Padre Pio* (Edizioni Padre Pio da Pietrelcina, 2005), 88.

13.   C. Bernard Ruffin, *Padre Pio: The True Story*, rev. and exp. 3rd ed. (Our Sunday Visitor, 2018), 23.

14.   *Voice of Padre Pio* 7, no. 2 (1977): 5.

15.   Interview with Pia Forgione, Padre Pio's niece, as quoted in Ruffin, *Padre Pio*, 30.

16.   Author's interview with Dónal Enright, based on his conversation with Padre Pio, County Cork, Ireland, June, 2010

17.   Gherardo Leone, *Padre Pio: Infanzia e prima giovanezza* (1887–1910)(La casa sollievo della sofferenza, 1973), 28.

18. Alessandro da Ripabottoni, *Pio of Pietrelcina: Infancy and Adolescence* (Edizioni Padre Pio da Pietrelcina, 1969), 100.

19. *Voice of Padre Pio* 4, no. 3 (1974): 1.

20. Preziuso, *I Genitori di Padre Pio*, 147

21. Ibid., 148.

22. Leone, *Padre Pio: Infanzia e prima giovanezza*, 31.

23. Lino da Prata and Alessandro da Ripabottoni, *Beata te, Pietrelcina* (Edizioni Padre Pio da Pietrelcina, 1976), 112.

24. Francesco Castelli, Vittorio Messori, and Archbishop Raffaelo Carlo Rossi, *Padre Pio Under Investigation: The Secret Vatican Files*, trans. Lee and Giulietta Bocham (Ignatius Press, 2011), 276.

25. Preziuso, *I Genitori di Padre Pio*, 12.

26. Leone, *Padre Pio: Infanzia e prima giovanezza*, 41.

27. Alessio Parente, *The Holy Souls: Viva Padre Pio* (Edizioni Padre Pio da Pietrelcina, 1988), 67.

28. Da Prata and da Ripabottoni, *Beata te, Pietrelcina*, 186.

29. Augustine McGregor, *Padre Pio: His Early Years* (Edizioni Padre Pio da Pietrelcina, 1981), 83.

30. Mary F. Ingoldsby, *Padre Pio: His Life and Mission* (Veritas Publications, 1988), 15.

31. Da Prata and da Ripabottoni, *Beata te, Pietrelcina*, 185.

32. Ibid.

33. Ibid., 186.

34. *Voice of Padre Pio*, 34, no. 9 (2003): 28.

35. Ingoldsby, *Padre Pio*, 10.

36. Ibid., 11.

37. Da Prata and da Ripabottoni, *Beata te, Pietrelcina*, 239.

38. Alessandro da Ripabottoni, *Padre Pio da Pietrelcina: Un cireneo per tutti* (Centro Culturale Francescano—Convento Immacolata, 1974), 62.

39. Ingoldsby, *Padre Pio*, 21.

40. All quotations relating to the vision in this section are taken from *Padre Pio of Pietrelcina, Epistolario I: Corrispondenza con le direttori spirituali (1910–1922)*, San Giovanni Rotondo, 1973, 1281–1282; translation into English: Ingoldsby, *Padre Pio*, 17.

41. Ingoldsby, *Padre Pio*, 21.

42. Patricia Treece, *The Joyful Spirit of Padre Pio: Stories, Letters, and Prayers* (Franciscan Media, 2014), 163.

43. As quoted on the Caccioppoli website, https://caccioppoli.com/03a%20Padre%20Pio%20and%20temptation,%20devil,%20confession;%20meditation,%20prayer,%20rosary.html.

44. Carty, *Padre Pio: The Stigmatist*, 248.

45. Ibid.

46. Ingoldsby, *Padre Pio*, 17–18.

47. Padre Pio of Pietrelcina, *Letters*, vol. 3, *Correspondence with Spiritual Daughters (1915–1925)*, 1016.

48. Frank M. Rega, *Padre Pio and America* (TAN Books, 2005), 11.

49. *Voice of Padre Pio* 42, no. 1 (2012), 13.

50. Carty, *Padre Pio: The Stigmatist*, 229.

51. This and subsequent quotations from the vesting ceremony are taken from Leone, *Padre Pio: Infanzia e Prima giovanezza*, 14.

52. Nesta De Robeck, *Padre Pio* (Bruce, 1958), 11.

53. *Voice of Padre Pio* 42, no. 2 (2012): 13.

54. Da Prata and da Ripabottoni, *Beata te, Pietrelcina*, 224.

55. Ruffin, *Padre Pio*, 49.

56. Ibid.

57. *Voice of Padre Pio* 19, no. 10 (1989), 6.

58. Alessandro da Ripabottoni, *Padre Pio of Pietrelcina: Everybody's Cyrenean* (Our Lady of Grace Capuchin Friary, 1987), 41.

59. All the quotations in this section come from Alberto D'Apolito, *Padre Pio of Pietrelcina: Memories, Experiences, Testimonials* (Edizioni Padre Pio da Pietrelcina, 2013), 391.

60. Ibid.

61. Gennaro Preziuso, *The Life of Padre Pio Between the Altar and the Confessional* (Pauline Press, 1999), 50.

62. Dorothy M. Gaudiose, *Prophet of the People: A Biography of Padre Pio* (Alba House, 2018), 275.

63. D'Apolito, *Padre Pio of Pietrelcina*, 253.

64. Preziuso, *Life of Padre Pio*, 53.

65. Ibid., 54.

66. Padre Pio of Pietrelcina, *Letters*, 1:218.

67. Padre Pio of Pietrelcina, *Letters*, 1:211.

68. Padre Pio of Pietrelcina, *Letters*, 1:204.

69. Padre Pio of Pietrelcina, *Letters*, 1:203.

70. Padre Pio of Pietrelcina, *Letters*, 1:204.

71. John A. Schug, *Padre Pio* (Franciscan Herald Press, 1983), 31.

72. Author's interview with Dónal Enright, County Cork, Ireland, June 2010

73. Author's conversation with religious sisters who were spiritual daughters of Padre Pio, Disciples of the Cenacle / Discepole del Cenacolo, Via Madonna degli Angeli 78, 00049 Velletri, Rome. August 2008

74. Rega, *Padre Pio and America*, 19.

75. Da Prata and da Ripabottoni, *Beata te, Pietrelcina*, 209.

76. Graziella DeNunzio Mandato, *Padre Pio: Encounters with a Spiritual Daughter from Pietrelcina* (A.M.D.G., 2002), 10.

77. Winowska, *True Face of Padre Pio*, 62.

78. Padre Pio of Pietrelcina, *Letters*, 1:264.

79. Ibid., 1:265.

80. Fr. John A. Schug, *A Padre Pio Profile* (St. Bede's Publications, 1987), 65.

81. Padre Pio of Pietrelcina, *Letters*, 1:234.

82. Ibid., 1:235–236.

83. Padre Pio of Pietrelcina, *Letters*, vol. 2, *Correspondence with Raffaelina Cerase, Noblewoman (1914–1915)* (Edizioni Padre Pio da Pietrelcina, 2019), 122.

84. Padre Pio of Pietrelcina, *Letters*, 1:480.

85. Padre Pio of Pietrelcina, *Letters*, 1:230–232, 248, 254.

86. *Padre Pio of Pietrelcina*, Ibid., 1:375.

87. *Padre Pio of Pietrelcina*, Ibid., 376.

88. Ingoldsby, *Padre Pio*, 113.

89. Brother Leo of Assisi, *The Mirror of Perfection* (Burns and Oates, 1902), 101.

90. Padre Pio of Pietrelcina, *Letters*, 1: 242

91. Agostino of San Marco in Lamis, *Diario*, 58.

92. Ibid.

93. Padre Pio of Pietrelcina, *Letters*, 1:300.

94. Ibid.,1:284.

95. Ibid., 1:288.

96. Ibid., 1:307–308.

97. Ibid., 1:308.

98. Ibid., 1:308.

99. Ibid., 1:329.

100. Ibid., 1:329.

101. Ingoldsby, *Padre Pio,* 110.

102. Padre Pio of Pietrelcina, *Letters*, 1:362.

103. Ibid., 1:377.

104. Ibid., 1:1156.

105. Ibid., 1:1169.

106. Ibid., 2:73.

107. Ibid., 2:63.

108. Ibid., 2:72.

109. Ibid., 2:63–64.

110. Ibid., 2:169.

111. Ibid., 2:10.

112. Ibid., 2:108.

113. Ibid., 2:114.

114. Ibid., 2:114.

115. Ibid., 2:101.

116. Ibid., 2:112–113.

117. Ibid., 2:116–117.

118. Ibid., 2:130.

119. Ibid., 2:130.

120. Ibid., 2:303.

121. Ibid., 2:140.

122. Ibid., 2:122.

123. Ibid., 2:141.

124. Ibid., 2:88.

125. Ibid., 2:131.

126. As quoted in Suzie Andres, "The Triple Novena to Join Padre Pio's Spiritual Children," Catholic Exchange, September 19, 2019, https://catholicexchange.com/the-triple-novena-to-join-padre-pios-spiritual-children/.

127. Carty, *Padre Pio: The Stigmatist*, 252.

128. Padre Pio of Pietrelcina, *Letters*, 2:99.

129. Ibid., 2:72.

130. Ibid., 2:307.

131. Ibid., 2:307.

132. Ibid., 2:307.

133. Ibid., 2:309.

134. Ibid., 2:308.

135. Ibid., 2:308.

136. Ibid., 2:308.

137. Ibid., 2:309.

138. Ibid., 2:309–312.

139. Ibid., 2:310.

140. Ibid., 2:309-310.

141. Ibid., 2:311.

142. Ibid., 2:312.

143. Ibid., 2:310.

144. Ibid., 2:313.

145. Ibid., 2:313.

146. Ibid., 2:308.

147. Ibid., 2:314.

148. Ibid., 2:314.

149. Ibid., 2:314.

150. Ibid., 2:314.

151. Ibid., 2:314.

152. Ibid., 2:314.

153. Ibid., 2:314–315.

154. Ibid., 2:315.

155. Ibid., 2:315.

156. Ibid., 2:315.

157. Ibid., 2:315.

158. Ibid., 2:315.

159. Ibid., 2:315-316.

160. Ibid., 2:316.

161. Ibid., 2:317.

162. Ingoldsby, *Padre Pio*, 10.

163. Padre Pio of Pietrelcina, *Letters*, 2:278.

164. Padre Pio of Pietrelcina, *Letters*, 2:277

165. Ibid., 2:649.

166. Ibid., 2:446.

167. Ibid., 2:178.

168. Ibid. 2:458–459.

169. Agostino of San Marco in Lamis, *Diario*, 258.

170. Ibid., 261.

171. Ibid., 261.

172. Padre Pio of Pietrelcina, *Letters*, 2:274.

173. Agostino of San Marco in Lamis, *Diario*, 261.

174. Paolino of Casacalenda, *Le mie memorie intorno a Padre Pio* (Edizioni Padre Pio da Pietrelcina, 1978), 236.

175. Parente, *Holy Souls*, 37.

176. Parente, *Holy Souls*, 37.

177. Lucia Fiorentino, *The Diary of Lucia Fiorentino: Mystic, Visionary and Early Spiritual Daughter of Padre Pio*, trans. Bret Thoman, O.S.F. (Icona Press, 2024), 38.

178. Padre Pio of Pietrelcina, *Letters*, 3:185.

179. Letter to spiritual daughter Antonietta Pompilio, as quoted in Andres, "Triple Novena"; and Morcaldi, *La mia vita vicino a Padre Pio*, 165.

180. D'Apolito, *Padre Pio of Pietrelcina*, 189.

181. Padre Pio of Pietrelcina, *Letters*, 1:1170.

182. Ibid., 1:1168.

183. Ibid., 1:157.

184. Ibid., 1:1172–1173.

185. Ibid., 1:1172.

186. Ibid., 1:1170.

187. Ibid., 1:1155.

188. Ibid., 1:1156.

189. Ibid., 1:1176.

190. Ibid., 1:173.

191. Ibid., *Letters*, 1:1186.

192. Ibid., *Letters*, 1:1186.

193. Ibid., *Letters*, 1:1186.

194. Ibid., *Letters*, 1,1191.

195. Ibid., 1:218.

196. Ibid., 1:219.

197. Agostino of San Marco in Lamis, *Diario*, 59–60; and Padre Pio of Pietrelcina, *Letters*, 1:223.

198. Preziuso, *Life of Padre Pio*, 111.

199. Ruffin, *Padre Pio*, 138.

200. Ibid., 130.

201. Da Prata and da Ripabottoni, *Beata te, Pietrelcina*, 230.

202. Ingoldsby, *Padre Pio*, 138; and Padre Pio of Pietrelcina, *Letters*, 1:1167.

203. *Voice of Padre Pio*, 29, no. 3 (1989): 29.

204. Ingoldsby, *Padre Pio*, 139–140.

205. Renzo Allegri, *Padre Pio: Man of Hope* (Servant Publications, 2000), 53.

206. Castelli, Messori, and Rossi, *Padre Pio Under Investigation*, 46.

207. *Voice of Padre Pio*, 19, no. 3 (1989), 29.

208. Padre Pio of Pietrelcina, *Letters*, 1:1277.

209. Ibid., 1:1305.

210. Ibid., 1:1307.

211. Frank M. Rega, *Amazing Miracles of Padre Pio* (pub. by author, 2019), 4.

212. Rega, *Amazing Miracles*, 4.

213. Author's correspondence with the Jewish Community Center of Florence. During this correspondence, I asked if such a miraculous occurrence moved the rest of Lello's family to seek Baptism. None of Lello's family, however, followed him in being baptized.

214. Castelli, Messori, and Rossi, *Padre Pio Under Investigation*, 163.

215. Ruffin, *Padre Pio*, 431.

216. Ruffin, *Padre Pio*, 389–390.

217. Carty, *Padre Pio: The Stigmatist*, 241.

218. Ruffin, *Padre Pio*, 344.

219. Ruffin, *Padre Pio*, 389

220. Gherardo Leone, *Padre Pio and His Work* (Casa Sollievo della Sofferenza, 1986), 69.

221. As quoted in "One Eye," Padre Pio's Facts, https://www.caccioppoli.com/Padre%20Pio%20facts.html.

222. Ruffin, *Padre Pio*, 372.

223. Ruffin, *Padre Pio*, 372–373.

224. Winowska, *True Face of Padre Pio*, 139.

225. Winowska, *True Face of Padre Pio*, 115.

226. Giorgio Festa, *Misteri di scienza e luci di fede le stigmate del Padre Pio da Pietrelcina* (Ferri, 1949), 160.

227. All quotations in this section on Cesare Festa come from Carty, *Padre Pio: The Stigmatist*, 91–94.

228. Unless otherwise indicated, all quotations in this section on Emanuele come from Giuseppe Pagnossin, *Il Calvario di Padre Pio*, vol. 1 (Pagnossin, 1978), 4–7.

229. Ibid., 24–25.

230. Savario Gaeta and Andrea Tornielli, *Padre Pio L'Ultimo Sospetto: La Verita sul frate delle stimmate* (Piemme, 2008), 185–186.

231. Morcaldi, *La mia vita vicino a Padre Pio*, 27.

232. Pagnossin, *Il Calvario di Padre Pio*, vol. 1, 41.

233. Padre Pio of Pietrelcina, *Letters*, 3:59.

234. Ibid., 3:250–251.

235. Ibid., 3:251.

236. Ibid., 251.

237. Padre Pio of Pietrelcina, *Letters*, 2:199.

238. Ibid., 2:449.

239. Ibid., 2:155.

240. Ibid., 2:142.

241. Ibid., 2:142.

242. Agostino of San Marco in Lamis, *Diario*, 265–266.

243. Francesco Chiocchi, *I nemici di Padre Pio* (Reporter, 1968), 46.

244. Pagnossin, *Il Calvario di Padre Pio*, vol. 1, 128.

245. Castelli, Messori, and Rossi, *Padre Pio Under Investigation*, 144.

246. Rega, *Amazing Miracles*, 118.

247. Ibid.

248. Ibid., 119; and Castelli, Messori, and Rossi, *Padre Pio Under Investigation*, 208.

249. Pagnossin, *Il Calvario di Padre Pio*, vol. 1, 139.

250. Ibid.

251. Ibid., 144.

252. Gaeta and Tornielli, *Padre Pio L'Ultimo Sospetto*, 136.

253. Ibid., 135.

254. Ibid., 135.

255. Ibid., 136.

256. Zsolt Aradi, *Pope Pius XI: The Pope and the Man*, Hanover House, New York, 1958, 74

257. Pagnossin, *Il Calvario di Padre Pio*, vol. 1, 170.

258. Ibid.

259. Castelli, Messori, and Rossi, *Padre Pio Under Investigation*, 93.

260. Ibid., 96.

261. Ibid., 95.

262. Ibid., 106.

263. Ibid., 87.

264. Ibid., 93.

265. Ibid., 95.

266. Ibid., 107.

267. Ibid., 154.

268. Ibid., 108.

269. Ibid., 46.

270. Ibid., 120.

271. Ibid., 122.

272. Ibid., 99.

273. Ibid., 110.

274. Ibid., 82.

275. Ibid., 115.

276. Ibid., 132.

277. Ibid., 239.

278. Ibid., 98.

279. Ibid., 132.

280. Ibid., 124.

281. Ibid., 125.

282. Ibid., 93.

283. Pagnossin, *Il Calvario di Padre Pio*, vol. 1, 153.

284. Gaeta and Tornielli, *Padre Pio L'Ultimo Sospetto*, 113–114.

285. Pagnossin, *Il Calvario di Padre Pio*, vol. 2 (Pagnossin, 1978), 168.

286. Pagnossin, *Il Calvario di Padre Pio*, vol. 1, 128.

287. Ruffin, *Padre Pio*, 211.

288. Francesco Castelli, *Padre Pio e il Sant'Uffizio, 1918–1939: Fatti, protagonist, documenti inedita* (Studium, 2011), 128.

289. Costantino Capobianco, *Detti e aneddoti di Padre Pio* (Edizioni Padre Pio da Pietrelcina, 1973), 61.

290. *Voice of Padre Pio* 1, no. 3 (1971): 13.

291. Pagnossin, *Il Calvario di Padre Pio*, vol. 1, 182.

292. Ibid., 189.

293. Ibid., 208.

294. Ibid., 252.

295. Ruffin, *Padre Pio*, 225.

296. Padre Pio of Pietrelcina, *Epistolario IV: Corrispondenza con diverse categorie di persone* (Edizioni Padre Pio da Pietrelcina, 2012), 734.

297. Allegri, *Padre Pio: Man of Hope*, 189.

298. All quotations in this section on Giovanna come from D'Apolito, *Padre Pio of Pietrelcina*, 396–406.

299. Dorothy M. Gaudiose, *Mary's House. Mary Pyle: Under the Spiritual Guidance of Padre Pio* (Alba House, 1993), 44.

300. Ruffin, *Padre Pio*, 236.

301. Bonaventura Massa, *Mary Pyle: She Lived Doing Good to All* (Leone Grafiche, 1986), 94.

302. *Voice of Padre Pio*, 30, nos. 8/9 (2000): 15–16.

303. Ibid., 16

304. Ibid., 16

305. Massa, *Mary Pyle*, 21.

306. Dorothy M. Gaudiose, *Mary's House. Mary Pyle: Under the Spiritual Guidance of Padre Pio* (Alba House, 1993), 44.

307. Winowska, *True Face of Padre Pio*, 49.

308. Massa, *Mary Pyle*, 28.

309. Gaudiose, *Prophet of the People*, 47.

310. Carty, *Padre Pio: The Stigmatist*, 236.

311. Gaudiose, *Prophet of the People*, 50.

312. Winowska, *True Face of Padre Pio*, 49.

313. Da Prata and da Ripabottoni, *Beata te, Pietrelcina*, 50.

314. Carty, *Padre Pio: The Stigmatist*, 96.

315. Ibid., 97.

316. Unless otherwise indicated, all quotations in this section on the Abresches are from Winowska, *True Face of Padre Pio*, 51–54.

317. Alberto Del Fante, *Per la storia* (Anonima Arti Grafiche, 1931), 162, cited in Carty, *Padre Pio: The Stigmatist*, 106.

318. Pagnossin, *Il Calvario di Padre Pio*, vol. 1, 272.

319. Ibid., 283.

320. All quotations from the conversion story of Ricciardi are from Winowska, *True Face of Padre Pio*, 140–141.

321. *Padre Pio of Pietrelcina, Epistolario IV*, 93–94.

322. Ibid., 95.

323. Ibid., 96.

324. Mary Pyle, unpublished manuscript, 1990, as quoted in Ruffin, *Padre Pio*, 252.

325. Ibid.

326. Padre Pio of Pietrelcina, *Letters*, 1:1170.

327. Pagnossin, *Il Calvario di Padre Pio*, vol. 1, 583.

328. Ibid., 573.

329. Ibid., 605.

330. Ibid., 605.

331. Agostino of San Marco in Lamis, *Diario*, 79.

332. Ibid., 93–94.

333. Morcaldi, *La mia vita vicino a Padre Pio*, 50

334. D'Apolito, *Padre Pio of Pietrelcina*, 229.

335. Ingoldsby, *Padre Pio*, 136.

336. Morcaldi, *La mia vita vicino a Padre Pio*, 55.

337. Ingoldsby, *Padre Pio*, 102.

338. D'Apolito, *Padre Pio of Pietrelcina*, 116; and Morcaldi, *La mia vita vicino a Padre Pio*, 49.

339. Winowska, *True Face of Padre Pio*, 181.

340. "The Man of God who Offers," *Voice of Padre Pio* 7, no. 4 (1977), 15.

341. Morcaldi, *La mia vita vicino a Padre Pio*, 48.

342. D'Apolito, *Padre Pio of Pietrelcina*, 129.

343. "The Man of God who Offers," 15.

344. *The Stigmata of Faith, Thoughts of Padre Pio*, Pauline Press, 2000, 65

345. Gerardo Di Flumeri, *The Mystery of the Cross in Padre Pio of Pietrelcina*, National Center for Padre Pio, Barto PA, 16

346. D'Apolito, *Padre Pio of Pietrelcina*, 225.

347. As quoted at "Our Lady of Grace Chapel," National Center for Padre Pio, https://www.padrepio.org/visit/our-lady-of-grace-chapel/.

348. D'Apolito, *Padre Pio of Pietrelcina*, 65.

349. Ibid., 64–65.

350. Pagnossin, *Il Calvario di Padre Pio*, vol. 2, 667.

351. Ibid., 667.

352. Padre Pio of Pietrelcina, *Epistolario IV*, 740.

353. Allegri, *Padre Pio: Man of Hope*, 123.

354. Carty, *Padre Pio: The Stigmatist*, 94.

355. *Voice of Padre Pio*, 32, no. 3 (2001): 23.

356. Gaudiose, *Prophet of the People*, 101.

357. Ibid., 101.

358. Giuseppe Pagnossin, *Il Calvario di Padre Pio*, vol. 2, 24.

359. Robbie Woliver, "Haunted and Redeemed," *New York Times*, October 1, 2000, https://www.nytimes.com/2000/10/01/nyregion/in-person-haunted-and-redeemed-by-a-jewish-heritage.html

360. Ruffin, *Padre Pio*, 279.

361. Leone, *Padre Pio and His Work*, 24.

362. Ibid., 32.

363. John McCaffery, *Tales of Padre Pio: The Friar of San Giovanni* (Andrews and McMeel, 1978), 21.

364. Leone, *Padre Pio and His Work*, 24–25.

365. Carty, *Padre Pio: The Stigmatist*, 300.

366. Ibid.

367. Ruffin, *Padre Pio*, 285.

368. Gaudiose, *Prophet of the People*, 163.

369. Angelo M. Mischitelli, *Padre Pio: Un uomo un santo* (Sovera, 2015), 593.

370. Ruffin, *Padre Pio*, 284.

371. Mischitelli, *Padre Pio*, 593.

372. Ruffin, *Padre Pio*, 283.

373. Gaudiose, *Prophet of the People*, 162.

374. Mischitelli, *Padre Pio*, 593.

375. Gaudiose, *Prophet of the People*, 162–163.

376. Agostino of San Marco in Lamis, *Diario*, 163.

377. Pagnossin, *Il Calvario di Padre Pio*, vol. 2, 101.

378. Ruffin, *Padre Pio*, 130.

379. Rega, *Padre Pio and America*, 114.

380. Agostino of San Marco in Lamis, *Diario*, 162.

381. Ruffin, *Padre Pio*, 284.

382. Allegri, *Padre Pio: Man of Hope*, 131.

383. Pascal Cataneo, *Padre Pio Gleanings*, Quebec, 1991, page 99

384. Ruffin, *Padre Pio*, 287.

385. Rega, *Padre Pio and America*, 209.

386. John A. Schug, *Padre Pio: He Bore the Stigmata* (Huntington, IN: Our Sunday Visitor, 1976), 155–156

387. Ruffin, *Padre Pio*, 290.

388. Ibid.

389. Mischitelli, *Padre Pio*, 594.

390. Ibid., 593.

391. Ruffin, *Padre Pio*, 295.

392. Rega, *Padre Pio and America*, 196.

393. Ibid., 158.

394. As quoted at "Close Encounters of the Special Kind of Americans with Padre Pio," Caccioppoli website, https://caccioppoli.com/Close%20encounters%20of%20Padre%20Pio%20and%20the%20American%20Servicemen,%20Mary%20Pile.html.

395. Ibid.

396. Rega, *Padre Pio and America*, 161.

397. Ibid., 171.

398. Ibid., 199.

399. Ruffin, *Padre Pio*, 346.

400. Ibid., 350.

401. Ibid., 297.

402. Rega, *Amazing Miracles*, 38.

403. Ruffin, *Padre Pio*, 302.

404. Ibid., 303.

405. Ibid., 305.

406. Ibid., 338–339.

407. Rega, *Amazing Miracles*, 38.

408. Ibid., 37–38.

409. Jim Gallagher, *Padre Pio: The Pierced Priest* (Harper Collins, 1995), 127.

410. Ibid., 129.

411. Ibid., 130.

412. Ibid., 131.

413. Ibid., 132.

414. Rega, *Padre Pio and America*, 194.

415. Allegri, *Padre Pio: Man of Hope*, 197.

416. Carty, *Padre Pio: The Stigmatist*, 236.

417. Ruffin, *Padre Pio*, 325.

418. Francesco Napolitano, *Padre Pio of Pietrelcina: A Brief Biography* (Edizioni Padre Pio da Pietrelcina), 153.

419. D'Apolito, *Padre Pio da Pietrelcina*, 98.

420. All quotations from this section on Bianchi come from Ingoldsby, *Padre Pio*, 78–79.

421. Pagnossin, *Il Calvario di Padre Pio*, vol. 1, 95.

422. Ibid., 95. This was a reference to Jehovah's Witnesses who had infiltrated the area.

423. Ibid.

424. Ibid., 94.

425. Ibid.

426. Leone, *Padre Pio and His Work*, 69.

427. *New York Times*, July 29, 1956, as cited at "Casa Sollievo della Sofferenza," Caccioppoli website, https://caccioppoli.com/St.%20Padre%20Pio%20Casa%20 Sollievo.html.

428. John A. Schug, *Padre Pio: He Bore the Stigmata* (Our Sunday Visitor, 1976), 226.

429. Ibid., 222.

430. *Voice of Padre Pio* 8, no.3 (1978): 14.

431. Ibid.

432. Ibid.

433. Leone, *Padre Pio: Infanzia e prima giovanezza*, 72.

434. Leone, *Padre Pio and His Work*, 72.

435. Ruffin, *Padre Pio*, 386.

436. As quoted at "Novena in Honor of Saint Padre Pio of Pietrelcina," Padre Pio Prayer Groups USA, https://www.pppg.org/?page_id=339.

437. D'Apolito, *Padre Pio of Pietrelcina*, 208.

438. Winowska, *True Face of Padre Pio*, 146.

439. Ibid., 146–147.

440. Ibid., 147.

441. Padre Pio of Pietrelcina, *Letters*, 2:511.

442. Carty, *Padre Pio: The Stigmatist*, 72.

443. Capobianco, *Detti e anedotti di Padre Pio*, 75–76.

444. All quotations in this section on Giacomo Gaglione are from Rega, *Amazing Miracles*, 91–93.

445. All quotations in this section on Vincenzo Mercurio are from D'Apolito, *Padre Pio of Pietrelcina*, 290–291.

446. Ingoldsby, *Padre Pio*, 122.

447. Agostino of San Marco in Lamis, *Diario*, 225.

448. Ruffin, *Padre Pio*, 430.

449. Pagnossin, *Il Calvario di Padre Pio*, vol. 2, 26.

450. Ibid.

451. Gaeta and Tornielli, *Padre Pio L'Ultimo Sospetto*, 202.

452. Stefano Campanella, *Il Papa e il frate* (Edizioni Padre Pio da Pietrelcina, 2005), 85–86.

453. Ibid., 122.

454. Ibid., 152.

455. D'Apolito, *Padre Pio of Pietrelcina*, 257.

456. Ibid.

457. Marcellino Iasenzaniro, *The "Padre": Saint Pio of Pietrelcina; Charismatic Priest: Testimonies* (Edizioni Padre Pio da Pietrelcina, 2006), 661.

458. D'Apolito, *Padre Pio of Pietrelcina*, 248.

459. Padre Pio, Meditation Prayer on Mary Immaculate (TAN Books, 1974), 5.

460. Winowska, *True Face of Padre Pio*, 181.

461. Padre Pio, *Meditation Prayer*, 6.

462. Ibid., 7.

463. D'Apolito, *Padre Pio of Pietrelcina*, 249–250.

464. Ibid., 251.

465. Winowska, *True Face of Padre Pio*, 181.

466. Ibid.

467. Ibid.

468. D'Apolito, *Padre Pio of Pietrelcina*, 253.

469. Patricia Treece, *The Joyful Spirit of Padre Pio: Stories, Letters, and Prayers* (Franciscan Media, 2014), 93.

470. Ibid., 95.

471. Padre Pio, *Meditation Prayer*, 6.

472. Ingoldsby, *Padre Pio*, 132–133.

473. Carty, *Padre Pio: The Stigmatist*, 250.

474. Ibid.

475. Ibid.

476. D'Apolito, *Padre Pio of Pietrelcina*, 247.

477. Winowska, *True Face of Padre Pio*, 181.

478. Ingoldsby, *Padre Pio*, 128.

479. Winowska, *True Face of Padre Pio*, 181.

480. Padre Pio of Pietrelcina, *Letters*, 1:672–673.

481. Ibid., 1:673.

482. All quotations in this section on Pellegrino are from Funicelli, *Padre Pio's Jack of All Trades*, 352–366.

483. José María Zavala, *The Best Kept Secret of Fatima* (Ediciones Martínez Roca, 2017), as cited in "Chief Exorcist Father Amorth: Padre Pio Said That the Third Secret of Fatima Was About a 'False Church' in the End Times," *Catholicism Pure & Simple*, August 2, 2017, https://catholicismpure.wordpress.com/2017/08/02/chief-exorcist -father-amorth-padre-pio-said-that-the-third-secret-of-fatima-was-about-a-false-church -in-the-end-times/.

484. Meriol Trevor, *Pope John: Blessed John XXIII* (Gracewing, 2000), 77.

485. As quoted in Jonathan Fleischmann, "Lucia of Fatima, Part 3: The Infamous Third Secret," One Peter Five, October 13, 2017, footnote 16, https://onepeterfive .com/lucia-fatima-infamous-third-secret/

486. Marco Tosatti, *Quando la chiesa perseguitava Padre Pio* (Piemme, 2005), 93.

487. Ruffin, *Padre Pio*, 420.

488. Tosatti, *Quando la chiesa perseguitava Padre Pio*, 89.

489. Ibid., 55.

490. Ibid., 59.

491. Campanella, *Il Papa e il frate*, 121.

492. Ibid., 121–122.

493. Tosatti, *Quando la chiesa perseguitava Padre Pio*, 77.

494. Ibid.

495. Ibid., page 203–204.

496. Carty, *Padre Pio: The Stigmatist*, 235.

497. Schug, *Padre Pio Profile*, 93–94.

498. Tosatti, *Quando la chiesa perseguitava Padre Pio*, 349.

499. Campanella, *Il Papa e il frate*, 135.

500. Tosatti, *Quando la chiesa perseguitava Padre Pio*, 92.

501. Pagnossin, *Il Calvario di Padre Pio*, vol. 2, 99.

502. Morcaldi, *La mia vita vicino a Padre Pio*, 190.

503. Ibid., 148.

504. Ibid., 150.

505. Ibid., 38.

506. Tosatti, *Quando la chiesa perseguitava Padre Pio*, 95.

507. Ibid., 100.

508. Pagnossin, *Il Calvario di Padre Pio*, vol. 2, 101.

509. Campanella, *Il Papa e il frate*, 152–153.

510. Pagnossin, *Il Calvario di Padre Pio*, vol. 2, 100.

511. Tosatti, *Quando la chiesa perseguitava Padre Pio*, 96.

512. Ibid., 99.

513. Ibid., 100.

514. Ibid.

515. Ibid., 108.

516. Ibid., 108, 117–118

517. Ibid., 108, 106.

518. Sergio Luzatto, *Padre Pio: Miracles and Politics in a Secular Age* (Metropolitan Books, 2007), 276–277.

519. Ibid., page 267.

520. Campanella, *Il Papa e il frate*, 126.

521. Eusebio Notte, *Padre Pio e Padre Eusebio: Briociole di Storia* (Foggia, 2008), 218–219.

522. Pagnossin, *Il Calvario di Padre Pio*, vol. 2, 133.

523. Schug, *Padre Pio Profile*, 118.

524. Notte, *Padre Pio e Padre Eusebio*, 267–268.

525. Ibid., 114–115.

526. Schug, *Padre Pio Profile*, 119.

527. Campanella, *Il Papa e il frate*, 177–179.

528. Ibid., 179–180.

529. Allegri, *Padre Pio: Man of Hope*, 220.

530. Campanella, *Il Papa e il frate*, 184.

531. Fernando da Riese Pio X, *Padre Pio da Pietrelcina: Crocifisso Senza Croce* (Postulazione Generale dei Cappuccini, 1975), 384.

532. Notte, *Padre Pio e Padre Eusebio*, 241.

533. Campanella, *Il Papa e il frate*, 229.

534. Padre Pio of Pietrelcina, *Epistolario IV*, 747–748.

535. Gabriele Amorth, *Padre Pio: Stories and Memories of My Mentor and Friend* (Ignatius Press, 2016), 112.

536. Ruffin, *Padre Pio*, 430.

537. Pagnossin, *Il Calvario di Padre Pio*, vol. 2, 26.

538. Tosatti, *Quando la chiesa perseguitava Padre Pio*, 174.

539. Pagnossin, *Il Calvario di Padre Pio*, vol. 2, 322

540. Campanella, *Il Papa e il frate*, 160.

541. Gaeta and Tornielli, *Padre Pio L'Ultimo Sospetto*, 200.

542. Notte, *Padre Pio e Padre Eusebio*, 255.

543. Allegri, *Padre Pio: Man of Hope*, 153.

544. Author's interview with Dónal Enright, County Cork, Ireland.

545. Carty, *Padre Pio: The Stigmatist*, 231.

546. Ibid., 231–232.

547. Treece, *Joyful Spirit*, 101.

548. Unless otherwise indicated, all material in the rest of this section comes from the author's interview with Dónal Enright, County Cork, Ireland, June 2010.

549. Author's interview with Dónal Enright, County Cork, Ireland, June 2010.

550. Funicelli, *Padre Pio's Jack of All Trades*, 205–206.

551. Winowska, *True Face of Padre Pio*, 161.

552. Ibid., 160–161.

553. Ibid., 161.

554. Carty, *Padre Pio: The Stigmatist*, 83.

555. Winowska, *True Face of Padre Pio*, 135.

556. Ibid.

557. Ibid.

558. Ibid., 136.

559. Carty, *Padre Pio: The Stigmatist*, pages 87–88.

560. Ibid., 88.

561. Ibid.

562. Ibid., 231.

563. Ibid., 231.

564. Ibid., 248.

565. Ibid.

566. Ibid.

567. Ibid., 236.

568. Ruffin, *Padre Pio*, 438.

569. Carty, *Padre Pio: The Stigmatist*, 248.

570. Carty, *Padre Pio: The Stigmatist*, 230.

571. Winowska, *True Face of Padre Pio*, 119.

572. Ingoldsby, *Padre Pio*, 85.

573. Carty, *Padre Pio: The Stigmatist*, 236.

574. Ingoldsby, *Padre Pio*, 85.

575. Ingoldsby, *Padre Pio*, 85.

576. Carty, *Padre Pio: The Stigmatist*, 235.

577. Carty, *Padre Pio: The Stigmatist*, 249

578. Ibid.

579. Ruffin, *Padre Pio*, 348.

580. Treece, *Joyful Spirit*, 89.

581. Castelli, Messori, and Rossi, *Padre Pio Under Investigation*, 28.

582. Ingoldsby, *Padre Pio*, 84.

583. Carty, *Padre Pio: The Stigmatist*, 230.

584. Da Prata and da Ripabottoni, *Beata te, Pietrelcina*, 203.

585. Carty, *Padre Pio: The Stigmatist*, 229.

586. Ibid.

587. Ibid., 242.

588. Ibid., 243–244.

589. Ibid., 244.

590. Ingoldsby, *Padre Pio*, 116.

591. Schug, *Padre Pio*, 55.

592. D'Apolito, *Padre Pio of Pietrelcina*, 100.

593. Ingoldsby, *Padre Pio*, 115.

594. Notte, *Padre Pio e Padre Eusebio*, 199.

595. Ibid., 413.

596. *La Casa*, no. 2 (1974), 21.

597. Ibid.

598. Ruffin, *Padre Pio*, 441.

599. Ibid., 442.

600. Da Ripabottoni, *Pio of Pietrelcina: Infancy and Adolescence*, 356.

601. Author's conversations with religious sisters who were spiritual daughters of Padre Pio, Disciples of the Cenacle / Discepole del Cenacolo, Rome, August 2008

602. Funicelli, *Padre Pio's Jack of All Trades*, 343.

603. *Acts of the First Congress of Studies on Padre Pio's Spirituality* (Edizioni Padre Pio da Pietrelcina, 1972), 149.

604. Morcaldi, *La mia vita vicino a Padre Pio*, 213.

605. Ruffin, *Padre Pio*, 438

606. Notte, *Padre Pio e Padre Eusebio*, 449–457.

607. Morcaldi, *La mia vita vicino a Padre Pio*, 213.

608. Ruffin, *Padre Pio*, 444–445.

609. Ruffin, *Padre Pio*, 443.

610. Ibid.

611. Morcaldi, *La mia vita vicino a Padre Pio*, 214.

612. Ruffin, *Padre Pio*, 444

613. Ruffin, *Padre Pio*, 444

614. Da Ripabottoni, *Saint Pio of Pietrelcina: Everybody's Cyrenean*, 241.

615. Acts of the First Congress of Studies on Padre Pio's Spirituality, 1972, 149

616. Gaudiose, *Prophet of the People*, 179.

617. Massa, *Mary Pyle*, 56.

618. Ruffin, *Padre Pio*, 158

619. Ruffin, *Padre Pio*, 158

620. Padre Pio and Pietrelcina, *L'Osservatore Romano*, English Edition, October 10, 1968, 9.

621. Ibid.; and Da Ripabottoni, *Saint Pio of Pietrelcina: Everybody's Cyrenean*, 233–234.

622. Morcaldi, *La mia vita vicino a Padre Pio*, 209.

623. Ruffin, *Padre Pio*, 73.

624. D'Apolito, *Padre Pio of Pietrelcina*, 223.

625. Schug, *Padre Pio*, 232.

626. Morcaldi, *La mia vita vicino a Padre Pio*, 222.

627. Gallagher, *Padre Pio*, 206.

628. Carty, *Padre Pio: The Stigmatist*, 236.

629. Ruffin, *Padre Pio*, 448.

630. Schug, *Padre Pio*, 237–238.

631. *Voice of Padre Pio*, 1, no.1 (1971): 11.

632. Alessandro da Ripabottoni, *Padre Pio of Pietrelcina: Everybody's Cyrenean* (Our Lady of Grace Capuchin Friary, 1987), 243

633. Andrea Tornielli, "The Great Promise of St. Padre Pio," *Gente*, June 27, 2002, 21–25, trans. Frank Rega, http://frankrega.com/sanpadrepio/promise.htm.

634. Ibid.

635. Morcaldi, *La mia vita vicino a Padre Pio*, 161.

636. Quoted in "Padre Pio da Pietrelcina," Vatican website, https://www.vatican.va/news_services/liturgy/saints/ns_lit_doc_20020616_padre-pio_en.html

637. Pagnossin, *Il Calvario di Padre Pio*, vol. 2, 93.

638. Campanella, *Il Papa e il frate*, 34.

639. Renzo Allegri, *I Miracoli di Padre Pio* (Oscar Mondadori, 1993), 193, as quoted in Frank M. Rega, "Pope John Paul II, St. Padre Pio, and the Miracle That United Them," *Catholic Digest*, December and January 2008 (2 parts), http://frankrega.com/sanpadrepio/poltawska.htm.

640. Wanda Poltawska, "Padre Pio the Saint of Our Time," *Lay Witness*, October 1999, as quoted Rega, "Pope John Paul II, St. Padre Pio."

641. *Voice of Padre Pio* 29, nos .7–9 (1999): 33.

642. Ibid., 40.

643. Ruffin, *Padre Pio*, 77.

644. *Voice of Padre Pio* 29, nos. 7–9 (1999): 40.

645. *Voice of Padre Pio* 32, no. 2 (2002): 21.

646. Morcaldi, *La mia vita vicino a Padre Pio*, 56.

About the Author

Mary O'Regan is a writer who was born and raised in County Cork, Ireland. After graduating from the University of Limerick, she worked as a teacher and then as a journalist in London for several years. She has blogged at *Mary's Blog* for fifteen years and had the honor of being invited to the Vatican, where she held forth on the role of more traditional Catholic bloggers. Her passion is to make accessible a synthesis of the teachings of saints, stigmatists, and scholars so that as many people as possible can inherit their wisdom, holiness, and charity. She edited the memoir *Drunks and Monks* and has spent the last eight years working on this book about St. Padre Pio. The Rosary and the Sacred Heart Novena are her favorite prayers. A social animal, she enjoys fun with her friends, fashion, stand-up comedy, and reading Agatha Christie. She lives in Los Angeles.